DANGER!
EDUCATED GYPSY

DANGER!
EDUCATED GYPSY

SELECTED ESSAYS

IAN HANCOCK

Edited by Dileep Karanth

University of Hertfordshire

First published in Great Britain in 2010 by
University of Hertfordshire Press
College Lane
Hatfield
Hertfordshire
AL10 9AB

British Library Cataloguing in Publication Data
A catalogue record for this book is available from the British Library

ISBN 978-1-902806-98-3

Design by Geoff Green
Printed in Great Britain by Henry Ling Ltd, Dorchester, DT1 1HD

Frontispiece: Ian Hancock by Romani artist Ferdinand Koci, 2008.

Contents

About the Editor

Dileep Karanth is a lecturer at the Department of Physics, the University of Wisconsin-Parkside, Kenosha. He received a doctorate in computational solid state physics from the University of Arkansas in 2005. He studied linguistics at The University of Texas and was introduced to the field of creolistics by his teacher, Ian Hancock. He was initially interested in the Roma because they are people; now he takes interest in them because they are *his* people. Through his association with Ian Hancock, he was privileged to meet some members of the Romani community in Austin and to correspond with several others in Europe and North America. Karanth speaks Hindi and Urdu (in addition to his native Kannada) and is proficient in French, Russian, Persian and German. With his background in Indic languages and Persian, he has now embarked on a study of the early development of Hindi-Urdu and its implications for the Romani language.

Ian Hancock is a marginal man. Like all Romani intellectuals, he has had to live torn between the pariah status of his people and the embrace of a dominant culture which can hardly conceive of such a monster as an educated Gypsy.

Professor Thomas A. Acton
Chair of Romani Studies
University of Greenwich

Foreword

My teacher, Professor Ian F. Hancock, is an unusual man: unusual in his background, in the breadth of his interests and in the range of his accomplishments. He was the first Gypsy to be awarded a doctorate in the UK; he is perhaps the only person to hold three doctorates without having finished high school. His book *The Pariah Syndrome* (1987) – the first to document the enslavement of Roma in Europe – came as a revelation to those who were accustomed to think of slavery as an institution restricted in modern times only to Europe's colonies. Another of his books, *We Are the Romani People* (2002), also the first of its kind (and now translated into several languages), has become an authoritative source for teachers who wish to present the Romani self-statement to their students. Author of over 400 publications, esteemed teacher to generations of students and tireless spokesman for the Romani peoples of the world, Ian has achieved much fame and even some notoriety in his eventful lifetime.

This collection of select writings is an attempt to introduce this dangerously educated and educating man through the medium of his work. Within its covers you will find poetry and song, stories and scholarship, bitter criticisms and friendly advice. The characters that speak through the pages of this book include scholars and 'concocters', oppressors and victims, promoters of equality and racial supremacists. Some characters, such as the seductive Gypsy woman of lore, turn out to be entirely imaginary upon closer examination. Others, such as a racist police officer, turn out to be all too real.

The book is inaugurated by *Djabravoki*, in which Ian brings his translator's craftsmanship to bear on the famous poem by Lewis Carroll.

This is followed by an introduction to his family, which he narrates in the first person. Raconteur then turns rebel (although his 'vorpal sword' is his pen) in one of his earliest essays from the 1960s, giving us a taste of his still-forming rhetoric, a rhetoric clearly influenced by the emerging Black Power movement to which he was exposed as a student in London.

In the next section, Ian dons the cloak of linguist and historian and clarifies the Indian connections of the Roma, explaining how an Asiatic people came to be transplanted into Europe. His vast knowledge of the Romani language gives him a vantage point from which to make useful suggestions for its standardisation. Speaking as an academic and educator, Ian shares his unique insights into the problems confronting the Roma in their quest for formal education. Then, embracing the role of social commentator, he rehabilitates the true image of his people, by rescuing Romani reality from the encroachment of the fictional 'Gypsy' stereotype.

In the last section, as advocate and human rights activist, Ian draws attention to the many impediments the Roma have endured over the centuries, especially during the *Porrajmos* (Holocaust) in the twentieth century and takes their case to the courts of justice to which they have long been denied access. Finally, as a watchful elder and shepherd of his people, he ends with a piece of sobering advice for the Roma: to live with dignity, to promote harmony and to discourage fractious tendencies among the various Romani groups.

In some of these writings, an undercurrent of anger and frustration is apparent. Anger at the sense of entitlement academics and others assume in studying, manipulating, defining and thinking for his people; frustration that Roma lack the adequate means to address this, while remaining victims of the stubborn and one-sided representation perpetrated by the all-controlling media. But the anger and frustration are channeled and sublimated and pour themselves finally into a message of accommodation, reconciliation and hope.

Ian's life story is anything but ordinary. Born into a British and Hungarian Romani family in London, he went with them to live in Canada for four of his teenage years and returned to England by himself at the age of nineteen. While in Canada he attended school briefly, but found his effort to 'fit in' an unrewarding experience. One teacher in particular, a Mr Tippett, told Ian that he was wasting his time getting an education and that he would never amount to anything. Mr Tippett would say this often and before the whole class, and Ian left after less than a year. But the stinging words lingered, and he told me that they motivated him fiercely to prove the man wrong. After his stint at school he found various jobs in Canada – in an automotive supply store, as a darkroom assistant on a daily newspaper, as a pin-setter in a bowling alley and as a Ferris wheel assembler, all the while saving his money to return to Britain. Back in London, he found jobs in the factories along the Great West Road as a plastic garment cutter, a windscreen-wiper packer and a spray painter. Later, he worked for the late Joe Meek as a roadie for a prominent band called the Outlaws. One of his jobs was working for an antiquarian bookseller called Luzac, opposite the British Museum. The shop specialised in secondhand language books, and Ian used his lunch breaks to go through the stock and learn what he could about philology.

The house in which he rented a room was also home to a number of students from Sierra Leone, and he spent many evenings in their company, getting to know them and their unwritten language, Krio. The Sierra Leonean community was large in that part of the city, and very supportive of his attempts to commit Krio to paper. Egged on to publish his efforts, Ian sought the advice of the Sierra Leonean writer Eldred Jones, then a visiting scholar at the University of Leeds. In turn Jones put him in touch with the editor of the *Sierra Leone Language Review*, Dr David Dalby, who was based at the School of Oriental and African Studies (SOAS) at the University of London. Dalby was impressed and asked to hold onto the notes that Hancock had brought along so that he could show them to the head of the college.

When Ian went back a second time, Dalby asked him to consider enrolling as a student at the University of London, a proposition which seemed so unreal that it angered Ian at the time, given his limited educational history prior to that. This was at a juncture when entry to a British university was still the preserve of the privileged and not considered suitable for school 'dropouts'. Dalby explained his thinking, however: in the absence of any formal linguistic training Ian had produced an impressive body of research, this despite the fact that he had never actually visited Sierra Leone. Dalby assured Ian that the University considered him capable of great things if given the opportunity.

On account of his Romani background, Ian qualified for a short-lived experimental affirmative action programme created by Prime Minister Harold Wilson. Wilson's socialist government wanted to make higher education available for minorities and other 'special case' individuals and Ian, along with just one other person (the late Abdul Karim Turay, who went on to become Sierra Leone's Minister for External Affairs) were selected. Ian's tuition was paid for and he was given a small amount of money to purchase books, although throughout his time at SOAS he continued to hold a variety of jobs to support himself.

Two other people also attended SOAS whose work later had an impact upon Ian's academic development: Lorenzo Dow Turner, who wrote a seminal book on African elements in the Gullah Creole spoken on the south-eastern coast of the US, and Ian's contemporary the late Walter Rodney, who reshaped current understanding of the first fifteenth-century European contacts with Africans on the Guinea Coast. Ian readily attributes his 'domestic hypothesis' of Creole origins to Rodney's work, and in 1976 Ian also discovered and later described an archaic variety of Gullah that is spoken to this day in south Texas and northern Mexico in two widely separated communities. The present volume includes a selection of his Roma-related writings, but he also has over two hundred publications dealing with Creole languages. His very first was about Sierra Leone Krio, and appeared in a 1964 issue of *The Linguist* magazine.

Ian's involvement in the Romani struggle began at about the same time that he became a student. Although he had grown up in an urban Romani household, he was not politicised. But then several incidents occurred in Britain's West Midlands that warranted brief mention in the *Evening Standard* newspaper, and they so upset him that he felt moved to become involved. In the first, a Gypsy man needed to pull his trailer off the road because his wife was going into labour, but was ordered to move on by the police. When the man refused he was driven away and thrown into a prison cell where he was badly beaten by the same officers, his pregnant wife and small children having been left alone on the side of the road. In a similar incident, both of the parents were taken into custody, leaving the children by themselves in the trailer. A paraffin lamp was knocked over and a fire spread that resulted in the death of all three Gypsy children. This was during the 1960s, when the police would contract professional teams using bulldozers, axes and other brutal means to move people on, a phenomenon that Ian describes in his book *The Pariah Syndrome*.

Ian made contact with the Gypsy Education Council, through which he met three non-Romanies who were to have a profound influence on the direction his life was taking: Thomas Acton, Donald Kenrick and Grattan Puxon. They encouraged his participation in Romani advocacy and rights issues and he found himself playing a key role in the first World Romani Congress, held near London in 1971, where he first met some of the major figures in the Romani movement.

In the same year Ian left the University of London with a PhD, the first in Britain to be awarded to a Gypsy. It was in African linguistics, with a specialisation in creole languages. As it happened, The University of Texas was looking for an expert in creolistics, and Ian was offered a job there while speaking at a conference in Washington DC in 1972. This was once again the result of his being in the right place at the right time – the original speaker invited to that conference lived in Hawaii and was unable to attend, so gave his ticket to Ian to go in his place. If Ian had not gone to Washington, he would have missed the offer. With his new doctorate, Ian had applied to over seventy universities for jobs, but had got nowhere. And here was an offer from one he had not even applied to. He had to borrow the money to fly to Austin.

As a new assistant professor at The University of Texas, Ian was taken under the wing of a senior faculty member, the late Edgar Polomé, who gave him the same advice, offered in good faith, that Ian had previously received from his supervisor at SOAS – that drawing attention to his Gypsy identity would hinder him academically. He consequently kept quiet about it until he received tenure – and hence job security – in his fourth year, a process which generally takes six years. He immediately began to compile the Romani Archives and to publish widely on Romani topics, both linguistic and sociopolitical. The Archives, which line the walls ceiling-high and are piled up on the floor of Ian's office at The University of Texas, are now known as the Romani Archives and Documentation Center, and is the biggest collection of its kind in the world, though it has never been officially recognised by his university.

Despite these remarkable achievements, Ian has become a controversial figure in some quarters. His linguistic theories have come under attack, and his sometimes outspoken criticism of the non-Romani monopolisation of Romani Studies has alienated him from some of those specialists. But it has been his effort to bring the details of the *Porrajmos*, the Romani Holocaust, to popular and academic attention which has caused him to be viewed with the most suspicion. Can it be that his determination to uncover the truth of what happened to the estimated million or more of his own people has caused discomfort in some quarters? He provides a wonderful Romani proverb in his book *We Are the Romani People*: 'He who is about to tell the truth should have one foot in the stirrup.' In recent years Ian has found himself dropped from the US Holocaust Memorial Council (to which he had been appointed by President Clinton in 1998), the Anne Frank Institute and the Project on Ethnic Relations Roma Advisory Board. Why was this?

One of Ian's most strident positions is found in *Responses*, which you will find in this volume, an essay which has provoked controversy and generated debate in no small measure. Ian is asking difficult questions here. Are Gypsies once again being accused of trespassing, of stealing the property of others? Have those age-old accusations now spilt over into the academic realm? Or is it the 'overly nationalistic' position that he and other Romani intellectuals espouse which raises hackles? Can it be that those non-Gypsy organisations which seek the assimilation and ultimate disappearance of Roma have no truck with him because he speaks instead of integration and self-determination? Is this the more profound truth that remains at the edges of the modern-day diaspora experience? Many European-based organisations, Ian argues, refuse to acknowledge the complexity of Romani history and the reality that Roma are a global people, and not simply a collection of disparate groups scattered throughout Europe.

If his scholarly views are perceived to be a threat by some intellectuals and scholars, then this is hardly a surprise. The 'Other' who ventures bravely in will always be a threat. The wheel of life turns, but it turns slowly. The most important fact to remember is that the wheel does turn. And the reader of this volume is free to judge Ian Hancock for himself — his views and the people for whom he speaks. This is an important step forward. Once, and it was not so long ago, the Roma were enslaved and their linguistic and cultural inheritances derided or ignored altogether. Today, both Roma and non-Roma are freer to read and debate, and come to better informed conclusions.

Ian's achievements, though, overwhelmingly override those of his detractors: he accepted the prestigious international Rafto Foundation human rights prize in Norway in 1997; he received the Gamaliel Chair in Peace and Justice from the University of Wisconsin in 1998; and in the same year was appointed by President Clinton to represent Roma on the

US Holocaust Memorial Council. He was part of a four-man team led by the late Yul Brynner that presented the petition to the United Nations for Romani membership in 1978, and has served as the representative on the UN Economic and Social Council and in UNICEF. He was awarded an honorary doctorate with distinction from Umeå University in 2002, and another from Constantine University in Slovakia in 2009. A scholarship in Holocaust and Genocide Studies has been established in his name at West Chester University in Pennsylvania, and a Roma organisation in Zagreb, Croatia, has been named *The Roma Education Centre "Ian Hancock"*. In March 2003, he was invited by the Dalai Lama to a private meeting in India. He has received certificates of recognition from Yeshiva University and other institutions. He has a place in Leland Robison's *Calendar of Prominent Ethnic Americans* and an entry in Barkan's *Making it in America: A Sourcebook on Eminent Ethnic Americans*. He is consulted regularly by the BBC World Service and by National Public Radio in the US; he has spoken before special Congressional hearings in Washington DC, and has addressed audiences in North and South America, Europe and Japan.

The honours and recognition attest to the existence of much goodwill felt by enlightened members of the larger society toward the Roma. Ian's own life and work have gone a long way in promoting this goodwill where it existed, and in creating it where it did not. However, despite his many accomplishments, it would be too early to say that Ian's work is done. While there is a verbal and intellectual acknowledgement of the Roma's plight, the lot of millions of Roma is still one of oppression. Atrocities against them continue to be reported in the press, especially in Eastern Europe. Even in the academic discipline of Romani studies, the Roma are not masters of their own destiny. Non-Romani linguists have discovered the Romani language and are being given huge grants to study it, to the tune of half a million pounds and more. Meanwhile, Romani families are forced to deal with Romaphobia on a daily basis while struggling to find decent jobs, housing, education and healthcare, seeking no less and no more opportunity than that enjoyed by their non-Romani neighbours. It is surely a collective insult to the twelve million Roma that no university to this day in North America sponsors a chair of Romani Studies, while much smaller populations enjoy such privileges, as in the Basque Studies Center at the University of Nevada, which is devoted to the half-million-strong Basque people. It is a collective slight to the Roma that Ian has had no formal recognition from The University of Texas, where he works, although his contributions have merited recognition by the Texas House of Representatives in a public ceremony in the state Capitol, and where he is a member of the State Commission on Holocaust and Genocide.

This book is a compendium of Ian Hancock's view of the Romani experience. No one will agree with everything he has to say but, undeniably, it is the first-ever book of its kind written by a Romani person for a non-Romani audience, and must surely pave the way for a new genre of 'Gypsy Literature'. His main historical contributions have been to correct widely and wrongly assumed theories, by establishing that the conventionally accepted scenario of a single, ancient, first Romani migration that split into three diverging branches is not correct; that participants in that migration were not one people speaking one language; and that the migration could not have pre-dated 1000 AD. Ian is also the first to have articulated the profound paradox that lies at the heart of Romani identity and which accounts for the 'square peg' conflicts that divide the Gypsy and non-Gypsy worlds – that the Roma are an Asian people, 'speaking an Asian language and maintaining an Asian culture', but that they are also a people who have only ever existed in the West.

Ian Hancock's impact upon Romani Studies has been truly remarkable, both in terms of its historiography and in its reassessment of Romani identity within the Western cultural fabric. In the words of Professor Thomas Acton OBE, Chair of Romani Studies at Greenwich University in London, Hancock is leading us into 'a major period of intellectual transition in the perspectives which govern Romani Studies'. In the process, he is forcing us to 'reshape our own views of the canon from which we are selecting'.

Ian's biggest impact, surely, has been amongst Roma themselves, and perhaps this is the true measure of success: recognition within one's own community. In 1993 he created *Romnet*, the first interactive Romani website, which became the model for those that came after. He is a member of the International Romani Parliament based in Vienna. His position as a university professor brings him emails every week from Roma who are either in college or who hope to attend in the future and are looking for advice and encouragement; those young people are not only entering unfamiliar territory, but sadly and too often have to deal with indifference or even scorn from their very own families. Ian has served as a model for other Romani leaders, too: teacher and activist Gregory Dufunia Kwiek wrote that after reading *The Pariah Syndrome*, he 'underwent a radical change; I understood the history behind my problems and realised it was time to live my life as I was – a Rom. Being equipped with this knowledge I am now able to fight both my fears and the fears of the non-Gypsies as well.' The Argentine Romani leader Lolya Bernal wrote, 'In the early 1980s I received a letter from Professor Ian Hancock. Who was this man who showed me a totally different world of which I could be even prouder? There in my hands through his letters an entirely new world was appearing, the origin of our culture, traditions, language, the clues to our Indian origin and many other things, none of which were taught us by the *gadže* (non-Roma). It encouraged me to continue working on our tales, language and, later, politics in searching for our destiny.'

As Ian's circle of influence expands, testimonials such as these are sent with unflagging regularity. As the sincerest tribute that could be given to Ian's life and work, I have collected a few more of them in the pages that follow. To them, I add my own salutations.

Me dav Tut and'o rrundo patjivale Rroma, te le Del na terdjon te den zor Tjire lavenge.

Dileep Karanth
Kenosha, Wisconsin
June 2009

Testimonials

The first time I met Ian Hancock was in 1992, at an international Roma conference in Stupava, Slovakia. At that time I was a young scholar, just starting my academic career in the field of Romani Studies. In communist Bulgaria we did not know anything about Western and American scholars, especially Roma, who were working on Roma issues. We did not have their publications, so the name Ian Hancock for me was as a legend. When I met him we spoke only in Romani, because at that time I did not yet speak any English.

As a PhD student at the University of Amsterdam in 1994, together with two non-Romani colleagues I organised the Second International Conference on Romani Linguistics, and Ian Hancock was one of the participants. It was then that I had my first opportunity to talk to him in person in English, and I was very much impressed by his contribution and with his very natural way of communicating with me. Since then, we have enjoyed a very close relationship and a mutaul exchange of scientific ideas. He visited me in Bulgaria, and I stayed in his home when I visited the Romani Archives in Texas. Some of the ideas which we shared we have realised, and others we still plan to work on. Throughout the years I was very much inspired by his writings and modern ideas about researching Roma, our language, and our history. Most of his publications in the field of Romani language and Romani *Porrajmos* (Holocaust) became classical readings in different university courses on Roma issues.

Nowadays, Ian Hancock is much more known in Eastern Europe and elsewhere than he was twenty years ago. The young Roma generation has more access to his publications than my generation had, and they are still so much inspired by them and by the basis they give for rethinking the place of Roma in the modern world.

Parikerav phrala Yanko!

Associate Professor Dr Hristo Kyuchukov
Institute of Romani Studies
Constantine the Philosopher University, Nitra, Slovakia

———

My name is William A. Duna. I am a Romani American. I was born and educated in the US, in the Bashaldo, or Hungarian-Slovak Roma, community. In 1987, I was appointed by President Ronald Reagan to the US Holocaust Memorial Council (USHMC). My position on the Council was to represent the Roma who suffered in the Holocaust. Also, I was there to ensure that the information and history of our people's suffering would be included in the museum that was later built in Washington DC.

Prior to my appointment to the USHMC, around 1985, I met Dr Ian Hancock, who taught at The University of Texas and continues to do so. He too was of Romani descent, and had been active for many years in human rights issues concerning the Roma people. Dr Hancock suggested that I get involved with the USHMC, and helped me to get appointed to the Council.

In my opinion, he is the most knowledgeable historian on the history of the Roma. In addition, he has worked for many years as an activist to change the public perspective about who we Roma are as a people. He has made a greater awareness as to how we have been persecuted and mistreated by people in power throughout history to the present time. Dr Hancock has brought great changes through his writings and lectures, and through working with different NGOs, and by attending many conferences around the world concerning Roma people. His name is synonymous with the word 'Roma'.

Dr Hancock and I have worked on different Roma projects together. I am proud to say he is a friend of mine, and one of the most intelligent and dedicated Rom I know. As a Rom, I will also say that Ian has done more for Roma than anyone I know.

William A. Duna
President, Sa-Roma, Inc.
Minneapolis

I first contacted Ian Hancock and met with him over two decades ago. I am proud to state that I have the honor to call him my friend. Over the years we have worked together on countless issues involving the persecution and oppression of Roma, commonly known as Gypsies.

He has worked tirelessly in these matters, and his books and papers are recognised throughout the world. He has been dedicated to improving the lives of Roma at great sacrifice to his own personal life, and I am sure that history will be more appreciative of his works than the intellectuals he has tried to work with throughout his life. After all, together the words 'Gypsy' and 'professor' go against the image of Romanies the world has created and has ingrained in their minds. It's almost as unthinkable as it would have been to elect an African American President not so long ago. That fact today gives hope that Ian's effort will someday in the future improve the terrible plight of his people.

John Nickels
American Ruso Romani leader
Vice President, Nickels Midway Pier
Wildwood, New Jersey

———

My name is Tamara and I am a born and raised tribal member of the Kalderash Nation and *Mineshti Vitsa*. My grandfather was the official leader of the American Kalderash, and before him, six generations ago, my great-grandfather Slotcho held the government papers as the leader of the American Rroma. Although I am a sixth-generation American Rromni, English is my second language, and my family lived within the subculture of western America, within our own private culture. Many who know the American Rroma feel they know 'all about them', but this would be a mistake.

Yanko [Ian] brought together a very big part of the peoples from all over the Rromani world, and as you and we only know, you helped to bring all the millions of pieces together. You witnessed firsthand with our generation that our parents and grandparents were not as incorrect as we all thought they were, and although we are aware to evolve spiritually, we do know prejudice is still living, is alive and well, when we have lived it ourselves. You already did more than most of our own race, Yanko. You already have done so much. They say about the presidents, how history will show in time.

In history *Prala*, every *Rromengi glata* will know your name. I know you didn't do that for these reasons and I know you hurt so much like so many of us for our people, for a voice to be heard, for respect and kindness.

You have a right to be tired and should pay attention to what brings you happiness and joy; life is too short, my brother, and like I said before, *na bister te trayis o mai shukar zakonulya thodya tu amaro Del te aves Rrom te halyares thai ashunes. Tu musai te pakyav anda amende vi tu.*

Tamara Stanley

Introduction to Section One

The paper *Family tales* introduces the reader to the world into which Ian was born. He pieces together the story of his life, beginning with his own stock of memories, and supplementing them with reminiscences tape-recorded by his father's sister, Aunty Nell. To this mix Ian adds the fruits of several years of patient historical and genealogical research, and evidence both documentary and anecdotal. The central figure in the story is his grandfather, Marko, who passed away when Ian was just leaving childhood. Ian is part of the picture he skilfully paints, and the reader can not only catch a glimpse of his world, but also feel the stirrings of his mind, and sense the intensity and power of his memories; memories which would, in later years, drive him to tell the story of his larger family, the Roma people, with the same quiet passion and unhurried urgency.

If *Family tales* is an account of the early events that shaped Ian's life, *Talking back* is a reflection of the young man moulded by these events. It was an early diagnosis of the several maladies that afflicted the study of Romani culture by outsiders, who either lacked understanding of *Rromanija*, or sympathy for it, or both. This paper was also a blueprint for a course of action that Ian was to follow for the rest of his life. In the later papers in this volume, and indeed in all his other writings, Ian expands on the ideas in this blueprint. Ian addresses the paper to his fellow Roma, and exhorts them to stand up and be counted as people and as Rom, not as mere 'Gypsy' subjects of anthropological research, whose image is defined and controlled by outsiders: the *gadže*. With a wry sense of humour that barely conceals his exasperation, Ian calls upon the Roma to be assertive; work with genuine Romanologists; challenge the misinformation peddled by gypsilorists; and help the *gadže* develop a balanced view of *Rromanija* by making the authentic voice of the Roma heard through their own publications and spokespersons.

Several of Ian's opinions have been modified and qualified in the light of new scientific evidence that has accumulated over these last three decades. His focus and emphasis have also shifted in response to changing circumstances. But in broad outline, he still stands by what he expressed so forcefully so many years ago, both because these ideas were very relevant at the time of their formulation, but also because these criticisms unfortunately remain valid to this day.

CHAPTER ONE

Djabravoki

Briliko o djes, e slajdale thov
And'o vabo gajrin thaj gimblin
E borogovura sa mimsale, 'aj
Avri le momutne ratura grabin

> *"Arakh e Djabravokostar čhava*
> *Thar dand'ren, vunži rrande'*
> *Čhiriklja djudjup gonisar, thaj naš*
> *E bandersnačostar frumale!"*

> *Lja p'o vorpalo xanrro vastal*
E dušmanos manksale but rod'las
Ap hodinisajlo paš'e rukh tumtum
Thaj tordilo vrjamasa te gind'las

> *Thaj sar gindilas ufišlones*
> *O Djabravok, jakh phab'rindo*
> *Viflisardja p'o tulutno veš*
> *'Aj burblinas sar 'vilo*

Jekh duj, jekh duj, andre, andre
Vorpali čhuri šnikšnak'sardjas
Mukhlja les mulo, lja o šero
Palpale galump'sardjas

> *"Thaj mudardjan Tu Djabravokos?*
> *Bimaleja, dav Tut angali!*
> *Frabutno djes! Kalu kalej!"*
> *Loš'nes asaja avri*

Briliko o djes, e slajdale thov
And'o vabo gajrin thaj gimblin
E borogovura sa mimsale, 'aj
Avri le momutne ratura grabin.

CHAPTER TWO

Family tales

Marko died in 1956, when I was barely into my teens. He was just 'Grandad' then, and I suppose I took his presence pretty much for granted. It wasn't until later that I began to realise what a source of interesting stories his varied life had been. For a number of years I have been collecting narratives, oral and sometimes written, about Marko in his earlier years; from talking to family members, and others who knew him, I began to put together a picture of his life.

On a visit back to England in 1984 I persuaded my Dad's sister, my Aunty Nell, who was then seventy-seven, to tape-record whatever recollections she had of her father, and before her death in 1994 she would periodically send me a cassette of these.

My own father was taken from my grandparents by the welfare authorities in 1918 at the age of six and a half, and put into a home where there were numbers of other Romani children similarly taken away from their parents, supposedly for their own good. While the removal of Gypsy children from their families for placement in institutions is well documented for countries such as Sweden, Slovakia or Switzerland, the fact that it was happening in Britain too, and that British Romani women may even have been coercively sterilised, is less well known. The late Len Smith, a Traveller acquaintance who lived in Hampshire, had begun to document such instances.

This particular home was at 'The Mote', Charlton House, part of a national organisation known as the Caldecott Community. It was originally about a mile and a half from Sutton Valance (in Kent, not the

Originally published in *Lacio Drom*, 21(3/4) (1985), 53–61.

Reginald Aubrey 'Marko' Hancock (Grandad)   Marko in his street clown regalia
                                              (Galford, 2001: 62)

same place as Sutton in Surrey where my mother was born), ten minutes from Headcorn Station, although it was relocated to Hertfordshire in 1929. It still exists; its website describes it as being there to 'help children grow emotionally ... repairing some of the damage brought about by abuse, trauma, disruption or deprivation' in their early childhood. In her description of The Mote, written while my father was there, Josephine Ransom told how 'the children take part in everything, house, garden, looking after the donkey and the pig, and waiting at table where the domestic workers join in the meals' (1919: 24).

In 1925, when he was thirteen and a half, my father ran away to join the training ship *T.S. Mercury* and later the *T.S. Arethusa*, both of which were docked at Hamble near Southampton, two miles from the Netley railway station. There he was put in charge of the wire gantlines, the gantry cables used for carrying a harness up to the masthead. He also took up boxing, and spent the rest of his life with a broken nose because of it. He later left the training ships for the merchant navy, and visited Australia, West Africa and the Caribbean; with the outbreak of World War II he transferred to the Royal Navy, where he served mainly in the

Reginald 'John' Hancock (Dad)

eastern Mediterranean, until he was demobilised in 1946. After that he found work as a travelling salesman in paper products for a company called T.B. Ford, and kept this job for the next ten years, until we left England in 1957.

His memories of Caldecott Community were not unhappy ones. He remembered the two headmistresses, Miss Phyllis Potter and Miss Leila Rendel, and none of the children wearing shoes (although all were provided with shiny matching shoes for the official photograph!), and their being made to plant and harvest their own crops to eat. I visited The Mote just once as a boy with my father, and only recollect seeing fields with neat rows of vegetables, and passing through a low archway into a big central courtyard.

My dear Dad was the most valuable source of information about our family, even though my mother, Kitty, usually managed to steer the topic of conversation away from my Grandfather Marko whenever it was broached in her presence. Her own father was Arthur 'Jack' Palmer, a Romanichal who sometimes stayed at 5 Beauchamp Road in Sutton in

The Mote

The Mote

Surrey, four or five miles from Epsom Downs where he knew Marko well, since they both used to spend a lot of time in that district. There is a new book of photographs of Romanies in the Sutton area, including some of the Romani visitors to that town from Hungary (Evans, 2003). Jack was a rag-and-bone man (a 'totter') as well as an amateur boxer. The Palmer family, which is very large, was a branch of the Smiths, and originated in the area around Windsor and where the Heathrow Airport

The Mote

now is, west of London. Her mother was a girl named Cicely who was either Irish or English, and who was in service in a mansion close to Sutton; she was only in her mid-teens, and my mother's father Arthur was with his second wife at that time, a woman named Harriet. After she was born, Cicely gave her baby, my Mum, into the care of Arthur's sister Rose, because Harriet refused to take her, and then she left Surrey permanently for somewhere in the Midlands.

When she was fifteen, by this time having already met my father, my mother was taken away to stay with Edith ('Ede'), the eldest daughter from Harriet's first marriage, and Edith's husband Bob Jolly, a postman. Their house was at 90 Nowell Road in Mortlake, not far from Barnes Common and Watneys Brewery, and connected to Chiswick on the north side of the Thames opposite by a footbridge. This was the area where a series of gruesome murders was to occur (described in detail, with a map of the area, by Seabrook, 2006), around the same time that we left Chiswick to go and live in Canada.

Edith was puritanically strict. Mum tells of hiding lipstick and stockings in her handbag and having to put them on in secret once outside the house then later removing them before going home, because they were absolutely forbidden by Arthur's tyrannical stepdaughter whom, for the rest of her life, she would only refer to as 'the deadly

Gypsy wagons in Chiswick, *c.*1900 (Heard & Cameron, 1978: 9)

aunt'. She remembers running into Edith somewhere unexpectedly while wearing lipstick and nylons, and getting a sound and public slap in the face for it. It was just a few months before my mother seized an opportunity to get away from Barnes and the Jollys for good.

She had found a job at John Barker's department store in Kensington High Street, and there met a girl named Madge Orpwood who lived in Shepherds Bush, with whom she became great friends. Madge's mother Frances lived in Acton, and she asked my mother to come and stay there with her in Kingscote Road, since life was so miserable for her in Barnes. Madge's mum was very kind to my mother, and when I was a little boy she was my 'Nanny Orp'; it is after her that I was given my middle name Francis. They called me 'Hinkhonk' because I couldn't pronounce 'Hancock' properly, and that was my nickname for many years. A surprising Hancock reference turns up in Barbara Nadel's novel *After the Mourning,* where the 'hero', an Anglo-Indian detective named Francis Hancock, solves a gruesome Gypsy murder in Epping Forest.

To get to Kensington, my mother would walk each day along the towpath to Hammersmith Bridge, then cross the river to catch the bus in Hammersmith Broadway. By this time my father had moved in with Aunt Jess, Marko's sister, where he slept in a closet under the stairs, and would arrange his time so that he'd be putting the daily papers in the rack

Hungarian Roma in Sutton, *c.*1935 (Evans, 2003)

outside when my mother, whom he'd originally met in Sutton, came past the shop. Later on he found another job selling books and papers in a shop in Ladbroke Grove closer to the family in Notting Dale. With the outbreak of war he went back to sea, this time to join the Royal Navy where he eventually became a lieutenant, a remarkable achievement considering his background. For the first three years of her marriage during the Second World War, before I was born and while my father was away at sea, my mother left Nanny Orp's house and went to stay with some Romani Palmers who lived near a village called Cookham, which is north of Maidenhead and some six miles from Windsor Castle.

Although my grandfather (and my father, when he was on leave) both spent a lot of time in the Sutton and Epsom area before I was born, I went back there with my mother to visit my grandfather and Aunty Rose fewer than ten times altogether as a child in the late 1940s and early 1950s. Rose had married a man named Bill Harland, and their children were Molly, Frank, Terry and Joan; Molly was my parents' bridesmaid and Terry was then a 'Desert Rat' serving in the army in Egypt. I remember Uncle Bill carrying me around on his shoulders in their house, and going up to a stuffed animal's head mounted on the wall, saying "Boo!" and me being terrified.

Jess, Marko's sister   Iris, Jess's daughter

My mother has never been enthusiastic about the Romani part of her own background and was also openly critical of my father's side of the family for being what they were. Now in her nineties, she has mellowed considerably and has begun to talk more about it. There was always friction there because she didn't really care for most of my father's relatives, especially Marko, and her animosity had a lot to do with our eventually moving away from Britain altogether and going to live in Canada. The circumstances of her birth, out of wedlock at a time when this was viewed with far more disapproval than it is today, has also distanced her emotionally from her childhood.

My parents married in 1939 in St Andrews Anglo-Catholic Church, Staveley Road, Chiswick, although my mother was a Baptist. I was conceived in Birkenhead in December 1941, when she visited my father there during his Christmas shore leave, but I was born in London. We lived in Chiswick at 34 Esmond Road, although in the early forties we stayed for different periods of time in a number of other towns too, including South Shields and Glasgow.

The first German V-2 rocket to be aimed at Britain landed a mile or two from our house, but mercifully it didn't explode. Every time my mother would take me on the number 55 bus to the free clinic in Meon

Iris, Jess's daughter

Nellie, my father's sister

Sylvia, Nellie's daughter

June, Nellie's daughter

Jim Harrison (Uncle)   Arthur 'Pedlar' Jack Palmer

Road and we'd pass under the railway bridge on Acton Lane, she'd say, 'That's where the rocket fell'. This got a mention in a book about the development of space travel: 'On September 8, 1944 the first rocket bomb, or V-2, fell near Chiswick in London, like a meteor out of space. This event marked the beginning of a new era in warfare' (Coggins and Pratt, 1952: 30).

Others in particular who have given me useful information about Marko are George Marriott, who was a contemporary of his and who organised the Gypsy Ex-Servicemen's Association; Manfri Fred Wood, Keith Nichols, Toni Nathan Lee (who began, but never finished, recording a cassette tape of his reminiscences of Marko for me), Barrie Taylor, and most of all a family friend and 'uncle', Albert Cook. We lost contact with Uncle Albert when we left for Canada in 1957, but Thomas Acton put us back in touch by mail in the early 1970s. Albert was Inmate Number 096510 in the Wandsworth Prison at that time, for the alleged theft of a shirt from Marks and Spencer, and Thomas Acton, working with the Gypsy Council, was attempting to effect his release. He was also visited by noted Romanologist Donald Kenrick and by Anne Sutherland, now Professor of Anthropology at the University of California and author of *Gypsies, the Hidden Americans* (1975), who was living in Britain at that time. She, too, spoke for his release; in all of his letters, he

Kitty Hancock (Mum)

Me in my teens

determinedly maintained that he had been wrongly convicted, and was only guilty of being a Gypsy.

Uncle Albert periodically travelled with Marko as a young man, and had also been in Hungary, where his own and part of our family both originate. His name is an anglicisation of 'Kocs'. Information he provided in this connection has been especially valuable, and I have supplemented it with the help of Dr Várnagy Elemér of Pécs, who has made a study of Hungarian Romani genealogy. Of course Marko's other children, as well as my grandmother and his sister Jess, both of whom survived him by several years, also spoke of him frequently, although not all of them at all kindly.

When I was very young, after the end of the war, groups of families, including my grandparents and my aunts and uncles, would go down into Kent and Surrey to pick hops, an occupation known to them as 'scrooping' (see Bignell, 1977 and Schweitzer and Hancock, 1991). My recollections of this are not very clear, but I do remember sleeping on a blanket on the floorboards of a long building in Farnham; a lot of noisy children; and the times at the end of the day when the adults would gather at one or another public house, and we would be left outside for interminable periods under a blanket in the backseat of a car and usually mollified with gifts of potato crisps (but not the extra

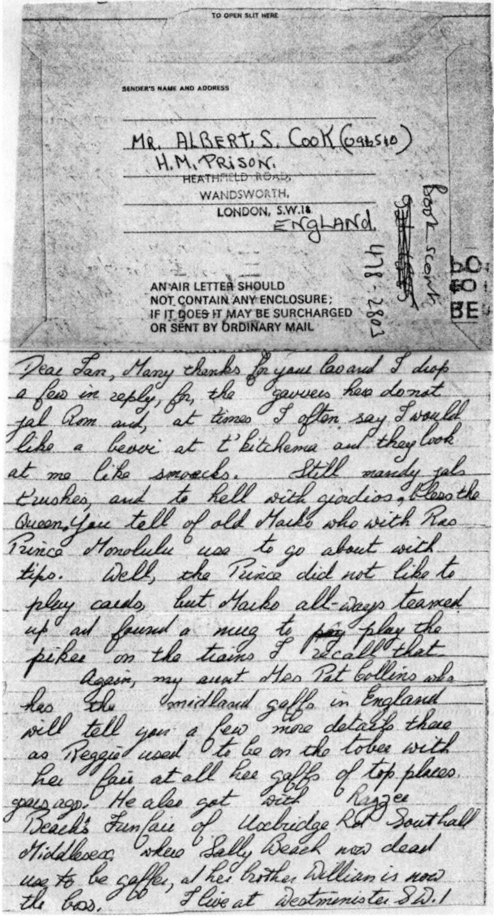

Letter from 'Uncle' Albert Cook

salty blue ones) and bottles of Tizer and fizzy Idris lemonade. 'I drinks Idris when I's dry!' went the racist advertisement, matching the paper gollywog I remember would be under the lid of each jar of Robertson's marmalade.

I really remember my Grandfather Marko well only when he was an old man; in fact he was just 67 when he died, but I suppose to me as a boy he seemed quite old. I'm told that as a younger man he had a great deal of charm, and was something of a womaniser. He was thin, with black hair and angular features, and because of his musical skills and nice voice (a talent shared by his sister Jessie) was very popular. For a while he was a street clown, performing tricks with balloons for children

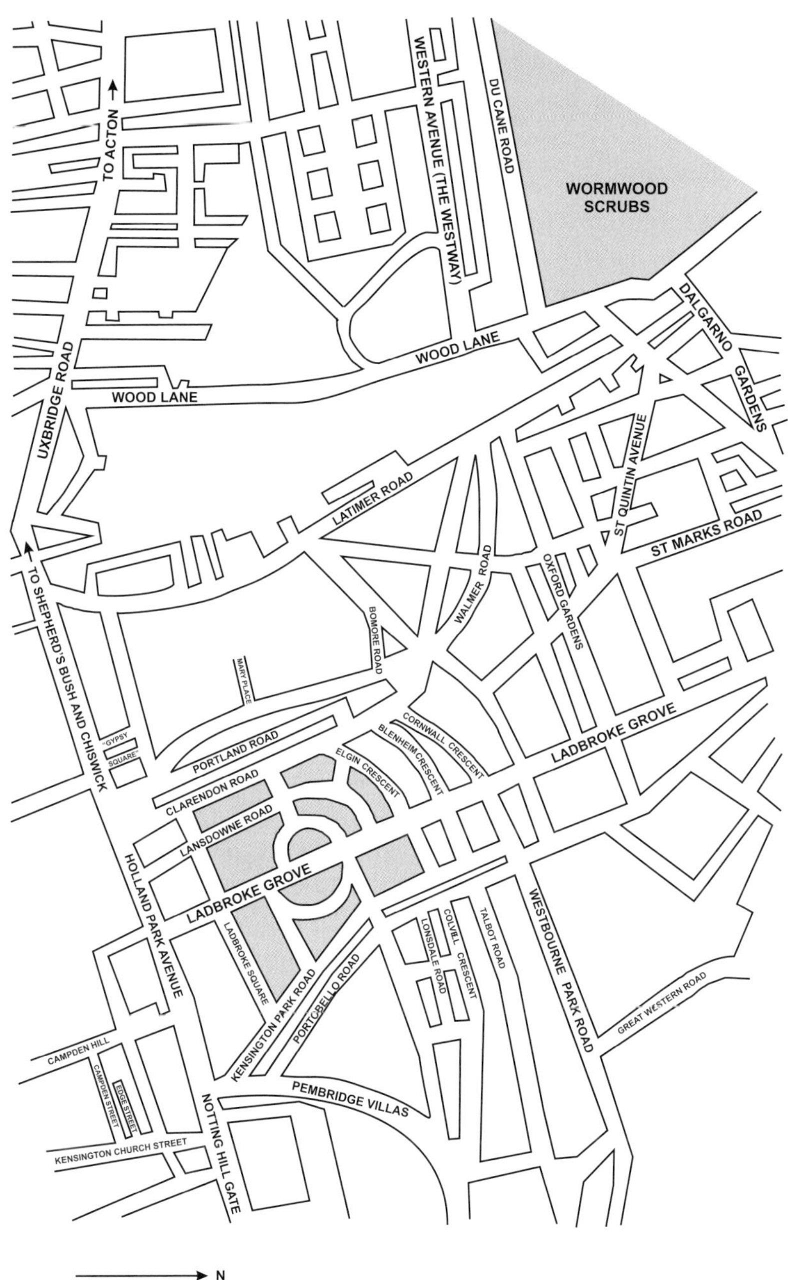

Notting Hill, London

(the picture of him doing this is from Galford, 2001: 62), but he was a rat-catcher during the last years of his life, and my grandmother's death certificate lists him as a 'rodent operator'. I don't imagine he ever used such a fancy title himself. Aunty Nell tells a funny story of Grandad's rat-catching days:

> When he was still new at it, he was in the basement of a bakery with an older hand who was showing him the tricks of the trade. Old Bill got a torch and said to my Dad, "Now when I shine this torch onto the pipes, you get the neck of the sack ready, and when I shout out, *right!*" Well, it all went okay until Dad saw these bloody big rats coming towards him. He dropped the sack and ran, and a rat went with him. And Dad fell on him, and killed it. And the outcome was, "I've seen some funny rat-catchers in my time, but never one 'oo kills 'em wiv 'is arse!"

Aunty Nell and Uncle Fred had two daughters, my cousins Sylvia (now deceased) and June (now June Butcher, and living in Barnsley). Most of my family, including Marko and my Grandmother Gertrude, lived in North Kensington and in Notting Hill near 'Gipsy Square' (no longer on current maps) in an area that used to be known as The Potteries, in streets such as Bomore Road, Latimer Road, Edge Street and Western Terrace (now renamed Lonsdale Road, where Marko lived at number 17, and where my father was born). Before the First World War there used to be kilns for the manufacture of bricks and clay pots, as well as a number of pig farms, between there and nearby Shepherds Bush. The area around Latimer Road was known back then as 'the piggeries and potteries', although it is highly gentrified now. On Saturdays and Sundays throughout the 1960s I would regularly ride the number 88 bus along Goldhawk Road to Shepherds Bush Market, a place where you could hear Romani, Yiddish, Urdu, Bengali, Jamaican Patois and several other languages being spoken around the stalls along by the arches below the Metropolitan Line tube station.

On one tape, Aunty Nell describes how they would periodically do a 'moonlight flit' from one place to another because they couldn't pay the rent; they would throw their belongings down from the upstairs window into a handcart and steal silently away in the middle of the night to a new place. On another, she describes how the police suddenly showed up in the middle of the night at a place where they were staying in Acton, looking for Marko, who had managed to disappear via the backyard just moments before.

Notting Hill (Notting Dale) was one of the 'metropolitan Gypsyries' of the Victorian era, described by Reverend John Hall and by George Smith (see also Gladstone, 1969), and was occupied by Romanies during the middle of the nineteenth century after a catastrophe in south London forced the resettlement of many Gypsy families from there to other parts of the city. According to George Hall (1915: 198), in 1853 some thirty Romanies returning from hopping in Kent lost their lives; their horses had evidently panicked while crossing a bridge over the Medway, sending their waggons into the river. This sad association brought many families into London, particularly North Kensington, Hammersmith and Wandsworth. Taylor (1983: 1) also attributes the decline of rural means of livelihood as a factor contributing to this relocation. An article in *Queen* magazine from 1861, however, says that its residents 'immigrated to this ground some sixty years since', that is, around 1800 (Anonymous, 1861).

An article in the *Illustrated London News* from 1879 reported that some two thousand Romanies inhabited the London Gypsyries in that year. An interesting description of the area appeared in the same magazine:

> The ugliest place we know in the neighbourhood of London, the most dismal and forlorn, is … Shepherd's-Bush and Notting-Hill. There it is that the gipsy encampment may be found, squatting within an hour's walk of the Royal palaces and of the luxurious town mansions of our nobility and opulent classes … It is a curious spectacle in that situation, and might suggest a few serious reflections upon social contrasts at the centre and capital of the mighty British nation, which takes upon itself the correction of every savage tribe in South and West Africa and Central Asia.

Rodney Smith wrote about Shepherds Bush (1901: 49), and George Smith mentions a Gypsy mission in Latimer Road which today is an Islamic centre. George Borrow described the very street, Portland Road (then called Pottery Lane) in his *Romano Lavo-Lil*, where Marko lived for some time, at number 145 (see also Chesney 1970: 3923). The whole area, with its once large sedentary Romani population (subsequently displaced by immigrants from the West Indies and elsewhere), was the subject of a study by Michael Taylor. Borrow (1874: 228–9) wrote:

> Going more than halfway down Notting Hill, you turn to the right, and proceed along a tolerably genteel street and which is on the left hand, and

Hungary

bears the name of Pottery Lane. Go along this lane and you … will see, on
your right hand, a little, open bit of ground, chock-full of crazy, battered
caravans of all colours – yellow, some green, some red. Dark men,
wild-looking, witch-like women, and yellow-faced children at the doors of
the caravans … you have now arrived at the second grand Gypsyry of
London – you are amongst the Romanichals of the Potteries.

Marko's maternal grandfather was Imre Róbert Bencsi (or Benczi:
Bálint Sárosi spells the name of the musician Benczi Gyula this way in
his book *Gypsy Music* (1983:204)). Marko's descendants in Hungary
today, or at least as late as the 1960s, according to Uncle Albert in a letter
postmarked 8 December 1972, have:

> [A] travelling fair of two shooters, a big wheel and shot gallery, plus a
> small set of gallopers. They travel the villages and have a yard at a village
> called Peste about 35 km. from Budapest. The old fellow Imree is the son
> of an earlier Imree whose sister married an English traveller years ago,
> and worked for a time on their gaff. They have, by the way, a few relations
> at our park on Liszbet Ilan.

According to other letters from Uncle Albert, and to information from
Dr Várnagy, the Bencsi family travels (or travelled) mainly in Győr
Sopron County in north-western Hungary around Mosonmagyáróvar and
in the region between the Einser Canal and the Rábca River near the

South East England

Austrian border some fifty miles from Vienna and Bratislava. The town of Peste he refers to is Uj Pest, twenty miles to the north-west of Budapest, and Liszbet (properly Erszébet) Ilan is an island in the Danube right in the centre of Budapest which has a big amusement park and funfair; I visited it in 1997 but it was closed for the winter. In one letter, he referred to the Bencsis being on the Gestapo list for incarceration by the Nazis during 1937 and 1938.

The sister Albert mentions was Marko's great-aunt, who also came to England as a young woman with some of her family and with the Kocs' in the second half of the nineteenth century; a third family which came in with them at the same time were the Laszlos. This migration was prompted by the *Ausgleich* (*vyrovnanie*) or Compromise of 1867 under which the Austrian Habsburgs agreed to share power with a separate Hungarian government that was being pushed for by members of the former Magyar nobility and clergy, dividing the territory of the former Austrian Empire between them. Gypsies, as usual, got caught in the middle, and the situation became intolerable for them. Their move may have also been stimulated by the huge migrations out of south-eastern Europe of the Danubian Romanies, not long liberated from Romanian

Parish register for Corsham, Wiltshire, records the birth of Welleno Hancock to John and Fellowphany Hancock on 22 June 1808

slavery and who, during the same period, spread to all parts of Europe and the Americas. Some went to France, but most went to the US, families such as the Dunas, Godlas, Horvaths and Baloghs; a family of Bencsis lives in Cleveland (Hancock, 1994). Kocs' in the US have respelt their name as Koch. Like Imre Senior's sister, some of these married into British Romanichal fairground families, and since the publication of the earlier version of this essay in 1985 I have received mail from members of one British Romanichal family telling me that they also incorporated Hungarian Romanies into the family line in the late 1800s.

Albert Cook himself stayed two streets away from Aunty Nell and her husband Fred Saker in Winchester Street for some of the time, but was living in a trailer at the Wardley Street Caravan Site in south London when he got arrested.

In 1888 Marko's mother Mary Maria married a man named Luther (they were born in 1868 and 1866 respectively), son of an earlier Luther from the sprawling family of West Country Hancocks from Romsey in Hampshire, on the eastern edge of the New Forest. His grandfather, John

Handcock, born in 1816, is listed as a 'tallow chandler' in the 1851 registry, and lived at 124 Middbridge Street. John's father, James Hancock (a 'hemp dresser and sack weaver') also had a daughter Hannah, who married a Christopher Smith, listed as a 'hawker and traveller' in the Somerset House records.

The Hancock family seat seems to have been in the neighbouring county of Wiltshire, with a movement to Hampshire and the Southampton area in the 1800s, and then on to London. The parish Register for Corsham in Wiltshire registered the birth of one Wellano (a variant of Wellenough?) Hancock on 22 June 1808 as the daughter of John Hancock, born in 1777 and the brother of James, and his wife Fellowphany, and lists the family as 'people commonly called gipseys'. His father was yet *another* John Hancock, born in the New Forest, near Ringwood, in 1740. I haven't been able to go back further than this; Edmonds (2001: 11) lists a traveller named Richard Hancock who was buried in Wimbotsham, Norfolk in 1738, but provides no further information.

Fellowphany is an unusual name; there was also a Thurza Hancock, Luther's sister who was born in Romsey in 1848, and other more recent family names include Ailsa, Fear, Blackadder, Wippetty and Cotlaba. Bob Dawson, who researches British Romani given names, says (in personal correspondence) that it is likely to be a form of Fallowfield with the common Gypsy name ending -phany, but Lavinia has been recorded as Laphany too. We christened our youngest daughter Fellowphany.

Mary Maria and her sister Sara, Imre's daughters, were both born in a waggon in Pimlico near Vauxhall Bridge Road, where my Aunty Nell and Uncle Fred later lived (in John Islip Street) for many years. She and her husband Luther went to live in Campden Street, off Kensington Church Street on the other side of Holland Park Avenue in Notting Hill, and their son Reginald Aubrey (Marko) was born a year later in 1889. According to the 1901 Census, they had moved two streets away to number 7 in Cousens Court, off Edge Street. Perhaps it was nearby Aubrey Walk that provided the inspiration for Marko's given middle name.

We remember Mary Maria, Marko's mother, as 'Granny Benge'. She had a daughter Jess and another son Frederick besides Marko, and she is described as having been a tiny woman who had a pet parrot. She and her sister were always dressed entirely in black, and kept their heads covered

Gertrude King (Nan)

all the time. Aunty Nell wrote about her Granny's and her Aunt Sara's unusual clothes in a note in the *London News and Post* (Saker, 1982: 6).

Marko's sister Jessie married a non-Gypsy, Fred McVety, and they lived at 68 Hammersmith Bridge Road where they had a cobbler's shop and tobacconist next to the Oxford and Cambridge pub, across the road from the river (it was outside the shop that my Dad would wait for my Mum to come by, but there's nothing but highrises in the area now). For some of the time they would leave it to stay in a trailer near Sunbury-on-Thames outside of London. As for their brother Frederick, he was killed in the First World War on the first day of fighting at the Battle of the Somme on 1 July 1916, but had already fathered Caroline, Calvin and Ellen, none of whose descendants I have so far been able to locate.

When he was eighteen, Marko married an English Traveller woman named Gertrude, my Nan, whose mother Elizabeth Lucy (her father's first wife; he had three altogether), daughter of Liddie, was a King from the branch of that Romanichal family that lived in the Leatherhead area. Her half-sister Nell also married a Romanichal, Sammy Cook, from the Kent and Surrey Traveller families and not related at all to Albert Cook (Kocs). Their son Charlie kept a stall in the Portobello Road Market, sometimes selling china, sometimes vegetables. The family was still there when I visited them in the 1960s, but was gone by the time I visited in 2009. Another Cook, Ronnie, wrote a book, published in 2005, about his life before turning to Christianity. Certainly the best-known Cook is singer David Essex, patron of the British Gypsy Council.

Nell Cook hated my grandfather, although she and her husband lived upstairs right next door to him in Bomore Road. She was angry because

Gertrude's relatives, 1970s (photograph courtesy of Barrie Law)

he had put her sister 'in a family way'. At the time that she married Marko, my Nan and some of her relatives were living in Upham Park Road in Chiswick, a borough which, along with neighbouring Brentford, still has quite a few Romani families resident today, particularly in the area where the two districts meet near Gunnersbury Park. A picture of some Travellers' waggons taken here a century ago is reproduced in Heard and Cameron (1978: 9). Barnes, Hammersmith and Chiswick were all listed as stopping places for Romanies in the *London City Mission* magazine (2 January 1860). Lots of other Romani families lived in the same road, the Smalls and the Lights among them. Other Chiswick Romani families included the Spraggs, Manceys, Collins, Worths, Burtons, Hollands, Hearns, Huxleys and Balls; the caretaker at the Chiswick Town Hall was a King (Mary Horner, in personal correspondence); a wonderful and familiar account of Gypsy life in Chiswick in the 1930s and 1940s was published by the Romany and Traveller Family History Society (Hearn, 2001).

My Nan was stone deaf, and towards the end of her life in 1979 she had lost most of her sight as well. When I would visit her in the 1960s I would have to guide her to the framed photograph of me on the wall and put her hand on it, so she would know who I was. Her wall was covered with family photographs that she could no longer see, but she knew exactly where each one was placed. Their children were Reginald John (my father, 1911–2000), Jessie Edith (1896–1975), and Frederick, who died of meningitis in 1915 at the age of nine months. 'Reg' and 'Redjo' were what my grandparents called my father, who outside the family was everywhere known by his middle name, John. Following the Vlax practice – and since I learnt Vlax Romani after going to America – I have somewhat fancifully given myself the Romani name Yanko le Redjosko, 'Ian, son of Redjo', that I use in some of my writings.

I came to realise early on that the British Gypsy families who had married with the Hungarian Romanies were something of a shunned group; the British Travellers were not at all well disposed to their own who 'married out' with the foreign Gypsies. A group of Hungarian Gypsies came back to Sutton again in the 1930s (Evans, 2003: 13).

It was only when we were with them – Nan and Grandad and Uncle Albert and some of his friends, people I didn't know, as well as Aunty Nell and Uncle Fred and everybody, usually at holiday times – that I would hear 'real' Romani being spoken by several people all at once. Marko knew at least some inflected Romani, and so did Uncle Albert, some of whose letters contain Romani, English Romanichal dialect and Hungarian mixed in with the English, but he spoke Pogadi better. He called it 'Pikey talk', but the word 'Pikey' has become so 'non-PC' now that its use is cause for legal action (Balfe, 2008: 1). I remember a little song my grandfather would sing to me to make me go to sleep while the gaslights were hissing, no doubt sung to him by his own mother, which began '*nan ma maro, nan ma mas, nan ma kotor balovas*', which means 'I have no bread, I have no meat, not even a piece of bacon'.

Marko had a reputation as a 'sponge', and Aunt Jess used to say that he must have inherited his habit of cadging money from people from their dad Luther, whose name in her Cockney pronunciation came out 'loofah', like the sponge.

I also learnt to swear in Gypsy at that early age from listening to Marko. At school – Southfield Road School in Acton, and later at the Chiswick County School for Boys – I and another boy called Billy Gray, who was from a Gypsy family that lived in Oxford Road, would get a

'Bird pub', Club Row

kick out of calling our classmates rude names in Romani. Oxford Road was beyond Turnham Green, along Chiswick High Road, where many Travellers used to stop; George Smith describes it in his book (1880: 277). In the earlier version of this essay I included some of those words, but it infuriated one old Romanichal man to see them in print. He told his son not to talk to me again, even though I'd previously been successful in getting that same son out of prison in Virginia by organising a petition to the State Governor.

Marko also knew Yiddish, as for some years he was a peddler of sheet music, and would sell for the Jewish music agencies in the district around Aldgate in London's East End, in Middlesex Street (Petticoat Lane) and elsewhere. He called himself Reggie Marks, and passed himself off as being Jewish. My exposure to Romani and Yiddish began with being around my grandfather. One of the first articles I ever had published, over forty years ago in 1964, was in *The Linguist* and dealt with Yiddish in London. When I was a boy, Yiddish posters in Hebrew letters were a common sight on the walls and fences in bomb-damaged Whitechapel, and they fascinated me. In later life I made it a point to learn how to read and write that language, and I even gave a

Club Row Market

one-semester course in it at my university. In the early 1960s I was able to get lessons through an organisation in east London called Di Fraynt fun Idish from an old couple, Soyre and Moishe Beckerman, who coincidentally lived in Ennismore Avenue, Chiswick, just one block away from Upham Park Road where my grandmother had lived as a child. I would show up at their home at seven o'clock each Wednesday evening, and they would give me soup and Yiddish lessons at the dining room table. Both are long gone now. *A brokhe af zeyer zikoren*.

Billy Cribb, an Essex Gypsy man, also mentions Marko and one of his favourite hangouts, a street named Club Row in Shoreditch, not far from the music companies he worked for in Aldgate. There, a man used to sell sarsaparilla and hot banana fritters out of the back of a van, and the Romanichals would sell the caged finches they'd caught that morning, outside the 'bird pub', as the Kings Head (now fancily renamed *Les Trois Garçons*) was then called. This practice is in fact illegal: the newspapers ran an article as recently as 2005 about a police raid on another 'bird pub' in Bethnal Green where fourteen men were arrested on charges of 'animal cruelty' (Seenan, 2005: 5). The area looks very different now, with many of its old buildings having been torn down or replaced, but the Club Row Market is still there and on Saturday mornings it still serves as a meeting and trading place for Romanies, although today they are mostly the post-1990 immigrants from Central and Eastern Europe.

Since my father was a merchant seaman during those early years and was away at sea for long periods after he left the Caldecott Community, I spent a lot of time with my grandparents and my paternal aunts, uncles and cousins. I remember very clearly Nan and Grandad's flat in Peabody Buildings, a subsidised housing estate with endless cement stairs, whitewashed walls, and long brick balconies in Dalgarno Gardens, down the road from the Wormwood Scrubs prison (where Marko had spent some time).

There was no electricity in the Peabody flat, and the pervasive smell and peculiar harsh yellowish-green glow of the gas mantles on the wall are still a memory. I remember that there was highly polished brass everywhere. Under his bed, also made of brass, my grandfather kept two or three battered tin trunks, filled with 'treasures' appropriated in the course of his day's work as a rat-catcher. Often he would let me choose an item to keep from these trunks – once a broken fob watch, once a piece of Roman tile – and to me they were treasures indeed.

When I stayed there, I would be given a bath in a zinc tub in the middle of the parlour floor, filled from buckets of water heated on the gas stove. There was in fact a bathtub, but I don't remember its ever being put to its proper use. It was in the kitchen next to the gas-stove, and had a board placed over it that served as a table. Washing and cooking in the same area was not appropriate in a Romani home. Marko used to make different things on that board to sell.

I remember also what I'd be given to eat: bread and dripping sandwiches, sugar sandwiches, bread soaked in hot milk, fried bread, and even an odd combination of bread dipped in milk and *then* fried, with jam on it – lots of food, but always lots of bread. My dad even used bits of bread as a pencil eraser, and as a poultice when I was sick. The milk was called 'sterilised' and came in bottles that had beer caps. My Nan had big lids on the windowsills, on which she sprouted mustard seeds on bits of damp flannel; she would use the sprouts (which she called 'crease') to make sandwiches. I remember also that both of them would pour their tea out of the cup into the saucer and drink it from there, and also dip their bread into their tea.

Christmas time and Easter were very big family events: I'd see relatives then that I never saw at any other time. Marko would sing his songs, usually very rude ones, and my mother was always uncomfortable at such gatherings. I remember one Christmas, at Aunty Nell's house in John Islip Street, my mother edging me into a corner and engaging me in conversation to divert me from listening to Marko. He would sing all kinds of songs, and compose them, too. He used to sing *Jealous of You, Come Inside You Silly Bugger, Turn a Winkle Upside Down*, and Noel Gay's *The Sun Has Got His Hat On*, songs hardly remembered today. I learnt a lot of them from my Dad who'd inherited them, and who had a song for every occasion.

Come Inside You Silly Bugger

I was workin' once in a lunatic asylum
breakin' up some stones
An' along come a lunatic 'oo says to me
"Good mornin' Mr Jones.
'Ow much a week do yer get for doin' this?"
Firty bob I sighed,
Then the ol' man looked an' 'e scratched 'is 'ead
an' this is what 'e cried –
"Come inside yer silly bugger come inside,
I fought you 'ad a bit more sense –
workin' for a livin'? Take my tip,
Act a little silly an' become a lunatic;
You gets yer meals quite reg'lar,
an' two noo suits besides,
Firty bob a week, no wife an' kids to keep
Come inside yer silly bugger come inside!"

Turn a Winkle Upside Down

You must turn a winkle upside down
To stand it on its 'ead
Stand it on its 'ead
Before it goes to bed,
In '83 when aht at sea
It's true what Nelson said,
You must turn a winkle upside down
To stand it on its 'ead.

The Old Kent Road

Last week dahn ahr alley come a tawf [a toff]
Nice old geezer wiv an 'ackin' cawf
Sees my missus, takes 'is topper awf
In a very gentlemanly way.

"Wot cher!" all the neighbours cried
"'Oo yer gonna meet, Bill
'Ave yer bought the street, Bill?"
Laugh! I fought I should've died
Knocked 'em in the Old Kent Road.

Ev'ry evenin' at the stroke of five
Me and the missus takes a little drive
You'd say, "Wonderful they're still alive"
If you saw that little donkey go!

When we starts the blessed donkey stops
'E won't move, so aht I quickly 'ops
Pals start whackin' him, when dahn 'e drops
Someone says 'e wasn't made to go

"Wot cher!" all the neighbours cried
"'Oo yer gonna meet, Bill
'Ave yer bought the street, Bill?"
Laugh! I fought I should've died
Knocked 'em in the Old Kent Road.

One of Grandad's party pieces was a rude version of *Bye Bye Blackbird* ("made her take off all her clothes, 'cept her shoes and her hose …"). Aunty Nell talked once about his days as a minstrel:

When I see the buskers of today, I compare them with Dad, as he used to have three pals, who played the harmonium, ukulele, and concertina. Dad sang, and sold the music and words, of a song sheet. He also was the bottler, and that's the one that takes the money. Sundays was their best day; they would go all round the East End. He would even get money wrapped round a note asking for a certain song to be played and sung. People in those days would throw the money from the window. There were a lot of buskers in and out our street, such as two sisters … they used to push the barrel-organ all the way to the West End, every day. Then there was a man and wife, with a large harp, on the baby's pram. She played, and he sang.

The accordion player was a West Indian whose name I don't know, and the man who played the harmonium was a Romani named Peter Ball, but no one can remember anything at all about the man who played the ukulele. Aunty Nell referred back to that anecdote at the end of one of her tapes:

When I told you about your Grandad, used to be a minstrel, well I didn't
tell you this bit, about when I said to all the girls, twelve and thirteen,
"that's my dad, that nice-looking one, that handsome one; you see when
he looks round! Dad! Dad!" D'you think the bugger would turn round? He
ignored me, because he didn't want the girls to know he had such a
grown-up daughter. That's your Grandad! Now that shows you what a
bugger he was, dunnit!

One of the things Marko used to make on the board on the bathtub was
team favours for the yearly Oxford and Cambridge boat race. On the boat
race days he would make a big board, and cover it in black velvet, and pin
on the little dolls and favours, he'd buy a gross of dolls, so many yards of
pale blue and dark blue ribbon, and pom-poms for the head, then glue and
tie the ribbons round the tummy of the dolls, then stand down Portobello
Market in the morning of the boat race selling them. Then afterwards; on
the towing path at Hammersmith Bridge calling out "Don't forget your
favours! Oxford or Cambridge!" Pity all those customs has died out now.

Something else he used to make, and sell very successfully around the
public houses, was artificial dog excrement. He used to call this 'faking
jookal inder for the gawjas'. He had a coarse sense of humour, my old
Grandad, and it was no doubt this that put off a lot of people. It was a
private source of amusement to him that people would actually pay
money for this. He would make several of these small piles out of flour
paste and pulped newspaper, and paint them when they'd dried. I
remember seeing these objects in a row on the board over the tub; in fact
I kept one myself as a souvenir for a long time.

During the War, people were subject to search by the police at any
time if they were seen carrying anything suspicious. One night, coming
home from his rounds of the pubs, Marko had two of these things left
unsold, wrapped in a piece of newspaper, tucked under his arm. He was
spotted by a policeman who, seeing the small package, demanded to
know what was in it. Marko told him – plainly – and of course the
officer thought he was being a smart alec, so he asked him to open it up.
When he saw what they were, he bought them both. On another
occasion, in a pub, some of Marko's pals got him to leave one of these
on the counter, to trick the barmaid. When she saw it she screamed,
swept it up and promptly disposed of it down the toilet, where it got
stuck and blocked up the plumbing. Marko was never allowed back into
that particular pub.

My Nan remained illiterate all her life because there was no educational provision available for the deaf, but Marko went to Fox School in Notting Hill for a while – it is still there – and developed a very artistic copperplate hand. Those who remember him all remark on this. "If any of the costers in Portobello Market wanted a letter wrote," said Aunty Nell, "they would ask Dad to write it, and would give him a guinea for his trouble." George Marriott remembers Marko from his days with the travelling shows when, for a small sum, he would with several pounds of heavy lead weights hanging from his right wrist write out your name, beautifully and without faltering.

One show with which Marko travelled belonged to Razzee Beach. Uncle Albert was with him in those days, and wrote of some of the times they had in a letter postmarked 25 October 1972:

> Pat Collins, who had the Midlands gaffs in England, will tell you a few more details there, as Marko used to be on the tobee with his fair at all his gaffs of top places years ago. He also got with Razzee Beach's fun fair of Uxbridge Road, Southall, Middlesex, where Sally Beach, now dead, used to be gaffer, and her brother William is now the boss … Nell and Fred did go down Kent in 40s and you may ask them if they recall John Lee of Epping, the Palmers, Hollands, Loveridges, Biddies and Francombes, who with a few Penfolds made a proper seven days booze up every minute of the day with the board out for dancing, till nearly the whole police force of England were praying on their knees for us to leave off as they stopped all the booze coming into the village at Romford, so as we would have to go back to the vardo. I remember my vardo was taken and left in Trafalgar Sq. and I do not know today who drove it there. I have a sus. it was Consuella Lee, but I do not know, as it left me speechless for £250.

Pat Collins was a well known and very wealthy carnival owner between the two World Wars, mentioned a number of times in Allingham's book *Cheapjack* (and see especially Allen and Williams, 1991). A branch of the Hancocks that moved to Australia changed their name to Collins, for some reason. The Romanichal poet and spokesman Eli Frankham (Francombe) who passed away in 2001 was another one who remembered Marko.

Another of my grandfather's means of livelihood was that of racing tipster. He did this much of the time, especially during the big race events such as the Grand National and the Epsom Derby.

> I was sent over to the shops to get a packet of BVD cigarettes, *Sporting Life* paper, and a couple of bloaters for Dad's breakfast. Then out would

come the John Bull Printing Set, sixpence in Woolworth's, and the scratch-pad, then Dad would pick out the Nat choice from the *Sporting Life*, and would stamp out the selections on all these pieces of paper and go down the market, again Portobello Road, selling them for half a crown a time, which is 25p.

Aunty Nell got this last bit wrong; decimal money was still new. Twenty-five pence is twice that: five shillings. Grandad found his most profitable times on Epsom Downs and was frequently there, especially on Derby Day. (The picture Hall painted of Gypsies converging on this famous racecourse each year hardly need be changed seventy years later, although there have been a number of attempts to forbid their doing so.) There, he called himself Marko the Tip, and teamed up with an African bookmaker called Ras Prince Monolulu. Monolulu was quite a well known figure in his day. He came from Somalia or Ethiopia, and dressed himself in leopard skins and coloured feathers to attract a clientele. Uncle Albert remembered this too, in a letter postmarked 8 January 1973: 'Old Marko who was with Ras Prince Monolulu used to go about with tips. Well, the prince did not like to play cards, but Marko all-ways teamed up and found a mug to play the piker on the trains. I recall that. To hell with gordios, and god bless the queen.'

In fact Marko once had a falling out with some of the other Gypsies over this, since there was constant resentment between the Gypsy and non-Gypsy tipsters, and he was accused of getting too pally with the opposition. Not infrequently Monolulu was the cause of fights that had to be broken up by the police. It was because Marko repeatedly used my father, then just a child, as a bookie's runner, that he was taken away and sent to the Caldecott Community. Bare-knuckle fighter Billy Cribb (2001: 64) wrote about both Prince Monolulu and my grandfather:

> With Prince Monolulu there would also be a Romani Gypsy man known as 'Marko the Tip'. Not only did we see them at the [Petticoat] Lane but they would be at every race track I remember visiting … Both Monolulu and Marko were real characters, the like of which the modern world appears to be lacking. Granddad often bought horse tips from these men until he sussed that they would sell the name of several horses to be the winner in the same race.

Some of my relations continue to move around the south-eastern and south-western counties of England, and periodically I hear about one or

Ras Prince Monolulu

another of them in letters, and sometimes the names of King and Cook and Palmer crop up in news items from the British press which are sent to me. I have met or corresponded with Palmers in Texas and Oklahoma, too, and have been told by Romanichal friends in Houston that Cooks related to them lived at one time in Shreveport, Louisiana. Together with Butch Lee, whose mother is a Palmer, I'm organising a touring workshop on language, history and culture exclusively for the many Romanichals who live in the Texas-Arkansas-Louisiana region. But it is with my kin in London and Southend that I remain especially in touch.

Another of Marko's grandchildren, my cousin Jacqui Harrison, married a scrap metal merchant, Lenny, who has a yard in Fulham; they both came to visit us in Texas in 1998. Her daughter Vicki married a Romanichal called Edward Rumball (a variant of the family name Gumbold), and works with Travellers on the Westway site near Notting Hill – the subject of an excellent 2008 book by Christopher Griffin. Jacqui's dad was my Uncle Jim, a Harrison on his father's side and a Marshall on his mother's: the union of two prominent north-east London Romani families.

In the late 1980s I received a letter from a Romanichal now living in Santa Clara, California, telling me that some of his people, the Bonds

CERTIFIED COPY of an ENTRY OF DEATH

Issued at a fee of 2/- in pursuance of and for the purposes of the First Schedule to the
INDUSTRIAL ASSURANCE AND FRIENDLY SOCIETIES ACT 1948

DEATH	Entry No. *183*

Registration district KENSINGTON · Administrative area

Sub-district KENSINGTON · ROYAL BOROUGH OF KENSINGTON AND CHELSEA

1. Date and place of death *Twelfth February 1979. St Charles Hospital Kensington*

2. Name and surname *Gertrude King HANCOCK.* · 3. Sex *Female* · 4. Maiden surname of woman who has married *King.*

5. Date and place of birth *8th September 1885. London.*

6. Occupation and usual address *Widow of Reginald Aubrey HANCOCK. Rodent Operator (retired). M.15 Peabody Estate. W.10.*

7. (a) Name and surname of informant *Mavis Vera HARRISON* · (b) Qualification *Daughter.*

(c) Usual address *M.15. Peabody Estate. W.10.*

8. Cause of death *I (a) Hypostatic Pneumonia. Certified by K. Clare Roberts. M.B.*

9. I certify that the particulars given by me above are true to the best of my knowledge and belief *Mavis Harrison.* Signature of informant

10. Date of registration *Twelfth February 1979* · 11. Signature of registrar *L. Staal Deputy Registrar.*

Death certificate of Gertrude King

and the Crowes, have married into the Hancocks, and that in 1978 he attended a family reunion of Hancocks at which there were so many people that a football stadium (also in Fulham) had to be rented for the occasion. I've found no evidence of that gathering. I received another letter (dated 4 October 1999) from some Hancocks in New Zealand who knew of their Romani background and were looking for more information about it, and from a Jimmy Hancock in Marietta, Georgia (dated 13 May 1999), also a Romanichal, whose mother was a Gordon. Ernest Hancock wrote to me from London for information on the family after learning that his surname 'is also borne by gypsies in Britain' from *The Oxford Names Companion* (Hanks *et al.*, 2002: 276), an odd piece of information since Hancock is by no means a widespread Romani surname, and the same wording does not accompany the entries for Lee, Locke, Herne, Price, Boswell and so on.

Some Hancocks, relatives according to Aunty Nell, operated a travelling funfair and bioscope in Wiltshire, Devonshire, and Cornwall at the turn of the century called 'Hancock's Gigantic Carnival' and 'Hancock's Living Pictures'. It was burnt down in Plymouth shortly before the outbreak of the First World War by suffragettes and never rebuilt; they had started a small fire in a neighbouring lumber yard to protest the arrest of the women's rights activist Emmeline Pankhurst, and it quickly spread to the Hancock property, which was uninsured (see Brown, 1988: 109–12; Braithwaite, 1999: 104–5; and Scrivens and Smith, 2006: 126–9). It was the first funfair to feature the 'Golden Galloper' roundabout, which was accompanied by a handcranked calliope, and after it was destroyed its place was taken by Whitelegg's Fair. Sophie Hancock, who co-owned the fair with her brothers Bill and Charles (an epileptic), could reputedly swear for half an hour nonstop without repeating herself once, and lay out flat any troublemaker. Any family connection with those Hancocks, however, would date at least to the early 1800s. Not all the births in our family are on record by any means, but so far I haven't been able to find the link that Aunty Nell said connects ours to Sophie's.

The only address listed for several of the Hancocks in our own family record was the workhouse. One ancestor went down with the *Titanic* and drowned on 15 April 1912 when he was only eighteen – that was Percy, the son of another Hannah Hancock and a man named Robert Rice.

There have been two formal acknowledgements of Marko's multi-faceted life: besides the Galford book, the *Facing History and Ourselves* annual European summer workshop on racism has created an educational module using the earlier version of this essay as its model (Zemo, 1997).

It has been said more than once that Marko lives on in some of his children and grandchildren, but times and circumstances have changed, and it's not likely that anyone quite so memorable as this 'Romani legend', as Ellen Galford called him (2001: 62), will come this way again in our family. I can't argue with Billy Cribb who wrote that the likes of him in the modern world is lacking entirely.

CHAPTER THREE

Talking back

*If we are going to depend upon anthropological studies to define
our history and our culture and our 'future', then we are lost.*
(Kasaipwalova, 1973: 454)

Américo Paredes' timely discussion of the 'current quarrel … between
minority groups and the social sciences' (1971: 1) is especially
applicable to our own situation. With the Third World Romani Congress
imminently upon us, the question of how to deal with those who are
increasingly seeking to define us and the legitimacy of our social and
political action is one urgently requiring attention, and one which will
occupy much of the discussion in Göttingen this May. I attempt in this
preliminary paper to analyse the situation, and to propose an explanation
for it. The solution, also proposed below, is rather more easily dealt with.

It is no revelation that those in a position to label or define a group are
invariably in a dominant position *vis-à-vis* that group (see Hancock,
1975: 10–11). The white power structures have manipulated Romanies
since our very arrival in Europe eight centuries ago (Hancock: 1981);
intolerant of our existence, simultaneously envious of and hostile to the
Romani way of life, Europeans have shipped our people as slaves and
felons to Africa and the Americas; tortured and killed our people; and
continue to subject our people to the most antiquated and senseless laws.
This point cannot be emphasised too strongly: no single human group, so
widely and so consistently, has suffered or continues to suffer at the
hands of others as have the Rom. The reasons are clear:

Originally published in *Roma*, 6(1) (1980), 13–20.

In terms of group psychology, there is always a need to create an outgroup, onto which the majority projects its own fears and suppressed desires, and reassures itself by blaming that outgroup for criminal, licentious or other forbidden behaviour. In terms of social anthropology, any minority group seen to be distinct, whether physically or otherwise, may be feared as a threat to accepted norms because its mere existence demonstrates that these norms are not universal. (Burney, 1968: 2–3)

Lacking military and political strength and a geographical homeland, and being forced to travel in small groups for self-preservation, we have, over the centuries, developed through contact with different European peoples into a number of sub-groups, divided by dialect, retention of *Rromanija*, and by physical appearance. We were one people when we left India, and one people when we arrived in Europe a thousand years after that. An increasing number of Rom seek to restore that lost unity; many *gadže* ridicule our desire to do so.

Several of the *gadžikane* spokesmen offering observations on Romani nationalism have, significantly, been associated with the Gypsy Lore Society. The late Honourary Secretary of that organisation, Dora Yates, asked in reference to a nationalist movement, 'except in a fairy tale, could any hope ever have been more fantastic?' (1953: 140). Twenty years later, the former sub-editor of the same society's journal, Brian Vesey-Fitzgerald, called the notion 'romantic twaddle' (1973: 2). Werner Cohn (1973: 66) in the same year wrote quite bluntly that, 'the Gypsies have no leaders, no executive committees, no nationalist movement … I know of no authenticated case of genuine Gypsy allegiance to political or religious causes'. Most recently another Gypsy Lore Society member, Matti Salo, observed that, 'political activists, both those who claim Gypsy identity and those who do not, have attempted to construct a pan-Gypsy identity, dismissing as irrelevant the ethnic categories of the actors themselves', then stated that he found 'a lack of common ethnic consciousness' among his informants (1977: 2).

This kind of blindness to what has been a growing movement among Rom in Europe for a hundred years, and in the USA since the late 1960s, reflects not ignorance but fear. *Gadžikane* scholars of *Rromanija* are victims of what Douglas has referred to as 'Bongo-Bongoism' (1970: 15–16), 'the trap of all anthropological discussion. Hitherto when a generalisation is advanced, it is rejected out of court by any fieldworker, who can say "this is all very well, but it doesn't apply to the Bongo-Bongo"'.

Gypsylorists, unlike Romanologists – and there is a difference – have jealously protected 'their' Gypsies and 'their' intimacy with them, content that any potential argument from their fellow gypsylorists could be countered by applying the techniques of Bongo-Bongoism, and especially secure in the knowledge that the objects of their study, 'fortunately and safely illiterate' (Paredes and Stekert, 1971: 16), would be nowhere in sight, and certainly not invited, to comment.

'Gypsylorists remain the arcane priests of an oriental mystery quite removed from the thinking of educated Rom who are dismissed almost as a contradiction in terms' (Acton, 1980: 3). It is difficult to know which group is the most damaging, those *gadže* who cling to the golden earrings stereotype, or those who know enough to acknowledge its falseness, but who nevertheless belittle or ignore what is happening outside of their own narrow, self-applied academic confines. Perhaps the latter, since they have more contact with the scholarly world and are therefore more frequently approached by other *gadže* as sources of information about the Rom. Examples of their glib dismissal of educated Rom as 'not real gypsies' need not be repeated here. Where else would the compilers of the *Oxford English Dictionary* (1956), for instance, go to obtain their information for the entry 'gypsy': 'members of a wandering race [who] make a living by basket-making, horse dealing, fortune telling…'. This clearly excludes as Rom such prominent individuals as Vanko Rouda, Django Reinhardt, Vanya de Gila, Matéo Maximoff, Jan Cibula, Šaip Jusuf, and thousands of others who have never been in doubt as to their Romani identity. A leading medical journal published in New York contains an anonymous article on Rom which offers the information that 'a gypsy is born in an open field and dies in the same fashion' (Anonymous, 1977: 27). This would certainly come as a surprise to the tens of thousands of American Rom who were born in hospitals. Clébert observed that, 'The myth of the romantic Gypsy continues on its grotesque course, which future societies will have great difficulty in stopping' (1963: 95), and he was right.

It cannot seriously be believed that those in the unification movement are unaware of the divisions now separating the Romani population, as Salo claims. This is of vital concern to members of the World Romani Congress.

The point being made here is that we do not need *gadže* to think on our behalf, or to tell us what aspirations or occupations are authentically 'gypsy'. It is presumptuous to assume that Rom need to be told how to manage their own affairs, and who is or is not a Rom. Although Acton, at whom Salo's comments were directed, is not himself a Rom, he was reporting accurately what he knew to be taking place within Romani politics (1977).

Just as unreal, although diametrically opposed to Salo's interpretation, is the older view represented by Graffunder, who tells us (1835: 52) that, 'when Gypsies meet, even if they have come from widely separated parts of the earth, they greet one another with the familiar cry *"Han dume Romnitschel"* Are ye Romničel? – and straightway begins the dance of joy'. This is wishful thinking, but it has been repeated endlessly over the years by novelists and journalists who prefer to believe such nonsense. In the same way, Bercovici first began the fiction that no words existed in Romani for duty or possession (1929: 15, and see Chapter 10 in this volume), which was repeated by von Stroheim in his amazing novel *Paprika, the Gypsy Trollop* (1935: 12), an anonymous writer in *Coronet* (1950b: 126) and Marie Wynn Clarke (1967: 210). It seems that once a notion achieves the sanctity of print, it is assumed to be true. It is not thought necessary to check the sources at first hand – and in this way misconceptions are perpetuated.

It has not been easy for Rom to speak against these things. Widespread illiteracy, political ineffectiveness, social separation, and non-participation in academic life have all allowed the status quo to be maintained. But it must not be assumed that the present state of things is completely new, or that the Romani intelligentsia has lost a part of its identity by acquiring *gadžikane* educational skills. Firstly, Rom have survived from the beginning by learning the behaviour of the *gadže*, and have kept a step ahead because of it. The emerging situation is merely a continuation of this. Secondly, there are social reasons for the apparent sudden blossoming of Romani political and scholastic activity; this in fact got its initial stimulus in central and eastern Europe, but as a result of the devastation caused by the Second World War (Hancock, 1980) it was fragmented in Europe generally. The repercussions are still being felt. Although reorganisation began in France in the 1950s, all Romani activities were made illegal by De Gaulle when he came to power in 1958, and have only been reinstated since his resignation in 1969. Since then the Komitia Lumiaki Romani, now incorporated into the World Romani Congress, which has today eastern European, western European and North American branches, has made great strides forward. Our international congresses in London, Geneva, and now Göttingen, have attracted the attention of many countries to our situation, and in the past four years alone we have achieved official recognition as an Indian people by the Government of India, national minority status in Yugoslavia, and permanent representation in the United Nations Organisation. We also now have our own Indian Institute of Romani Studies, and this journal, *Roma*. None of this could (or would) have been achieved if we so-called 'educated gypsies' didn't exist, and if our brothers and sisters were not anxious to see our efforts bear fruit. The excuse, should it ever be proffered, that ignorance of these things is due to their having happened so recently, would be unacceptable, since World Romani Congress offices have kept the media informed of events. That there has nevertheless been a tendency to minimise their significance underlines the theme of this essay.

It is true that much of the 'gypsy myth' has been intentionally created as a smokescreen by Rom themselves to insulate *Rromanija* from *gadžikanija*. Perceptive Romanologists have realised this, and have dealt with it in its proper perspective, that is, in its function as a survival technique. Gypsylorists differ from the latter group in the extent to which they are unaware of the separation of the myth from the reality.

Today, things are different. If a *gadžo* wants to learn about Rom or *Rromanija* or know something of our language, he need only go to the library to find many titles on these subjects. We cannot stop them from doing this, nor do we have any control over their selectiveness, their ability to distinguish scholarly work from trash; but we can maintain our integrity by making accurate information available to the *gadžikane* scholars, and to the journalists, so that it is obtained at firsthand, rather than via the garbled ramblings of Borrow, Bercovici, Maas and others. There was a time when smoke-screening served its purpose, and to some extent, it still does. It does in many human societies where outsiders are concerned (Jansen, 1959); but times are rapidly changing.

I stated at the beginning of this paper that providing a solution to this situation was easier than attempting its analysis. The solution lies in *talking back*, loudly and clearly, wherever possible through our own publications such as *Roma* and *E Loli Phabaj*, and through our own conferences and our own scholars. Paredes (1971: 15) discusses this well in his reference to the Detroit folklore symposium, where he illustrates his point that the outsider working with urban folklore is finding that 'the subjects of his research are able to talk back to him':

> One of the most interesting results of the Detroit symposium was the way
> the main speakers were challenged ... the remarkable thing was the
> number of speakers (some scholars and some not) who rose to challenge
> the learned doctors as spokesmen for their ethnic group, questioning not
> points of theory and method, but the whole view of the subject under
> research, and at times questioning even the right of the scholar to do
> studies outside his own ethnic group.

The *gadže* know more about us today than they ever have, and to keep ahead we must study our own history and make our own pronouncements where and when they concern us. This is no cultural sellout; it is necessary if we are to resist being manipulated and defined by outsiders (Lomax, 1977). It is necessary if we are to gain respect. It is necessary if we are to stop being gypsies and start being Rom.

Editor's note: Fourteen years after writing the above, Ian gave a presentation in Warsaw before the Organisation for Cooperation and Security in Europe entitled *The consequences of anti-Gypsy racism in Europe*, in which he elaborated upon the dangers of Romaphobia (see Chapter 16 below). It was clear then that we were travelling on a dangerous road. And now, a further ten years ahead, little change is in sight.

Introduction to Section Two:
History and culture

The origin of the Roma was for centuries shrouded in mystery. The idea that they came from Egypt gave them the name 'Gypsies' – a term tainted with many negative connotations. From studies beginning in the eighteenth century, a scholarly consensus has emerged which traces the ancestors of the Roma to North West India. This claim was first based on linguistic research which revealed the profound similarities between Romani and several neo-Indic languages. Cultural practices shared by Roma and by Indians added to the weight of this argument. In recent years, geneticists have further confirmed the Indian connection with the help of haematological and bio-anthropological studies of European Roma and some Indian populations.

The fact that the Roma are kin to North Indians came as a surprise to both, and the news evoked much solidarity. Indian scholars began to regard Roma almost as overseas Indians, and at least some Roma began to look upon India as their own homeland. However, despite the warmth Indians and Roma might feel for each other, their separation is now a permanent fact. Centuries of life in the lands stretching west from India to Europe have wrought far-reaching linguistic, cultural, and even genetic changes in the Roma's Indic heritage. They are now citizens of the lands they live in. Roma profess the religions of their neighbours – most Roma are Christians or Muslims, and most Indians are Hindus. When the Roma's memories take them back to an ancestral land, it is not India, but merely the previous station in their long march.

For the Roma, emphasising their exotic origin too much is fraught with danger, as it plays into the hands of xenophobes who would 'send them back to India'. (The postscript to Chapter 16 shows that this possibility is quite real.) A recent dissertation sums up some of Ian's feelings on this matter: 'the Roma are a European people and ... their Indian origins, over a thousand years old, do not require association with India as a place of return' (Sachdev 2008: 107). This is only half the story, for Ian regards acknowledgement of the Indian connection as crucial for an understanding of the Roma's identity as a people. Without an awareness of their Indian origins, the Roma would be deracinated individuals, who can easily be portrayed merely as deviants from the norms set by the larger society, with no culture of their own.

The monographs in this section are studies of the Romani past and its links with India. In *The Hungarian student Vályi István and the Indian connection of Romani*, Ian attempts to uncover the identity of the person who is usually credited with making the fortuitous discovery that Romani was related to Indic languages. The monograph *On Romani origins and identity* is a summing up of the *status questionis* regarding the origins of the Roma. Ian's own views have changed over the years; he has rejected the Sampson and Turner scenario of a joint Rom/Dom connection seeing separate origins for the Romani and the Domari language of the Middle East. He also hypothesises that the proto-Roma originated in the Indian armies and their retinue taken captive by the Ghaznavid invaders in the early eleventh century, or else who fought for the Ghaznavids as *ghulams*, thus challenging the prevailing view that the ancestors of the Roma were drawn from the *ḍom* castes of India. This rethinking of an old problem necessitates a closer examination of words denoting labels or identity, such as *Rom* or *gadžo*, which is the subject of the paper *Gypsies, gadže, languages and labels*.

Romani religion is an overview of the religious practices followed by the Roma. While the ancestral religion of the proto-Roma must have been some form of Hinduism, the religious practices of the Roma are similar to those of their neighbours. But some beliefs and practices akin to those of the Hindus yet survive in Romani culture.

CHAPTER FOUR

The Hungarian student Vályi István and the Indian connection of Romani

It has become established lore in Romanological Studies that the discovery of the Indian affiliation of the Romani language should be attributed to Vályi István, a Hungarian theological student who is said to have attended the University of Leiden in the early 1760s. Vályi was the son of a landowning family living in Komora County that employed numbers of Romani labourers on its estate, from whom he had learnt some of the Romani language. There is no account of this directly from Vályi himself, however; the story is ultimately traceable instead to a printer named Stephan Pap Szatmar Nemeth, who had evidently come into possession of Vályi's handwritten notes.

In a conversation in late 1763, Nemeth told one Count Szekely von Doba, an army captain and amateur archivist, about Vályi and his discovery, and presumably gave or sold those notes to him. Szekely was also an amateur philologist, so recognised the value of the discovery, and eventually passed it along to the Austrian academician Georg Pray. Pray in turn published it as a short notice that finally appeared in the *Vienna Gazette* (the *Wiener Anzeigen* or *Gazette de Vienne*) in 1776, in Latin, and in Szekely's own words, as follows:

> Die 6 novemb. visitauerat me Stephanus Pap Satmar Nemethi, Typographus Karoliensis, habito ad inuicem discursu mihi retulit: Est in Comitatu Comaromiensi, in villa Almas, Pastor Reformatus, Stephanus Vali, is eidem retulit; dum Lugduni Batauorum studiorum academicorum caussa suisset constitutus, se usum suisse familiaritate trium iuuenum Malabaricorum, qui simper terni ibi solent studere, nec nisi aliisternis

Originally published in *Roma,* 36 (1992), 46–9.

venientibus redire possunt ad suos. Ex horum amicitia hunc fructum hansit Stephanus Vali, quod mille et plura vocabula eorum linguæ, cum significatione eorumdem, adnotauerat, obseruando plura notris Zingaris esse communia. Ipsis enim Malabaribus afferentibus, in Insula Malabaria, esse prouinciam vel districtum (qui tamen in mappa non conspicitur) quæ Czigania vocatur. D. Vali redux a Zingaris Jaurinensibos perquisiuit, eas voces a Malabaribus sibi dictatas quarum significations Jaurinenses Zingari absque vila difficultate eidem dixerunt; vnde Czinganos seu Czinganos ex prouincia Malabarica, Czigania, ortos conclude potest.

Velim autem scias, dulcis amice, Stephanum hunc Pap Nemethi esse vnum ex eruditis Patriæ nostræ, qui, antequam, ad academias Belgicas exiuisset fuerat ciuis, et ex post senior Colegii Lebrezinensis, nec ita credulum, vt fibi passus fuisset imponi a Valio Pastore Almassiensi.

The story, however, only became widespread following the publication of Heinrich Grellmann's 1783 book *Die Zigeuner*. That account was translated from the *Vienna Gazette* as follows:

Im Jahre 1763 den 6ten November, sagt der lirheber dieser Nachticht, besuchte mich ein Buchdrucker, Nahmens Stephan Pap Szathmar Nemethi. Indem wie so von Allerley plauderten, kamen wir auch auf die Zigeuner; und bey dieser Gelegenheit erzählte mir mein Gast, aus dem Munde eines Reformierten Predigers, Stephan Vali, zu Almasch im Komorner Komitat, folgende Anecdote: Als er, dieser Vali, auf den hohen Schule zu Leiden studiert habe, sey er mit den Malabarischen jungen Leuten, dergleichen beständig drey daselbst studiren müssen, und die nicht eher in ihr Vaterland zurückkeren dürfen, bis wieder andere drey an ihrer Stelle da sind, in genauer Bekanntschaft gestanden. Weil er nun bey ihrem Umgange bemerkt habe, daß ihre Muttersprache derjenigen, die unseren Zigeunern eigenthümlich ist, überaus ähnlich sey; so habe er diese Gelegenheit benutzt, sich mehr aus tausend Wörter, nebst ihrer Bedeutung, aus ihrem Munde aufzuzeichnen. Dabey hätten auch diese Jünglinge versichert, daß sich auf ihrer Insel ein Strich Landes, oder eine Provinz, Czigania genannt (die man aber auf der Charte vergeblich sucht) wirklich finde). Nachdem nun Vali von Universitäten wieder zu Hause gewesen wäre, habe er sich über die Bedeutung der mitgebrachten Malabarischen Wörter bey den Raber Zigeunern erkundigt, und diese hätten ihm jedes ohne Mühe und Anstoß zu dolmetschen gewußt.

In the year 1763, on the 6th of November, a printer, whose name was Stephen Pap Szathmar Nemeth, came to see me. Talking upon various subjects, we at last fell upon that of the Gipseys; and my guest related to me the following anecdote, from the mouth of a preacher of the reformed church, Stephen Vali, at Almasch in the county of Komora. When the said Vali studied at the university of Leyden, he was intimately acquainted with some young Malabars, of whom three are obliged constantly to study there, nor can they return home till relieved by three others. Having observed that their native language bore a great affinity to that spoken by the Gipseys, he availed himself of the opportunity to note down, from themselves, upwards of one thousand words, together with their significations. They assured him, at the same time, that upon their island was a tract of land, or province, called Czigania, but it is not laid down on the map. After Vali was returned from the university, he informed himself, among the Raber [from Raab] Gipseys, concerning the meaning of his Malabar words, which they explained without trouble or hesitation. (English edition, 1807: 170–1)

A number of Grellmann's contemporaries (Pallas, Rüdiger, Pauer, Büttner, Marsden) undoubtedly also read the same report that appeared in the *Vienna Gazette*. The possibility that he concocted his own story based upon it in order to claim a 'first' has to be discounted, for just one year before, the same story appeared, in very similar wording, in a lengthy two-part treatise by Samuel ab Hortis (1775: 85–96). It is that Hungarian-Slovak scholar from Gross-Lomnitz, rather than Grellmann, who must be credited as being the first to write a detailed ethnographic study of the Romanies. Grellmann does refer to the journal in which it appeared (the *Anzeigen aus Sämtlichen Kaiserlich Königliche Erbländeren*) in his own book (1783: 102), but does not mention ab Hortis as its author. Ab Hortis' text (1775: 82) is as follows:

Im Jahre 1763 den 6ten November besuchte mich ein gelehrter Buchdrucker, Nahmens Stephan Pap Nemethi, welcher mir bey unseren Unterredung zugleich entdeckte, wie ihm ein Protestantischer, in dem Kormornerkomitat dazumal zu Almasch befindlicher Prediger Stephan Vali erzählet habe: Als sich nämlich dieser Vali auf der hohen Schule zu Leyden befand, so hätte er mit dreyen malabarischen Jünglingen daselbst genaunen Umgang und Freundschaft gepflogen; indem es gewöhnlich ist daß beständig dreye von dieser Nation daselbst studerum andre drey an ihrer Stelle da sinn. Weil nun Vali merkte daß ihre Muttersprache mit der Sprache unserer Zigeuner nicht eine geringe Verwandschaft haben möchte, so suchte er aus diesem Umgang den Vortheil zu gewinnen, daß er aus ihrem Munde mehr den tausend malabarische Wörter nebst ihrer Bedeutung aufzeichnete. Vali wurde in seiner Muthmassung noch mehr gestärket, nachdem ihn Czigania genannt (die man aber auf den gewöhnlichen Landkarten vergäblichen suchen wird) wirklich vorhanden sey. Als nun Vali, daer sich wiederum in seinem Vaterlande befand, sich bey denen Raber Zigeuneren wegen der Bedeutung dieser malabarischen Wörtererkundigte, so wusten ihn die Zigeuner die Bedeutung aller dieser Wörter ohne alle Mühe und Schwierigkeit herauszusagen.

In 1763 on the 6th November I visited a learned printer named Stephen Pap Némethi, from whom I immediately discovered from our conversation, being like him a Protestant, that there was a preacher named Stephen Vali on the Kormora Committee in Almasch, and that he attended a college in Leiden where he knew three Malabari youths and had befriended [them] there; it was the usual practice for three from that nation to come here and for three others to take their place there. Now because Vali noted that their native language had more than a little affinity with the language of our Gypsies, he sought to take advantage [of the acquaintance] using the approach of recording from their mouths over a thousand Malabari words with their meanings. Vali was surprised even more in his conjecture when they mentioned 'Czigania' (but which you would not find on the usual maps), though it actually exists. When Vali went back afterwards to the Raber Gypsies in his own country because of the Malabari words he had asked for, he found that the Gypsies knew the meanings of all of those words without trouble or difficulty.

Certainly over the years since then, details of the episode have become quite muddled. Piasere has attempted to sort them out, although he predates the *Vienna Gazette* article by thirteen years and comes to no firm conclusion as to whom the discovery should be attributed (1988: 120), but suggests the phenomenon of 'simultaneous discovery' following Kroeber (1917). Sampson (1911) provided strong arguments that it was in fact Jacob Bryant who made the Indian connection earlier than, and independently of, Grellmann, and Matras (1999b) has made similar claims for Jacob Rüdiger.

Another of Grellmann's contemporaries, the cartographer James Rennell, must surely have read the 1776 account in the *Vienna Gazette* which mentions '*Czigania*' as being an actual place near the home of the three students, because he inserted it (as *Cingana*, adjusting the spelling even more closely to *Cingan*) into his map of India that appeared six years later – although he removed it from subsequent editions. Ab Hortis' account of Nemeth's story – the first – was presumably reproduced faithfully by Pray, and liberally embellished by Grellmann.

Given the findings below, we must question whether Vályi was even registered at Leiden University. No evidence has come to light so far demonstrating that he was, and the only details we have of the story are those found in ab Hortis and in Grellmann – and Pray's short piece in the *Vienna Gazette* lacks any linguistic material. Vályi's supposed thousand-word list has never been found.

In Grellmann's day Malabari, the language of the Malabar Coast, referred to Tamil rather than to Malayalam, as it does now (Caldwell, 1856: 4n). But like Malayalam, Tamil is a Dravidian language and therefore quite unconnected with Romani. Grellmann created the Indian students' identity as the sons of Brahmins, in order to be able to say that the language they were discussing was not their own but the 'Shanscritt' from which Romani does descend.

Nevertheless, while Romani certainly has its source in Sanskrit, in no sense has it remained so unchanged that it can be understood by a Sanskrit speaker 'without trouble or hesitation'. Even Swadesh's basic hundred-item lexical checklist for Romani demonstrates only an 80 per cent correspondence with contemporary Indic languages, and comparisons for sound-alike forms are better made with New Indo-Aryan languages such as Hindi or Punjabi rather than with Sanskrit. It could well be that the students were in fact discussing Hindustani rather than Sanskrit if the words were so readily recognised as being similar to Romani; presumably neither Vályi nor Szatmari had the expertise to identify any specific Indian language.

The following comparisons illustrate the proximity of Sanskrit, Hindustani, Romani and Sinhala (the Indic language spoken in Sri Lanka), together with the non-Indo-Aryan 'Malabari' (Tamil):

	Sanskrit	Hindustani	Romani	Sinhala	Tamil
dance	krīḍ-	khel-	khel-	kel-	āḍu
four	čatvāri	čār	štar	sataliha	nālu
hot	tapta	tatta	tato	rathvu	çūḍāna
house	gṛha	ghar	kher	gara	vīḍum
knife	kṣurikā	čhurī	čhuri	siriya	katti
milk	dugdha	dūdh	thud	dudu	pāl
nose	nāsa	nāk	nakh	nakutu	mūkku
salt	lavaṇa	lon	lon	lunu	uppu
twenty	vimśati	bīs	biš	visa	irubadu

In 1990 I visited the students' Common Room at the University of Leiden, the most likely venue for this supposed historic encounter to have taken place, and I attempted, during my stay in that city, to locate eighteenth-century records which might have provided further details. I also shared my interest with Dr Harm Beukers of the Faculteit Sociale Wetenschappen (Faculty of Social Sciences), and he promised to pursue the matter himself as time permitted. Some months later, I received a notice from Dr Beukers on his findings, and have incorporated them into this report.

According to the University records for that period of time, students entering the University were obliged to register their names at the Office of the Chancellor (the *Rector Magnificus*) on the same day that they arrived in Leiden. Furthermore, for as long as a student remained at the University, he had to renew his matriculation, that is, his registration application, each year on around 8 February. His name would then appear in a directory known as the *Recentzelissten*. Dr Beukers examined both the *Recentzelissten* and the *Volumina Inscriptzo* numbers for the years 1750 to 1763 (when, according to Grellman, the report of this event was first made), looking for the name István Vályi or Stephen (or Stefan) Vali, but found nothing. He did, however, turn up a clue to a possible line of further investigation.

Nearly every year, two students from Hungary were given the opportunity to apply to the University's Staten College, which had originally been founded by the Estates of Holland to enable students from poor Dutch families to acquire a higher education. The registry entry for 16 May 1761 noted that twenty-three year old Michael Pap Szathmari, '*Transsylvano Hungarus*' (from Hungarian Transylvania), was admitted as a theology student. Further investigation, this time of the Register of Examinations, listed two students with the family name Szathmari. For 28 September 1758 there was a Daniel, '*Hungarus, extra ordinem ab Ill. Curatoribus et Consilibus commendatus*' [Hungar, extraordinarily recommended by the curates and advisors], and for 4 June 1761, the same Michael Pap, '*commendatus a Professoribus Collegii Reformati Claudio-polotani in Transsylvanio*' [recommended by the professors of the redefined college of Koloszvar (Klausenberg) in Transylvania (Romania)]. But an examination of this particular register for the entire period between 1700 and 1790 failed to indicate any entry for a Vályi István or anything similar.

Upon first consideration it would seem that, without any actual evidence of the existence of Vályi István at Leiden University, the story might have been a fabrication on the part of Baron von Doba's acquaintance Szathmari. However, the printer's claims are strengthened by the fact that one of the Hungarian students, a theologian, also bore his somewhat uncommon family name, and may have been a relative who passed the story along. Furthermore, three students from the south of India – in fact, from the island of Ceylon – had been admitted during the 1750s and were 'obliged constantly to study' in The Netherlands. Their names were Johannes Jacobus Meyer, admitted on 4 September 1750; Petrus Cornelissen, on 7 October 1752; and Antonius Moyaars, on 23 September 1754. All were listed as '*Ceylonensis*', that is, as being from Sri Lanka, then a Dutch colony and which, like the homeland described in von Doba's account, is an island. The languages spoken there at the time were Tamil (which is Dravidian), Dutch, Lusoasian Creole, and Sinhala, which is distantly related to Romani but is radically different from it, as the above comparisons indicate. The names of the students suggest that they were Ceylonese Burghers, who were probably Christian and who would have spoken Dutch or Portuguese Creole as their native language(s). There is no way of knowing whether they spoke, in addition, any Indian language. The descendants of the Burghers today live in the area of Batticaloa, and speak Tamil as well as Creole.

It is also true that Vályi was not registered at Leiden but at the University of Utrecht, not in 1763 but ten years earlier in 1753 (contemporary with the three Sri Lankan students who were at Leiden), and furthermore he was not listed there as Vályi István but as Stephanus Waali. We can only guess that he visited Leiden from time to time, perhaps to meet with other divinity students. It is also possible, of course, that it was not Vályi at all who should be credited with this discovery, but one of the Szatmaris, who were also Hungarian, and who may also have known some of the Romani language.

As a final note, I should mention that much of this original information, which I first published in 1992, has been reproduced unreferenced in Willems (1997: 57–9). In the same book Willems reproaches Grellmann for not acknowledging his sources.

CHAPTER FIVE

On Romani origins and identity

A geneticist's summary of [our] data would describe the Gypsies as a conglomerate of Asian populations ... unambiguous proof of the Indian ancestry of the Gypsies comes from three genetic marker systems ... found on the same ancestral chromosomal background in Gypsy, Indian and Pakistani subjects. While confirming the centuries-old linguistic theory of the Indian origins is no great triumph for modern genetic research, the major, unexpected and most significant result of these studies is the strong evidence of the common descent of all Gypsies regardless of declared group identity, country of residence and rules of endogamy ... The Gypsy group was born in Europe. All marker systems suggest that the earliest splits occurred 20 to 24 generations ago, i.e. from the late 13th century onwards.

(Kalaydjieva *et al.*, 2005: 1085–6)

Those of you familiar with my work know that it has taken a circuitous route over the years in an ongoing effort to refine it, and no doubt it will be modified further as it continues. Thus in my earliest writing I supported a fifth-century exodus from India and accepted the established three-way Rom-Dom-Lom split; I no longer do. I argued for a wholly non-'Aryan' ancestry, but no longer believe this to have been the case nor, indeed, that 'Aryan' is even a genetically relevant label. I saw the migration from India to Anatolia as having been a slow one, consisting of a succession of military encounters with different non-Indian

Originally published as 'Re-examining romany origins and identity', in Adrian Marsh and Elin Strand (eds), *Gypsies and the problem of identities: contextual, constructed and contested* (I.B. Tauris/Swedish Research Institute, Istanbul, 2006), pp. 69–92.

populations; I no longer think that it happened in that way. I have argued, sometimes strenuously, that our people were one when they left India, one when they arrived in Anatolia, and one when they entered Europe. My findings are leading me more and more to believe that they were not.

Working especially closely with three other scholars, themselves also Romanies – Kenneth Lee formerly of Newcastle University, Ronald Lee at the University of Toronto New School and Adrian Marsh at Greenwich University – I have come to modify these positions considerably. The research of Marcel Courthiade and the late Jan Kochanowski in France has also been most useful in reaching these newer interpretations,[1] and I am especially grateful to Vardan Voskanian for generously sharing his materials and his ideas regarding Lomavren. Although this newer perspective differs considerably from my earlier one, I find myself obliged to accept it because I am wholly convinced that the history that is coming to light is, in its broad form, the correct history.

That the Romani people had a military origin is not in fact a new hypothesis; it was first addressed over a century ago by Burton, Leland, de Goeje, Clarke and others. My own contribution, besides attempting to flesh out the details, addresses rather the origins of the Romani language as a military *koïné* (Hancock, 2000). Certainly not everyone is persuaded by the direction my work is taking; Matras says:

> In a number of recent publications, Hancock claims that Romani was formed as a military koïné by a caste of warriors assembled to resist the Islamic invasions of India. In some circles, this view is gaining popularity as it pretends to revise what is referred to as potentially racist, or at least stereotypical images of the Rom. There is, however, neither linguistic nor historical evidence to support it. (2004a: 301) [See also 2004c for a harsher criticism][2]

Matras' own position – although itself accompanied by neither 'linguistic nor historical evidence to support it' – adheres to the traditional account:

> Indic diaspora languages [are] spoken by what appear to be descendants of itinerant castes of artisans and entertainers who are spread throughout Central Asia, the Near East and Europe. They include ... Romani. (1999a: 1)
>
> Proto-Romani was carried from India westwards by migrants who appear to have been members of service-providing castes, similar in status and occupational profile to *jatis* or service groups known in some parts of

India as dom ... the řom settled in the Byzantine Empire sometime around the tenth century CE. (2004b: 278)

More recently, Tcherenkov and Laederich (2004: 13) have leant toward the same conventionally accepted origin:

[It] is but a small step to support the hypothesis that these Indian *Dom* are the ancestors of the European Rroma. The professions exercised by the *Dom* in the Indian subcontinent – musicians, dancers, smiths, basket weavers, sieve makers, even woodworkers, are transmitted from father to son. From their similarity to the ones of the European Rroma these could or may be considered as the origins of the traditional Rroma trades! ... some authors claim that Rroma originated from either one of the upper castes such as the Rajputs or from a mix of different castes. With our current knowledge, this cannot be settled to satisfaction.

Even at time of going to press, the following appeared introducing a BBC series entitled *On the Road: Centuries of Roma History* (Radu, 2009):

Historians agree that the Roma's origins lie in north-west India and that their journey towards Europe started between the third and seventh centuries AD – a massive migration prompted by timeless reasons: conflicts, instability and the seeking of a better life in big cities such as Tehran, Baghdad and, later on, Constantinople. Some of these Indian immigrant workers were farmers, herdsmen, traders, mercenaries or book-keepers. Others were entertainers and musicians. They settled in the Middle East, calling themselves Dom, a word meaning 'man'. Large numbers moved into Europe, where the 'D', which was anyway pronounced with the tongue curled up, became an 'R', giving the word 'Rom'. Today's European Roma (the plural of 'Rom') are their descendants.

The present monograph raises a number of questions, some of which are posed further below. A central position underlying the discussion is that three salient, and hitherto not adequately considered, aspects of the contemporary Romani condition rest upon the facts of our history detailed here:

First, that the population has been a composite one from its very beginning, and at that time was occupationally rather than ethnically-defined;

Second, that while their earliest components are traceable to India, Romanies essentially constitute a population that acquired its identity and language in the West (accepting the Christian, Greek-speaking Byzantine Empire as being linguistically and culturally 'Western'); and

Third, that the entry into Europe from Anatolia was not as a single people, but as three (or possibly more) smaller migrations over perhaps as much as a two-century span of time.

Together, these account in part for the lack of cohesiveness among the various groups self-identifying as Romani, and for the major dialect splits within the language. We might see each major post-Byzantine group as evolving in its own way, continuing independently a process of assimilation and adaptation begun in North West India. Thus the descendants of those who were held in slavery until the nineteenth century and those whose ancestors entered Spain in the fifteenth century are today very different, the former – the Vlax Romanies – having been heavily influenced genetically, culturally and linguistically by Romanian and the Romanians; the latter on the other hand – the Kalé Romanies – having been influenced in the same way by Mozarabic and Spanish, and both populations have furthermore been separated by a more than six century span of time. Thus any originally acquired characteristics they might still share, which constitute the genetic, linguistic and cultural so-called 'core of direct retention', are greatly outweighed by characteristics accreted from the non-Romani world. The reunification (or more accurately, *unification*) movement urged by such organisations as the International Romani Union or the Roma National Congress seeks – as I do myself – to emphasise the original, shared features of each group rather than those acquired from outside which separate them; yet for some, that original material is now scant, and creating for them any sense of a pan-Romani, global ethnicity would require the kind of effort that is, sadly, very far down on the list of day-to-day priorities and, pragmatically, would be difficult to instigate. It also calls into question the legitimacy of the exclusionary and subjective position taken by some groups who regard themselves as being 'more Romani' than others.[3]

1. Who were the ancestors of the Romanies?

Using lexical data I demonstrated (Hancock, 1995c) that the assumed early single migration out of India with a subsequent split into Domari, Lomavren and Romani (Middle Eastern, Armenian and European Gypsy) once it had passed through the Persian language territories, could not be maintained in light of the percentages of shared and non-shared Iranic items evident in each today. This confirmation is already finding a place in the new scholarship; thus Windfuhr, in his entry on Gypsy languages in the *Encyclopædia Iranica* (2002: 415) refers to that 1995 study when stating that the Iranic items 'reflect three distinct historical layers of Indo-Aryan innovations, which suggests three successive westward migrations, rather than a single one'. It is of some significance since it overturns the generally accepted historical scenario current over the past one and a half centuries, and impacts directly on our understanding of early Romani. Higgie (1984) for instance, attempted a reconstruction of Proto-Romani by comparing Romani with Domari, as did Kaufman (1984); Higgie's work points to something like the sixth century BC as the time of the split from Indic, while Kaufman posits the separation from Indo-Aryan by 400–300 BC. This would be comparable to attempting a reconstruction of the original Latin by including (say) Umbrian or Oscan along with the modern Romance languages in the comparative data.

An examination of the earliest words in the Romani language suggests a number of things: firstly that there is little in the original, 'first layer' Indian vocabulary that reflects a nomadic or itinerant population, but rather it points to a settled one; and secondly that while there are not many original words for skills artisanal or agricultural, there are quite a few military terms. There are Indian words for *soldier* and *attack* but not for *farmer* or *harvest*; there are words for *sword* and *spear* but not for *plough* or *hoe*; there is a word for *horse* but not for *buffalo* and so on.[4] Given these lexical clues and the likely time period (both discussed below), and given that the Indian words and grammar in modern Romani point to the languages spoken in the north-western part of India and to nowhere else, an examination of Indian history for evidence of any military activity during that time and in that area is a natural next step; but first, the time period must be established.

2. The date of departure

It has been claimed repeatedly that the speakers of the language that developed into modern Romani left India sometime between the fifth and ninth centuries; those who support the traditional *Shah Nameh* explanation, which is routinely repeated in even the latest books on Romanies (for example, Sirmarco, 2000), would place it in the fifth century. Others, like myself, see military activity as the reason for leaving, but still argue for an earlier date of departure: 'they left perhaps as early as in the sixth century AD, probably due to repeated incursions by Islamic warriors' (Barany, 2002: 9).[5]

On the basis of lexicon, Kaufman (1984: 12) has asserted that:

There is no way that Romani could have avoided Arabic loanwords unless it had entered Iran before 700 AD. Speculations that do not operate within these constraints as axiomatic are idle; it is totally irrelevant that there may be some historical evidence of troubles in, and out-migrations from, India around 1000 AD, and I am getting bored with hearing again and again the speculation that the Gypsies may have left India at such a late date.

Vekerdi (1988: 13) says:

The Gypsies' ancestors began leaving northwest India probably about the seventh century AD. They are characterised as robbers, murderers, hangmen and entertainers. These professions were prescribed for them by the rules of the Hindu caste system. Thus they belonged to the so-called 'wandering criminal tribes' of India and were obliged to lead a parasitic way of life. Among the numerous outcast groups, they occupied the lowest rung on the social scale.

Salo (1997: 369) puts it sometime later, but includes Dom and Lom Gypsies together with Rom: 'All groups considered Gypsies are descended from ancestors who left India around 900 C.E. and arrived in the Greek-speaking areas of south-eastern Europe in the eleventh or twelfth century.'

Halwachs (2000: 5, 24) is also persuaded that the lack of adoptions from Arabic is a decisive factor in dating the time of departure:

As Romani lacks Arabic loans, it is to be assumed that the Romani speakers left the Persian area before its arabization ... and following this moved on to the Byzanthinian [*sic*] area of influence … Experts still disagree on the point of time of the Gypsies' emigration from the north-west of India. If we consider all the different statements, the resulting period of time is somewhere between the 5th and 10th centuries after Christ. In the second half of the first millennium, emigration most probably did not happen all at once but took place in the course of various waves.

In an earlier monograph (1977: 3), Kenrick too believed that '[t]he Romanies of Europe must have come through Iran before 600 AD – the first Arab invasions – this is the only possible explanation for the large number of Iranian words and the small (infinitesimal) number of Arabic words found in the Romani vocabulary'; although in a more recent statement (*Patrin*, 14: *viij*: 3) he moves that estimation two or three centuries forward:

> My basic theory at the moment is that the Roma of Europe are mainly offspring of the defeated Zotts of Zottistan [in AD 855]. These were divided by the Arabs into two groups; one was sent to Ain-Zarba where they were in due course massacred by the Byzantine Greeks – maybe the women taken as slaves. The other group went to Khaneikin and thence to Europe. They were mainly buffalo keepers (see Rishi's article 'Panjabi love of buffalo milk' [1976]) but obviously in Zottistan had developed other trades. We know there were musicians there. Some other Indians joined them and adopted Romani as their language, intermarried…

In a subsequent publication (2004: 10) he added to the social details but avoided speculating as to dates:

> My own belief, as stated earlier, is that Indian immigrants from various tribes intermarried and intermixed in Persia, forming into a people there using the name Dom, and that a large number of them then moved into Europe; their descendants are the Romany Gypsies of today.

In his newest book, however, he reverts to the Firdausi account (Kenrick and Puxon, 2009: 1–2), providing a map indicating migratory routes out of India into Arabia and Egypt, and where he says: 'The Persian poet Firdausi, writing in the tenth century, dates their arrival to some five centuries before his own time … Linguistic and other evidence shows that the Romanies of Europe belong to groups which left India between the fifth and eleventh centuries.'

In his UNESCO-sponsored book, Alain Reyniers (1998: 25) writes of

'*Une sortie étalée le Ve et le XIIe siècle ... Après une première étape en Perse, les Tsiganes se seraient divisés en deux groupes. Le premier se serait dirigé vers le Moyen-Orient et l'Egypte. Le second se serait déplacé vers le nord-ouest.*' [An exodus that spread out between the 5th and the 12th centuries ... after an initial stay in Persia, the Roma split into two groups. The first was driven towards the Middle East and to Egypt, the second shifted towards the north-west.] Another recent publication (Marushiakova and Popov, 2000: 5) supports the traditional view, and places the presence of Romanies in Persia before AD 900:

According to most linguists, the formation of the Gypsy language began sometime in the 6th or 7th century, while from the 8th–9th centuries onwards, it developed as a separate language under the influence of the majority languages spoken in the area: Persian, Armenian, Greek. Wandering for several centuries throughout the lands of what are today Pakistan, Afghanistan and Iran, and to the south of the Caspian Sea, the Gypsies (and their language) divided into two separate branches, speaking the so-called 'ben' and 'phen' dialects respectively, this being an important stage in the development of the Gypsy language and the Gypsy community as a whole. Reaching the land of northern Mesopotamia and the eastern boundary of the Byzantine Empire towards the end of the 10th and beginning of the 11th centuries, the Gypsies split into three major migration groups – the ben-speaking Dom, who took the southern route, or stayed in the Middle East, and the phen-speaking groups of Lom, who took the northern route, and Rom, who took the western route.

Achim (2004: 7–12) also accepts a ninth-century departure:

The migration took place over an extended period of time and was not dramatic in nature ... [i]t is generally accepted that the migration of Gypsies from India to Europe took place between the ninth and the fourteenth centuries, in a number of waves. It is believed that the Gypsies arrived in Persia in the ninth century. Persian sources call them *Luli* or *Luri.*

Blachut (2005: 26), using Barany (2002) as his source, says:

Gypsies had begun leaving the southern part of India in 1500 BC, when the Aryans invaded the country ... Gypsies originated in the Punjab region of northwestern India. They began leaving in the sixth century AD because of constant invasions by Islamic warriors.

Wogg (2006: 3), basing his position on the combined works of

Hübschmannová (2004), Kenrick (2004) and Matras (2002) says:

> The [*Shah Nameh*] legend about the Luri could thus very well refer to the
> Roma, who left Persia already in the fifth century, and India even earlier
> on their westward journey … most scientists today assume it was over a
> long period of time – between the 3rd and 10th century – during which the
> Roma left India, most likely between the 8th and 10th century.

The Consultants on Religious Tolerance, based in Kingston, Ontario,
Canada, recently stated that:

> The Roma people originally lived in northwest India in what is now
> southeastern Pakistan. They migrated to Persia between 224 and 642 CE.
> They lived under Arab rule in the Middle East from 642 to 900 CE, and
> eventually arrived in Constantinople … There are three language groups
> within the Roma: the Domari in the Middle East and Eastern Europe, the
> Lomavren in Central Europe, [and] the Romani of Western Europe.[6]

In discussing Romani history, Price (2000: 207) says that, '[a]t some
indeterminate period, not later than the ninth century AD, the Romanies
were on the move again [out of India]'. Miklosich (1874) put the date of
departure at somewhere between AD 500 and AD 700, while Sampson
(1923: 157) argued for the ninth century. Fonseca (1996: 94) provides an
account that concludes 'the earliest Gypsies would have left India at least
by 720 AD'. A recent interpretation has Romanies leaving India between
AD 1017 and AD 1030 as a result of Ghaznavid invasions, but splitting
into the three-way Dom-Rom-Lom (Jordan, Europe, Armenia) division
somewhere between Afghanistan and Persia (Knudsen, 2003: 22–3),
while Tcherenkov and Laederich (2004: 14), who also support the
one-migration three-way-split position, have most recently placed the
migration back six hundred years: '[A] time frame for the migrations of
Rroma from the Indian subcontinent … at what we believe is a
reasonable departure date, around the fourth and fifth centuries.'

Djurić (2003), on having determined that Romani has a middle voice,
has argued that the language must date back to before the time of Christ.
Any claim to a pre-AD 1000 date of departure, however, must be
challenged on the basis of the historical development of the Indo-Aryan
languages. Woolner's analysis (1916: 123) of the derivation of the
first-person singular personal subject pronoun *me*, and Bloch's similar
examination (1953: 24) of *kon* ('who') both point to a post-seventh
century development. We must also examine the reassignation of

neuter-gender nouns after that category began to disappear from the Apabhramśas by the end of the Middle Indic period. This is accepted as about the year AD 1000; Masica (1991: 8) gives the New Indo Aryan period as '1000 AD–present ... the modern Indo-Aryan languages properly and henceforth called New Indo Aryan ... date from approximately AD 1000'. The transition was clear-cut, and the date significant. Bloch (1965: 29) says 'it is of great importance to indicate the chronological break, which isolates the whole of neo-Indian [from Middle Indic]'. 'The three genders [of Old Indic] continue [in Middle Indic] but the masculine and the neuter come closer together' (Sen, 1960: 75). The OIA neuter gender was systematically lost, the change spreading towards the north-western part of India, where some three-gender NIA languages are still found to this day, such as numbers of Central (Śauraseni) languages like Bhili, Gujarati and Khandeshi, as well as some Southern (Maharasthri) languages such as Marathi. Nevertheless,

> ... the most widespread NIA system is a two-gender system, in which the old masculine and neuter have merged. (That is not to say that there have not been some reassignments of OIA gender ... e.g. the NIA descendants of OIA agni- 'fire', which is masculine, are mostly feminine), as is Romani jag, as well. (Masica, 1991: 221)

According to Burton (1851: 90–1), the neat shift of the neuter to the masculine set did not happen everywhere: 'In the Játaki dialect, nouns are of two genders, masculine and feminine. The neuter is not used, and words which properly speaking belong to that gender are made masculine and feminine, as usage directs without any fixed rule.' He describes Játaki, the language of the Jats, as 'a corrupt form of the Multání, itself a corruption of the Panjábī, tongue'.

It is significant that the languages most *like* Romani – Hindi, Panjabi and Rajasthani – are not three-gender languages. If pre-Romani had left India before the end of the first millennium AD, which is to say during the MIA period, it would have retained its three-genders, and the fact that it is a two-gender language today would oblige us to accept that the loss of the neuter, and its reassignation to either masculine or feminine, took place outside of India.

Kenrick is of this opinion, believing Persian to have been the factor of change: '*Il y avait trois genres (comme en allemand), au moment où les*

Tsiganes ont quitté l'Inde, mais le neutre a disparu au Moyen-Orient, sans doute sous l'influence du parsi.' [It had three genders (as in German) at the time that the Roma left India, but the neuter disappeared in the Middle East, no doubt under the influence of Persian.] (1994: 54). He repeats this position (in Kenrick, 2004: 104): 'There were three genders (like German) when the speakers left India, but the neuter disappeared in the Middle East, probably under the influence of Persian.' Out of contact with other Indian languages, such reassignment would have been random; however, comparing those Romani nouns deriving from neuter source forms in Sanskrit and/or Prakrit, with their equivalents in Hindi, we find that the match is 98.7 per cent (one mismatch out of thirty-five items compared) for the masculine set, and 60 per cent for the feminine set, 86 per cent for both masculine and feminine matches. The approximately 2:1 ratio of masculine to feminine Indian-derived nouns in Romani also accords with the reassignment of OIA neuters mainly to the masculine set. While he did not discuss the date of the presence of pre-Romani in India or recognise its relevance to ascertaining the time of its separation, Lesný had already noted the reassignment of OIA neuters in MIA nearly a century ago:

Die mittelindischen lautlichen Prozesse haben bekanntlich bewirkt, dass auch das Geschlecht eine Änderung erfahren hat. Marati und Gujarati haben noch die ursprüngliche Einteilung in drei Geschlechter behalten, Bangali unterscheidet eigentlich kein Geschlecht, Hindi, Panjabi, Sindhi, Kashmiri und Naipali unterscheiden nur das männliche und das weibliche Geschlecht. Diese nordwestlischen Gruppe reiht sich auch die Zigeunersprache an, indem sie auffallenderweise in bezug auf die Änderung des Geschlechtes mit derselben übereinstimmt. Ich will die zahlreichen Neutra, die zu Maskulinen geworden sind, übergehen und erwähne nur zwei Substantiva, die sowohl in der genannten Sprachengruppe als auch in den Zigeunermundarten Feminina geworden sind: agni masc. 'Feuer', MIA aggi, Marati, Gujarati, Hindi ag f., Panjabi agg, f., Sindhi agi, f., Kashmiri agun, m., Romani jag, f. aksi 'Auge', MIA acchi, n. oder f., Marati aksi n., Gujarati ankh f., Hindi ank f., Panjabi akkh f., Sindhi akhi f., Kashmiri acchi f., Romani jakh f. (1916: 422)

Phonological processes in the MIA languages included the well-documented shift in grammatical gender. Thus while Marathi and Gujarati continued to keep the original categorisation into three [m-f-n], Bengali differed in actually making no gender distinction, while Hindi,

Panjabi, Sindhi, Kashmiri and Nepali came to differentiate only between the masculine and feminine genders. This NW dialect group also parallels the Romani language which shares, remarkably, this same distribution of grammatical gender. I will ignore the many neuter nouns that became masculine, and only mention the two in particular that became feminine in both the group of languages mentioned here as well as in the Romani dialects: *agni* masc. 'fire', MIA *aggi*, Marati, Gujarati, Hindi *ag* f., Panjabi *agg*, f., Sindhi *agi*, f., Kashmiri *agun*, M., Romani *jag*, f. *aksi* 'eye', MIA *acchi*, n. or f., Marati *aksi* n., Gujarati *ankh* f., Hindi *ank* f., Panjabi *akkh* f., Sindhi *akhi* f., Kashmiri *acchi* f., Romani *jakh* f.

Since the loss of the neuter gender had begun to take place while the NIA dialect groups were still in formation, this means that pre-Romani was still in India at the time that this was taking place, that is, still a part of the Middle Indo-Aryan cluster. Even if pre-Romani were derived from various Indian languages, as I maintain, the case still holds; a gender match with Sindhi or Panjabi yields the same result.

If we assume that Sampson's (and my own earlier) 'single race speaking a single language' remained intact until it had passed through Persia, then we would expect the Persian words it picked up during that period to be shared by Romani, Domari and Lomavren; but they are surprisingly few: just 16 per cent between Romani and Domari, 7 per cent between Romani and Lomavren, and 12 per cent between Lomavren and Domari. By way of comparison, over 50 per cent of the Persian words in Romani are shared by Urdu (although the likelihood of some of these having been acquired by the language more recently must be considered).

3. Domari

That Romani, Domari and Lomavren constitute three branches of an original proto-language has remained the conventional wisdom in Romani historical linguistic studies for over a century, and continues to be repeated. That they had independent origins had already been suspected by Colocci (1907: 279), who urged caution in drawing too sweeping a conclusion from the available sources:

To imagine that just because the Gypsies of Europe and their brothers in Asia share a common linguistic core, one should therefore conclude that there was a single exodus of these people [out of India], and furthermore that the unity of their language argues against more than one migration, seems to be a conclusion which is only slightly weakened by the still nebulous state of the documentation. Unity of language might well prove unity of origin; but there could still have been different migrations, chronologically and geographically, without that fact being too apparent from the lexical adoptions acquired by the mother tongue in the countries through which they passed; all the more so since those migrations were very rapid. To conclude, therefore, that the unity of their exodus rests upon the recognition of the unity of the substrate of their language, strikes me as a proposition which shouldn't be universally accepted without [first incorporating] the benefit of a [lexical] inventory.

Some years before him, Pischel (1883: 771) had already written that 'in spite of the similarity of their name and customs, it is absolutely erroneous to identify the Dōm with the Rōm'. The late Angus Fraser also cautioned that 'despite Sampson's insistence that both sprang from a single source, some of Domari's dissimilarities from European Romani create doubts about how far we can assume that the parent community was uniform' (1992: 39).

In Hancock (1995c) I demonstrated that Colocci's and Fraser's doubts were justified, and the fact that Domari and Romani had separate origins is gradually moving toward general acceptance; Matras concludes, in the most recent overview of Domari, that together with Romani they 'were, to begin with, two distinct, albeit related Indo-Aryan idioms' (1999a: 55).

The additional claim I make that the Domari language and its speakers left India earlier than did Romani and its speakers might also be supported by the evidence of gender. Macalister (1914: 9, 11) says:

> There are three genders [in Domari], *masculine, feminine* and *neuter*. The last is now all but obsolete, but recognisable only by the form of the accusative singular … As in most Aryan languages, neuter substantives have no accusative form different from the nominative. This is now the only criterion for distinguishing neuter nouns. But even here they appear to be in process of assimilation to the masculine or feminine declension, and developing analogous accusative forms.

Sampson (1926: 125) has contested this, although it has to be assumed that he is only querying Macalister's claim that the modern Domari language has three genders; he would have known that three genders existed in the speech of the original population, which he maintained left

India 'at least as early as the end of the ninth century' (Sampson, 1926: 28–9). He said that 'the Nuri "neuter" of Macalister has no historical basis, and is to be understood merely as a term applied by this collector to nouns denoting inanimate objects in which, as in Eur. Gyp., the form of the acc. sg. is identical with that of the nominative'. Unfortunately, Macalister does not provide genders in his Domari vocabulary, although he lists some examples of each in his grammatical outline (1914: 15–16): *béli, záro*, 'friend', 'boy', m., *cóni, júri*, 'girl', 'woman', f., *páni, ag*, 'water', 'fire', n. Kenrick, however, in his current series of Domari lessons (2000b: 2), says 'some dialects also have a traditional (historical) neuter gender, ending in a consonant'.

Besides losing the neuter gender, Indo-Aryan also lost the dual number that characterised its Old period. Romani lacks this entirely, but according to Macalister (1914: 9), in Domari, 'faint traces are not wanting of the former existence of a *dual*, but this is almost wholly obsolete'. It is a pity that Macalister did not provide actual examples of these, since if they had indeed existed in Domari, it would suggest an improbably much earlier separation from India; thus Masica (1991: 226) says '[t]here are only two numbers, singular and plural, in NIA at best. OIA had three, but the old dual quietly disappeared at the beginning of MIA'; but he has MIA *beginning* around 600 BC (1991: 51), far too early to match with the rest of the linguistic data we have on Domari. If Domari does indeed show evidence of a dual number, this is probably an influence from Arabic, which has it (and not Persian or Kurdish, which do not).

4. Lomavren

On the basis of its lexicon Lomavren, the language of the Lom or 'Bosha' in eastern Turkey and the Caucasus would seem to stand somewhere between the two migrations that gave rise to Domari and Romani. On the one hand, it shares items with Romani which differ from their Domari equivalents, thus:

Rom	Lom	Dom	English
bul	*bul*	*blos*	buttocks
čumid-	*čum-*	*meštersk-*	kiss
devel	*level*	*goča*	god
džukel	*čükel*	*snōta*	dog

gili	*gilav*	*gref*	song
giv	*giu*	*gēsū*	wheat
khel-	*khel-*	*nač-*	dance*
kolin	*koli*	*šiše*	chest, breast
mol	*māl*	*pīrə*	wine
nasval-	*nasvav*	*meštak*	ill
per-	*par-*	*kwiyə-*	fall
pučh-	*pučh-*	*šo-*	ask
sov-	*səv-*	*setak-*	sleep
ther-	*thar-*	*waša-*	get, have
vaker-	*pakr-*	*šərde-*	speak
xandž-	*xant-*	*hərwšer-*	itch
xin	*xenav*	*higera*	feces

* Domari has *kēlər*, 'play', its secondary meaning in both Romani and Lomavren.

On the other hand, it shares items with Domari which are absent (or which have not been replaced) in Romani:

Rom	Lom	Dom	English
avrjal	*baraj*	*bare*	outside
dad	*bap*	*bap*	father
buti	*kam*	*kam*	work
čiken	*tel*	*tel*	grease
dar-	*bi-*	*bīər-*	fear
drom (Greek)	*panth*	*pand*	road
gav	*lei*	*dei*	village
kin-	*li-*	*li-*	buy
maškar	*mandž*	*mandž*	middle*
phabaj	*ansev*	*sev*	apple
pi(n)rro	*pav*	*paw*	foot
šel	*saj*	*saj*	hundred

* *Mindž*, *miž* has been euphemised to mean 'vulva' in Romani, if it is not originally an adoption from Lezgian (a Caucasian language) *miš*, ditto.

The complete lack of Greek lexical items in Lomavren shows that the ancestors of the Lom never made it into Anatolia, or else that they passed through it before Greek was established there. It furthermore shares only five items from Persian with Romani (some nineteen have been identified in Lomavren altogether (Voskanian, 2002), and over 100 in Romani (Hancock 1995c)). Significantly, not one such item in either language is from the Middle Persian (Pahlavi) period; all are from the modern period, which dates from the early tenth century, thus further undermining the argument for a fifth century passage through the area. Furthermore, there is only one indisputable item of Kurdish origin in Lomavren (perhaps ten in Romani). Most of the Iranic items in Domari are Kurdish, not Persian.

Fraser (1989: 14) has already noted that Lomavren and Romani share practically none of the same Armenian loanwords. Those Armenian-derived items in Romani for which both languages have words are as follows:

English	Romani (from Armenian)	Lomavren
button	*kočak*	*banthič* (< Indic)
chew	*kic-*	*čamxi karel* (< Indic)[a]
dog	*rikono*	*solav* (< Indic)[b]
dough	*xumer*	*nəmor* (< Arm?)
dust	*poš*	*thuli* (< Indic)
godfather	*kirvo*	*kavrav* (< Arm?)
horse	*grast*	*khori* (< Indic)[c]
land, region	*them*	*thenav* (< Indic)
oven	*bov*	*santhu* (< ?)
skin	*mortji*	*čam* (< Indic)[d]

a   Romani also has Indic *čamb-*
b   Romani also has Indic *džukel*
c   Romani also has Indic *khuro*
d   Romani also has Indic *čamb*

Another feature that distinguishes Lomavren is that in that language, New Indo-Aryan /a/ was not raised to /e/ as it was in Romani: (Lom: *khar, par-, phan-, saj, thar-*; Rom: *kher, per-, phen-, šel, ther-* 'house', 'fall', 'say', 'hundred', 'have', cf. Hindi *ghar, par-, bhan-, sau, dhar-*). However, numeral 'ten', which is *las* in Lomavren (Hindi *das*, Romani *deš*), has the *e-* form *de(s)* in its combinations: *de'-hu-dui* 'twelve', Romani *deš-u-duj*). A further indication of its later date of separation from India is in the behaviour of initial Middle Indo-Aryan /v/, which became /b/ in New Indo-Aryan (including Romani) but not in Lomavren or in Domari:

OIA/MIA	Dom	Lom	Rom	(cf. Hindi)	English
vāla	*wal*	*valis*	*bal*	*bāl*	hair
vaṭa	*wat*	*var*	*bar*	*baṭ*	stone
viś	*wesar*	*ves*	*beš-*	*bais-*	sit
vimśati-	*wīs*	*vist*	*biš*	*bīs*	twenty

On the other hand, both Romani and Lomavren share a sound-shift not evident in Domari – the devoicing of voiced aspirated stops, thus:

Rom	Lom	Dom	(cf. Hindi)	English
kher	*khar*	*gar*	*ghar*	house
khil	*khəl*	*gir*	*ghī*	butter
khuro	*khori*	*gori*	*ghoḍā*	horse
ph(r)al	*phal*	*bar*	*bhāī*	brother
phus	*phus*	*bis*	*bhūsā*	straw

Nevertheless, some Lomavren items appear not to have undergone this: *banth-*, *bakhot-*, 'shut', 'break'; Romani *phand-*, *phag-*; Domari *ben-*, *bæg-*. It is intriguing that both Romani and Lomavren share the secondary meaning of the verb 'sit' to mean 'reside', not paralleled in the modern languages of India, and that the early speakers of both languages relexified the original Indian *triśūla*, 'trident' (presumably in its religious context as the one held by the god Shiva) into new religious contexts: Romani *trušul*, 'cross' and Lomavren *tərusul*, 'church'.[7] It is also the case that the Romani word *xulaj*, 'host' (from Persian *xudāy* and not, as Voskanian (2002: 182) has convincingly shown, from Kurdish *xola*, 'god') exhibits the same phonetic rule that is general in Lomavren, that is, the shift of /d/ to /l/ (cf. Lom *xula*, do., and the items *level, lei, las* above), suggesting a common point of separation – although it is the only Romani item that does this; the possibility exists that the word may have entered each language independently from separate sources. Since /r/ does not go to /l/ in Lomavren, it can be argued too that *lom* is from **ḍom(ba)* rather than from *Rrom* or *Rum*.

If my argument is maintained that Romani only crystallised into an ethnic mother tongue under the influence of Byzantine Greek, and that prior to that it was a military *koïné* and not a native language, then we might suppose that this nativisation did not happen to pre-Lomavren, but rather that its speakers were quickly assimilated into the eastern

Armenian speech community, retaining Indian words solely as lexical items conforming to Armenian morphosyntax and phonology. Although the processes giving rise to each may or may not differ, this has resulted in an ethnolect similar in many ways to the Angloromani dialect of the British Romanichals (Hancock, 1984).

The present work is supported by Courthiade's independent research in France which even more specifically places the origin of Romani in Kannauj which, together with Ayodha further east, was the city in the central area which served as the home for the Rajput armies. A comparison of modern Kannauji with Romani shows less similarity between the two than that shared by Romani and Hindi; the same is true for Sindhi, the language of Sindh – the place of origin proposed by Marsh (2003), Marwari, proposed by Hübschmannová (2004) and Jataki (Jatki, Siraiki), the language of the Jats, a people proposed by Leland (1882) as the ancestors of the Romanies. While the Rajput conscriptees and their camp followers may well have spoken these and many other languages, the fact that Romani is nevertheless closer to Hindi/Urdu supports the shared origin these latter languages have in Rajputic. Domari equivalents have been included by way of comparison.

5. The military factor

A military origin for Romanies, generally as captives, is not a new idea; de Goeje (1876: 32) wrote that 'in the year 1000, we find bands of Zotts in the army of Abû-Naçr ibn-Bakhtiyâr, in Persia and Kirmân (Ibno-'l-Athîr, ix., p. 114). In 1025, al-Mançûra was conquered by Mahmûd al-Gaznawî, because the prince of this town had forsaken Islamism.' Clarke (1878: 134) wrote,

> [I]t was from the Ghaznevide conqueror and at home that the independence of the Jats received its death-blow. The victorious army of Mahmoud, when returning laden with spoil from the Somnauth expedition of 1025, was attacked and pillaged by them on the banks of the Indus. Their temerity was chastised with exemplary rigour. Broken and dispersed by the resistless arms of the Sultan of Ghazni, they were not, however, annihilated.

Leland (1882: 24) wrote that 'Jat warriors were supplemented by other tribes ... they were broken and dispersed in the eleventh century by Mahmoud'; and Burton (1898: 212) that 'Sultan Mahmoud carried with him in A.D. 1011 some two hundred thousand [Indian] captives, the spoils of his expedition.' Kochanowski later agreed (1968: 27–8) that 'our own inter-disciplinary studies have shown that the Gypsies are Rajputs who left northern India', and Vijender Bhalla's serological studies undertaken in India concluded that 'Rajputs occupy the [genetic] position nearest the Gypsies' (1992: 331–2). Nagy *et al.* conclude that there were 'non-significant differences' in haplotype frequencies between Haryana and Sikh Jats and Slovakian Roma, but 'significant differences with non-Romani populations' (2007: 19).

Over a decade ago the Polish scholar Lech Mróz had also considered a specific connection with the Islamic raids into India: '*Podsumowują: uważam za prawdopodobne że Cyganów dostali się do Iranu w czasach Mahmuda z Ghazny, w resultacie jego wypraw do Indii*' (1992: 40; 'I consider it likely that the Gypsies' ancestors arrived in Iran in the time of Mahmud of Ghazni, as a result of his raids into India'). Bajram Haliti (2006: 6) has come to the same conclusion:

> Sometime between the tenth and eleventh centuries, the largest groups of Roma left India and the main cause was invasion of the great emperor Mahmud Gazni, who led seventeen raids in western India. Running away from terror, Roma first stopped in Iran, and then separated in two groups, the first moving toward Spain, and the second toward Byzantium and Greece.

My own research also supports this, although it has been somewhat misinterpreted; Kenrick wrote that 'Hancock says ... the emigrants were not defeated soldiers but a victorious army ... he writes that the Kshattriya warrior caste did not in fact fight but organised other people to fight for them' (2000b: 39). Nevertheless, there continues to be resistance to the whole notion of any kind of military association; in 2004, in his own interpretation of Romani history, Viorel Achim wrote, 'The distinguishing feature of the Gypsy migration is that it was not of a military nature.' An examination of the circumstances of Indian and Middle Eastern politics and warfare during the relevant timeframe is thus called for.

For roughly the first quarter-century of the second millennium, north-western India came under a series of attacks by Muslim troops led by General Mahmud from his headquarters at Ghazna (today called Ghazni and located in Afghanistan). Between AD 1001 and AD 1026 these Ghaznavids, as they were called, made seventeen forays into the Hindu-Shahi kingdom as far as Kashmir with the intent to spread Islam; ultimately the Indian kingdoms of Nagarkot, Thanesar, Kannauj and Kalinjar were all conquered and left in the hands of Hindu vassals. There were seventeen battles altogether; the main ones during the Shahiya Dynasty being:

AD 1001   The Ghaznavids advanced against Peshawar and defeated King Jayapāla at Udbhāndapur, Afghanistan, going on to attack Multān, Gujarāt and Rājpūtānā, occupying Peshawar in the Panjab, where by their own account they took half a million slaves.

AD 1005–6   Jayapāla's successor, King Ānandapāla, defeated.

AD 1008   Ānandapāla called for backup from the Rajahs of Ujjain, Gwalior, Kalinjar, Kannauj, Delhi and Ajmer. 5,000 Muslims were defeated but they ultimately won the battle.

AD 1013   Ānandapāla's successor Trilochanapāla with the help of troops from Kashmir, fought the Ghaznavids but lost.

AD 1015   Bhimapāla and his son successfully fought off Mahmud from their capital in Lohkot.

AD 1017   The Ghaznavids occupied the city of Mathurā, birthplace of Lord Krishna, and the first mosque in India was erected.

AD 1018   Vidyādhara (whom the Muslims called Nanda) successfully repulsed the Ghaznavids.

AD 1021   Trilochanapāla killed.

AD 1022   Mahmud unsuccessfully attacks Gwalior and Kalanjar.

AD 1024   Mahmud destroyed the Somanāth Śiva temple and killed 50,000 Hindu troops, and built a second mosque.

AD 1026   King Bhimapala was killed, bringing an end to the Shahiya Dynasty.

And during the Chandella Dynasty (based at Kalanjar and Khajuraho),

AD 1026   Mahmud attacks King Chālukya Bhimadevi of Gujarat at Somanāth and sacks that city, but suffers heavy losses to the Jats at Mansura on his return to Ghazna.

They were successful; with only a couple of exceptions the Ghaznavids were able to win each confrontation with the Indian armies, sometimes taking many hundreds of prisoners, as in the encounters at Kabul and Peshawar.

In addition to being prisoners of war, Indians themselves also fought as *ghulams* in special units with the Ghaznavids as *mawālī*, or 'client' soldiers. Following Bosworth, Patricia Crone (2003) describes the special *Qiqaniyya* regiments, Hindu Indians in ethnic units fighting as Ghazis in the armies of Islam from the earliest periods. Indeed, Indians would not have reached Trans-Oxiana (on the plain of Dandanqan near Marv) had it not been that they were also a major and important part of the Ghaznavid army and palace guard. If Mahmud's son and successor Mas'ud had not been sidetracked by the Oghuz Türkmen, he would not have lost the western empire, and the beginnings of Romani history would have stopped there.

Ghulams were highly trained slave-soldiers, mostly Indian in origin, but included Khurasanis and others. The Ghaznavid army included an elite palace guard, consisting of four to six thousand *ghulam* heavy cavalry. The balance of the standing army was also comprised of *ghulams*, bringing the core force to an estimated 30,000 people. The cavalry were armed with bows, maces, battleaxes, lances and long curved swords, although their horses went unarmoured (Haider, Nicolle).

Wink (1991: 23) describes the 'large numbers of Indian captives [who …] under the Ghaznavids did become important'. That they were used to fight for the Ghaznavids is documented by Ikram (1989: 31) as well, who writes of the 'Hindu contingent' of the army of Mahmud's son Mas'ud 'fail[ing] conspicuously against the Seljuqs' during the 1038 confrontation (see also Reynolds (1858), Pipes (1981, 2000), Bosworth (1961), Crone (1980) and Haider (1990) for descriptions of mediaeval Muslim armies, and Lal (1994) and Levi (2002a, 2002b) for soldiery in India). It is to those Hindus, both captives and militia, that we must look for the ancestors of the Romanies.

Marsh (2008 and in personal correspondence, pointing to Bosworth, 2001: 37–9) notes that the Seljuqs were much more likely to have destroyed the ghulams that surrounded the sultan at the last stand; the *Seljuq-Nameh* (or *Book of the Seljuqs*, written by Ibn Bibi in the thirteenth century) recounts that he had previously been forced to flee the field of battle. Being the core of the Ghaznavid military machine, and infidels as far as the Muslim Seljuqs were concerned, they could have expected no mercy upon the defeat of the Ghaznavid sultan. The camp of the Ghaznavids was sacked after their defeat by the Seljuqs and their Turkoman allies, and the remaining Hindus (the armourers, grooms, tent-makers, cooks, entertainers, elephant-keepers, shield-bearers, women and children who would all have been present as mediaeval armies were societies on the move) fled the Seljuq onslaught westward, and would seem to have arrived in eastern Anatolia fairly soon afterwards using the Silk Road from Marv, Rayy and through Khorasan into Armenia. The next encounter in the sources seems to indicate the presence of nomads in black tents outside the city walls of Ani, the centre of the Bagratid kingdom, when the Seljuqs destroyed this in 1064 AD. This seems to me to be the last point at which the Hindus from Ghazna, together with a host of other refugees on the roads in eastern Anatolia (see Matthew of Edessa's *Chronicle* about this event and his reference to princes, noblewomen, and the mass of people wandering the highways of Asia Minor, a 'vagabond nation' is the term he uses) are defeated and lose their military capacity, being reduced to the artisans, entertainers and servitors and 'hangers on' that any army carried along with it during this period. The destruction of the Armenian Bagratid kingdom marks the end of Byzantine control of Asia Minor and the beginnings of what Vyronis has called the Islamification of the Anatolian region, and the settlement of the Turks. The references to the arrival of the 'Egyptians' in Sulukule (the recently destroyed Mesotechion section of the Constantinople walls near the River Lycus), is well documented and described in the secondary sources (Soulis, 1961: 142–65). The loss of the Hindus' military function and capacity was due to their defeat by the Seljuqs and the decimation of the warrior elite that were very close to the Ghaznavid sultans, although they always maintained their religion. The complex picture of further forced migration in the wake of the Ghurid destruction of Ghazna in the twelfth century remains to be investigated.

The Indian military detachments were made up of the fighters and their camp followers, the *śivirānugāmī*, people recruited to tend to the duties associated with war. They generally outnumbered the soldiers themselves, and like the soldiers came from many different backgrounds and spoke many different languages and dialects. That Romanies have a mixed Indian origin is not a new idea; over a century ago de Goeje (1876) wrote of the ancestors

> ... consisting in large part of the tribe of Jats, which occupied lands in the Indus Valley near Multan ... during the Omayad Dynasty they took a great number of their families, together with their camp followers, into the regions of the Lower Tigris ... organising a resistance to al-Motacim's government they were subdued and taken to Baghdad, and then taken to various places along the borders of the Byzantine Empire ... it is from these Jats that the European Gypsies originate.

This would have placed the date of departure at approximately AD 855. Although the Jat language, Jataki, is considerably less like Romani than is Hindi-Urdu – see Burton (1849) – a mixed (principally Jat) origin was also supported by Leland over a century ago, who wrote (1882: 332–3) that:

> Romanies speak an Aryan tongue, which agrees in the main with that of the Jats, but which contains words gathered from other Indian sources. This is a consideration of the utmost importance, as by it alone can we determine what was the agglomeration of tribes in India which formed the western Gypsy.

Woolner (1914: 123–6) has also referred to Mahmud of Ghazni's forays, leading, he said, to the 'wiping out' of the Indian dialects of Gandhāra (now north-western Pakistan and eastern Afghanistan) and the destruction of the Jats.

The soldiers themselves, whatever their social backgrounds, were given honorary warrior, or *kshattriya*, caste status and were called *Rajputs*, or 'sons of princes'. The administrative language of both the government and the military in the Hindu Shahi kingdom during that period was mediaeval Persian, although the local population spoke different Indian and Dardic languages natively; it is already widely (although not universally) accepted that such a situation gave rise to the Urdu language as a military lingua franca, combining elements from Persian and a number of different Indian languages. Even though the name 'Urdu' did not appear in print until the late 1700s, Bailey (1938: 1) – critically discussed at length by Faruqi (2001: 45–62) – wrote that 'Urdu was born in 1027; its birthplace was Lahore, its parent Old Panjabi; Old Kharï was its step-parent'. Abbas (2002: 2) wrote:

> The Ghaznavid origin of Urdu follows from the very name of the language: *Zaban-e-Urdu*, or 'Language of the Armies'. The word 'Urdu' is derived from the Turkic 'Oordou', meaning 'camps' or, as Khullar notes

above, 'armies'. Urdu was thus self-evidently the language of the soldiers of the armies of Mahmud-e-Ghazni, the only militarist sovereign of the era who maintained a large enough army for a considerable period to provide sufficient time for a new language to develop.

The connection between the formation of Urdu and the Ghaznavid invasions is not new. Khullar (1995: 1) wrote that 'The birth of Urdu language was the direct result of the synthesis between the invading armies of Mahmud of Ghazni with the civilian population of the Indian cities. The word Urdu itself means Lashkar, derived from the Turkish language meaning *armies*.'

And as long ago as 1888 Sachau wrote (Vol. II, p. 258) that:

Tilak, the son of Jai Sen … studied in Kashmir, [then worked as an] interpreter first to Kadi Shirazi Bulhasan Ali, a high civil officer under Mahmud and Masud (Elliott, II.117, 123), then to Ahmad Ibn Hasan of Maimand, who was grand vizier, 1007 AD–25 … and then 1030–1033 under Mahmud and Masud, and rose afterwards to be a commanding officer in the army (Elliott, II.125–7). This class of men spoke and wrote Hindi (of course with Arabic characters) and Persian (perhaps also Turkish, as this language prevailed in the army), and it is probably in these circles that we must look for the origin of Urdu or Hindustani.

We can speculate that Romani began to emerge under the same circumstances; for want of a name I have called this hypothesised contact language 'Rajputic' (Hancock, 2000). As demonstrated above, it shares over three times as many of the same Persian words with Urdu as it does with Domari. Military terms (or terms with a military application) of Indic and Persian origin in Romani, and which have thus been a part of the language from the very beginning, include:

'arrow' (*sulica*) < Skt śūla, Hi sūl, + Gk –ιτζα
    (Balkan dialects use Turkish *okja* for this).
'axe' (*tover*) < cf. Hindi and Persian *tabar* 'axe',
    and *Hi tarvār* 'sword', Kurdish *taver*.
'battle' (*kurripen*) < Skt kuṭṭayati + -tvana
'confront, oppose' (*nikl-*) < Skt nikālayati, Hi nikālnā
'decamp; move out' (*rad-*) < Skt rah- + dadāti
'fight' (*kurr-*) < Skt kuṭṭayati, Hi kūṭnā
'gaiters' (*patava*) < Skt patta-, Hi paṭṭī, cf. E. 'puttees'

'horse' (*khuro*) < Skt ghoṭa-, Hi ghoḍā
'military' (*lurdikano*) < Skt luṭṭati +
'plunder' (*lur-*) < Skt luṭṭati, Hi lūṭnā, cf. E. 'loot', *Luri*
'saddle' (*aster*) < Skt āstara-
'set up camp' (*lod-*) < Skt lagyati
'slaughter' (*manušvari*) < Skt mānuṣamārikā
'soldier' (*kuripaskero*) < Skt kuṭṭayati + -tvana + kro
'soldier' (*lur, lurdo*) < Skt luṭṭati, Hi lūṭnā
'spear, lance' (*bust*) < Skt bhṛṣṭi-
'spear, stab' (*pošav-*) < Skt sparśayā, Hi phasnā
'sword' (*xanrro*) < Skt khaḍga-, Hi khaṇḍā
'trident' (*trušul*, but now meaning 'cross') < Skt triśūla-
'whip' (*čupni, čukni*) < Persian čābuk
'battleaxe' (*nižako*) < Persian načak, cf. also Kurdish nijakh
'halter' (*ašvar*) < Persian abzār
'spur' (*buzex*) < Persian sbux
'saddle' (*zen*) < Persian zin
'stirrup' (*bakali*) cf. Kurdish paq, 'lower leg,' + alî(n) 'support, hook'

Given the comparatively small number of Indic items in Romani it is significant that there are two words in the language for 'silk', *phanrr* (Panjabi: *paṭṭ*, 'silk', from the same root as *patavo*, 'gaiter') and *kež* (Kashmiri: *kheš*, 'silken cloth', but also Urdu (<Persian): *kaz,* 'raw silk'). The military distinguished between two kinds of silk: that with a fine weave for outer clothing, and another with a coarse weave worn as an undershirt, designed specifically to entangle and impede arrowheads fired into the body (information courtesy of Adrian Marsh; the two layers of silk are clearly depicted in the illustration of a *ghulam* warrior in Nicolle, 1997). The various words for a non-Romani person also suggest a military/civilian relationship: the commonest, *gadžo*, is traceable to Skt *gārhya-*, Pkt *gajjha-*, 'domestic, non-military, civilian'; *das* may be compared with Pkt *dāsa*, 'slave, enemy, captive'; *goro* with Skt *gaura-*, cf. Siraiki and Sindhi *gora*, 'slave'; and *gomi* with Skt *gomi*, cf. Bag *gomi*, 'one who has surrendered'.

One connection with the Ghaznavids is found in the word for a mattock (a tool with a head consisting of an axe-blade on one side and a hammer on the other), one of the symbols of authority carried by the *Rrom baro*. This is *nižako* in the Vlax dialects and *njako* in Balkan

Romani. According to Nicolle (1996: 153), 'as usual there was considerable variety among the troops of the eastern Muslim countries, ranging from the Ghaznavids' elite heavy cavalry armed with *nachakh* (axes) to the Turkish horse-archers of thirteenth century northern India'.

The word is Iranic (cf. Gurani Kurdish *nijāk*, 'axe', Mokri, 1951: 134), and has passed into the Perso-Arabic military lexicon as *nachakh* (Nicolle, 1997: 306). The Rajputs' religious restriction on eating vegetables that grow below ground at a funereal feast is also maintained amongst Vlax Romanies, where potatoes and peanuts are forbidden at *pomèni*.

The military connection has been explored from the historian's perspective by Marsh (2008) who, rather than (or perhaps in addition to) seeing the *koïné* as having originated within the Rajput's own environment, says:

> The development of the military koiné happened, I suggest, in the Ghaznāvid armies amongst *mawālī* troops ('client' soldiers) of Indian units, *Qīqanīyya* or *Kīkanīyya*, as a result of the need to communicate across dialectical and regional differences ... The assaults on the region of northern India following the accession of Amir, later Sultan Mahmud of Ghaznā (Mahmūd b. Sebüktigin, sometimes Mahmūd-i Zābulī 998–1030), [and his part in] the dislocation of Indian peoples as infantry, elephant-drivers, prisoners of war, craftspeople and artisans, and their incorporation into the Ghaznāvid state, centred in what is now eastern Afghanistan. These were a continuation of his father's policy of raiding the sub-continent in assaults against Shi'ite Multan and other centres of the Ismā'īlī Muslims of Sindh, and also the pagan Hindus. The resources of India were needed in order to finance the professional, multi-ethnic standing army of the Ghaznāzvids. The expansion of Ghaznā during Mahmūd's rule followed the important *razzias* of 1018–1019 against the cities of the northern Ganges, including Kannauj.

The significance of Kannauj has been explored by Courthiade, who claims that it is the ultimate home of the Romanies (2004: 105–124 and 2007). He maintains that nearly all of the 53,000 inhabitants of that city, then the capital of northern India, were captured by the Ghaznavids in AD 1018 and enslaved in Khorasan, where they subsequently united with the Seljuqs and the Persians to overthrow Mahmud's son Masudi, killed near Lahore in AD 1040. Moving on to Baghdad in AD 1055, the combined troops then defeated the Byzantine troops at Manzikert, near

Vangjoli, in AD 1071 and later drove out the Fatimide Egyptians who held sway over this part of the Muslim world at that time. Courthiade's position has been pointedly – although unconvincingly – attacked by 'Im Nin'alu', who argues elsewhere for a Jewish origin for Roma (2004: 3):

> A recent theory that is having some success among the intellectual environment interested in the subject, and that is destined to be proven fallacious like all the preceding hypotheses, pretends to have discovered the original 'city' from where Roma might have come: Kannauj, in Uttar Pradesh, India ... the author founds the entire argumentation on an alleged linguistic proof that is quite insufficient to explain the Romany cultural features not related to language and that are undoubtedly much more relevant, and not any reliable evidence is given to support his theory.

The mixed nature of the Romani lexicon is exemplified by the numerals; 'one', 'two' and 'three' are traceable to the Central group, 'four' is Dardic, while 'five' and 'six' are of mixed origin (John, 2006: 6). To these, and as evidence of *koïnéisation*, may be added the two words for 'two', *duj* and *do*. These are distinguished by case, *do* being the oblique form (an innovation – no languages in India distinguish numerals by case). *Duj* is found in Nemadi, Kannauji, Pahari and Siraji, while *do* is found almost everywhere else; only Chhattisgarhi and Pangwali have both, although as synonyms, not as case-contrastive forms. The language includes numbers of synonyms traceable to separate Indian dialect groups, that is, it cannot be linked with any single Indian language but has features from several of them. There are three different words for 'burn': *xačar*, *thab-* and *phab-*. The first descends from OIA *ksāti*, the second from *daghda-* and the last from **bhabh-*. The first is mainly represented by the Central neo-Indic languages (Panjabi, Pahari, Jaunsari and so on), the second mainly by members of the eastern group (Bengali, Oriya and so on), while there are no descendants from the last other than in Romani. Except for Romani, no Indian language has descendants from all three forms, although the first and second exist in Shina, Sindhi, Panjabi, Kashmiri, Nepali and Gujerati. There are two words for 'wash', *xalav-* and *thov-* (from OIA *ksālayati* and *dhauvati* respectively). In India the first is restricted to Pahari and Kumauni; the second is widespread in all dialect groups. Only Kumauni (besides Romani) has both. There are three words for 'sing': *gilab-* and *bag-* (from OIA *gīta-* and *vādyāte* respectively) and *kixiv-* (? < OIA *kīkkati*, 'yell', listed in Courthiade and

Kányádi, 2007: *vij*). The first is restricted to Dardic and Sinhalese, the second to several mainly Central and Eastern Indian languages, but no language in India includes all three. There are three Romani words for 'to scare': *trašav-*, *darav-* and *šas-*, from OIA *trasati*, *dāryati* and *śāsati-*; only Romani has all three. The first is restricted to Sindhi, Lahnda, Panjabi and Kashmiri, the second to Assamese and Gujerati and the third to Bengali. The first and third occur in Nepali and Oriya and the second and third in Hindi alone. Numbers of these synonym clusters in Romani have been collected, and their analysis is still in progress.

We might assume that there were even more such lexical clusters among the speakers of Rajputic, some items from which were ultimately selected and others of which were discarded. This would account for the uneven distribution of some Indic items in the European Romani dialects – some restricted only to the Northern dialects (which includes Iberian) for example, and would explain, why Lomavren selected *hath* for 'hand' while Romani (and for that matter Domari) have the earlier (and Dardic) forms with /-s-/ (*vast, xæst*), or why Lomavren selected, inter alia, the Indic *ansev*, *solav* and *pantrič* ('apple', 'dog', 'bird') while Romani selected the Indic *phabaj*, *džukel* and *čiriklo*.

Typical of contact languages was the development of analytical numerals in Rajputic (cf. New Guinea Pidgin English *two-pela-ten-one*, *two-pela-ten-two*, Cameroon Creole English *two-tali-one*, *two-tali-two* = 21, 22 and so on) instead of its having retained the original Indian fusional forms; in the case of Romani the model was probably supplied by Persian, although for numbers above twenty the linking word *u* (< Persian o) is replaced by *ta* (< OIA *atha*, 'and, also'). Significantly the 'corrupt dialect of the jargon of Hindostan' described by Hadley and Fitrut (1801: 37) does have the analytical forms alongside the traditional ones: *eck bees ekh/ekkess* '21', *eck bees doo/baueess* '22', *eck bees teen/te-eess,* '23' and so on. In some dialects, *u* and *ta* are not used to link the Greek numerals seven, eight and nine, following the Greek model instead (for example, 19 = δέκ'έννέα); Indian models for six, seven, eight and nine are also lacking in Domari and Lomavren. In all three languages, the link-word for the teens differs from that for all higher numbers (for a general discussion of Romani numerals see Bakker, 2001):

	Hindi	Persian	Romani	cf. Lomavren	cf. Domari
1	ek	yek	ekh, jekh	yak, yek	yika
2	do	do	duj (do, obl.)	lui	dī
3	tin	she	trin	tərin	tærən
4	chhar	chæhār	štar	išdör	štar
5	panch	pænj	pandž	pendž	pandž
6	cheh	shesh	šov	šeš	šaš
7	sāth	hæft	ifta	haft	xaut
8	āth	hæsht	oxto	hašt	xaišt
9	nau	noh	inja[1]	nu	na

	Hindi	Persian	Romani	cf. Lomavren	cf. Domari
10	das	dæh	deš	las	des
11	gyāraha	yāzdæh	deš-u-jekh	de'-hu-yek	das-wa-yika
12	bāraha	dævāzdæh	deš-u-duj	de'-hu-dui	das-wa-dī
13	teraha	sizdæh	deš-u-trin	de'-hu-tərin	das-wa-tærən
14	chaudaha	chæhārdæh	deš-u-štar	de'-hu-išdör	das-wa-štar
15	pandraha	pānzdæh	deš-u-pandž	de'-pandž	das-wa-pandž
16	solah	shānzdæh	deš-u-šov	de'-u-šaš	des-šeyš
17	satra	hefdæh	deš-ifta	de'-u-hoft	des-xaut
18	athārah	hejdæh	deš-oxto	de'-u-hašt	des-xaišt
19	unnēs	nūzdæh	deš-inja	de'-u-nu	des-u-nu
20	bees	bist	biš	vist	wīs
21	ekis	bist-o-yek	biš-ta-jekh	vist-yek	wīs-u-yika
22	bāis	bist-o-do	biš-ta-duj	vist-ər-du	wīs-u-dī
23	teis	bist-o-seh	biš-ta-trin	vist-ər-tərin	wīs-u-tærən
24	chaubis	bist-o-chæhār	biš-ta-štar	vist-i-šdör	wīs-u-štar
25	pachēs	bist-o-pānz	biš-ta-pandž	vist-i-pendž	wīs-u-pandž
100	sew	sād	šel	saj	saj
1000	hezar	hezar	adjur[2]	illi[3]	illi

1   Borrow gives *nu* for Spanish Romani '9', although this has not been found
    in any other dialect.
2   Finnish Romani only, therefore probably not thematic.
3   From Arabic.

6. Appearance in the West

Having established a date for a continuing presence in India, we need
now to look for the earliest documentation of a Romani presence in the
West, because the window of time between both dates must cover the
time span during which their exodus took place. While most earlier

scholars have placed the migration out of India sometime well before AD 1000, some have placed it as late as the twelfth century – most recently Kochanowski, who argues for the date of departure of Rajputs following the Muslim invasions led by Mohammed Ghori in AD 1191[8] (2003: 341).

There are two likelier and earlier possibilities, the first, dated AD 1068, from Byzantium, reported the presence of 'Lors' in that city, but that may have been a reference to *Luri* (Dom) rather than Romanies; but the second, dated sometime in the latter part of the twelfth century, clearly refers to *Atsinganoi* and *Æguptoi*, then as now the most usual names for Romanies. Fraser's important lexico-statistical analysis of Romani puts the beginnings of its linguistic split into the different dialect groups in the Byzantine Empire at around AD 1040 (Fraser, 1989), while Kalaydjieva *et al.*'s more recent findings place the migratory divisions into Europe beginning in the thirteenth century (2005:6): 'The Gypsy group was born in Europe. All marker systems suggest that the earliest splits occurred twenty to twenty-four generations ago, i.e. from the late thirteenth century onwards.'

Yet further evidence supporting the dates of movement out of India and into Europe argued for in this study is provided by a recent examination of a number of 'private' genetic mutations that are exclusively responsible for the specific disorders in the Romani people (Morar *et al.*, 2004). One in particular is a mutation that causes congenital myasthenia, which is shared by Indian, Pakistani and Romani patients, and which was clearly brought out of India. Those researchers used their genetic data to posit the date of the founding of the entire Romani population, and estimated it to have taken place about 800 to 1000 years ago, with the subsequent splits (out of Anatolia) into individual groups occurring between 400 and 600 years ago, with no evidence of any such substructure prior to their estimated earliest date. These findings have generated some interest in the scientific community; see, for example, Sellah (2004) and Brownlee (2004).

7. The Seljuq factor

If this provides an explanation for where and how the pre-Romani population may have begun, we are left having to explain how it reached the Byzantine Empire, the period of its history barely ever addressed in the scholarship[9]; nor has the crucial period spent in Anatolia been properly acknowledged, although this is now being redressed with Adrian Marsh's current research and Nadia Demeter *et al.*'s 'new approach' to Romani history, which includes 'a profound analysis of the Romany people's three-century sojourn in Byzantium ... [which] period is always very cursorily dealt with in scholarly works' (2000: 321–34).

The Seljuqs, or rather the nomadic Sunni Türkmen who were the main military component in the Seljuq polity during this period, provide this link. They were the force behind the proto-Romani migration, driving the original Hindu army, defeated after Dandanqan (1040), ahead of them:

> On May 24th, 1040, the Seljuqid army attacked the Ghaznavids during their advance towards the castle of Dandanakan ... Sultan Mesud['s ...] command led to the disruption of the order of the Ghaznavid army and to the defeat ... slaves from the palace left the Ghaznavid army to pass to the Seljuqid side, joining the ones who had escaped before. Later, they attacked. This led to the collapse and dispersal of the already exhausted, tired and destitute Ghaznavid army. (Güzel *et al.*, 2002: 105)

They spread out into Khorasan, Armenia and eastern Anatolia because of the complete collapse of the Ghaznavids – which, it has been argued, was 'because of Mahmud's excessive reliance on Hindu soldiers and generals' (Rikhye, 2006: 2). They were part of an increasingly composite group consisting of, beside themselves, Persians, Armenians, Greeks and other 'refugees' from what the twelfth-century Armenian historian Matthew of Eddesa described as the 'perfidious nation of the Turks'. It was standard practice for the conquering armies in Mongol-Turkic warfare to push defeated populations ahead of them, in order to create fear and disruption to a maximum degree. The Seljuqs were not especially interested in Anatolia, except to distract the Türkmen from depredating the Persian lands and causing enormous problems for the sedentary population – which they succeeded in doing nevertheless, ultimately undermining the very fabric of their empire. Only those based in Konya (Iconium) in central Anatolia remained powerful enough eventually to set up the Rûm (Rome) sultanate, and only after the Mongols had invaded Baghdad and dealt a severe blow to the Great Seljuq Empire. The small Seljuq ruling class in Rûm governed a population that was mostly Greek-speaking Anatolian Christian.

After Mahmud of Ghazni was repulsed in 1008 in his attack on the

Qarakhanid Empire to his north, he enlisted the Seljuq Turks in southern Sogdia and Khwarazm to defend his kingdom from Qarakhanid retribution. The Seljuqs were an enslaved Turkic tribe that had been used as defence forces by the Samanids and had converted to Islam in the late tenth century. Having secured his homeland, Mahmud now turned his attention back to the Indian subcontinent. Despite their military successes on the Indian subcontinent, the Ghaznavids were unable to control the Seljuqs under them, and in 1040 the latter rebelled. The Seljuqs took over Khwarazm, Sogdia and Bactria from the Ghaznavids and, in 1055, conquered Baghdad, the seat of the Abbasid caliphs.

The Seljuqs were Sunnis and as adamantly anti-Shiite and anti-Ismaili as were the Ghaznavids. They were anxious to wrest the caliphs from the influence and control of the Buyid Shiites in Iran. In 1062, they finally conquered the Buyid Kingdom and, the next year, proclaimed their own empire. The final parts of the Seljuq Empire lasted until submitting to the Mongols in 1243. In the face of their defeat to the Seljuqs, the Ghaznavids withdrew to the east of the Hindu Kush Mountains, restricted to Ghazna, Kabul and the Punjab (Berzin, 2006).

Contact with speakers of Mongolian resulted in the adoption of the single word *mangin*, 'treasure' (< mōngōn). This was either acquired at this time, when the Mongols expelled the Seljuqs, or else during the trek across the Caucasus or northern Persia during the period of its occupancy by the Khanate of the Kipchaks, or the 'Golden Horde'. In either case, its adoption must have been later than around AD 1265, since Mongolian and Turkic languages were not spoken throughout northern Persia until after that date (Doerfer, 1970: 217ff.).

Ibni-Bibi describes how the Seljuqs forced the ghulams that surrounded the sultan to flee from the field of battle during their last confrontation in his Seljuq-Name (Bosworth, 2001: 37–9). As the core of the Ghaznavid military machine, and infidels as far as the Muslim Seljuqs were concerned, they could have expected no mercy upon the defeat of the Ghaznavid sultan. The camp of the Ghaznavids was sacked after their defeat by the Seljuqs and their Turkoman allies, and the remaining Hindus – as previously noted, an entire society on the move – fled westwards from the Seljuq onslaught and would seem to have arrived in eastern Anatolia fairly soon afterwards using the Silk Road from Marv, Rayy and through Khorasan into Armenia. The next encounter in the sources also indicates the presence of nomads in tents outside the city walls of Ani, the centre of the Bagratid kingdom, when the Seljuqs destroyed it in 1064 AD. Marsh suggests (in personal correspondence) that this was likely the last point at which the Hindus from Ghazna, together with a host of other refugees who joined them along the roads in eastern Anatolia are defeated and lose their military capacity, being reduced to the artisans, entertainers, servitors and 'hangers on' that any army carried along with it during this period.

The loss of the Hindus' primary military function and capacity was due to their defeat by the Seljuqs and the decimation of the warrior elite that were very close to the Ghaznavid sultans, although they always maintained their religion, or at least elements of it, and some military involvement was still in evidence at the time of the move across into Europe. Bosworth writes that 'Indian troops passed from the Ghaznavid to the Seljuq armies; troops, if not formally made prisoners of war, often joined the bandwaggon of the winning side', very willing to turn against their captors, while Leiser surmised that 'after the Seljuqs defeated the Ghaznavids they "appropriated" their prisoners of war; such action was fairly commonplace in those days' and, citing the work of the Turkish historian Köyman, which provides several sources, goes on to say that 'after the victory at Dandanqan, soldiers from throughout Khurasan, "some of whom may have served the Ghaznavids", joined the Seljuqs'. Marsh (2003) also notes that Sindhi warriors:

> … had been present in the Persian lands since the early fifth century AD, often as auxiliaries to the Sassanid armies of Persia or as remnants of a defeated and 'decapitated' military society … subsequently the Seljuqs of Rûm had acquired large numbers of these troops and their retinues, in the aftermath of their defeat of Mahmud's heir, Mas'ud on the steppes of Dandanaqan, 23rd May 1040. These combatants were, as all armies in the early mediaeval period, effectively societies on the move, with the fighting force making up approximately one third of the total number. The rest would have been the armourers, grooms, smiths and metalworkers, carpenters, military engineers, servants and servitors, tent-makers, cooks, bakers, washer-women, slaves, camp-followers and children.

Located to the south-east of the Byzantine Empire, Armenia fell to armies directed by the Seljuqs in AD 1071 and the foundation was laid for the establishment of a new sultanate called Rûm, occupying former Armenian and some Byzantine territory in Anatolia – the area that is today Turkey. Fraser, supporting the conclusion reached in the important earlier work of Soulis, wrote that 'the appearance of the Gypsies in Byzantine lands is *undoubtedly* connected with the Seljuq raids in Armenia' (emphasis added), although he would have been nearer the mark if he had called these instead Türkmen raids. It is also probably more accurate to regard the incoming Indians as part of the co-opted Ghaznavids and as allies, with the Armenians as the antagonists, and not as joint protagonists along with the Seljuqs.

Marsh goes on to suggest that the establishment of groups who were to become Romanies in Anatolia was the result of the Seljuqs' policy of establishing *beyliks*, that is to say, granting autonomous fiefdoms within Rûm to bands of their warriors. While this early connection with Sindh is well documented, it must be taken as geographical rather than as necessarily linguistic, since many languages besides Sindhi are (and were) spoken in that part of India. The comparative wordlists above do not demonstrate a particularly close lexical relationship between Romani and Sindhi.

While it is documented that 'Indians' were brought into Byzantine territory by the Seljuqs, 'usually in a military capacity', nowhere are those Indians referred to specifically as either Rajputs or Rom. We would not expect the former, since it is an Indian word and only a minority of the Indians would have been Rajputs in any case, and if, as is proposed here, the Romani population did not come into existence *until* the Byzantine period, then 'Rom' had not yet become a label.

One self-designation found among Romanies in the Balkans is *Romi* – a Slavic plural, although the word is also found in non-Slavic-speaking Romania. *Romi* (<ρόμοι, ρόμαιοι) seems to have been used consistently in Byzantium after about 1070 to refer to all the inhabitants of Rûm, especially after the history of Michael Attaliates, who wrote from the perspective of a military official in a twelve-year period leading up to Manzikert (1071). The Arabs used it in its Arabic form (*Rûmi*) from about the same time, as part of the titles in diplomatic correspondence between the Mamluk Sultans and the Byzantine Emperors, according to a recent article by Korobeinikov (2004). It was probably used regularly in Europe in the aftermath of the Great Schism (1054), as focus turned to concerns for crusades and the Holy Lands. Ibn Battuta refers to Rûm in his mid-fourteenth century account of travels through Asia Minor to Central Asia (Gibb and Beohingham, 1994) and specifically mentions that from the earliest times (that is, since the contact between Arabs and

Byzantium), it was called Rûm to designate the lands ruled, or once ruled in his time, by the Romans. In that sense, it seems that the Arab invasions and conflicts with the Byzantines in the seventh and eighth centuries probably resulted in the emergence of the notion of the *Rhomaioi* or *Rhomoi* by the eleventh century. Marsh argues that the Indian population in Anatolia became ethnicised into the *Romiti* by the 1300s, that is, into the forerunners of the Romani people. Significantly, there is a population of nomadic metal workers living in the West Bank who are referred to as 'Kurds', but who call themselves *rōm* or *rōmat* (Matras, 1999a: 7) (I have included a list of metalworking terms in Appendix 1 of this paper).[10]

Ioviţă and Schurr (2004: 275), whose very valuable article on genetic evidence for Romani identity goes far to support the proposals in the present paper, do question specifically my military *koïné* hypothesis (Hancock, 2000), arguing that 'the defeat of the Rajputs by the Muslim Ghaznavids in the twelfth century … is difficult to reconcile with historical data that places Gypsies in the Byzantine Empire before this time – around the tenth–eleventh centuries'. However, they have confused Kochanowski's later dates with my own; the Ghaznavid invasions took place between AD 1000–1027, not in the twelfth century as Kochanowski has it; furthermore, we cannot be sure that the earliest references to people identified as 'Gypsies' in the Byzantine Empire were Rom rather than Dom.

The late and much missed Milena Hübschmannová (2000; 2004) too was bothered by the time frame, questioning the linguistic evidence because it supports an eleventh-century exodus when the presence of Romanies in Byzantium is also recorded for the same century:

> Roma professor Ian Hancock *le Redžosko* of Texas University in Austin (USA) believes that Roma – originally Rajput fighters whose army was composed of a great variety of castes – left India because of the Muslim invasions. Tropes led by General al Qasim began the invasions with the conquest of Sindh in 712. The wars peaked with twenty-one border raids led by Mahmud of Ghazni (beginning of eleventh century). Hancock dates the departure of the Roma from India back to exactly the time of Mahmud. Hancock bases his theory on linguistics: according to him, modern Indic languages lost their neuter gender, and neuter words were absorbed by the masculine gender. Hancock (2001) presents a table in which he compares the genders of *Romani* words with related *Hindi* words. His theory is interesting, but if *Athingani* (very probably Roma) were already in

Byzantium in the eleventh century, they would scarcely have left India in the same century.

Of course the loss of the MIA neuter isn't according to Hancock, but to the specialists in this area such as Masica and Bloch, mentioned above. I have simply applied it to the Romani case.

Historical evidence points to the Seljuqs, or their main fighting force the Türkmen, as the link accounting for this span of time (which easily allows for such a migration to have taken place within a century); they defeated the Ghaznavids in AD 1038 and AD 1041 and took their prisoners of war to use as their own fighting force and as a frontline 'buffer' in their move towards Anatolia. Tsaggas (2006: 21–3) writes about the Seljuqs' arrival in Baghdad, Ani, Manzikert, Edessa, Nicaia, Antioch, Tripoli and Jerusalem in company with Indians from the Panjab ('Pentopotamia'), probably acquired in Khurasan or Manzikurt from the Ghaznavids. Lee has recorded *seldjùko*, meaning 'Turk', in the speech of his principal Kalderaš-speaking informant Russell Demetro.

Like the Shahi administrators before them, the Seljuqs too used Persian as their lingua franca. Kjeilen (2003: 1) says, 'The Seljuqs made Esfahan their capital, and they started to use the Persian language in the administration of their new state. The Seljuq sultans also sponsored Persian, and they were effectively propagators of the language to the entire Persian continent.'

8. Anatolia and the emergence of the Romani people and language

Almost a century ago Colocci (1907: 279) saw the move from India to the Byzantine Empire as having been 'very rapid'; but if that took only two or three decades, the stay in Anatolia itself lasted for over two centuries, and was crucial to the emergence of the Romani people. As an already ethnically and linguistically mixed population, bound together by former occupation and now social circumstance, the Indians not only intermarried with each other but with the local people as well. Social and caste barriers to marriage that are strictly maintained within India become relaxed in diasporic Indian populations; this is clearly evident in Indian communities in countries such as Fiji, Mauritius or Trinidad.

Byzantine society was ethnically diverse and included many different peoples and languages, although the lingua franca was Greek and the national religion Orthodox Christianity. It may be relevant that while Greek was the everyday language of Constantinople (Byzantium), situated on the European side of the Bosporus, and was the administrative language throughout the Empire, it was not the only language spoken at the popular level throughout the rest of the land. Children newly born into this community must have been exposed to a variety of languages, including the Rajputic of their own parents and the Greek being spoken all around them. We may well suppose that the Romani language, and the Romani people, came into existence in the Byzantine Empire during this time; this being the case, reconstructing proto-Romani as a discrete pre-Byzantine Indian language is not possible, although a more detailed description of Rajputic is underway.

The influence of Byzantine Greek in the makeup of the Romani language cannot be underestimated (see Grant, 2003); not only does it constitute the second largest percentage of the pre-European vocabulary after the Indian words, being found in every semantic area (even in the numerals), but it has also contributed to fundamental areas of the grammar, such as the different words for the definite article 'the', losing the Indian grammatical feature of ergativity, and the change of the basic NIA syntactic ordering from subject-object-verb to subject-verb-object. The middle voice which Rajko Djurić argues is evidence of Romani's great age may equally well have been acquired from Greek, as well as the shift of the Indic dative to the Balkan accusative. Athematic final and non-final affixes of Greek origin include inter alia *-in, -os, -is, -mos, -mata, -itza* (also Slavic), *-itko, -me(n)*, verbal *-as, -is, -azo, -izo, -isar-* and *-ar-*. The synthetic construction modelled on Greek πίο (in Romani, *po*, relexified by *maj, meg* and so on, in other dialects) before comparative adjectives (*po-baro*, 'bigger') replaces – or was selected – in some dialects rather than the Iranic/Ossetic enclitic *-der* (*bareder,* 'bigger'; see Hancock, 1995c: 33 for further discussion of this). A semantic calque may be found in the Romani verb *beš-*, which means both 'sit' and 'reside', paralleled in Byzantine Greek καθίζω, 'sit', and also 'settle in a place; (of an army) encamp' (Liddell and Scott, 1980: 339).[11]

9. Into Europe

The main move up into Europe was also the result of Islamic expansion, this time initiated by the Ottoman Turks, who eventually sacked

Byzantium in AD 1453 and extended their influence up into the Balkans, although it would be wrong to think that this migration happened all at one time. The bubonic plague (the 'Black Death') had reached western Anatolia by 1347 for instance, and forced a general migration across into Europe that surely included some Romanies, since they were blamed for having introduced it. Linguistic evidence points to the Romani language existing in three distinct overlapping strata across Europe (see Courthiade, 1994); there are very few Greek words, including the definite articles, in at least one European Romani dialect (Doljenska, spoken in Slovenia, see Uhlik, 1973 and Cech, 2006), suggesting a very early move out of Anatolia before the heavy lexical impact of Greek had affected it.[12]

Not only was Islam a key factor in the move into Europe, as it was in the move out of India, but both events also shared a military aspect, since the Ottoman Turks used the Romanies 'as direct participants (in their militia), mainly as servants in the auxiliary detachments or as craftsmen servicing the army', as Marushiakova and Popov have written. By the 1300s, there were specifically military garrisons of Romanies at both Modon and Nauplia, in Venetian Peloponnesia, today southern Greece. The Romanies had arrived in Europe.

We do not know how the various groups of Romanies first entered Europe. Most presumably crossed the isthmus at Constantinople, although it has been suggested that others left Anatolia by boat across the Aegean or even the Black Sea (Gheorghe, 1983: 13). In whatever way they reached the Balkans, they continued to move on in all directions, being reported in almost every country in Europe by 1500.

10. Questions

I am well aware that these hypotheses have been challenged by some of my colleagues, and I welcome that. We are all working towards the discovery and documentation of Romani history, and if theories can be shown to be baseless, then we can eliminate those lines of pursuit and move on in other directions. So far, however, I have not seen any *specific* counter-arguments (although some relevant questions are raised in Matras, 2004b), and would like the following points to be addressed. Perhaps a future conference might be organised to deal solely with these:

- If the migration out of India pre-dated AD 1000, how may we account for the reassignment of formerly neuter nouns in Romani and their matching reassignment in languages still spoken in India, as well as for other neo-Indic characteristics of the language?
- If the migration through Persia and the acquisition of Persian words took place in the fifth century, why are all such items in Romani, Lomavren and Domari from Modern (post-ninth or tenth century) Persian?[13]
- If the ancestors of the Romanies were not a military force, how may we account for the significant number of military terms of Indian origin in Romani, and the corresponding paucity of other terms, such as agricultural terms? If they were military but not Rajputs, who else could they have been? Consider also the further non-linguistic arguments for Rajput identity made in Hancock (2000).
- How may we account for the significant number of homonyms in Romani which are traceable to separate Indo-Aryan dialect groups, and which are not paralleled in languages still spoken in India (although Urdu is an exception)? And if they *did* parallel Romani at an earlier time but have been lost, where is the evidence for that?
- How may we account for the fact that Romani shares three times as many Persian-derived words with Urdu as it does with Domari?
- If the population left India in small groups spread out over several centuries as has been claimed, how did those groups manage to find each other and regroup subsequently?
- If the Indians left as entertainers, traders and so on, how did they get to Anatolia?
- We know that there were thousands of Indians in Anatolia as a result of the historical events outlined here; if they were not the ancestors of the Romanies, who were they, and what happened to them?
- How do we account for the apparent cognate relationship between the ethnonyms *Rom*, *Dom* and *Lom*, and the surviving Indic *jati* name *dom*? The fact that those Romani dialects that preserve a distinct reflex of retroflex /d/ use that reflex in Romani is significant.[14]

Appendix 1: Metalworking terms

alloy (v.)	ham-o-	< Gk. *σμίγ-*
anvil	amòni	< Gk. *ἀμόνι*
anvil	dòpo	< Rum. *dop*
anvil	kàpra	< Rum. *capră*
awl	dekàfti	< etym. unknown
bell	kudùni	< Gk. *κουδούνι*
bellows	mixàni	< Gk. *μηχανή*
bellows	pišot	< Arm. *փհէ փհնշ*
bellows-pipe	xoni	< Gk. *χωνί*
blacksmith	arčondo	< etym. unknown
bolt	klinčo	< Rum. *clenci*
brass	perdìda	< etym. unknown
bronze	brònžo	< Gk. *μπρούντζος*
cast iron	čugùno	< Bulg. *чугунь*
chain	lànco	< Rum. *lanţ*
chisel	kopìdi	< Gk. *κοπίδι*
cooling trough	kopàna	< Gk. *κοπάνα*
copper	xàrxuma	< Gk. *χάρχω*
copper solder	kolis	< Gk. *κόλληση*
cowbell	klopoto	< Rum. *clopot*
dross	zgorìja	< Gk. *σχωρία*
file	rin	< Gk. *ρίνη*
forge	kòvanica	< Slav. *кованица*
forge	kàmini	< Gk. *καμίνι*
forge	vìndja	< etym. unknown
furnace	furnìja	< Gk. *φυρνία*
gimlet	bùrgo	< Turk. *burgu*
gimlet	zumbas	< Gk. *ζουμπάς*
hailing hammer	kutùla	< Gk. *Κουτούλια*
hammer	čokàno	< Rum. *ciocan*
horseshoe	pètalo	< Gk. *πέταλο*
ignite	alav-	< Pers. الو
kettle	kekavi	< Gk. *κακκάβη*
key	klisin	< Gk. *κλειδί*
key	naxtàri	< Turk. *anahtar*
kiln, to fire	pir-o-	< Gk. *πυρώνω*
lead metal	molivi	< Gk. *μολύβι*
lock	leketo	< Rum. *lăcat*
lock up	klodj-o-	< Gk. *κλειδώνω*

nail	karfin	< Gk. καρφί
oven, furnace	bov	< Arm. ԷՈՄ
shoe a horse	pod-i-	< Gk. πόδημα
slag-shovel	skorjàlo	< Gk. σκωρία
sledgehammer	vàri	< Gk. βαριά
smithy	racìri	< Gk. ἐργαστήρι
steel	avcin	< Ossete. вcejнvг
tin	arčič	< Arm. шрԳհԳ
tinplate, to	han-o-	< Gk. γανώ
tinplate	teničava	< Gk. τενεκεδένιος
to file	vran-o-	< Gk. βράνι
tongs, pliers	klàšto	< Bulg. клешти
tripod	pirostìja	< Gk. πυρωστιά
wedge-hammer	sfiri(n)	< Gk. σφυρί
weld	ol-i-	< Gk. κολλω-
weld	vras-i-	< Gk. βράσι
wire	sìrma	< Gk. σύρμα

Gypsies, *gadže*, languages and labels

The category 'Gypsy languages' is not a linguistic one, nor an accurate one by any criterion that would group them in any meaningful way. There are numbers of quite distinct populations referred to as 'Gypsies', such as the Austronesian (Dayak)-speaking 'Sea Gypsies', the Irish Travellers, and the groups dealt with in Grierson's *Gipsy Languages* – Volume XI of his *Linguistic Survey of India* (1922) – which includes languages as unrelated as those of the Dravidian (Telugu)-speaking Bhamtas and the Indo-Aryan (Jaipuri)-speaking Pendaris.

The reason for the loose application of this label is traceable to nineteenth-century Britain, when the Romani population in that country was receiving considerable attention as the supposed keepers of a much missed and much romanticised pre-industrial rural way of life. They were also the focus of attention as an 'exotic' Asian population in the heart of England, as well as one considered greatly in need of Christian salvation. Both their language and their ancestry fascinated small groups of academics, folklorists and dilettantes, and over time *gypsy* (with a lower case initial) has come to stand more for an imagined way of life than for an ethnic people, since the 'True Romany' idealised by such individuals did not in fact exist.

The culprit would seem to be Sir Denzil Ibbettson, who used the word 'gypsy' in his 1881 *Census Report for the Punjab* to refer to certain indigenous Indian populations which, because of their itinerant way of life, reminded him of the 'gypsies' he was familiar with in England.

Despite this established use of the word, there may nevertheless still be a legitimate need for such a category if it be properly defined, since no other label otherwise exists for a large number of languages, or remnants of languages, spoken by populations that originated in India and who left before or during the mediaeval period.

There are many such groups which, on the basis of more or fewer Indian elements in their speech, and sometimes subjectively from their physical appearance, are included in this category. For most of these, however, the ability to be more specific about their identity is made difficult by two factors: the names applied to them, and the fact that whatever Indic linguistic material is evident consists only of a handful of lexical items otherwise used in the grammatical matrix of whatever the local language happens to be. Arnold noted that '[i]t is a remarkable fact that in the wide stretch of country from the Indus to the Ægean (Byzantine Gypsies) in the West and to Syria (Nuri) in the South, there exists no nomadic group which speaks a language corresponding with European Romani' (1967: 110).

Names

The only overview of such languages to date is Kenrick, where he reproduces the list provided by Arnold (Kenrick, 1976: 108–9) of the names for Middle Eastern 'gypsy' groups found in the literature. These are Alimah, Abdal, Aptal, Awgon, Awgon-Luli, Baluji, Banu Sassan, Barake, Beluchi, Berberi, Beshawan, Bosha, Catchar, Djugi, Dom, Dshukihar, Dummi, Faij, Fayjan, Fiuj, Gavbar, Geygel, Goudari, Ghagar, Gurbat or Kurbat, Kustani, Guaidiya, Haddad, Helebi, Hindustani Kentschlini, Köčer, Krishmal, Luli, Jat, Kabuli, Kaloro, Kara-chi, Tabriz, Kara Luli, Karashmar or Krismal, Kasibar or Mugat, Kenites, Kersi, Koli, Koudji or Kochi, Kouli, Lom, Luli, Lur, Luri, Masang, Mazang, Midreb, Motribiyya, Multani, Mutrub, Nawar, Odjuli, Pessewann, Posha, Qarabana or Qarabtu, Qarachi, Quenites, Qorbati or Ghorbati, Quf, Rawazi, Sagvand, Sahsawan, Sasan, Sayabigeh, Shurasti, Sozan, Suzmani, Tat, Tavoktarosh, Zangi, Zargari and Zott. For most of these we have only a passing reference in this or that document. Sometimes, quite different names are applied to the same population (such as the *Lom* or *Bosha*); sometimes – like the very label 'gypsy' itself – the same name is applied to quite distinct groups (for example, *Djugi* being applied to both the Iranian *Koli* and the Tajikistani *Mugat*). Sometimes they are clearly geographical (*Helebi* < Aleppo or *Kabuli* < Kabul) and sometimes they are occupational (*motribiyya* < Arabic 'musician'). The overriding commonality seems to be only that such populations are migrant, 'gypsy' referring to their behaviour rather than their ethnicity. An excellent bibliography, as well as some grammatical discussion, is to be found in Windfuhr (2002).

Paucity of linguistic material

In cases where no grammatical material has been retained, it is not possible to make an identification with any particular Indian language or even dialect group, nor even necessarily with other 'gypsy' languages. That two of these vernaculars may share the Indic word *pani* for 'water' demonstrates nothing beyond an Indian connection; in India itself, a hundred languages have the same word. Nor is it the case that all of them were ever 'full' languages at some earlier time; non-indigenous lexicon can be acquired in many ways and inserted into existing languages. That English, for example, contains the Chinese word *tycoon* does not mean that it is a Sinitic language or even that the Anglo-Saxons ever interacted at first hand with speakers of Chinese.

Romani Studies, which began to emerge as an area of scientific (mainly linguistic and ethnographical) endeavour in the 1780s, have traditionally regarded 'gypsy' languages as belonging to three branches: Romani, Domari and Lomavren (Hancock, 1995c). The Indian origin of Romani, the language of the Rom or European 'Gypsies', was first recognised by Western scholars in the late 1700s; by the middle of the following century Domari, the language of the Dom 'Gypsies' in Syria and elsewhere, had begun to be documented, and by 1887 Lomavren, spoken by the Armenian Lom, became a part of the discussion (Patkanov, 1887). It was initially assumed that all three were branches of the same original migration out of India, and attempts have been made to reconstruct protoforms based upon their combined analysis (Hancock, 1988a). This no longer appears to be the case, at least for Domari. There are structural and lexical features of this language that point to a much earlier separation from India than is evident for the other two.

The first published account of Domari was Pott (1846), where he summarised notes on the language sent to him by the Reverend Eli Smith, an American missionary working in Syria. The only extensive grammatical and lexical account remains Macalister (1914), although it is flawed and seriously out of date; a modern linguistic description is in preparation by Matras, who has also written on the present state of the language in Jerusalem (1999a).

The existence of Lomavren, spoken in Armenia, Georgia, eastern Turkey and probably elsewhere in the region, was first brought to the attention of European scholars in 1828 when a hundred-word list was published by von Joakimov (mentioned in Finck (1907: 2) which, together with Patkanov, (1887) and Papazian (1901), is the principal published source on the language).

Speakers of Domari refer to themselves as Dom, but are most often called *Luri* or *Nuri* (plural *Nawar*) or *Luli* in the literature. Like the Lomavren-speaking Lom and the Romani-speaking Rom, they have not retained the details of their own history, and attempts to reconstruct it have been mostly speculative. It is possible that their ancestors left India in response to fifth- and sixth-century raids into India by the Huns, when the Indian kings sent out fighters to resist them. The word for a non-Dom is *gačča* which, like its equivalents in Lomavren (*gačav*) and Romani (*gadžo*) derives from the Middle Indo-Aryan *gajjh-* meaning 'civilian; non-military person', and the word *luri* itself, although usually attributed to an Arabic origin, may be from MIA *luth-* 'plunderer' (compare Romani *lur*, ditto). Speakers of other varieties of Domari, among them *Karači* (a name possibly from Turkish *karaca* 'swarthy') and *Mıtrıp* (possibly from Arabic *motribiyya* 'musician') live elsewhere in the Middle East (Patkanov, 1887; Benninghaus, 1991; Hancock, 1995c: 31). Against this possibility and in support of a post-ninth century move is the fact that none of the Persian items in Domari (or in Lomavren or Romani for that matter) derives from the Middle-Iranic period.

Lomavren exists almost solely as a vocabulary, and is a register of Armenian rather than an Indo-Aryan language. For this reason the only clues as to its history and affiliation are in its lexicon. Nevertheless it shares much more of this, as well as of its phonology, with Romani than it does with Domari, and an argument might be made for their having been one before developing independently in separate directions in eastern Anatolia. In light of the *koïné* hypothesis (Hancock, 2000), it might also be the case that Lomavren was never a discrete language at any time, but has always existed solely as a cryptic lexicon.

Romani is the most widely spoken of all the Gypsy languages, and the most extensively studied. It supports an extensive literature, is used on a number of internet websites, and is taught regularly at several universities (Charles, Moscow, Texas, the Sorbonne). Some of its dialects, such as those spoken in north-eastern Europe, demonstrate after a thousand years a truly remarkable retention of Indic lexicon and morphosyntax, while others survive only as a limited lexical corpus in the structural and phonological framework of a European language, and are typologically no longer Romani, for example, *Pogadijib* in England or *Caló* in Spain (Bakker and Courtiade, 1991).

Romani was brought into Europe not with one migration but by at least three and probably more, over a period of perhaps two centuries. Courtiade calls these waves *strata,* the first and geographically most widespread in Europe stretching from the Balkans to the north, east and west, the second concentrated in south-central Europe and the third emerging from the Romani-speaking populations who had been held in slavery in Moldavia and Wallachia until the 1860s. These last have since migrated to all parts of the world, and are particularly well represented in North and South America. The earliest reliable reference to a Romani presence in the Balkans dates from around AD 1100. It is entirely likely that these broad dialect divisions reflect more than one different period of migration into Europe from the Byzantine Empire; some dialects for example show minimal lexical influence from Greek, suggesting an early move out of Anatolia. There are some eighty different Romani dialects today, and attempts are underway to create a universal written standard (see Chapter 8 of the present volume).

Romani words for Romanies and non-Romanies

The view that the ancestors of the Romanies emerged from the lees of Indian society was initiated by Grellmann and began to spread after 1841, when a man named Hermann Brockhaus suggested in a letter to Pott dated 16 July 1841, that the word *Rrom* had its origin in the Indian word *ḍom* (reproduced in Pott, 1844: *i*: 42) and translated here:

> In the collection of fairy tales of the Somadeva edited by myself, we find Tar.3 *çl.* 96 (page 169), and in Kalhana's *History of Kashmir, e.g.* V. 353, the word *Ḍòmba* (with retroflex *ḍ*), and Wilson makes at this point the comment that this name indicates a kind of pariah. Since this word is missing from the Sanskrit dictionaries, and thus is not considered to be classical by Indian grammarians, it must therefore belong to the words borrowed from the colloquial vernaculars. In Hindi, we actually find the

word *ḍ'oma*, feminine *ḍ'omni*, with which a person of the lowest class is labelled. Might not this word *ḍom* be the same as the Gypsy *Rom*? Doesn't this perhaps refer to a tribe originally living in north-western India which, being subjugated, were degraded to the status of pariahs? The fact that a people don't call themselves by a name indicating something dishonourable is obvious; only through subjugation can the name of a people become a name of opprobrium among the victors.

Ḍom refers to a class of people which the dictionary describes as 'a very low caste, representing some old aboriginal race, spread all over India. They perform such offices as carrying dead bodies, removing carrion, and so on.'

Sinclair, in his discussion of the etymology of the word, described the *ḍom* less charitably as 'the very dregs of impurity, the Helots of all, shameless vagrants, eaters of carrion, beggars and thieves' (1909: 40).

Very quickly, this origin became the conventional wisdom in Romani Studies, and is repeated even today without qualification. While on phonological grounds a case might be made for the word *Rrom* being derived from *ḍom* (< Skt डोम(डोम्ब) -, *ḍom(b)a-*, Hi *ḍom*), its semantics have been challenged by Kenrick (1995: 37), who maintains that it meant simply 'man' or 'our people' rather than 'others', and at the time of the exodus from India did not have Brockhaus' later interpretation. Leitner (1877: *i*: 6) has also shown that in some Dardic languages, the words *rōm* and *rŏm* mean simply 'race of people'; in Khowar it means a 'flock' (Sloan, 1981: 128), while Mookerji (1927: 66) says that in Bihari, 'the epithet for a *gentleman* is "Rouma", a contraction of the Sanskrit "Romya" (the beautiful)'. In addition, and given that in Indic its most likely Sanskrit etymology would be *ḍōmba,* which derives from a word meaning 'drum' (and thus 'drummer' – see Turner, 1966: 313), the first suggested meaning of, inter alia 'musician', cannot be entirely discounted; drummers in particular featured among the camp followers accompanying the Rājpūts, and Briggs (1953: 79), also discussing this as an origin for the word, writes of the Chandālas (Domba) in Kāśī being required to 'beat the drum before they entered the town to make higher-jāti people aware of their staining presence'.

This etymology for *Rrom* has been questioned however, Brockhaus' *ḍom* being rejected in favour of Sanskrit राम *rāma*, 'husband'; this is also its meaning in Romani (Rishi, 1976: 10–12). Rishi's suggestion, however, is very implausible, given that the word *Rāma* is a proper name. The word *ramana* ('delight of', 'lover of') is sometimes used in the sense of 'husband', but this usage is restricted only to poetry. Borrow had already considered this etymology in his *Lavo-Lil* a century before (1874: 56). Also Mookerji's suggestion above can be challenged. The Sanskrit term for beautiful is *Ramya* – pronouncing the 'a' as an 'o' is a characteristic of eastern Indic languages such as Bihari, Bengali and Assamese. In Western Indic languages the word would have been pronounced as 'Ramya'.

It is also entirely possible that the name is not Indian at all, but was acquired at the time of the formation of the people themselves, in the Sultanate of Rum (1071–97), whose inhabitants were called Ρομαΐβοι (*Romaivi)* and Ρομΐτοι (*Romiti*) by the Byzantine Greeks. A source in this name was first put forward by Sinclair (1909). Persian and Arab writers referred to Byzantia as *Rūm* and it appears in the writings of Firdausi (Abu Ol-Qasem Mansur) in the *Shāh Nāmeh*, although not as a reference to its people.

The weakness of the *dom* hypothesis on genetic grounds has been demonstrated by Bhalla, who reviewed and analysed a series of bio-anthropological and haematological studies of Romani groups in Europe, and of measurements of genetic distance of population groups in northern India. He uses these data to test the Dom, Jat and Rājpūt theories of Romani origin, concluding that:

> [T]he results of the distance analysis clearly refute the Dom theory. The gene pool of Eastern European Gypsies is more in line with the stock of Indian people represented by the Jat Sikhs, Punjabi Hindus and Rajputs ... the dominant ethnic element in the Doms and Kolis ... is not reflected in any sizeable proportion in the genetic make up of East European Gypsies. (Bhalla, 1992: 331–2)

Findings such as Bhalla's are particularly important since they challenge the dominant power/knowledge discursive formations by Romanies. If the generally accepted origin, that is, as a low-caste group of wandering musicians can be replaced by a paradigm of origin in a warrior caste, based on scholarship by Indian and Romani scholars, (that is, not part of the Eurocentric hegemony) and reinforced by 'scientific' analysis, this gives the contemporary Romani population a demonstrable and verifiable origin.

The idea that the Sinti have a separate history from the Rroma has gained some currency in recent years, but is not tenable on linguistic grounds. The origin of this belief is first of all found in the similarity between the words *Sinti* and *Sindhi*, and has no doubt been reinforced by the geographical isolation of the Sinti people in northern Europe which has led to the notion of separateness (found for the same reason amongst the Vlax Romanies, isolated in slavery for centuries, and who believe themselves to be the only 'true' Gypsies, and the Calé in Spain, geographically isolated, and who believe that they entered the peninsula via North Africa; see for example Bernasovský and Bernasovská, 1999: 12). The word *Sinti* has been compared with Hindi माँध *sāndh*, earlier Prakrit *sandhi* 'group, community'. The early Indic cluster /nt/ regularly becomes /nd/ or /nn/ going to /n/ in neo-Indic, and this hasn't been preserved. It is more likely that the word is of European origin, because of its non-final stress pattern and athematic plural (*Sinti*, rather than **Sinte*, from singular *Sinto*). It has the common variant form *Cinti*, pronounced [tsɪnti], which can be compared with German *Zinn* [tsɪn] 'tin', for example, the English 'tinker' (< 'tin'). The word is not found in the earliest Sinti samples, where the endonym is *Kale*. Still, it would have to be demonstrated that tin-smithing has been so much associated with the Sinti, historically, as to provide the established name for the population. A different Sanskrit source has been proposed by Turner (1966: 784a): सैन्धव- *saindhava-* 'pertaining to the River Indus' (yielding Hindi *sendhā*, Sindhi *sendho*), although we might consider a derivation from Sanskrit सैन्य- *sainya-* 'belonging to an army', as in Hindi *senā* 'general', Gujerati *sen* 'army', as being equally likely or unlikely. Megret (2000) has questioned whether a connection exists between the first syllable of the word, [tsin-], and *Tsingani*. That Sinti Romani (or for that matter Spanish Romani) came into Europe as part of the common migration described here, and only diverged after this event, is readily demonstrable through the process of linguistic reconstruction, and an examination of the respective lexical sources. The same argument for a separate origin is found among the Boyash (*Beas*) in Hungary, who are taught (at the Ghandi School in Pécs) that they descend from the Jats, unlike the Rom who descend from the Luri. The Beas language is a variety of Banat Romanian, and both the population and the language undoubtedly descend from the house slaves of the Wallachian *boyars* or landowners, who forbade the use of the Romani language within their households.

Military allusions are also found in the words for non-Romanies. The most common, *gadžo*, is said by Turner to derive from Sanskrit गाह्य- *gārhya-* via Prākrit गाज्झ- *gajjha* which means 'domestic'. The Serbian and the Italian words for 'civilian' (*civil* and *borghese* respectively) are used by Romanies in Slovenia and Italy to refer to non-Romanies, and occasionally American Romanies also refer to *gadže* as 'civilians'. In Lomavren, the language of the Lom Gypsies in eastern Turkey and Armenia, a non-Lom is called a ɟɑɕɑɲ (*gača-* + *-av*) from the same Sanskrit root. Pischel (1883: 370) noted that the Changars, whom he attempts to link with the ancestors of the Romanies, call all outsiders *goča*, which he compares with *gadžo*. Grierson (1922: *xj*: 96) makes the same argument for the words *kājwā*, *kājā* and *kajjā* in Dumāki, Nati and Sansi respectively. In Domari, the language of the Nawar, a non-Dom is also called a *kājjā* (*kádžža*); Ivanow (1914: 540) lists *gerze* as 'a non-Gypsy' but compares it to Pashto *garzedal* 'to travel'. Cognates in some other Indic languages are listed in Soravia (1988: 8). Diwana (1943: 32), Rishi (1976:13–16), Kochanowski (1994: 203), and Moreau (1995: 62) have all argued for the etymology of this word in *Ghazni* or its variant *Ghazzi*: 'Ghazzi would become Ghazzo and further transmute into the modern-day *Gaujo* or Gadjo' (Moreau, 1995: 123), although this would be difficult to support on phonological grounds. Among other things, the initial consonant is the uvular fricative [ʁ] in the original word, not the velar stop [g]. Yet another etymology is that proposed by Kostić, who sees its origin in Sanskrit ग्राम *grama* 'village' (from which comes R. *gav*), plus the common morpheme *-dža* meaning 'of' (1998: 27). A second word with the meaning of 'non-Rrom' is *das*, from Prakrit दास *dāsa* 'slave, enemy, captive'. Sharing some semantic overlap is a third term, *gomi*, like *das* found in the Balkan Romani dialects, and which has a parallel in Bagani *gomi* 'one who has surrendered', (presumably in battle). This word is traceable to Sanskrit गोमि *gomi*, a synonym for *upasaka,* an ascetic (Taranatha, 1970: 43), and the 'vows of gomi' which entailed the surrendering of physical pleasures (Roerich, 1983: *iij*: 56). Yet a fourth word for a non-Gypsy, *goro*, simply meant 'pale skinned' in the original Sanskrit *gaura* (गौर); in modern Siraiki and Sindhi, *gora* means 'slave', while in the European dialects of Romani it occurs as *goro* in Wales (meaning 'elderly non-Romani'), and *gero* in England (meaning 'non-Romani man'), which is also the meaning of *gori* in Zargari, the Balkan-type Romani dialect spoken in Iran (Djonedi,

1996: 55). As *guro* in Spain, it now means 'policeman'. *Goro* ('pale-skinned') contrasts with the native ethnonym *Kalo* ('black'), a self-designation among Romani populations in Spain, Wales, Finland and (earlier) Germany. Leitner (1877: 1) lists the *Kale* as one of the Rājpūt-descended Changar *jātis*, while Djurić points to their descending from a tribe in India called the *Kale* who 'probably originated in Kalistan' and who were driven from there by Mahmud of Ghazni (1996: 9). In Romani, Eastern Europe, with its massive Romani population, is called *Kali Oròpa* (or *Kali Eròpa*) while Western Europe is *Parni Oròpa* ('white Europe').

Listed as Indic by Wolf (1959: 131) is a fifth word for non-Rrom, or possibly simply meaning 'person', *xalo*, (with the Sinti variant *xujlo*). He derives this – unconvincingly – from Sanskrit *chalin* 'deceiver', via Prakrit *caïla* 'cunning, deceitful', cf. Pahari and Marwari *chala*, Hindi and Panjabi *cal*, with related meanings. Closer on phonological grounds is the Phalura *xaláka* 'people, nation' (Buddruss, 1967: 135), although this is ultimately from Arabic حلق, via Persian, and may not have been a part of the Phalura lexicon as early as the eleventh century. The word *gomež* for a non-Romani may or may not be an extended meaning of the same word that means 'horse', ultimately from Armenian.

One item that may or may not be related to this same word is *čal* or *čel* in combination (in various forms) meaning 'Romani person'. It has generally been considered restricted solely to the Northern group of dialects, thus *Rom(a)nichal* (Britain), *romanitchel* (France), *Rom(a)ni-čēl* (Germany), *rommani-sael* (Sweden), *romansēl* (Finland), *romanichel* (Basque country), *rumijele* (Spain); however Vaillant – if he did not lift it from Roberts' British list, as he did for other entries (see Hancock, 2004) – lists *romnic'el* from Romania, and Matras has found it in a dialect spoken in Greece (2004d: 23). Only Bischoff (1827: 108) seems to have recorded the word outside of this combination, viz. *mellĕli Tschehl* 'black Gypsy'.

Lomavren also has *gala-* (*kala-* < *kalarav*) 'foreigner, alien' for a non-Lom; two other Romani words for a non-Gypsy that remain to be explained etymologically are Caló *hambo* and *sesó*.

CHAPTER SEVEN

Romani religion

I never could meet with anybody that pretended to say what their private faith and religion may be.

(Hoyland, 1816: 25)

They have, as a people, no religion.

(Roberts, 1836: *xvij*)

The lack of religious ideas, and the want of a peculiar system of worship among the Gipsies, constitute remarkable features in the history of this strange people.

(Morwood, 1885: 281–2)

They cannot be said to have a religion of their own.

(Greenfield, 1977: 52)

Romani traditions ... are complex enough to be mistaken for their own religion.

(Dellal, 1999)

If religion is popularly perceived – as it so often is – to include a place of worship, a clergy, and a set of holy scriptures, then it is easy to understand why observers such as Hoyland, Roberts, Morwood, Greenfield and others should have reached the conclusions they did. If, on the other hand the usual dictionary definition is adhered to, such as Webster's 'belief in a divine or superhuman power or powers to be obeyed and worshiped as the creator(s) and ruler(s) of the universe [and

Originally published in Bron Taylor (ed.), *The encyclopedia of religion and nature* (Continuum, London and New York, 2005), pp. 1414–18.

the] expression of this belief in conduct and ritual' (1966: 1228), or Encarta's 'particular institutionalised or personal system of beliefs or practices relating to the divine' (1999: 1516), then it is clear that they were wrong.

It is not difficult to understand why outside observers were uniformly convinced that Romanies have no religion. Apart from there being no tangible evidence – a sacred text, a temple, or a priest for example – Romani society is tightly closed to outsiders, considerably reducing the opportunity to observe cultural behaviour at close quarters. Ethnographers attempting to enter Romani households report being kept at arm's length by various means, even by being met at the door with feigned epileptic seizures or frightening explosions of profanity. But it is in fact one of the aspects of Romani religious belief which keeps that barrier in place.

So entrenched is the idea that Romanies lack a religion, that it has become a part of European folklore: the story that 'the gypsies have little or no, if any, religion … their church was constructed of curds or lard and the dogs ate it' (de Peyster, 1887: 58) is widespread; Block repeated it half a century later: 'the gypsies, it is said, once possessed a church of their own built of cream cheese. On one occasion, however, when they were particularly hungry, they ate the church and for this reason are now without a national religion' (1938: 234).

Because Romanies come ultimately from India, it is in Hinduism that the roots of their religion are to be found. However, awareness of this has become lost over the centuries and is only now being relearnt by Romanies today. Likewise the daily cultural behaviour in which Indian-based spiritualism (called *Rromanipen*) manifests itself so clearly is not recognised as such; asked what his religion is, a Romani is likely to say Orthodox or Roman Catholic, Pentecostal, Mormon, Muslim, Bahá'í, or any one of the non-indigenous faiths acquired, voluntarily or not, since arrival in the West.

Woodcock, like so many others, was wrong when he wrote that 'The gipsies … are utterly without religious impressions … they brought with them no Indian idols … nor indeed Indian rites or observances, for no trace of such are to be discovered amongst them' (1865: 84). While Kounavine claimed to have found Brahma, Indra, Lakshmi and other Hindu deities continuing to be worshipped by name among Romanies in Russia (Elysseeff, 1882), this has been shown to be fabricated.

Nevertheless other connections with Hinduism are in evidence, although the names of only three deities have survived: Sara-Kali, Vayu and Maruthi. Shiva's trident, called *trisūla* in Sanskrit, changed its role from Hindu symbol to Christian symbol and has become the Romani word for 'cross' (*trušul*). This probably happened when the migration first reached Armenia; in the Lomavren language *trusul* means both 'church' and 'priest'. Similarly, *rašaj* '(Christian) holy man' represents a shift of meaning from Sanskrit *ṛṣi* '(Hindu) holy man'. The word for 'God' is *Devel*, (from Sanskrit *devatā* 'divinity', compare Hindi *dev*), while the Devil is known as *o Beng* (from a Munda root meaning a malevolent spirit).

Some Romani groups in Europe today appear to maintain elements of Shaktism or goddess-worship; the Rajputs worshipped the warrior-goddess Parvati, another name for the female deity Sati-Sara, who is Saint Sarah, the Romani Goddess of Fate. That she forms part of the yearly pilgrimage to La Camargue at Stes. Maries de la Mer in the south of France is of particular significance; here she is carried into the sea just as she is carried into the waters of the Ganges each December in India. Both Sati-Sara and Saint Sarah wear a crown, both are also called *Kali*, and both have shining faces painted black. Sati-Sara is a consort of the god Śiva, and is known by many other names, *Bhadrakali, Uma, Durga* and *Syama* among them.

The names of two Indian deities have been preserved in some Romani riddles. Reference to the Vedic god of the wind and the air, *Vāyu* (also called *Marut*), is retained in a number of these: *Kana hulavel peske bal o Vajo, legenisavol e čar* ('When Vayu combs his hair, the grass sways'); *Amaro Vajo hurjal tela savorrenge podji, aj konik našti t'astarel les* ('Our Vayu flies under everyone's petticoats, and no one can catch him'); and *O pharo vurdon e Vajosko cirdajlo ekhe šele grastendar kaj phurden ande'l rrutunja* ('Vayu's heavy waggon is pulled by a hundred horses blowing through their nostrils'). The answer to each is *e balval*: 'the wind'. In Indian theology the task of Vayu's son *Māruti* (also called *Hanumān*) is to tear open the clouds and let the rain fall, and in Romani the expression *marutisjol o Devel* means 'the sky [*lit.* 'God'] is growing overcast'. The reference to a hundred horses may also be of Vedic origin; there are several references in the scriptures to the *aśvamedha yajña* or 'horse sacrifice', whereby in ancient India the king would release one hundred horses to roam freely through his kingdom. Stopping them or blocking their path was forbidden.

The female spirits or fates, in Romani called the *vursitorja*, hover in its presence three days after a child is born to determine its destiny and to influence the choice of name the parents will decide upon. They may be compared with the Indian *matṛkā* or 'little mother' spirits who also possess a baby's destiny at the time of its birth. The red thread (the *loli dori*) tied around a newborn's ankle or wrist and worn for two or three years afterwards to guard against the *jakhalo* or 'evil eye' reflects the protective properties of that colour, which is also worn or painted on the body in India.

The burning of one's possessions after death and even, among some populations at least into the twentieth century, the ritual suicide of the widow, have striking parallels with *sati* in India.

Time spent in the non-Romani world (the *jado)* drains spiritual energy or *dji*. Sampson (1926: 257) gives the various meanings of this word as '[s]eat of the emotions, heart, soul; temper, disposition, mood; courage, spirit', comparing it to Sanskrit *jiva*, Hindi *ji*, 'life, soul, spirit, mind'. In some dialects it has the additional meaning of 'stomach'. One's spiritual batteries can only be recharged by spending time in an all-Romani environment – in the normal course of events, in family homes. It is in the area of spiritual and physical well-being (*baxt*) that the Indian origin of the Romani people is most clearly seen.

In the preparation of food, and in one's personal hygiene and deportment, it is absolutely essential that a separation between 'pure' and 'polluted' conditions be maintained. A pure state is achieved by maintaining spiritual 'balance' or what is called *karma* in India (and in Romani *kintala*, or in some dialects *kintari* or *kintujmos*) in one's life and avoiding shame (*ladžav* or *ladž*), being declared unclean or, in extreme cases, being shunned by the community. Maintaining balance or harmony between God (*o Del*) and the Devil (*o Beng*) pleases the spirits of the ancestors (the *mulé*), and they are there to guard one and help one to do it, but if they are displeased, they will mete out punishment by way of retribution (*prikaza*). Depending upon the nature of the transgression, this may be mild, such as stubbing one's toe, or so severe as to involve sickness and even death. The consequences of *prikaza* underlie the universal Romani belief that nothing is an accident; that nothing happens simply by chance.

The penalty for extreme pollution is being banished, or made an outcast, and an out-caste, from the community, for which different

Romani words are *durjardo, gonime* or *stražime*. 'Banishment' is variously *durjaripe, gonimos* or *straža*, which may or may not imply a state of pollution, being imposed also for other reasons, such as disregard for territorial claims. Being in a state of pollution is being *magerdo, marime, pokhelime* or *makherdo* (*lit.* 'smeared', as with menstrual blood). These words can be contrasted with *melalo* which also means 'dirty', but only from physical dirt.

Prikaza brings bad luck (*bibaxt*) and illness (*nasvalipe*), and it can be attracted even by socialising with people who are not *vuže* (< *vužo* 'clean'). Non-Romani people are not seen as *vuže*, which is why Romanies avoid contact which is too intimate. But this is not an inherited condition of non-Romanies, it is because these cultural practices are not maintained. A non-Romani woman who marries into a Romani family is expected to adopt them, and in doing so becomes in that context *vuži*.

The Ayurvedic concept of ritual purity and ritual pollution, so central to Romani belief, existed in the eleventh-century caste system and continues to exist today; thus members of the same *jāti* (sub-caste) may eat together without risk of contamination, for example, but will become polluted if they eat with members of other *jāti*; and because the *jātis* of one's associates might not always be known, contact between the mouth and the various utensils shared with others at a meal is avoided, just to be on the safe side. In conservative Romani culture, liquids are poured into the mouth from a container held away from the lips, so that the rim of the vessel (the *kerlo*) is not touched; smoke from a shared tobacco pipe is drawn through the fist clenched around its stem, again to avoid making contact with the mouth. The surest way not to touch utensils used by others is to eat with the fingers, and every one of these habits is to be found among Romanies today.

Like the Rajputs, some Romani groups divide foods into 'ordinary' and 'auspicious' or 'lucky' (*baxtalo*) categories (the Rajputs' terms for these two categories mean 'cold' and 'hot', although these have nothing to do with either temperature or pepper); this distinction reflects the close relationship between food and health, a particular ingredient being not only beneficial to the physical self but also to the spiritual. *Baxtale xajmata* or 'auspicious foods' include those which are pungent or strongly flavoured, such as garlic, lemon, pickles, peppers, sour cream and so on. The use of red pepper in some traditional Romani dishes is typical of Rajput cuisine particularly, and such food is called *ito* or 'piquant' in Vlax Romani, contrasting with the word *tato*, '(heat) hot'. Also in common with Indian culinary behaviour is the practice of not preparing dishes far in advance of their being eaten, and of not keeping leftover food. Dishes set for the dead at a *pomana* (wake) table or a *slava* (Saint's Day) table are eventually disposed of by being offered to passersby, never just thrown away. There are very many customs associated with food and eating: there cannot be an even number of chairs at a *pomana* table. Potatoes (*kolompirja*) are not eaten at a *pomana*, comparable with the Rajputs' religious restriction on only eating vegetables that grow below ground at their own funereal meals. Serving peanuts is also forbidden at *pomeni*; greens (*zelenimata*) are not eaten while one is in mourning, or expecting a baby or breastfeeding (probably because they induce colic) and so on. Various Romani populations in Europe and America also maintain *nacijange semnura* or group symbols, such as the sun (representing, for instance, the Serbian Romanies) and the moon (representing the Lovara), which may be found drawn or carved onto the *stago* or 'standard' at a wedding, and on the *sèmno* or *rupuni rovli* ('silver baton'), that is, the clan leader's staff, and which are appealed to at the consecration of the *mulengi sinìja* or 'table of the dead' at a *pomana*. Here, the invocation is '*Khama, Čhona thaj Devla, ašun(en) man!*', which means 'Sun, Moon and God, hear me'. The significance here is the fact that the Sun and the Moon were the two symbols worn emblematically on the armour and tunics of the Rajput warriors to identify them in battle from all others.

Because access to physicians and hospitals is only sought in extreme cases due to their polluting association, safeguarding the health of the community *within* the community is of special importance. Like groups in northern India such as the Banjara, some Romani populations distinguish illnesses which are natural to the group (*rromane nasvalimata)*; these are such things as heart complaints, rashes, vomiting, hiccups, insomnia or irritability, from those which are the result of over-familiarity with the *jado* or non-Romani world (*gadžikane nasvalimata*). These latter include, for example, all sexually transmitted diseases. For such afflictions, a non-Romani physician needs to be consulted; but for 'Romani afflictions', traditional cures are provided by a *drabarni* or female healer. This is the same as the Hindu *siana*. The root of the word *drabarni* is *drab* which means 'medicine' (from Sanskrit *dravya* 'medication', compare the Hindi word *darb*). It is also the root of the verb *drabar-* which is usually translated in English as 'to tell fortunes', but which from the Romani perspective means 'making well'. When speaking English, Romanies prefer to call this skill brought from India 'advising' rather than 'fortune telling', for which another verb, *duriker-* exists.

If it is necessary for a person who has contracted a *gadžikano nasvalipe* to be admitted to hospital, relatives and others will go to him, often in considerable numbers, to provide *dji* and help restore balance. 'Relatives, their relatives, and friends of a Gypsy flock around his hospital bed because [of] their culture' (Anderson and Tighe, 1973: 282); only recently have hospital administrations begun to recognise this as cultural behaviour and to accommodate it (Salloway, 1973; Shields, 1981; Thomas, 1985). Depending upon the nature of the non-Romani affliction, the individual may be declared defiled; not visited in hospital but instead banished from the community. This is invariably the response when it is such diseases as syphilis and AIDS. Infections of this kind are a clear indication of a too-personal involvement in the non-Romani world, since it is assumed that they could never be contracted within the ethnic community.

Islam

The journey across the Middle East took place too rapidly for Islam to have had an impact on Romani spiritual belief, as well no doubt because it was the religion of an enemy people. There is no linguistic impact at all directly from Arabic, and none from Persian's religious vocabulary. Nevertheless there are hundreds of thousands of Romanies throughout the Balkans and Turkey who are Muslim, having converted, or having been converted, during the centuries of Ottoman rule in the area.

Zoroastrianism

Zoroastrianism existed in north-west India at the time of the exodus at the beginning of the eleventh century, and in Persia through which that migration passed, and a number of writers (Kounavine, Clébert, Wood and Rishi among them) have suggested that Rromanipen has acquired at least some aspects of that religion, particularly its dualism and the significance of fire. It is unlikely that this was the case, however, given the circumstances of early Romani history, the time and location involved, and the fact that these are also characteristics found in Hinduism.

Judaism

There are numbers of Romanies who profess the Jewish faith, although in each documented case it has been the result of conversion following marriage to a Jewish spouse. Reportedly, during the Second World War several Romani-Jewish marriages took place in a concentration camp (known as the 'marriage camp') close to the Serbian border, although the fate, and religious persuasion, of any survivors is not known.

Christianity

The vocabulary of Christianity has inherited two Hindu concepts: *rašaj* 'a priest', compare Indian *r̥si* 'a holy man', and the word for the cross, *trušul*, which is derived from the word *triśūla*, the god Shiva's trident. The Romani word for a church, *kangeri*, is from the Persian or Hindi word for a battlement, because of a perceived architectural resemblance. Christianity was first encountered in Armenian-speaking Anatolia, at the eastern end of the Byzantine Empire. The Romani words for 'Easter', 'co-father-in-law', 'incense' and 'godfather' are of Armenian origin, all concepts specific to Orthodox Christianity. Whether it was adopted at that time or not is unknown; in the Christian Byzantine Empire, professing Christianity clearly brought benefits to the outsider Romani population, and later presenting themselves as Christian penants and pilgrims in Europe was also a means of distancing themselves from the Muslim threat. But in Ottoman Turkey, being Christian was a liability, and the seriousness with which either religion was embraced is open to question.

In Europe, it was not uncommonly the Church that was most openly hostile to Romanies. In 1568 Pope Pius V banished them from the entire realm of the Holy Roman Empire, and priests in the Eastern Rite church could be excommunicated for performing Romani marriages. Monasteries in the Romanian principalities were reportedly the cruelest of all towards their slaves, and in Western Europe, Romanies were routinely forbidden from entering churches to worship, and had to listen from outside through the windows. Such incidents are not entirely unheard of today.

Some Romani groups in France relate the story of how Christianity first came to their people. Originally, they say, the woman leader of a group of Romani metalworkers who lived along the Rhône and whose name was Sara, saw a boat on the river which was sinking. In it were Saint Mary Salome, Saint Mary Magdalene and Saint Mary Jacobi, the three Marys who comforted Jesus as he died on the cross. Sara was expecting this since she had seen it in a dream, and she waded out into the water and threw out her cloak which became a raft, and which enabled the three Marys to reach the riverbank safely. As a reward, they made her their servant, and converted her to Christianity. This story, however, seems to originate in European, rather than Romani, tradition. Generally speaking, the Romani population of an area will claim to follow the predominant religion of that area: Protestant in Protestant lands, Roman Catholic in Roman Catholic lands, and Orthodox in Orthodox lands.

In the early 1950s in north-western France, a Breton evangelist named Clément le Cossec began preaching Pentecostal Christianity to Romanies in that region, and it spread rapidly through France and Spain, then the rest of Europe, and to North and South America. Today, 'Born Again' Pentecostalism is the fastest growing and most widely found religion among Romanies. It has been suggested that there are two main reasons for this: first, that it is a church that tells its congregants that they are loved, a personal aspect not characteristic of more formal churches, and a message not formerly heard by Romanies. Second that, compared with the Roman or Orthodox churches, it is easy to become a pastor, and to establish a church of one's own. There are today hundreds of Romani churches, with pastors and congregations who are Romani, who preach in Romani and who even have Romani-language evangelical radio programmes and who distribute Romani-language sermons on audiocassette tapes. Significantly, the growth of 'Born Again' Christianity has caused a split in the Romani population, some of whom believe it is a major factor in the loss of traditional *Rromanipen*. One successful Pentecostal church in Dallas, Texas, developed a programme which has deliberately integrated references to dualism, balance, ancestral spirits, and other aspects of Rromanipen which do not conflict with Christian doctrine, stressing parallels rather than differences.

Other religions

There are Romanies who have embraced Mormonism, and the Bahá'i faith has acquired numbers of converts, especially in Spain. But with the exception of those completely assimilated to the non-Romani world, whatever religion may be professed, it will exist syncretistically with more or fewer elements retained from the original set of beliefs and practices which find their origins in India.

Introduction to Section Three:
Language standardisation and education

Language standardisation and education are domains in which the great task of uniting and empowering the Roma will be carried out. The Roma, being traditionally among the disadvantaged groups in their home countries, are not very well-versed in international languages such as English, French and German, and often not even in the national languages of the lands in which they live. In very many cases, the Roma are comfortable only in their own varieties of Romani. Educational facilities and a modern literature do not exist in most of these dialects. Before the Roma can come together to articulate their aspirations, they need a common medium. This common language can, it is hoped, help the Roma educate, uplift, and unite their people.

The essay *The standardisation of the Romani language* deals with the challenging task of developing a single standard form of the Romani language, out of as many as eighty dialects which can be grouped into five or six branches. This standardisation will have to be brought about without committing violence to identities such as that of a Sinto or Romanichal. While some Romani dialects have many speakers, their original Indic core has undergone so much attrition that they no longer overlap very much with other Romani dialects. Such is the case with the numerically important Kalderash dialect (the most widespread Romani dialects in Europe and the Americas), which has been heavily influenced by Romanian. While international languages such as English and French may be logically the ideal source for coining neologisms, Romani speakers for the most part come into contact with East European (especially Slavic) languages.

Ian proposes that the standard Romani dialect be based on Polish

Lovari, which retains many features of the core Romani linguistic heritage; has less phonological interference from Romanian than other Vlax dialects; and which offers the possibility of greatest mutual intelligibility with other Romani dialects. Since Ian has in recent years modified his earlier stance that the Roma were one people when they left India, and now believes that the Romani identity and language crystallised in Anatolia, the contributions of Persian and Byzantine Greek should be regarded as being as fundamental to the Romani language as the Indic element, and must be included in the core.

The Roma's own varied experiences in history influence their outlook towards schooling in the world of the *gadže*. The various Romani groups have preserved their languages and culture to varying extents, and each group presents a different set of challenges to the would-be educator. The monograph *The schooling of Romani Americans: an overview* is an account of attempts made in the US to establish schools to serve Roma communities, and an analysis of the reasons for their success, or more often, their failure. Basing himself on the cases he has studied, Ian makes several specific recommendations which can help ensure that such attempts will meet with more enduring success in the future.

CHAPTER EIGHT

The standardisation of the Romani language: an overview and some recommendations

Te astaras o jekhipe amara čhibake avela o angluno phir karing amaro jekhedženengo khetanipe. 'To achieve the unity of our language will be the first step toward achieving our unity as a people'.

(*author,* speaking at the first World Romani Congress, 1971)

And Yahweh said: 'So this is what they can do when all share one language! There will be no limit on what they can accomplish if they have a mind for it'.

(Genesis X)

Since my first monograph on the standardisation of Romani which appeared in 1975, the topic has gathered considerable momentum. In that essay, the opening statement in its historical and social summary maintained that we were one Romani population when our ancestors reached the gates of Europe, and that we spoke one language. Half a lifetime later, I have changed that position, although that change does not alter the points that followed it; rather, it helps explain the roots of the situation that we are here to discuss. Briefly, I have come to accept that both the Romani people and the Romani language were formed in Anatolia out of a conglomerate of Indian, Byzantine Greek and other elements, and that in the period during which that was taking place, from the late eleventh to the mid-fourteenth centuries, there were at least three major moves out of Asia Minor into Europe. I believe that the

Originally published as 'Language corpus and language politics: the case of the standardization of Romani', in Farimah Daftary and François Grin (eds), *Nation-building, ethnicity and language politics in transition countries* (Open Society Institute and Local Government and Public Service Reform Initiative, Budapest, 2003), pp. 267–86 © ECMI, 2003.

consequences of this are fundamental to our understanding of both the social and linguistic history of our people. I repeat here what I first stated over thirty years ago:

a. Because of historical and ongoing factors, not least of which are antisocial pressures from the host societies that continue to divide the Romani-speaking populations, there are today a great many widely differing dialects of that language.

b. Perhaps the greatest obstacle in achieving political and cultural unity is the lack of communication among the various Romani populations throughout the world.

c. It may be assumed that progress towards reunification would be more easily made if a common dialect were available to all groups. And the problems in creating a standardised dialect were identified thus:

1. No single dialect spoken anywhere is so close to the common protoform spoken upon arrival in Europe that it may be adopted with no modification. In other words, whatever dialect is chosen will have to be adapted to a more internationally acceptable form – especially phonologically and lexically.

2. Using existing means of education, the propagation of such a standard will be very unevenly achieved. Sedentary, already literate Roma, such as predominate in Eastern European countries, will have a far better opportunity to acquire such a standardised dialect. For illiterate and nomadic Roma, the task would be very much harder.

3. Not all Roma everywhere will ever learn, or be disposed to learn, such a dialect. This will create a 'linguistic elite' composed solely of those who have learnt to use the international standard.

Addressing the problem

When gypsilorist Matt Salo stated that his research revealed 'a lack of common ethnic consciousness' among the different Romani groups (1977: 2), he made it clear nevertheless that each is aware of a common ethnic and linguistic link, but that group identity beyond that is negligible. What Salo should have said was a lack of a *constructive* sense of ethnic consciousness. While this may be explained in light of the chronology of Romani history, sociolinguistic and sociohistorical evidence incontrovertibly demonstrates a fundamental shared linguistic, cultural and genetic history. Only now, with increased education, is this history beginning to be learnt and accepted, by both Roma and *gadže* alike.

As a result, this lack of concern on the part of our people for members of groups other than their own is changing; we may cite the European Roma and Travellers' Forum as an example of such cooperative change. Still, Porter (1975: 186–7) and others have commented upon the marked tendency of those who study Romanies to deal with a single group, and then to apply their findings to all groups, or else not to acknowledge any group other than the one they have studied, an example of which is what Thomas Acton has called 'Kalderašocentrism'. Salo (1977: 2) made this clear:

> Recently, political activists, both those who claim Gypsy identity and those who do not, have attempted to construct a pan-Gypsy identity, dismissing as irrelevant the ethnic categories of the actors themselves ... some scholars have reacted by adopting the ethnocentric perspective of the group they have studied, dismissing the others as not true Gypsies.

This Kalderašocentric attitude is central to the formation of a standardised dialect, and it is important that the definitions and attitudes established in the *gadžikano* mind be revised, since cooperation from the non-Romani population is essential if moves forward are to be made. This became a central issue, in fact, at the Rom and Cinti Union National Congress, which was held in Mülheim-Ruhr in November 1990, and at which the foundation was laid for our international Romani Parliament. Among its demands was the call for 'the immediate dissolution of non-Romani organisations who speak for the Roma and who help perpetuate a circumscribed definition of who we are'.

As I say, our current findings support the likelihood that the divisions within the population have existed from the different times of the very arrival in Europe (in Romani referred to as the *aresipe*; I suggest too use of the word *teljaripe* for the exodus from India, *nakhipe* for the crossing over from Asia into Europe, and *buxljaripe* for the migrations out into the West, when we write our own history in our own language); Marcel Courthiade's three strata demonstrate this. While Graffunder's 'grand reunion' has to be seen as an impossibility, a 'grand *union*' – an awareness of common origins – is happening, and is desirable. Without sacrificing identity as a Sinto or a Romanichal or a Xoraxano, it is possible to be aware of sharing a common linguistic and cultural heritage, and of the blood which binds Roma together as one people. And without that, we are drastically weakened as a whole people to confront and deal with the massive social problems that beset us today. At Babel, the confusion of tongues wrought upon humanity by God was *precisely* to prevent communication and cooperation. It is imperative that we do something about our own linguistic confusion.

Selection

There are only two workable options available in selecting a standard dialect: the creation of an artificial Union variety, or the selection and cultivation of a dialect that already exists. There are arguments to be made for each of these, and arguments against each. In order to tackle the problems of standardisation, it is necessary first of all to determine which dialect or group of dialects is to constitute the basis for the new standard, whether it be an *a priori* or an *a fortiori* choice.

According to the model proposed by Haugen (1974), the initial stage in language planning is selection, and it rests primarily upon social and political considerations. Romani exists in some eighty dialects, which fall into five or six branches. These share a high proportion of common grammar and lexicon, but because of the fragmentation of the population in Europe, there are also far-reaching differences apparent among them. These are the result of external, rather than internal, factors, something I have elaborated upon in a paper dealing with the Romani reunification movement (Hancock, 1988c). Some varieties of Romani have become so attenuated that their morphosyntax and phonologies belong now to other languages; Caló and Pogadijib are examples of this and have been discussed in print by Marcel Courthiade. Like Courthiade, I would also omit such varieties from consideration (except perhaps lexical consideration) since their retention of native Romani grammar, phonology and semantic content is minimal or nonexistent. Internal factors, on the other hand, account for natural divergence: for the development of /h/ from /s/ in some Northern Romani dialects, for instance; for vocabulary loss, such as *masak* 'month' and *vraker-* 'talk' in the Vlax group; or for morphological reduction, such as loss of the first and second person singular and plural emphatic subject pronouns in all but Welsh Romani and dialects in the Southern branch.

External differences are the result of contact with the various *gadžikane* idioms spoken in the environment of the various Romani dialects and also includes phonological modification, such as the loss of the aspirate/non-aspirate distinction in French and Italian Sinti, the acquisition of palatalised sounds in Kalderaš Vlax, and morphological intrusion, such as the incorporation of a narrative suffix *-li* (from Bulgarian) in Drindari, as well as extensive calquing-upon and relexification. It is the latter factor in particular, as I said earlier, that constitutes the greatest barrier to inter-dialectal intelligibility, for even where morphologies may differ, a shared lexicon will usually continue to provide a basis for communication.

It is unlikely that an artificially created dialect, perhaps a linguistic reconstruction of Proto-Romani such as that attempted by Schultz (1974) or Higgie (1984), would attract much support. It will be interesting to see the extent to which reconstructed Iberian Romani, such as that used for a translation of the Spanish Constitution (Heredia, 1988) will be learnt by Kale Roma in Spain. On 14 December 2006 a strongly worded response was posted on the Roma Virtual Network protesting an attempt by one Indian linguist to create a highly Indianised standardised dialect of our language:

Romale!

This gadjo aims at destroying our language and it is evident that there is a Hinduist political agenda throughout his letter. You can see by yourself, Romale, how does he write words that do not exist in our language, and that not a single Rom in the world knows such terms. Please do not pay attention to his letter, that is pure silliness.

Whoever among you who knows any Rom who greets saying 'namaste', please tell us. Our greeting is 'lashó dzhes' (Kalderaš), 'lacho dives' (Sinti) or other similar expressions. We do not say 'lekh', this word is not Romany but Hindi. We Roma do not know what does 'antarashtri' mean, written in this gadjo's letter. *It is not Romany what is written in his letter!*

Our Roma in the whole world, those who have lost our language, now want to learn Kalderaš so that they can communicate with Roma wherever they go, as Kalderaš is the best known tongue among Roma worldwide.

But baxt thai sastimós savorhenge.

The varieties of Romani used most extensively for purposes of documentation at the present time are Central Vlax (such as Kalderašitska), the Erli dialect of Balkan Romani and the Slovak variety of Central Romani. The Balkan dialect, spoken in Niš and Skopje, among other places, supports a considerable local literature, including the translation of Kenrick and Puxon's *The Destiny of Europe's Gypsies* (1990). Indeed, a recent conference at which our colleague Hristo Kyuchukov was present dealt with the specific issue of creating a regional standard – something I shall return to. The Central dialects are being increasingly used for written media by a growing number of Czech and Slovak activists, and are the principal variety used in the journal *Džaniben*. Northern dialects appear frequently these days in emails from Poland, where the current President of the IRU, Stanisław Stankiewicz, lives.

Elsewhere in Europe, however, as well as in North and South America and in Australia, it is Vlax that appears to serve as the vehicle for the widest communication, since its speakers are most widely scattered geographically. All Romani-language materials published in the US are in Kalderašitska, as well as most of those being published in Europe. There are more contemporary grammars and dictionaries available for Vlax than for any other dialect, and more unpublished theses and dissertations. It is quite clear that, for the most widely applicable practical use, a Kalderaš-based dialect would be the logical choice for a standardised dialect. Balkan dialects differ from Vlax more than conservative Central dialects do, and their geographically restricted use argues against their adoption. Differences between Vlax and Central dialects can be minimised with only a small risk of creating too artificial a dialect native to no one; differences which are primarily phonological and lexical. The lexical differences are the subject of a monograph by Kochanowski (1989).

Codification

Haugen's second stage is called codification, defined by Fishman *et al.* (1968: 295) as dealing with 'the normalisation (standardisation) of regional, social, class or other variation in usage via the preparation of recommended (or 'official') grammars, dictionaries, orthographic guides, etc.' At the Fourth World Romani Congress, which was held in Warsaw in April 1990, the Language Commission (*o Kolo le Alomaske la Rromana Čhibake*) voted upon an orthography to serve for the standard dialect now being developed. It made use of the archiphonemic characters <ç> (to represent either /s/ or /ts/) in the postposition –*sa*; <θ>

(to represent either /t/ or /d/) in the postpositions *-tar* and -te 'at'; and <q> (to represent either /k/ or /g/) in the postposition *-ke* and the adjectival series in *-k-* + V, the second in each pair following the masculine and feminine plural oblique marker /-n-/. Consonantal modifications are indicated with an acute accent, thus alveolar <s> contrasts with palato-alveolar <ś>; uvular /r/ is written as <rr>, contrasting with the front /r/ written with a single character <r>, and a second non-Romani symbol <3> has been introduced to stand for the voiced palatoalveolar fricative. What are voiceless aspirated palatal fricatives in some dialects are articulated with retroflexion by speakers of others; one grapheme <ćh> represents both possibilities. <c> represents /ts/ and <x> is a voiceless uvular fricative. The new orthography also incorporates the accents < ˇ > (Eastern Europe) or < ` > (Western Europe) and < ¨ > to indicate /j/ onset (for example, <ǎ> = /ja/), non-predictable, non-final stressed syllables on athematic stems and vowel centralisation, respectively.

Even if a Vlax dialect, say, Russian Kalderaš, were to be selected as the basis for a new standard, we ought ideally to have at our disposal a complete grammatical and lexical study based upon all of the Romani dialects from which to draw in order to supplement the base dialect selected. Vlax has a number of forms lacking in some other branches, such as causative and inchoative verbs, but it has lost in turn the thematic comparative construction, for example, and supplementation or replacement of these should ideally be with thematic (that is, pre-European) models.

There are a number of ways in which the base lexicon might be augmented: (a) incoining, (b) phrasing, (c) native retrieval and (d) foreign adoption.

Incoining is already a widespread mechanism for lexical expansion in Romani. This involves combining already existing morphemes in the language in innovative combinations either having no exterior model, or else being calques on another language. Examples are American Vlax *šudro-bakso* 'refrigerator' (*lit.* 'cold box') and *gadžengo pleso* 'public' (*lit.* 'place of the *gadže*').

Phrasing involves replacing a single, athematic (non-native) item where it has become lost with a descriptive phrase-employing native vocabulary. Examples from American Vlax include *glinda te dikhen palal* 'rearview mirror' (*lit.* 'mirror that you [use to] look behind') and *mačhina kaj ramol* 'typewriter' (*lit.* 'machine which writes').

Native retrieval has been used for a number of developing languages, such as Malay and Hebrew, and consists of reviving obsolete words from the historical native stock to augment the contemporary lexicon. For Romani, this would mean the resurrection of Sanskrit words, for example **merdika* or *mestipen* 'freedom' – this latter already having been introduced – for which only adoptions from European languages exist (such as American Kalderaš *frijimos*, Russian Kalderaš *slobuzenja*). It would then remain a problem as to whether such items would retain their Sanskrit form or be modified according to the rules of change that have produced modern Romani phonology, in which case **merdika* (<Sanskrit *mrdīká-*) would have the form **mareko* in Romani. This presupposes considerable linguistic sophistication on the part of the linguistic committee whose task it would be to select and modify such items. An alternative has been proposed by Kochanowski (1971: 76–7), who suggested modern Hindi as a lexical reservoir for Romani.

Foreign adoption means simply the acquisition of new lexical items from any athematic source. Kochanowski (1971) again suggested that international vocabulary be adopted and, where these are insufficient, words common to French and English be incorporated, in each case made to conform to Romani grammar. This is already happening in the European dialects, where it is not always possible to identify the immediate source of such widely occurring items as *tilefono* 'telephone' or *mikroskopo* 'microscope'. The choice of Vlax is particularly useful in this regard, since it has both a thematic and an athematic grammatical paradigm, any new items already having their morphological behaviour determined for them. But while it is true that both French and English have wide international currency, neither is commonly heard in Eastern Europe, where pan-Slavicisms would seem to be a more logical source to supplement the language.

To obtain an idea of the proportion and character of the non-core lexicon of Romani, a breakdown is provided here of two different paragraphs chosen at random from letters that have been sent to me. In each, the non-core items are italicised, and the spelling remains as received:

> Bičhalava tuke jekh *foto-kopi* katar o *žurnali* i *Arena*, kai vakerela o Prof. S.J. baš i *Indija* -kaj vov arakhla o M.D. ano *London*, kaj i *Indija* vazdinda amari *rezolucija* ko *U.N.O.*, taj so ka kerel, so rodel, o Duito *Kongreso* ani *Ženeva* avutno bers. (Balkan, from southern Yugoslavia)

I'm sending you a photocopy from the journal Arena, where Professor S.J. talks about India, where he found M.D. in London, where India supported our resolution to the UN, and what he'd do, and what he sought; the second Congress in Geneva another year.

Sayekh mangav tutar tay me či bišalav tuke *šoha* khanči. Te *trubul* tu vareso, te na lažes, *numa* motho. Si tu kodi *knyiga* katar o V. tay M. pa e šib le *Lov*arengi ando *Ungr*iko? Te niči, bišalav tuke *fotokopiya* te kames; but *interežnyime* [= *interežno*] si. (Vlax, from Trieste)

In the same way I want (it) from you and I'll never send you anything. If you need something, don't be shy, just say. Do you have that book by V. and M. about the language of the Lovara in Hungary? If not, I'll send you a photocopy if you like, it's very interesting.

Of the two passages, non-native elements constitute about 20 per cent of the whole, although over half of this consists of proper names. Of the remainder, the majority may be considered to be 'international vocabulary', (*foto-kopi, fotokopiya, žurnali, rezolucija, kongreso, interežnyime*), two are grammatical particles (*šoha* 'never', *trubul* 'need'), and one a local adoption from Serbian (*knyiga* 'book'), with which a native form, *lil*, alternates. Thus, less than a tenth of the vocabulary is derived from external sources in these passages, exclusive of proper nouns. In less conservative dialects the percentage is much higher; thus in this sample of French Sinti, some 40 per cent of the lexicon represents accreted material:

Mē am trin *nebudi*, žjam te rodas *šáfreba* ačas kek. Ijo '*Jean-Jean*', bišštar beršengro, '*Niglo*', bišjek un o '*Ratam*', bišberšengro čače morš, *ledige* čave. *Memke hart šáfreba* darā *gar, safráxa fort*. Vejam so *fus* trianda panč *kilomēngri* ano foro. Ačam *gar* o rašaj, *krat* dui *batríja* un i *pisla* sastar *pur* te xas i kotar māro.

The three of us are cousins, we went looking for work, [but] we didn't find any. There was Jean-Jean, twenty five, Niglo, twenty-one and Ratatam, twenty – real men, unmarried. Even if the work is hard, they're not afraid, and they'll do the job even if it is far away. We came on foot, 35 kilometres, to the town. We didn't find the priest, just two batteries and a piece of scrap iron to buy [lit. eat] a bit of bread.

Of the 3,600-item glossary of Swedish Kalderaš by Gjerdman and Ljungberg (1963: 193–396), some 1,750 words, or almost 48 per cent of the total, derive from non-native sources, overwhelmingly from

Romanian. But, as the authors point out (1963: *xx*) 'the vocabulary originally brought by the Gipsies from their Indian motherland is, despite its paucity, of much greater significance. For this is, after all, the material from which the principal features of the Romani language are derived.' In this respect, it compares with the Anglo-Saxon component of modern English, less than 30 per cent according to dictionary count, but as high as 85 per cent in ordinary discourse.

Conclusion

Having discussed some of the issues related to the selection and implementation of an international standard for written Romani, I suggest that the following scheme be adopted in the creation of such a dialect:

a. A number of representative Romani dialects from the most widespread or numerically most important branches be selected. This would include a conservative dialect of Vlax (such as Kalderaš), as well as Balkan (such as Erli), Central (such as Bašaldo) and Northern (such as Sinti).

b. All foreign material (lexical, phonological, morphosyntactic and so on) be removed from each of these representative dialects, and codification made of the remaining thematic material. Shared and non-shared features would be listed separately.

c. Features absent in the natural dialect selected as the base of the Standard, which I suggest be Polish Lovari, be supplemented from other dialects where they exist.

d. A standard lexicon be developed using the techniques outlined above. My own position, and that of a growing number of my colleagues, is that Romani crystallised in Asia Minor, not in India, from a conglomerate of pre-Anatolian languages in the matrix of Byzantine Greek. I believe therefore that all of the languages that have contributed to this are equally valid as constituting the 'core' lexicon. That the speakers were leaving under different circumstances and entering Europe at different times across the span of perhaps three centuries clearly accounts for the different representations of these core items from one present-day dialect group to the other. Nevertheless if we are to scour all the dialects for Indian-origin items in order to supplement the lexicon, we must equally well look to items derived from Greek, Armenian, Persian and other pre-European languages. It is only *after* the arrival of the different early groups into Europe and their subsequent dispersal that the different dialect groups began to acquire separate, non-core words.

e. If *regional standards* are to be developed, as was the focus of the conference in Skopje on 17–19 December, which discussed a common variety intended to serve populations in Macedonia, Serbia, Kosovo and Bulgaria, then the same recommendations apply as those made here, but limited to the specific area.

f. My suggestion regarding orthography is that we follow the lead that is being taken naturally in our emails to each other: rather than using diacritics, English graphemes be employed, thus <sh> rather than <š>, <ch> rather than <č> and <zh> rather than <ž>. I would retain <x> for the voiceless uvular fricative and <rr> for the voiced. I would retain <j> for [j] and <c> for [ts], but allow the optional use of <y> and <ts> in their place in English-speaking countries.

CHAPTER NINE

The schooling of Romani Americans: an overview

who ever gets this mesage please help me i live in los angles calif i am a Gypsy that needs to go to school i saw this site and i want to be somebody and also help other peaple like my self please email me
(Email message to a Romani website, 28 May 1999)

In contrast to the European situation, efforts to establish schools for Romanies in the US have been both few in number and – with only a couple of limited exceptions – unsuccessful. There are approximately one million Romanies in North America, a number which is slowly growing. Romani presence in the western hemisphere dates from the fifteenth century, but large-scale migration from Europe began only in the late 1800s. The makeup of the Romani population mirrors the eclectic nature of North American society as a whole; Canada and the USA are nations composed of immigrant groups from all over the world, and Romanies too have come here from all parts of Europe, and reflect that diversity.[15]

The largest two populations are the Vlax, whose migrations were prompted by the ending of slavery in Romania after about 1860, and the Romanichals, who began reaching America in relatively large numbers after the 1840s. Members of both populations have continued to come into the country. The next two largest groups are the Bashalde, who left the Hungarian and Slovak-speaking regions of the Austro-Hungarian Empire after about 1870, and the 'New Wave' of Romanies who have come here, mainly from Hungary, Poland and Romania (and in Canada

Originally published in H. Kyuchukov (ed.), *New aspects of Roma children education* (Diversity Publications, Sofia, 2002), pp. 30–51.

especially, from the Czech Republic), since the fall of Communism around 1990. There is thus no homogeneous Romani population but a number of sharply disparate groups differing from each other in numbers, in degree of acculturation, and in aspects of their language and priorities. All of these factors have a bearing on Romani education.

Characteristics of the different Romani American groups

A. *The Vlax*. The Vlax Romanies are easily the largest Romani group, constituting perhaps two-thirds of the overall Romani American population. All descend from ancestors held in slavery in the Romanian principalities of Wallachia and Moldavia. The impact of over five centuries of enslavement has very deeply affected the identity and character of the contemporary Vlax-speaking Romanies. Being socially – and for most groups physically – isolated as slaves for almost their entire existence in the West, Vlax Romani language and culture, while extensively influenced by Romanian, have at the same time remained conservative in comparison with those of other groups. Vlax Romanies too, regard the use of the ethnonym Rom as applying exclusively to themselves, despite the fact that its use as a self-ascription is found among non-Vlax populations as well, such as the Bashalde. Perhaps because the condition of slavery placed the Romanies in a category clearly distinct from the rest of society, and perhaps because isolation lent itself to the conservation of traditional Romani cultural practices, Vlax Romanies in America are far stricter in maintaining social distance from the non-Romanies than are members of other groups. American Vlax Romanies, in fact, because they came here soon after abolition and, following their arrival having been able to maintain Romani culture practically unhindered (albeit invisibly) are considered rather old-fashioned by Vlax visitors from Europe. The Vlax population is itself further divided into eastern and western groups, the 'Russian' Romanies, most of whom are Kalderasha, and the 'Serbian' Romanies, most of whom are Machvaya. There are groups identifying themselves differently, but these are by far the largest. The Russian Kalderasha tend to be less assimilated and more mobile than the Machvaya, who include individuals following mainstream professions among their number; both groups regard the Machvaya as the more prestigious. Kalderashitska (the Kalderash Vlax dialect) and Machvanitska/Machvanska are easily mutually intelligible. The speech of the recently arrived Lovara, also Vlax, differs considerably from the long-established American varieties of Vlax.

B. *The Romanichals.* The Romanichals, Romichals, or 'English Travellers', no longer speak inflected Romani, but an ethnolectal variety of English nevertheless referred to as Romani or Romnis which may contain from a few dozen to a few hundred (mostly) Romani-derived words. For this reason, they count among the native English-speaking population, and special provision for teaching English as a Second Language would not be a factor if schools for them were to be established. While the majority of Romanichals are physically indistinguishable from the general Anglo-American population, they nevertheless maintain a strong sense of separateness from the *gaujas* or non-Romanies, and can maintain pollution taboos with some strictness.

C. *The Bashalde.* The Bashalde or 'Hungarian-Slovak Roma' as they refer to themselves, arrived in America as part of the larger late-nineteenth century immigration of non-Romanies from central Europe, who came here among other reasons to work in the steel mills in the north-eastern part of the country. The Bashalde (the word means 'musicians') found employment in the mills and in the ethnic cafés, clubs and restaurants as entertainers. Although that world has long since gone, many continue to work as musicians. Bashaldo Romani is of a Central type, and perhaps only 60 per cent mutually intelligible with Vlax Romani. It is no longer spoken by people below middle age. Because of assimilationist policies directed at Romanies in the Austro-Hungarian Empire, Bashalde Romani Americans maintain pollution taboos to a lesser extent than other groups, and the rate of out-marriage appears to be somewhat higher.

D. *The Xoraxane.* Established mainly in the Bronx where they have established two mosques, the Xoraxane are an Islamic population originating in Macedonia and surrounding areas of the Balkans, several hundred families that came to America beginning in the late 1960s. Several thousand other Xoraxane Roma have come later as part of a Bosnian refugee programme initiated by the city of Saint Louis, Missouri, and are settled there. They maintain minimal ties with other

Romani American populations, include engineers and teachers among their number, and have established soccer and other social clubs.

E. *The Russian/Serbian Lovara.*   Some two thousand or more who belong to this group live today in the Chicago area. They descend from Russian Roma who fled to Yugoslavia during the First World War, travelling back and forth into Hungary and intermarrying with Lovara from that country. After deciding to leave Europe a group of families arrived in Montreal on a Russian ship from France but were targeted for deportation, and so in 1973 moved to St. Louis and then on to Chicago to find relatives. Since that time those families have been joined by numbers of other relatives from Europe, who continue to arrive.

F. *The 'New Wave' Romanies.* These include Romanies representing many different European groups, all of whom have come to North America in the past ten or fifteen years. They have an imperfect command of English, and speak a number of different dialects of Romani. Many of them speak no Romani at all, especially the Romungre from Hungary and those from certain groups in Romania such as the Catani. They tend to be concentrated in New York and Chicago. There is little social contact within these groups, and with American Romani groups, although alliances are beginning to be formed in New York. Their priorities at the present time are less directed at establishing special schools than at getting established in homes and jobs in their new country.

Who is the focus of schooling issues?

The fact is, that it has only been members of the Vlax-speaking Romani population who have been involved in any of the previously established schools. Of the six groups listed above, those Romanichals and Bashalde who are of school age are English monolinguals, and while their parents share the same concerns as those of the Vlax parents, referred to below, it is easier for their children to attend at least the first few years of public (state-provided) schooling. Nevertheless some of the problems encountered are the same as those that Vlax Romani children must contend with, and the same reasons exist for taking the children out of school in the early teen years, and indeed for an overall reluctance for civic engagement. New Wave Romanies do not constitute a homogeneous group, and are only now becoming organised. It remains to be seen whether special school provision will be sought – the number of children among these immigrant groups remains small. Members of other (long-established) Romani populations, such as the Sinti or Kale, are too few in number and too scattered to participate in ethnically directed school programmes.

The reason that the only Romani American population to consider such schooling were (and still are) the Vlax, may have to do with a perspective on society conditioned by centuries of enslavement; only the Vlax Romanies were slaves in Europe. For those people, everything, from food to clothing to accommodation, often choice of marriage partner and even their very existence, was provided by the non-Romani slaveholders: the *gadže*. For more than five hundred years, Vlax Romanies had no decision-making powers. This has created a worldview which sees the situation of the Romanies as having been created by non-Romanies who, having caused the problems arising from it, must be responsible for solving those problems. Having no internal autonomy or problem-solving power, the Vlax had to go to the *gadže* for intervention. The success with which a slave could persuade his owner to grant him favours personally, or to his community as a whole, gained him considerable status. While this is not a characteristic exclusive to Vlax Romanies in the US, it is far more typical of them. Also typical is the desire not only to have influence with powerful individuals in the non-Romani world, but to acquire influential positions within it, particularly in law enforcement. Displaying their deputy sheriff's badges is a not uncommonly observed ritual among the men at Vlax Romani gatherings. Other considerations aside, schooling, however, has not been regarded as a positive thing by the Vlax Romanies. I discuss the reasons for this below.

The beginnings of schooling for Romanies

The involvement of Romanies with special schooling ('alternative' or parochial schooling) dates from about 1965, and began in Richmond, near San Francisco in northern California. The 1960s was the decade of emerging ethnic self-assertion, and minority programmes were beginning to flourish, supported by affirmative action. But the Romanies were a special case, because while the larger society was entirely familiar with the African American and Hispanic American minorities – populations numbering in the millions – it had only the vaguest of notions of the infinitely smaller Romani American presence, to the extent of being unaware of its very name Roma(nies). The concept of 'Gypsies', on the other hand – a name also used in self-reference – was widespread, although based in fictionalised stereotypes rather than in real-life experience. For this reason, the agencies which were approached and which were willing to accommodate Romani students, such as the Municipal Social Services Department, the Volunteer Bureau, the California State Service Center and so on, made no special provision for them. No permanent programme was established, nor were these provisions centralised, and no school resulted. Nevertheless, this brief exposure to the classroom was sufficient to stimulate the interest of both the students involved and their parents, who were aware that at least some formalised basic education was becoming necessary in an increasingly technological world. It was in this framework that the first successful Romani school in America was eventually established, a school which lasted for seven years.

Acknowledgement must also be made of the pivotal role played by Miller Stevens in 1968, then living in Tacoma, Washington. After learning of the Richmond initiative, he travelled to Washington DC to meet with officials of the Department of Health, Education and Welfare (DHEW) to make them aware of the needy situation of the Romani American population. He saw that other minorities were getting recognition and assistance, and wanted the same for Romanies. Indeed it was Miller Stevens who was responsible for getting Romanies recognised as an official ethnic minority by the DHEW. He began a Head Start programme for fifteen Romani children in Tacoma out of his home in the summer of 1968, funded by the Office of Economic Opportunity.

The first school

In the case of the families in Richmond, the stimulus was not initially a desire for education, but because the truant officers were targeting Romani families for their children's non-attendance and eventually arrested numbers of parents and took them into custody. Sending the children to school was a trade-off.

Two things happened: the children found that they enjoyed classroom activities, within limits, and their fathers found that association with the school board brought them a status useful in their interaction with city officials. When news of this spread to Romani communities further north on the West Coast, it stimulated the establishment of Romani schools in Portland, Seattle, Tacoma and Spokane, and spread eastwards to Chicago and Baltimore.

Romani attitudes towards schooling

From the traditional Vlax point of view, formal schooling has not been regarded as a good thing. It requires that Romanies enter the non-Romani world, which is seen as polluting and counter-cultural. Not only is the environment unclean, particularly with regard to the toilet and cafeteria facilities, but equally unacceptable would be the seating of boys and girls in the classrooms, and the topics addressed in the curricula. It would also require formally identifying oneself and filling out paperwork, and spending a fixed amount of time in a non-Romani-controlled environment. The classroom is seen as a place to learn to become *gadžikanime* or 'Americanised'. This fear of assimilation is not only an American phenomenon. A Romani singer from Ostrava in the Czech Republic lamented that parents 'don't send their kids to school because they don't want them to be white' (Furlong, 2008: 2), an attitude distressingly mirrored among some African Americans. But it is true that there is nothing in the schoolbooks about Romani history or contributions, and when 'Gypsies' turn up in the classes they are invariably represented negatively in works of fiction – especially children's fiction – and the historical figures presented as heroes in Western culture are all too frequently the same individuals who sent Romanies into exile or even to their deaths. Schools are seen not only as environments that do nothing to teach a child to be a better Gypsy, but which seem determined instead to homogenise and de-ethnicise that child. Stories about children's interaction with domestic pets, for example, send a different message to the pupil from the values taught in the home. Stories about structured mainstream domestic life present a picture foreign to the Romani child, and newer, diversity-conscious storybooks about, for example, same-sex parent families, are completely confusing and disturbing. School records may be used to keep track of the whereabouts of Romanies in a community by the authorities; Romani children are often targeted by their classmates once their ethnicity is known; one Romani adult remembered with bitterness, 'Oh God, it was murder going to school; they wouldn't sit beside you in the seats' (Anonymous, 1973: 5). Nick Dimas addressed these issues most directly (Hancock, 1975: 45–6):

> In the US, the continuing internal solidarity and resistance to acculturation of the American Rom is a phenomenon that merits closer attention. Although the underlying social dynamics of this cohesion are as yet obscure, one of the prime techniques which maintains this cohesion is not. They avoid the school system like the plague. While most other US minorities are boycotting, busing and organising to obtain better education for their children, the Rom are, by any means at their disposal, keeping their children at home. As a result of this mass truancy, the majority of adult Rom in the US are illiterate or, at best, functionally illiterate (fifth-grade reading level). If the origin of this practice of education-avoidance is rooted in custom and tradition rather than in a consciously organised group policy, the results of the practice are no less effective in maintaining the solidarity of the group. And if we use the tolerance of marriage outside the group as an indication of group solidarity, they are solid indeed. The school-avoidance tradition and its resulting illiteracy acts in five specific ways to maintain the non-acculturation of the Rom:
>
> a. The minimalisation of time at school reduces proportionately the influence of the teacher's value system on the Romano child, and effectively eliminates the peer group pressure of the other children, two of the tremendous forces in the socialisation process;
>
> b. Illiteracy prevents any socialisation in the direction of the majority culture through the written word. It forestalls identification with historical and cultural heroes in books and novels;
>
> c. Illiteracy ensures that Romani will remain the first language of the individual Rom, with the resulting reinforcement of group values which occur when he speaks mainly to and in the company of other Rom;
>
> d. Illiteracy limits the defection to the majority culture via the occupational route, as only the most physical, menial and low-paying jobs are accessible to an illiterate in the US;
>
> e. Illiteracy tends to discourage intermarriage between Romani males and

non-Romani females since the husband's income is severely limited, and tends to remain so.

It is plain that the integrity of the American Romani community is maintained in great part, by severely circumscribing the options of the individual Rom. It goes without saying, however, that any socialised member of the Romani community does not himself feel oppressed or deprived by his lack of reading and writing ability – rather he feels 'liberated' from the 'craziness' of the gadjo community, much of which he ascribes to reading and writing.

Sometimes the singling-out of a Romani pupil can be for other reasons, motivated not by animosity but by paternalism, but discriminatory all the same. I can relate an anecdote concerning my own daughter Melina who some years ago at the age of about eight, came home from school one day terribly upset. She was hurt and confused because one of her teachers, of whom she was very fond, had told a boy in the class who was misbehaving that if he didn't settle down she would 'sell him to fifty Gypsies'. Melina wondered why a teacher she admired so much would have such negative feelings about Gypsies. I called the woman at her home that night and explained to her that Melina was a Romani girl, and that she had been very upset by the remark. The teacher was embarrassed and profusely apologetic, claiming that she didn't know Gypsies were a real ethnic population. The next day, however, she told the class that she had a 'surprise' for them; that they had 'a little Gypsy girl in the class; Melina is a little Gypsy'. From that point on schooling became increasingly difficult for my daughter, and we eventually removed her for placement in a different school. When I asked the principal in that second school to remove certain children's books from the school library which presented Romani characters in a damaging stereotypical way – this was prompted after receiving a self-congratulatory circular from the school announcing that in the interest of sensitivity to ethnic diversity numbers of books (such as *Little Black Sambo*) had been taken out of circulation – I received a letter telling me that the characters in the books were Gypsies, not Romanies, and that Gypsies were fictional beings, distinct from Romanies who were an actual ethnic people. The books remained.

Attempts to accommodate Romani culture

The Richmond school was fortunate to have as its first principal Anne Sutherland (then Louis, and later to become author Sutherland, 1975). Ms Sutherland recognised the importance of incorporating the priorities of the Romanies, which were both culturally and pragmatically determined. Culturally, Romanies needed to be on the school board itself, to oversee behaviour, meals, class topics and so on. Boys and girls were to sit separately from each other, for instance. Pragmatically, they wanted such topics as reading and writing to be taught, but were not interested in history (of no practical value) or mathematics (already known) or gymnastics (inappropriate culturally). Because this school, which materialised in 1970 out of the various earlier programmes, was initially unfunded and wholly supported by volunteers, the school board was not subject to control by any funding body. Ms Sutherland had the wisdom to sit back at the board meetings and let its Romani members make the decisions. In 1972 the new principal, Janet Tompkins, was able to obtain the first state funding for the school, which lasted until 1977.

Other programmes

A year after the Richmond school closed down John Ellis, the leader of the Portland, Oregon, Romani community went to the State Governor to ask for a community centre for the Romanies in his area. Ellis wanted a building for social events, but which would also incorporate a classroom, in which traditional Romani values, as well as literacy, would be taught. There were 250 school-aged Romani children in Portland at that time. The response was positive, although the Portland School District's relations officer was adamant that such a project could only be a transitional set-up to prepare Romani children for their eventual entry into the public (state) school system. A compromise was reached, after other Romani leaders were brought into the debate, and a three-part programme developed: first, a summer school at Portland Community College for young adults over the age of eighteen; secondly, a vocational training programme for younger children, funded by the State Welfare division; and lastly, afternoon and evening classes for Kindergarten through eighth grade. These were held in the Romani business district of the city, and began in the summer of 1978, supported by funding from the Portland School District, the State Fund for Disadvantaged Children, Federal Impact Aid and Title One. But it was always made clear that the intent was clearly to prepare the children to enter mainstream schools as quickly as possible. While John Ellis enrolled his own three children in school (the Vestal School), he was in a distinct minority; most Romanies in Portland were just not interested. Others pulled their children out of the classes because they were being ridiculed and bullied. This was worse for the older children, those who were unable to read, since the rest of their non-Romani classmates could. Their non-native command of English also made them stand out from the rest of the class. At the point of its greatest enrollment, there were only thirty children attending, and then sporadically.

The problem was tackled by the School District's decision to put two Romanies on the payroll as 'Special Gypsy Counsellors'; they acted as liaison between the parents and the administration, and worked with a non-Romani American who specialised in 'disadvantaged' pupils. While the Romani children, as young as four and five, attended regular school, they only stayed for two or three hours at a time, following the wishes of their parents and the recommendation of the counsellors. The school board was happy to comply.

Some of the children in Portland still go to school, but most don't. The Vocational Training School programme foundered after the second year (Rubin, 1980: 72–3).

In the same year (1973) that John Ellis approached the Oregon State Governor, in Seattle in Washington State another Romani leader, Ephraim Stevens, was attempting the same thing. Civic-minded like his brother Miller, he worked during the early 1970s as a community organiser for the King County Economic Opportunity Board, which he asked for funding to establish a Gypsy Multi-Service Center, a move stimulated in part by John Ellis' action, and by the fact that Seattle's Chicano community had just received over $130,000 for such a centre. He was initially refused, being told that the Romani population was too small to qualify – it didn't exceed 500 at its maximum – to which it was countered that to favour one minority over another on grounds of numbers was discriminatory. The administration bowed to the criticism, and the response was that the Gypsy Community Center was set up in the city, headed by Stevens and funded by the Urban, Rural, Racial and Disadvantaged Education Program, which contained a day school for young children and an evening literacy class for adults. There were six children to begin with, a number which quickly grew to twenty-five. Stevens hired a female university student to teach, and according to his own testimony, she took over the programme and gradually eased him out. She was followed by three more non-Romani directors in succession, Lesley Easton, Barbara Cemeno and Carolyn Hall. By 1981 the Gypsy Alternative School occupied two buildings and had two teachers, with forty students registered, although only twenty-six came regularly to class. By 1983, there was just one teacher employed there because of lack of funding (Whistler, 1983: 14). The Culture Center eventually closed down, but the school continued to exist, for many years with the involvement of Dorothy (Bora) George, a local Romani, and later Paul Stevens, brother of Kaiser Stevens of Tacoma. It was the longest running Romani alternative school in the country, but it has been closed for over three years now. The late Dorothy George spoke to the author often of re-opening it, but had not been successful in finding the means to do so.

At the same time, another Romani leader, the late James Marks, in Spokane, Washington, obtained funding from the Spokane Work Exchange Program for Young Adults, and established the Gypsy Cultural Center in a disused army barracks. For a short time it offered an evening class for small children, although no day classes, and very quickly it transformed to a community and sewing centre for women, eventually closing down altogether after about six months. Marks' three children attended both state school by day and the Gypsy school in the evenings. James Marks could not himself read or write. The existence of a similar venture in Tacoma, Washington, begun by Kaiser Stevens and funded by the Division of Vocational Rehabilitation, was more successful – although stimulated by a 1975 juvenile court ruling that Romani children not attending school were liable to be placed into foster homes. This led to the submission of a proposal entitled the *Gypsy Educational Development Program*, which asked for $152,000. Its authors are not specified, but the proposal is flawed in its understanding of the Romani American population, and its design suggests strongly that it was meant, at least in part, to provide a framework for somebody's doctoral thesis. What did survive in Tacoma was an evening school programme in which the students were able to earn a General Education Diploma (GED), a high-school graduation equivalent. The three other school projects which have received attention were in Chicago, Philadelphia and Baltimore, although there have been short-lived ventures in Boston, Fort Worth, Austin and elsewhere. The Chicago project was initiated by Tom Nicholas, supposedly motivated by Ephraim Stevens who went from Seattle to that city to spread the word. Miller Stevens obtained travel money from the DHEW to visit Romani leaders around the country to tell them about Romani schools and to try to establish new ones; but his greatest success had been several years earlier, when he visited Washington DC in 1968 with Stanley Stevens, a Romani leader from Baltimore, Maryland. In Chicago, a grant of $26,000 from state bi-lingual funds was initially provided for the 1973/1974 school year, during which time refinements were made to the programme and a proposal drawn up for submission for further funds. It required, among other things, that:

a. A Rom be named director and be given full authority in the selection of personnel;
b. An equal number of Romani and non-Romani teachers be employed;
c. No distinction be made in salaries received by the teachers, whatever their academic credentials;
d. Equal time be given to the teaching of Romani language and culture by the Romani teachers, as to literacy and computational skills, taught by non-Romanies;
e. All classes were to be held at night;
f. Students of all ages were to be admitted equally;
g. No attendance or enrolment records were to be kept;
h. Students were not to be required to identify themselves;
i. Classes were to be small, and acquisition of any skill was to be achieved by repetition;
j. There was to be no formal discipline;
k. Male and female students were to be seated separately, and females were never to be placed in competitive situations with males;
l. Non-Romani teachers were to leave the room when sessions on Romani language and culture were taking place;
m. The programme was to admit the students regardless of their place of residence, and with no reference to the actual school district to which he or she belonged.
(Kearney, 1981: 50–1)

The Chicago School District rejected the proposal, which was then picked up by the Northwest Education Cooperative which provided $13,000 for a three-month pilot bi-lingual programme. This was entitled Gypsy Village Hindsight and was located at the Halsted Urban Progress Center; it had seventy-five students to start with and eight teachers, half of whom were Romanies, and it seemed to be off to a good start. The evaluation at the end of this period was positive enough to obtain an extension of a further three months. The Chicago School Board was asked to sponsor a permanent school but, despite the success of the pilot, it declined. Other agencies approached by Nicholas, including the various urban colleges throughout the city and the University of Chicago, were not in a position to sponsor projects requiring bi-lingual funding. Different agencies such as the Small Business Administration, the Right to Read Program and the Division of Vocational Rehabilitation were all solicited, but none was willing to underwrite a Gypsy project. The school closed down.

In Philadelphia in 1970, Kalderash Romani leader Johnny Thompson got together with city officials to work out a compromise with them, because they had begun to withhold payments from those Romani families having children who were not attending school. A highly effective leader, Thompson was not only able to obtain a $50,000 grant from the federal government to establish a Gypsy school, but he was also able to persuade newly arriving Romani families that, as the *forosko baro* (community leader) he would only help them find homes and establish businesses if they agreed to enroll their children in the programme. He even went so far as to arrange for regular minibus transportation for the children to and from their homes. The school was located in the basement of St Rita's Catholic Church at Broad and Rittner Streets. With the help of diocesan Cardinal Crowe, and later one Father Bevelacqua, classes for as many as 200 children lasted for more than ten years. All of the teachers were the nuns associated with the St Rita's Convent, and their main focus was literacy skills and religious training. When Thompson died in 1982, no one was equipped to take over the work of this dynamic man, and the school closed down. Waning interest on the part of the government also ensured that here, as elsewhere, no particular effort would be made by the authorities to urge school attendance. The impetus of the sixties and seventies was a thing of the past. Today, Thompson's sister Barbara Nicola has plans to re-institute the school on the premises of her own church outside Atlantic City in New Jersey, but the problems of finding teachers and funding have yet to be overcome.

In August 1968 in Baltimore, Miller Stevens met with Stanley Stevens after responding to a telephone call asking how a Gypsy school might be established on the East Coast. Together these two men visited a professor in the Department of Social Relations at Johns Hopkins University and Maryland State Senator Joseph Tydings. Senator Tydings wrote to the Mayor of Baltimore strongly recommending that social services programmes be established for Baltimore's Romani community; this in turn led to the Office of Economic Opportunity and the Baltimore City Community Action Agency organising a joint discussion of the situation. From this meeting it was determined that a survey of the Romani American population of Baltimore be undertaken, to assess needs and numbers. This was not successful. Most of the community refused to participate, and only members of Stevens' extended family seemed interested. It was decided nevertheless to proceed with a proposal to establish a school since the parents interviewed were unanimously supportive of such a programme. This was put together in 1968, and it asked for $14,300. Its requirements were that:

a. One teacher having sufficient background in linguistic skills and with sympathy for cross-cultural problems be appointed to be an effective instructor and innovator;
b. A female aide be selected from the Romani community to assist the teacher as an interpreter and control link;
c. Space for a classroom be located within the Romani community and be provided by the Romani leadership;
d. Educational materials and equipment be held in the custody of the teacher between classroom sessions.

The evident Romani/non-Romani imbalance of authority, the biased wording in parts of the proposal, and its one-family focus combined to assure that the project would not succeed.

Institutional resistance to Romanies and Romani culture

Fear of Romanies in the classroom in America is mild compared to reactions in Europe. A British parent told a newspaper reporter that 'It came as a tremendous shock when we heard that Gypsy children were to be taught at the school. They smell, I'm afraid, and have the educational standard of retarded children' (Anonymous, 1965: 5), while in Italy, car tires were heaped in the middle of the road and set on fire to prevent Romani children from reaching the school. In Spain, local residents pelted Romani children who were attempting to attend school in Zaragosa with bricks (Anonymous, 1984: B7). In Hungary, at least in the mid-1980s, about 15 per cent of Romani children are put into schools for the mentally deficient (Satory, 1986: 5).[16]

Although the western US schools for the most part received positive support initially from the surrounding non-Romani community, their establishment was not entirely free from elements of anti-gypsyism. In Seattle, for example, when non-Romani parents learnt that there would be Gypsies in their schools, they became alarmed, and demanded meetings with the Parent Teacher Association (PTA). 'In addition to the fear engendered by the prejudiced view of the Rom, there was also a feeling of resentment at having school territory impinged upon' (Kaldi, 1983: 21).

Both Ephraim Miller and James Marks were angered by the lack of enthusiasm and concern they encountered from the establishment once the initial fascination with the Gypsy schools had passed. While other minorities continued to received attention and financial support, the administration and the funding bodies simply lost interest (Tyrnauer-Stastny, 1977: 32–4), and James Marks, personal correspondence).

The situation today

We may trace the initial impetus for creating alternative schooling for Romanies in America to the mid- and late-1960s, when it was stimulated by the general increase in interest in the civil rights of American ethnic minorities; and we may trace its decline to both internal and external factors: externally to declining available funds and (eventually) changing governmental policies towards minority support, and to general ignorance on the part of the establishment of who and what Romani Americans are. Internally, schools failed to maintain themselves because of fundamental cultural and social differences separating the worlds of the Romanies and the non-Romanies, and the lack of trained personnel within the Romani population to serve as administrators and educators. The Reagan administration (1981–89) severely curtailed minority funding, blocking the Texas Proposal just weeks before it may have become a reality (see Appendix 1 of this paper); the Hopwood Decision which brought an end to affirmative action (1997) has further ensured that federal and municipal funds for parochial schools are out of reach.

Some classes have been created informally in different cities attached to the Charismatic Christian ('Born Again') churches which have proliferated since the 1970s. While Romani community life is shrinking in terms of numbers because of changes in family structure and distribution, Gypsy churches are now providing locations in which Romanies still gather in considerable numbers, and on a regular basis. Indeed, this may be one overriding reason for their popularity. But such classes still lack trained teachers, or appropriate workbooks, or accreditation, and they tend to focus on literacy centred upon Bible stories in English to the exclusion of anything else.

There is a thirst for education among young Romanies, but satisfying it means making it available in an accessible and attractive way. It must hold their attention, it must be compatible with everyday life outside of the classroom, and it must be reassuring to the older generation. Ideally this means an all-Romani environment, with trained teachers who are themselves Romanies, who can not only teach various subjects but also oversee the behaviour and well-being of the students. A start has been made in New York with the informal weekly classes organised and run by Gregory Dufunia Kwiek, significantly a *themengo* Rom, that is, from a European rather than American-born family. American Vlax Romanies came here following emancipation from slavery, and have not experienced the Holocaust and other events in Europe which have politicised and educated European Romanies.

The New Wave Romanies are already bringing innovation with them, but the extent to which it will spread into the American Romani population remains to be seen. A greater sense of ethnic unity, bringing all Romani populations to an understanding and acceptance of shared origins and unity, is itself something which will have to be learnt in the classroom.

Appendix 1: The Texas Proposal
(Hancock, 1975: 47–8)

1. That a school be established for Romani children in Texas, up to the age of *ca* 15 years, with adult classes also made available if required. The school would be known as *E Romani Skola and'o Teksas*.

2. That, in view of the nature of the distribution of the Romani population in Texas, this school take the form of a bus or buses equipped as travelling classrooms.

3. That the school's jurisdiction be restricted to serving an area which encompasses Houston, San Antonio, Dallas/Fort Worth, Waco, Austin, Temple and Bryan.

4. That, whenever possible, Romani teachers be trained to conduct this class or these classes.

5. That all subjects taught meet with the approval of the Kris (Tribunal) and that they not run counter to Romani culture and values, or be ultimately assimilationist in content.

6. That such subjects include:
   (i) Literacy and writing skills in English and Romani;
   (ii) Basic mathematical skills;
   (iii) History of the Romani people;
   (iv) History, culture and laws of the US.

7. That because of frequent earlier instances of failure in establishing Romani schools elsewhere in the country, a pilot project be instituted to ascertain the potential success of such a venture.

8. That a bi-lingual primer, or series of primers initially be compiled, and a small group of children work with these primers, before proceeding to a more far-reaching plan.

9. That a meeting be arranged to discuss the content and applicability of such a teaching aid, and that such funds as may be required be made available for the preparation of same, the amount of such funds being determined at this meeting.

10. That in the event of the pilot project's being successful, proposals one through six above be implemented.

Introduction to Section Four:
Image

The Roma have endured the dubious distinction of being the most misunderstood people in history. Almost every aspect of Romani culture has been perceived by outsiders through a lens coloured by prejudice and misinformation. Even the names by which they are called attest to a lack of understanding of the Roma. The English name 'Gypsy' and the Spanish '*Gitano*', for example, derive from a misconception that the Roma originated in Egypt. More ominously, a coincidental similarity of the Romani word for God, *devel*, to the word 'devil' has fuelled suspicion that the Roma are devil-worshippers. This is all the more tragic because the word *devel* is in fact cognate with the word for God in many European languages, and is related to words such as 'divine' and 'deity'.

Throughout history, Roma have been subjects or subalterns. Lacking a homeland of their own, they have been the/an Other in every land they have lived in. The image of a 'Gypsy', then, has been shaped more by outsiders than by the Roma themselves, and has been subject to much manipulation and distortion, based as often on malice as on ignorance and inertia. A caricatural image of the Roma has been integrated into a culture of oppression on the part of the larger society, and one of mute acquiescence by the Roma. To break this vicious circle, it is of utmost importance that the Roma reclaim agency in formulating their own self-image, and lead non-Roma to a just appreciation of their identity.

In this section, Ian attempts this monumental task, beginning with the chapter *Duty and beauty, possession and truth: the claim of lexical impoverishment as control*. Ian surveys the literature about the Roma produced in the course of a century by writers, including linguists and criminologists, scholars and lay writers. He documents the persistent claim that the Roma lack words for such concepts, routine and commonplace in the 'civilised world', as *duty* and *beauty,* with the implication that the Roma simply do not understand these things. It is insinuated or even blatantly claimed that the poverty of the Roma's lexicon is a reflection of the poverty of their thought and culture. These ideas are common to all cultures, and so in claiming that the Roma lack them, the very *humanity* of the Roma is denied. These claims are plainly false. Since the truth could have been easily determined by consulting members of Romani society, one can only conclude that the writers in question have no knowledge of the subject at first hand.

George Borrow's Romani introduces the reader to a writer, raconteur and linguist whose malefic influence has loomed over Romani Studies for a century and a half. Ian pays tribute to Borrow's very considerable literary and even linguistic skills, but is critical of his pronouncements about the one language for which he is best remembered. Borrow had a penchant for embellishment and creativity, and wrote for a readership that most definitely did not include the 'gypsies', whom he is said to have both 'despised and intensely loved'. Borrow's immense prestige as a linguist prevented a widespread recognition of the fact that he mixed Romani dialects recklessly and also made up his own linguistic evidence, which misled scholars who took his academic writings seriously. His sensational popular writings, on the other hand, have left a legacy of prejudices which Roma activists now struggle to dispel.

The concocters: creating fake Romani culture is an overview of attempts that have been made by outsiders to shape the image of the Roma. It lays bare some of the motivations that drive people to speak about the Roma, or on behalf of the Roma instead of letting the Roma speak for themselves. The concocters include such diverse types as writers seeking exotic characters for their plays, or zealous policemen engaged in personal missions to fight organised crime, or folklorists in search of a thesis, or peddlers of erotica operating discreetly behind a website. The concoctions are not necessarily deliberate: for instance, a linguist who was trying to learn the Romani word for 'glass', recorded the word for 'window'. On the other hand, another linguist who found lexicography to be more demanding a task than he expected, decided that it must be the result of the average Gypsy's stupidity. Ian skilfully exposes several of these concocters by highlighting logical contradictions in their writings (such as putting British Romani words into the mouths of Roma who are supposed to be from the Continent), or by a meticulous search for original sources which uncovers trails of misquotations and misunderstandings.

Gypsy Mafia, Romani saints: the racial profiling of Romani Americans is a document in support of a person (identified only by a pseudonym) who has been the victim of racial profiling by the police. In this paper, Ian exposes a tendency on the part of the police to create a specious distinction between the words 'Gypsy' and 'Romani', analogous to the distinction between 'Mafia' and 'Italian'. This distinction has not succeeded in liberating the term 'Romani' of the unfair associations evoked by the term 'Gypsy'. This is not only because the two terms continue to be used as synonyms (although only the term Roma is deserving of that privilege), but also because the police themselves recognise a class of crimes called 'Gypsy Crimes' – a noxious term in which inheres the notion that 'gypsies' are merely deviant individuals of any background.

The last paper, *The 'gypsy' stereotype and the sexualisation of Romani women*, deals with the contentious issue of race relations and miscegenation, which erupted in extreme fashion in the twentieth century. But the ground for the racially motivated genocide had been prepared for centuries, in the form of racial stereotypes about the Roma. A number of different and sometimes mutually contradictory sources feed these racial myths. An early idea was that the Roma had unhygienic habits, and were dark simply due to dirt. A medieval belief held that darkness of skin denoted evil. During the age of slavery, the enforced social inferiority of the Roma strengthened racist attitudes. Colonial dominance reinforced feelings of white superiority, and heightened fears of 'race mixing', which was thought to be both genetically contaminating and socially disruptive. By virtue of the fact that it was forbidden, miscegenation acquired a peculiar attraction, which was exploited in literature and later in cinema. While white females were depicted as needing protection from the lustfulness of the darker races, females of coloured peoples were shown as being available to white males, or even as needing to be rescued from their own societies. A stereotypical 'gypsy' woman, who is sexually immoral and loose, who does not live in the real Romani cultural universe with its high regard for chastity and modesty, lives on in literature and at Disneyland.

CHAPTER TEN

Duty and beauty, possession and truth: the claim of lexical impoverishment as control

Language is essentially the control of thought. It becomes impossible for us to direct our future until we control our language. The sense of language is in precision of vocabulary and structure for a particular social context. (Asante, 1988: 31)

The manipulation by societies in power of the identities of subordinate groups is achieved in many ways. One such way is through discriminatory legislation, such as that enacted against the Romani people in almost every land, including the US. Another is through media representation, both factual and fictional. This last category, the portrayal of 'Gypsies' in poetry, film and novels, is the most effective in establishing such negative feelings because they are absorbed subliminally by children, at a time when they are most susceptible to acquiring the attitudes of mainstream society. Apart from descriptions of Romani people and their life, which are legion, the Romani language has also been the target of comment, invariably worded as fact rather than supposition. In his *Tales of the Real Gypsy*, Paul Kester gives his readers those 'real' facts about it (1897: 305):

> The Gypsies, like the birds and all wild things, have a language of their own, which is apart from the language of those among whom they dwell … the Gypsy['s] … language is deep and warm and full of the charm of the out-of-doors world, the scent of the clover and the ripple of streams and the rush of the wind and the storm. For the Rommany speech is full of

Originally published as 'Duty and beauty, possession and truth: lexical impoverishment as control', in Thomas Acton and Gary Mundy (eds), *Romani culture and Gypsy identity* (University of Hertfordshire Press, Hatfield, 1997), pp. 182–9.

all this, and although the Gypsy has few traditions, his rich mother tongue must embalm in each word a thousand associations that thrill in the soul.

Kester was not a linguist, and it is easy to see how he was able to allow his fantasies about the Romani people to shape his preconceptions of the language. Doris Duncan, however, presumably is, and can claim no such excuse. Writing seventy years later in a journal of popular linguistics, she made the following observations (1969: 42),

> All authentic gypsy [*sic*] communication is, and must be, oral. As they settle for a time in a new country, they acquire some of that country's words and incorporate them into *Roum*, more popularly called Romany. It is believed that the *Roum* language began as a very small one, concerned with the family, the tribe, the horses and herd, words required for a simple existence. It must be very old, for *Roum* is highly idiomatic, and the complication of verbs and genders is endless. There is no way to write it except phonetically, and some sounds of the gypsy tongue simply defy our twenty-six letter alphabet ... *Roum* is a disorderly language, and must be learned phrase by phrase. Even the syntax differs from one occasion to another. Verbs are very difficult ... no one can explain why the verb changes so radically. A major problem is that no gypsy really knows what a verb is, and it wouldn't matter anyway if he did, because this is the way it must be said. The idiom is paramount in *Roum* and cannot be changed.

Duncan is right in maintaining that Romani has adopted words from those with whom its speakers have come in contact – this is a natural process affecting all languages, and one which has caused English, for example, to lose nearly three-quarters of its original Anglo-Saxon lexicon by dictionary count. But Bayle St John couldn't simply discuss this phenomenon as lexical adoption when referring to Romani (1853: 141), which, he said 'contains traces of an original character, [but which] is encrusted, as it were, with words borrowed – it might be more appropriate to say stolen – from a dozen different dialects'.

A number of authors have claimed that because of our character as a people, we lack certain virtues, and that this is reflected in our Romani language which cannot even express them. Those which have been discussed by different writers include 'duty', 'possession', 'truth', 'beautiful', 'read', 'write', 'time', 'danger', 'warmth', 'quiet', 'God', 'soul' and 'immortality'. How negatively must the non-Gypsy world regard our people, to think that we cannot express such basic human concepts and skills, or that we don't even know the difference between good and evil!   Eleanor Smith (1943: 59) wrote that 'in the gypsy language the words "divine" and "devilish" are the same'. On a *Geraldo Rivera Show* which dealt with Gypsy confidence crimes broadcast on CBS Television in April 1990, one invited 'Gypsy expert', former Associate Professor John Dowling of Marquette University in Wisconsin, asserted in all seriousness that 'Gypsies don't know the difference between right and wrong, like the rest of us' – a man who has never met a Romani and whose qualifications originate with statements such as Eleanor Smith's.

Jószef Vekerdi, in his intensely racist article (1988: 15), said,

> The vocabulary of all Gypsy languages is astonishingly poor … even such simple phenomena as names of flowers, trees, bushes, birds are completely absent in all Gypsy idioms; and, there are no Gypsy words (even loan-words) for lightning, thunder, shower, storm, cloud, mist, fog, frost, dew.

There are of course many words for flora and fauna; far too many to list here. 'Lightning' is *strafin,* 'thunder' is *rrondjeto* or *vrontipe,* 'shower' is *brišindorro,* 'storm' is *furtuna,* 'cloud' is *nuvero,* 'mist' is *maglica,* 'fog' is *bruma,* 'frost' is *morrozo* or *paho* and 'dew' is *drosin* or *projni.*

Even efforts on the part of Romanies to stop the use of the word 'Gypsy' (or more often 'gypsy') when it is used to characterise wildness or wandering or cheating are met with resistance. The word was banned from use in any further official Roma-related documentation at our First World Congress in London in 1971 by Roma themselves, but many non-Roma have decided that they will continue to use it anyway. *The New York Times'* Will Shortz, for example, defended the inclusion of *gyp* for 'cheat' in his crossword puzzle dictionary because 'it is only part of the word gypsy' (letter received dated 21 August 1996); but then so is *Jap* for a Japanese, a word he *doesn't* include in his dictionary. In response to a letter objecting to her stereotyped use of the phrase 'professional gypsy' to refer to anyone having to leave and seek new employment at a moment's notice, Deborah Morse-Kahn (2007: 1) defended her choice by stating that 'the Romani peoples are well known' to her, and by referring to the definition of 'gypsy' in three separate dictionaries. If Roma had compiled those dictionaries, of course, the definitions would have been quite different. Significantly, she did not include the one found in the *Encarta World English Dictionary*, which lists *Gypsy* as 'an offensive term for a member of the Romani people' (1999: 800).

Over a century ago, Adriano Colocci – taking Grellmann as his cue – introduced a notion which has since become a part of gypsilorist folk wisdom. In his extensive discussion of the Romani people in his 421-page book *The Gypsies*, he maintained that Romanies 'have no more conception of property than of duty; "I have" is as foreign to them as "I ought"' (Colocci, 1889: 156). Citing Colocci as his source, Italian criminologist Cesare Lombroso elaborated upon the statement in his widely used book on Gypsies as a criminal race, and made the jump from concept to actual language, by saying that 'The word *ought* does not exist in the Gypsy language. The verb to *have* is almost forgotten by the European Gypsies, and is unknown to the Gypsies of Asia' (Lombroso, 1918: 41).

In 1928, Konrad Bercovici, probably also using Colocci but not acknowledging any source, repeated this notion on the first page (and again on the third page) of his book *The Story of the Gypsies*, and also interpreted the original observation linguistically, saying, 'I am attempting to unravel the story of a people whose vocabulary lacks the words for both "duty" and "possession" (1928: 1, 3). He goes on to rationalise this by explaining that 'what we own possesses us, jails us'. This was then picked up from Bercovici shortly afterwards by Erich von Stroheim who, in his racist Gypsy novel *Paprika*, told his readers that 'The Gypsy mind is timeless. The Gypsy tongue has no words to signify duty or possession, qualities that are like roots, holding civilised people fast in the soil' (von Stroheim, 1935: 12).

Fifteen years later, the anonymous author of an article in *Coronet Magazine* plagiarised and reworded the same statement:

> Even today, there are two important English words for which the Gypsy vocabulary has no known equivalent, and for which the Gypsy people have never exhibited any desire or need. One of them is the word 'duty', the other is 'possession'. (Anonymous, 1950b: 126)

In a 1962 reissue of Leland's *Gypsy Sorcery and Fortune Telling*, Margery Silver wrote in her introduction to that edition:

> [In Germany], where they had been chronically subjected to the most relentless and brutal oppression of their European experience since their

first appearance in 1417, five hundred thousand 'sons of Egypt' – whose vocabulary a recent writer has described as 'lacking two words: "duty" and "possession" – died in the Nazi ovens beside six million sons of Jacob, whose history was founded on just those concepts, duty to God and possession of his law. (Leland, 1962: xx)

Five years after that, in perhaps the most invidious way of all since the plagiarism has been recast in such a way as to suggest an actual verbatim interview, the statement turns up again in an article by Marie Wynn Clarke, predictably entitled *Vanishing Vagabonds*: 'A young Gypsy wife said "there is no word in our language for 'duty' or 'possession', but I'm afraid there will be soon"' (Clarke, 1967: 210).

In her introduction to the 1983 edition of Bercovici's *Gypsies: Their Life, Lore and Legends*, Elizabeth Congdon Kovanen repeats this yet again, although adding the suggestion that because of this, Gypsies themselves are responsible for the discrimination against them:

> The Gypsy vocabulary lacks the words 'duty' and 'possession'. This reflects their unwillingness to settle down, live in houses, obey the law, educate their children, be employed by others – and helps to explain their almost universal persecution. (Bercovici, 1983: *viij*)

The eighth repetition of this strange idea is found in a novel by Piers Anthony, *Being a Green Mother*. The fact that the words 'Gypsies! … Beware – they steal children!' appear at the very first mention of the Romani characters when they are introduced (1988: 18) is an indication of the depiction of Roma throughout the rest of the book. The author describes someone's attempt to learn Romani, but who 'discovered that the Gypsy language had no words for what in her own were rendered as "duty" and "possession". This was because these concepts were foreign to the Gypsy nature' (Anthony, 1988: 39).

Next we find the statement turning up in Roger Moreau's *The Rom*:

> One thing the Romani *chib* never acquired, though, was a future tense. Maybe this was a reflection of their attitude to life? . . . Neither is there the verb 'to have' or a word for 'possession' in Romanes, which I suppose makes sense if you don't happen to own anything. (Moreau, 1995: 127–8)

The tenth is found in Agnes Vranckx' *Declaration of a Lost People*, where she states that 'the words "possession" and "submission" did not exist in Romani' (Anisha, 1997: 18–19). The eleventh and most recent, although no doubt not the last, of these repetitions is in an online history of Roma by Ionas Aurelian Rus of Rutgers University, posted in 2007:

> Europeans regard 'private property' as sacrosanct, whereas gypsies do not have a word for 'possess,' which gives rise to two incompatible ways of life and a continual problem of gypsies being regarded as 'thieves' from the European's view.[17]

Another word which Romani has been said to lack is 'truth', as maintained by Jim Phelan, author of many books about Romanichals in which he describes his intimate life with British Travellers, and in which he claims to have been 'long ago admitted to the brotherhood'. In his book *Waggon-Wheels* he says 'There is no word for "truth" in the romani [*sic*] language. There is the crux of the matter' (1951: 81).

The concept 'beautiful' is denied in the language in Virginia Woolf's novel *Orlando*: 'One evening, when they were all sitting around the camp fire and the sunset was blazing over the Thessalian hills, Orlando exclaimed "how good to eat!" The gipsies have no word for 'beautiful'. This is the nearest.' (1956: 142).

In their *American Cyclopaedia* entry on Romanies, authors Ripley and Dana (1873–76: 8, 357) write that we are a people with 'few redeeming characteristics [who are …] treacherous, cowardly, revengeful and cruel', and who have 'little or no religious belief and no word in [their] language to signify God, the soul, or immortality'.

About the language, and also referring to religion, the nineteenth-century evangelist George Smith, himself of Romani descent, although evidently ashamed of the fact, said,

> There is certainly nothing very elevating about [Romani]. Worldliness, sensuality and devilism are things helped forward by their gibberish. Words dealing with honesty, uprightness, fidelity, industry, religion, cleanliness and love are very sparse. (1880: 196)

Another claim to a lack of certain basic human responses or skills is found in Isabel Fonseca's *Bury Me Standing: The Gypsies and their Journey*, where she maintains that there are no words in Romani for 'read' and 'write'. Elsewhere in the same book she states that there are no words for 'time', 'danger', 'warmth' or 'quiet' either, because these are foreign concepts for us (1996: 98). Even before the book reached the bookstores, reviewers were accepting and repeating these false assumptions: '[the Gypsy's] is a world ... where there are no words for "time" (or for "danger," "warmth" or "quiet") ... where no day is different from any other' (Kobak, 1995: 14).

The assumption that the Romani way of life is evidence of some kind of evolutionary arrested development that accounts for an inherent disregard for ownership – and by implication justifies a 'license to steal' as Marlock and Dowling (1994) call it – has found its way into at least one standard textbook on anthropology at my own university. In words recalling those of Charles Davenport half a century before him (1915: 10–11), Cyril Dean Darlington wrote in 1969 that,

> [T]he gipsy communities which eventually wandered into Europe ... still betray the evidence of their paleolithic ancestry ... the lack of interest in property or understanding of ownership. For this reason, many of them are regarded by settled societies as criminal tribes or castes. (1969: 364)

One individual who actually presents himself as a Romani and as a Romani speaker (he is neither) is Eugene Hütz of the band *Gogol Bordello*. He told National Public Radio (in an interview on 15 August 2007) that our language has the same word for *yesterday* and *tomorrow* – a notion picked up from reading George Borrow.

The idea that we live 'only for today', and that any other days mean nothing, to the extent that both 'yesterday' and 'tomorrow' are translated by the same word in our language is a fanciful stereotype often repeated in books by *gadže* about 'Gypsies', but it is not true. In all dialects – including those spoken in the Ukraine where Mr Hütz is from – 'yesterday', 'today' and 'tomorrow' are three distinctly different words; some dialects even include separate words for 'the day after tomorrow' and 'the day before yesterday'. It is foolish to imagine that any human group is unable to express the difference linguistically between yesterday and tomorrow, or that the inability to do so is, as he claimed, 'important for the Gypsy psychology'. No Romani would say such a thing. What has been misunderstood as meaning both 'yesterday' and 'tomorrow' is the word *taisa* (with variants) which means 'morning' (from the Greek ταχια 'morning'). The word is then modified with other words if necessary according to dialect in order to specify which morning or day is meant.

Like Bayle St John, who saw lexical *thefts* as a more appropriate label than lexical *adoptions* in his discussion of the non-native element in the Romani vocabulary, none of the above writers sufficiently overcame his or her stereotypical preconceptions of Gypsies or of what he or she *expected* of the language, to ask a Gypsy whether these words existed, or even to consult a Romani dictionary, of which dozens exist. For a people who were enslaved in the Romanian principalities for five and a half centuries, a people whose lives were an interminable succession of duties and obligations, and for whom possessions were a precious thing, it should not be surprising that there are in fact many words for these two concepts. For 'duty' there are, in the various dialects, the words *musajipé, vója, vužulimós, udjilútno, udjilipé, kandipé, slúžba, kandimós, thoximós* and *vudjlipé*; for 'possession' there are *májtko, aračimáta, sersámo, trjábo, butjí, aparáti, kóla, prámi, djéla, djélica, joságo, istarimáta, ičarimós, astarimós* and *theripé*. The words for 'truth' include *tačipén, čačimós, vortimó, siguripé* and others, while 'beautiful' is *šukár, múndro, rínkeno, jakhaló, orčíri, pakváro* and so on in the various dialects, 'tomorrow' is *tehara*, while 'read' is *djin-* or *gin-* or *čit-* or *giláb-* or *drab-*, 'write' is *ram-* or *jazd-* or *lekh-* or *pišú-* or *pisát-* or *čet-* or *škur-* or *skrij-* or *čhin-*. 'Time' is variously translated by *vaxt, vákti, vrjámja* or *čéros*, 'danger' by *strážno*, 'warmth' by *tatičosimós* or *táblipen* and 'quiet' by *míro* or *mirnimós*. The word for 'God' is *Devel*, 'soul' is *dji* or *ogi* or *obúro* or *dúxo* and 'immortality' is *bimerimasko*; although in truth the fallacy of such a belief, that such words don't exist in our language, should scarcely need refuting.

Many of these words come from the ancient Sanskrit stock of the language, while others, like *prámi* or *míro*, have been adopted from Greek and Slavic. Isabel Fonseca concedes in her book that Romani had to adopt the words for 'read' and 'write' from other languages, but apparently doesn't recognise that English, too, has had to borrow most of its lexicon from other languages (incidentally, the word for 'read' is of native Sanskrit origin in Romani). Indeed, a dictionary count of English word origins indicates that only 28 per cent of that language is traceable to its original Anglo-Saxon stock; should we assume from that, therefore, that the concepts of 'duty', 'possession', 'beauty', 'quiet', 'danger' and so on, were foreign to the English, since all of these words have been 'stolen' from French? Furthermore, English also 'lacks' a future tense, in the sense meant by Moreau, but constructs it, just as Romani does, with a word which expresses the intention or desire to undertake the action ('will' or 'shall'; in Romani, *ka(m)*). There is clearly a double standard operating for these writers.

The blind repetition of someone's statement without checking the original source is a mark of shoddy scholarship; perhaps it is felt that less rigour is needed in Romani Studies than in other areas of research. A list of writers who, one after the other, have quoted the Romani proverb about not being able to sit on two horses with one backside, could also be assembled – all traceable without acknowledgement to Jan Yoors' book *The Gypsies* (1967), or the story about the Gypsy in jail who weeps for his jailer who must stay there, or the story of the nails used to crucify Jesus. Victorian writers unashamedly lifted material from each other too. These descriptions of the Gypsy children on the Romanian slave estates are far too similar to be coincidental, and appeared in the British and American press at the time that the fictionalised image of the Gypsy was taking shape, although its inspiration seems to be traceable to a German source dating from 1841:

> The children are seldom provided with clothing before they are ten years old. This is especially true of the wandering Gypsies … they find every kind of meat good: dogs, cats, rats, mice and even sick farm animals are eaten by them. (Brockhaus, 1841: 801)

In the same year, George Borrow too, described Gypsies as 'a raging rabble of fierce and animal propensities, men and women and children, some of them of nearly negro blackness, most of them half naked; some, especially the children, entirely so' (1841: 124).

Collie (1982: 250) commented that it was 'difficult to determine' whether Borrow had merely copied this from a pre-existing work, or whether he based it on something actually seen. In British literature just a few years later, and more clearly attributable to Brockhaus, we find,

> The children wear no clothes until the age of ten or twelve years; and resemble imps rather than human beings as they run beside the carriage of the traveller shrieking for alms, with their long matted hair flying in the wind, and their black limbs shining in the light. (Pardoe, 1848(i): 168)

> The children go naked up to the age of ten or twelve, and whole swarms of girls and boys may sometimes be seen rolling about together in the dust or mud in summer, in the water or snow in winter, like so many black worms. (St John, 1853: 140)

> The children to the age of ten or twelve, are in a complete state of nudity, but the men and women, the latter offering frequently the most symmetrical form and feminine beauty, have a rude clothing. (Gardner, 1857: 58)

In its 8 January 1992 issue, *The New York Times* published the results of a public opinion poll surveying national negative attitudes to fifty-eight different racial and ethnic populations in the US over a twenty-five year period. For the entire quarter-century, 'Gypsies' were ranked at the very bottom of the list, the most discriminated-against minority in the eyes of the general population. Since most *gadže* have no personal or social contact with the Romani population, such attitudes can only be based upon how we are presented in literature. The persistent, relentless portrayal of Romanies as rootless, lawless, immoral, childlike thieves, as a people for whom the basic human concepts of truth and beauty, obligation and ownership do not exist, who don't know right from wrong and who are ignorant of danger and never seek warmth or peace or quiet, is attributable to such individuals as Colocci, Lombroso, Bercovici, von Stroheim, Silver, Clarke, Kovanen, Dowling, Smith, Anthony, Woolf, Phelan, Fonseca, Moreau, Ehrlich and others, whose investment in defining our character will ensure that anti-Gypsy prejudice will remain firmly a part of Euro-American racist attitudes.

CHAPTER ELEVEN

George Borrow's Romani

Introduction

George Borrow (1803–81) has stood as the acknowledged source of inspiration for countless Romophiles (as well as Romophobes) ever since his literary heyday in the nineteenth century; in fact Brian Vesey-Fitzgerald saw himself as quite 'unfashionable' (1944: x) because he was one of the few who *didn't* make his 'first acquaintance with [Gypsies] in the pages of George Borrow'. From Prosper Merimée, who 'drew from Borrow his inspiration for Carmen' (Ridler, 1996: 55), to criminologist Detective Samuel Haines whose monograph on American Gypsy crime relied largely on the '*Romano La Volil*' (*sic*; 1989: 2), George Borrow's writings have stimulated the creative muse for innumerable writers about Gypsies for more than a century and a half.

Borrow spent the greater part of his life studying languages, a love which was kindled while he was a boy learning Latin and Greek at Norwich Grammar School, and he was already able to translate some twenty languages as diverse as Armenian and Middle Welsh 'with facility and elegance' by the end of his teen years (Ridler, 1996: 451–3). By the time of his death at the age of seventy-eight, he had dealt in greater or lesser detail with eighty more (1996: 427).

As one of two sons of a military family, he moved about England with his father's regiment and developed a love for the British countryside

Originally published in Yaron Matras, Peter Bakker and Hristo Kyuchukov (eds), *The typology and dialectology of Romani* (John Benjamins, Amsterdam and Philadelphia, 1997), pp. 199ff. Reprinted with kind permission from John Benjamins Publishing Company, Amsterdam/Philadelphia. [www.benjamins.com].

and its inhabitants later reflected so elegantly throughout his writings. So strong indeed was the lure of rural England that instead of pursuing the legal education his father had intended for him, he left his parents to take up with Traveller families on the roads, acquiring a taste for the Romani language which he subsequently took with him to Spain, Hungary, Romania, Russia and elsewhere.

Few figures in Romani Studies have been so roundly praised nor yet so heartily criticised as George Borrow, or have prompted such extremes of reaction. His all-consuming interest in Gypsies condemned him to serve as a prime example of 'feebly inhibited genetic development' in a report by the Director of the US Department of Experimental Evolution (Davenport, 1915: 23) for example, while on the other hand John Sampson, the greatest scholar of Romani ever to have lived, was moved to dedicate his monumental grammar of Welsh Romani to Borrow. His inscription, in Devanagari script, reads *ki Borrow, kai but beršendi dudyerdas m'o drom akai, ta akana asala 'pre mande peske brišindeskeriate* ('to Borrow, who for many years lit my way here, and who now smiles at me from his rainbow', 1926: *iv*).[18] Yet his contemporary Laura Smith wrote (1889: 134) that his book was 'most incomprehensible' and 'could content no one [because] it hovers between romance and reality, and can have done but little towards establishing a more friendly feeling between Gorgios and Romanies'. A century later Audrey Shields, in her study of the Gypsy stereotype in Victorian literature, believed that Borrow's idealisation 'did as much harm as writers who denigrated Gypsies' (1993: 167), a sentiment echoing that of British Member of Parliament, John Wells, one of the few government representatives sympathetic to the Romani situation, who claimed that 'George Borrow has done more harm to the cause of those of us who wish the Gypsy community well than almost anyone else' (quoted in Reid, 1962: 37).[19] John Geipel, on the other hand, more recently lauded him as the 'savant … who provided posterity with its largest single source of information on the Indian roots of the "secret" language of the gitanos' (1995: 112). That he has prompted such widely differing responses probably accounts for the fact that the study of the man and his life remains so intriguing to this day; and it was his involvement with the Romani people and language in particular which has left the most indelible mark.

George Borrow and the Romani language

Three features in particular characterise George Borrow's relationship with Romani: firstly, that his knowledge of its structure was surprisingly poor, given his acquaintance with so many other languages; secondly, that he freely mixed dialects, and thirdly, that he was not above creating lexical entries and grammatical forms of his own. Behlmer (1985: 241) criticised both Borrow's knowledge of English Romani and Spanish Romani, saying that his *Romano Lavo-Lil* was 'shot through with absolutely ludicrous errors in etymology', while Francis Hindes Groome (1900: 5) wrote '[t]he meagreness of his knowledge of the Anglo-Gypsy dialect came out in his *Word Book of the Romany*'.

True to his style, Borrow spared no pains in cloaking the origins of Gypsies and the Romani language in mystery, a mystification which in fact was forced, at least in one respect, for he was aware of the Indian identity of the Roma by the time that he published his work *The Zincali* in 1841, being already familiar with the works of Grellmann, Whiter, Marsden and Richardson, which last work also contains the vocabulary collected by Bryant. He had even seen Andrew Boorde's book, which he mentions in *The Romany Rye* – although he seems to have missed the Romani it contained. So in the second volume of *The Zincali* (1841: 104) he stated quite plainly that 'Gypsies ... are the descendants of a tribe of Hindus, who, for some particular reason, had abandoned their native country'.

Despite already being aware of this, he asked in *Lavengro*, published ten years later in 1851 (in Chapter 17), 'Rommany Chals! ... whence did they come originally? ah! there is the difficulty'; and the concluding statement of *The Romany Rye*, which appeared six years later in 1857, clearly gives the impression that the Indian connection had only at that moment occurred to him: '"I shouldn't wonder," said I as I proceeded rapidly along a broad causeway, in the direction of the east, "if Mr Petulengro and Tawno Chickno came originally from India. I think I'll go there."'

Nowhere in those two books is the Sanskrit origin of Romani discussed, although there and elsewhere Borrow does compare other languages with Sanskrit, for example Welsh, in *Wild Wales* (1862: 599–600). Even in the *Lavo-Lil* (1874: 4), his final work, he did not elaborate upon his observation that 'the Gypsy language ... [is]

decidedly of Indian origin, being connected with the Sanscrit or some other Indian dialect', although he did wonder in *Lavengro* (p. 316) whether it was perhaps 'the mother of all languages in the world'. Angus Fraser suggested to me that this notion may have had its origin in Whiter (1800: *xxvij*; see also Grosvenor, 1908; Fraser, 1995; and Ridler, 1996), who himself believed that Romani 'as it is now spoken, may probably be considered as the most ancient form of Speech, which is at present extant in the world', and whom he toasts in the same book in Chapter 24.[20]

Borrow's knowledge of Romani

Because of his penchant for embellishment, and because so many of his samples are transparently of his own creation (although he was by no means such a sprucer as was his contemporary Leland), it would be useful to ascertain the extent of his knowledge of Romani, as well as the degree of its accuracy.

Perhaps his first exposure to it took place according to his own account about 1810, when he was seven years old, and when he met Jasper and his family for the first time. The words he heard during that initial encounter were *bengui* 'devil', *tawny* 'young', *sap* 'snake', *sap-engro* 'snake-charmer', *Romans* [*sic*] 'Gypsies', *gorgeous* 'non-Gypsy', and the non-Romani Cant word *mumper*. Although he didn't recognise the language being spoken around him, he knew enough to say "it wasn't French". He was not to meet Jasper again after this for nearly ten years.

Although this episode was described in *Lavengro*, which was published in 1851, it was not the first time that Borrow had introduced Jasper, whom he had already mentioned ten years before in an appendix to the second volume of the second edition of *The Zincali*. In those pages he provided vocabularies and texts in British Romani, and compared it with the dialects spoken in both Spain and Hungary. Jasper Petulengro and his brother Tawno Tickno were, in real life, Ambrose and Faden Smith; but changing the names of people and places, or sometimes hiding them behind initials, was part of Borrow's mystifying style. Furthermore, while Jasper is presented in the stories as being older than George Borrow, he was in fact one year younger.[21]

Borrow visited Russia in 1833 when he was thirty, and remained there for two years. After a period of time spent back in England, he left again for Spain, and between 1836 and 1840 made three visits to that country. In 1844, he took an extended trip through Hungary and Romania to Turkey, in each place seeking out Romanies and collecting linguistic material from them. It was clear that he recognised the linguistic unity of Romani, thinking of it as one language consisting of many dialects differing by more or less retention of the original vocabulary and original grammar. Perhaps this is why he felt at liberty to mix them so freely, although it is more likely that he in fact believed that his readers would be unable to distinguish one dialect from another. Thus in *Wild Wales* (Chapter 98) he had Romanichals speaking Hungarian Romani, and elsewhere he put Spanish Romani in the mouths of Transylvanian Romanies (see the entries *busno* and *errai* in Winstedt, 1952), and British Romanichals; the very first Romani word in *Lavengro, bengui*, in fact, has the Spanish Caló spelling and pronunciation rather than the British Romani *beng*. This means, of course, that he was not reporting accurately, which seriously diminishes the value of his material – referred to by Thomas Acton (in personal correspondence) as 'deeply unauthentic' – for Romanologists, a number of whom in the nineteenth century based their own work at least partially upon it. Smart and Crofton remarked upon this in their own book, referring to 'the intrinsic evidence in his writings that many of his words have been procured from various and widespread sources' (1875: *xij*). This is evidenced by the fact that well over half of the approximately 120 words they give as unattested in English Romani (1875: 157–63) are listed as having originated in the works of Borrow. Knapp, his biographer, called it 'a kind of philologico-literary gazpacho' (1899: 23).

The creation of Romanies and Romani

In a paper I wrote some years ago (see this volume, at Chapter 3), I made reference to Douglas' notion of 'Bongo-Bongoism', the practice of some scholars of faking or misrepresenting data with the assumption that their audience knew nothing about the topic, and was therefore not in a position to challenge their claims. Borrow was especially guilty of this, although he should not be judged too harshly for that. Approaching his work on Romani as linguists may be frustrating and disappointing, or even amusing sometimes, but coming to it from the point of view of the literary critic is something else entirely. Borrow's writings are widely enjoyed precisely for their ponderous and self-involved style; Croley (1996: 186) calls it 'precious'. He had a particular fondness for this, and modelled his prose upon the numerous eighteenth century works his library contained. He was, after all, writing for a particular audience. Helyear sums this up very well when she says (1972: 82) that Borrow 'complied, consciously or not, with the requirements of Victorian society, to the detriment of realism. He obviously sought literary success, and consequently had to satisfy his public's tastes and suit its intellectual esthetics.'

Nemeth (2002: 230) adds to this: 'Victorian times were notably pretentious and lacking in originality, and it is against the inertia in this backdrop that Borrow's audacious actions involving Gypsies seem to stand out.' Victorian readers relished being titillated by tales of the savage and the exotic in the Sunday afternoon safety of their drawing rooms, and Borrow's writings typified very well the popular middle class literature of the period. In fact, he tended to overdo it, and was criticised in the press for being too prone to philosophising and flights of moralistic fancy. In retrospect, we might reproach Borrow for presenting the Romani population in too romanticised and idealised a light – Helyear points out that nowhere does he 'drop a single hint about the hardship of their life', instead sustaining the more attractive image of 'picturesque outsider'. Like Frederick Ackerly, whose only observation in his review of Potra's volume on the enslavement of Gypsies in Romania (1942: 69–71) was that it was a pleasure and a delight to read and that it gave him a chance to practice his Romanian, Borrow too had nothing to say about that ultimate violation of humanity. Although he visited Romania while slavery was still everywhere in effect, for example, he was not moved sufficiently to comment upon it:

> I visited Wallachia with the express purpose of discoursing with the Gypsies, many of whom I found wandering about, the men supporting themselves by smithery, and the women by telling fortunes, but the generality [were] employed in the brick-fields making bricks like the Ishmaelites of old in Egypt. (Knapp, 1899: ii: 44).

Although *Lavengro* and *The Romany Rye* were not especially well-received at the time of their publication, and Shields (1993: 113) believed that in particular it was the 'long, virulent diatribe against Scott and Catholics ... that readers found excessive', and that the 'picaresque style, lacking moral earnestness, was less fashionable than it had been in the previous century', they nevertheless had a singular effect upon both contemporary and later writers. Borrow's style was very cleverly parodied in an article in the *Pall Mall Magazine* by Sir Arthur Conan Doyle of Sherlock Holmes fame, in an article entitled *Borrow-ed Scenes* (Conan Doyle, 1913).

Lavengro appeared in 1851, the year of the Great Exhibition in London, when the British Empire was enjoying the height of its power on every continent. Meyers noted (1966: 40) that Borrow's books were 'intensely nationalistic'. *The Romany Rye* was published in 1857, only two years after the appearance of Gobineau's *Essay On the Inequality of the Human Races* and two years before Darwin's equally influential *Origin of the Species*. Colonialism and new ideas about evolution and racial superiority stimulated a particular interest in foreign, and especially non-Western, peoples and cultures. Readers' imaginations did not need to be transported to Borneo or Zululand or Nepal, when this dark and mysterious eastern population occupied their very doorstep. The *Illustrated London News* (Anonymous, 1879: 503) drew attention to this. Describing a Gypsy community 'within an hour's walk of the royal palace', it urged 'a few serious reflections upon social contrasts at the centre and capital of the mighty British nation, which takes upon itself the correction of every savage tribe in South and West Africa and Central Asia'.

Ideas about these 'savage tribes' and the superiority of the colonising powers gave rise in time to the kind of racist dogma expounded by Houston Chamberlain (1899) and specifically elaborated upon against Romanies by Alfred Dillmann (1905), in a document which laid the foundation for the National Socialists' concept of Gypsies as sub-humans *vis-à-vis* the German master race, and which later paved the way for the racial policy of ethnically cleansing the Third Reich by attempting to exterminate the entire Romani population – adopted in modified form since the Holocaust by Ceauşescu in Romania into the 1980s (Hancock, 1993: 27).

The Industrial Revolution (1730–1850) had also brought tremendous changes to urban society by the time of Victoria's reign, having created a foul and unhealthy mechanised environment vividly described in the works of Dickens and others. But Borrow's idealised Gypsies lived apart from all this and above it, noble savages untouched by civilisation, representatives of a vanishing rural era who had refused to relinquish it for the sake of progress. This has been well-discussed by Wilson (1986: 33–9). Shields (1993: 113) calls Borrow's attitude towards his Romani acquaintances 'preachy and condescending', and says that he was 'worried that their aspirations to gentility [would] corrupt them'. That the real experience of British Romanies didn't mirror the literary descriptions of it presented no dilemma, since those who obviously didn't match the idealised image were simply dismissed as being 'not real Gypsies', but mumpers, diddicais, pikeys, people with little or no Romani ancestry who got the 'True Romanies' a bad name (see in particular Mayall, 1988). Here again, the particular devaluation of individuals regarded as being genetically mixed between Gypsy and white was to re-emerge in a frightening way in Hitler's Germany half a century later.

Although many authors before Borrow's time incorporated Romani characters into their works, it was not until the appearance of George Borrow's books, as Angus Fraser states (1993: 15),

> ... that the literary and dramatic clichés received a clear and credible challenge. Borrow conveyed something of the real nature of Gypsies and their life-style, language and attitudes, and provided a picture that offered an exciting alternative to the previous hackneyed views.

But Fraser was choosing his words carefully when he referred to Borrow's exposition of '*something* of the real nature of Gypsies', for his writings are an exasperating mixture of fact and fancy, and separating the two is not easy. Borrow clearly imagined that he had some special status, reflecting what Shields has appropriately called 'the rye phenomenon' (1993: 164). For Borrow this provided something of a conflict because, as Helyear says, 'he mingled with ruffians and people of the road, but insisted upon his being [regarded nevertheless as] a scholar' (1972: 82). It might say something of his aloofness that he missed entirely learning of the existence of inflected Romani in Wales – a discovery that would have been of tremendous importance to him – despite his exploration of that country and the book resulting from it. Ken Lee brought my attention to the information in Jarman and Jarman's book *The Welsh Gypsies* (1991: 151), that,

> George Borrow missed the opportunity of hearing this language when he was in Bala, for he drank in the front room of the inn, while the local

Wood family of Gypsies drank in the rear room with the rest of the ordinary Welsh people of the town.

To be fair to Borrow, he spent only three days in Bala altogether, and there is no evidence that the Woods were in the inn while he was there, or that they were even in the district. Nevertheless, during his entire stay in Wales, he encountered Gypsies only once, and those were Boswells, from England.

Despite his rather distant behaviour, he regarded himself as a 'brother', at least in his own terms, almost certainly a self-designation just as his status as a 'rye' was. We shall never know whether his Romanichal acquaintances saw him as he saw himself, but Mrs Hearne's attempt to murder him with a poisoned cake (*Lavengro*, Chapter 71)[22] is a good indication of their general attitude. Philip Allingham (1934: 5) came to realise what seemed never to have occurred to Borrow, despite his being told repeatedly and in many ways to mind his own business: 'I decided to steal out of London as quietly and as quickly as possible and join the Gypsies. That the Gypsies would not be too keen to have me, did not then occur to me.' Paspati (1870: 30) too admitted to receiving a less than warm reception on occasion: 'Some have chased me from their tents with nasty words and gestures. Others haven't responded to my questions, continuing with their work without acknowledging my presence.'

Two more recent accounts in the same vein are Kent (1992) and Hofman (2008). This perception of Gypsies simply as sources of data, as objects of study, rather than as people with sensibilities of their own, was one characteristic of the early ryes. Describing his visit to the Baltic lands in 1908, for example, Bernard Gilliat-Smith (1909: 154) wrote, 'I could see clearly five or six black tents pitched on the left side of the road under some birches. I would fain have stopped, waked the *Baro*, and there and then collected material of interest for the Gypsy Lore Society.'

Like some modern ryes, Borrow was not above giving others the impression that he was himself a Gypsy; in *Lavengro* (Chapter 110), when asked by the man in black Reverend Fraser 'Are you then, a Gypsy?', he replied, 'What else should I be?'[23] He has also been taken to task for putting far too cultured a brand of English in the mouths of the Romanichals (Helyear even calls it 'pompous'). Pakomovna tells him, when she visits him in the dingle, 'do you allow me to officiate upon your hair' – a hortative construction obsolete in English even by Borrow's day – while in the Book of Wisdom in the *Lavo-Lil*, the heavily class-marked pronoun 'one' turns up in his list of homilies in Romani, justifying the charge that 'his Gypsies all spoke like bishops', thus *when yeck's tardrad yeck's beti tan oprey, kair'd yeck's beti yag ta nashed yeck's kekauvi* … ('when one's put one's little tent up, made one's little fire and hung up one's kettle …'). Equally transparent are the English origins of his translations, thus *the mush savo kek si les the juckni-wast oprey his jib*, 'the man who has not got the whip-hand of his tongue'. While calquing upon English idioms certainly characterises Angloromani, constructions of this kind lack the ring of authenticity (see Tilford (1953) for a discussion of the English spoken by the Romanies of Borrow's acquaintance).

Borrow as Romani scholar

As a linguist, Borrow was prone to exaggeration and sometimes quite impressive creativity; Ridler (1981: 329), referring to Caló, relates how, in a letter to the British and Foreign Bible Society, Borrow wrote that within a day of having first arrived in Spain, he located some Gypsies and 'we began conversing in the Spanish dialect of [Romani], with which I was tolerably well acquainted'. It is significant that in his defence of *Lavengro*, which appeared as an appendix in *The Romany Rye*, he chided his critics for not having spotted his 'deliberate' mistakes in the Armenian and Welsh samples in his books, but he did not mention Romani. It is possible that some of his errors in the latter language were likewise deliberate – certainly they have allowed us to spot plagiarism in the writings of others. Collie (1982: 231) gives examples of Borrow's becoming flustered and actually running away when confronted with questions concerning his knowledge of foreign languages.

Ridler also remarked upon his ability to undertake a complete re-translation of his earlier version of *St Luke* thirty years after having left Spain and any further contact with Caló speakers. Her implication is that much of his new version was in what we might call Borromani, a concocted dialect not actually spoken by anyone. Ridler goes on to provide examples of such created forms, such as his word for 'incense' for which he used the Spanish word *incienso* in the original version, and which became *usur-gudlo* in the new version, compounded from *usur* 'smoke' and *gudlo* 'sweet'. The first item, *usur*, occurs only in Pott, who got it from Borrow's *Zincali* in the first place; it isn't in any other Caló wordlist. And the second item, *gudlo*, has the English and not the Spanish Romani form, which is *gulo*. Another example of lexical creation Ridler cites is *Brono Aljeñicato* for 'Pontius Pilate', or *Pòncio Pilato* in Spanish. To Borrow's ear, the name (in English more so than in Spanish) sounded like *puente* and *pila*, which mean 'bridge' and 'fountain' in Spanish. According to Borrow, the Caló words for these are *brono* and *aljeñicato* respectively, and both have been listed in his *Zincali* lexicon as legitimate Caló, and were furthermore entered as such, like *usur*, without comment by Pott in his dictionary (1844: ii: 433); but in his correspondence with the British and Foreign Bible Society, Borrow indicated that he made up both words himself, from Sanskrit and Arabic.

The same creativity is evident in his English Romani versions. Thus in the appendix on this dialect in the second volume of *The Zincali*, he includes his translation of the Apostle's Creed; to the line 'I believe in the Holy Ghost', he appends the following note:

> The English Gypsies, having, in their dialect, no other term for ghost than mulo, which simply means a dead person, I have been obliged to substitute a compound word. Bavalengro signifies literally a wind thing *or form of air.*

This word, respelt as *bavol-engro*, then turns up as the only entry for 'ghost' in the *Romano Lavo-Lil*, published in 1874, while at the entry *mullo* in the same vocabulary, which is the *actual* English Romani word for both 'ghost' and 'dead', only the meanings 'dead man' and 'dead' are given.

Our image as liars and deceivers got a major boost from George Borrow, who documented the *hokkano baro* or 'great trick' perpetrated upon the gullible Europeans as the early Romanies conned their way across the continent. Surprisingly, Fraser repeated this uncritically in his own book (1992: 62) where he called it 'the greatest trick of all'. But Borrow was the first to use the phrase, and his poor knowledge of Romani reveals that he invented it. It mixes Continental and British syntax and form, and misinterprets *hokkano* as 'lie' when it means 'liar'. A lie is a *xoxajipe, xoxavipe, xoxajimos, xoxipen* and so on in the various

Continental Romani dialects; a 'great lie' in British Romani is a *boro hokkiben*.

While it would be possible to reconstruct the lexical and grammatical characteristics of the kind of British Romani Borrow was hearing, such an undertaking might be more usefully achieved by looking at the work of others, such as Whiter or Vallancey, because of Borrow's tendency to mix dialects. But even from his own material it is clear to see that English Romani is a member of the Northern European dialect group, sharing much in common with Sinti (including such items as *džin-, tikno, miro, grai, hajer-, ma, čomoni, džuvel, stif(o)-p(r)al, mukh*: 'know', 'small', 'my', 'horse', 'understand', 'don't', 'something', 'woman', 'brother-in-law', 'let' – compare Southern Romani *džan-, cino, mu(n)rro, gras, hatjer-, na, vareso,džuvli, salo, mekh*). Like Sinti, the infinitive seems to be modelled upon the third person singular indicative (Sinti *kamav te džal* 'I want to go', rather than *kamav te džav* – cf. Central Romani *kamav te džan*), although Welsh Romani, like Vlax, does not do this. Like Vlax but unlike the Central or Northern dialects, Welsh Romani negates 'is/are' as *naj*, recorded by both Borrow, and Smart and Crofton, for English Romani. Borrow correctly analyses this as *na + hi*, although unlike Northern and Central Romani, British (Welsh, Scottish and English) Romani, like Vlax, belongs to the /s/ group, thus *si, san, lesa, sår* rather than the /h/ group (*hi, hal, leha, har*, 'is/are', 'am', 'with it', 'like/as'). British Romani preserves the original negative construction with preverbal *na*, now lost in most dialects of Sinti, which has postverbal *ga(r)* (< German).

The most authentic Angloromani Borrow reproduces, recorded verbatim from Romanichals, is probably found in his 'beti rockrapens' and to a lesser extent in his collection of English Gypsy songs in the *Lavo-Lil*, but even here, material of his own creation is quite evident. Thus in the section entitled 'The English Gypsies', he includes a song called *Tugney Beshor* which contains the line *cauna volélan* 'when they fly', using the Spanish root for 'fly', an item he does not enter in his dictionary. In the same song is the word *artavàvam*, glossed as 'we'll forget'. His knowledge of Romani grammar seemed to have deserted him by 1874, since this is an aorist construction, not a future one, and he also appears to have forgotten its real meaning, which is 'forgive' rather than 'forget' (in English Romani *bister*), but even as early as 1844 he was confusing tense and number endings, listing *camenna* 'they (will) love' as 'I love' and *chorava* 'I (will) steal' as 'I have stolen' (Winstedt, 1952).

In the dingle episode in *Lavengro* (Chapter 83) he is describing the manufacture of a horseshoe, and refers to the fire's 'tongues of flame' as *vagescoe chipes*, using the Caló word and plural for 'tongues' and the wrong gender and number for 'fire' (*vagescoe* is probably a misprint for *yagescoe* here, although the form is continental rather than British, which would be *yogakere*, *yog* being plural and an inflected feminine noun), and to an anvil as a *covantza*, a Slavic-derived item listed in his Hungarian Romani vocabulary (Winstedt, 1952) and by Paspati (1870), and recorded by Smart and Crofton (1875, along with *volélan* and *artavàvam*) as only having been encountered by them in print in Angloromani, and in the works of Borrow.

Borrow was evidently influenced by the Romani he heard in Eastern Europe, for even Jasper's wife Sanspirella Heron was renamed with the Balkan-sounding *Pakomovna* in his stories. The same Continental influence is evident in three unusual words which occur in Chapter 26 of *Lavengro*, where Jasper Petulengro is muttering to himself about the weather: *dearginni* 'it thundereth', *villaminni* 'it flameth' (referring to the lightning) and *grondinni* 'it haileth'. With the exception of *vílamo*, 'lightning' in Bohemian Romani (Ješina, 1886), the items themselves turn up in no other recorded dialect,[24] although it is clear where Borrow found them, for their origins are, respectively, in Hungarian *dörga* and *villám* and Romanian *grindini*. It might now be possible to temper Winstedt's caution that 'it would be rash to attempt to define the precise dialect of Borrow's "Czigány"' (1952: 49); the morpheme {-*in*-} is characteristic of Hungarian Lovari loanverbs (like {-*sar*-} in other Vlax dialects), and the athematic termination {-*i*} (more properly {-*ij*}) for third person singular {-*il*} is likewise indicative of Hungarian phonological interference in the Lovari Vlax spoken in that country and in Transylvania. Clearly these items were recorded during his visit to Hungary and Romania in 1844, seven years before he wrote *Lavengro*, although only *rondíni* 'hail' turns up in his Hungarian Romani vocabulary (Winstedt, 1952: 56). The spellings both with and without initial /g/ may reflect trouble Borrow had in attempting to represent the Vlax voiced uvular fricative in this word. In Welsh Romani, 'thunder' is *devléski gódli* 'God's noise' and 'hail' is *brišindéske bára* 'rain stones'; 'lightning' is *molóna* (from Slavic).[25] Smart and Crofton include all three of Borrow's words, but mark each of them as unattested; the fact that two of the items don't occur in Winstedt's list lends support to his suggestion (1952: 47) that Borrow may have collected more material in Cluj than has so far been located.

Borrow errs in his explanation of the plural morpheme, which he spells <-or> and which he sometimes applied to words indiscriminately and incorrectly (for example *bauor* 'mates', from English dialect *bor* 'chum').[26] Because he spoke a non-rhotic dialect of English, /r/ was not articulated in his speech except before vowels; after vowels, it merely indicated length. This confusion is evident in such conflicting orthographic representations as both <*saulo*> and <*sorlo*> 'early', <*sap*> and <*sarp*> 'snake', <*villaminni*> and <*villarminni*> 'lightning-flashes' and so on. Thus what he wrote as <-or> in fact represents the sound '-aw', which corresponds to the Common Romani plural post-consonantal morpheme {-*a*} and reflects the regular phonetic shift of [a] to 'aw' (Sampson's <å>) in British Romani (e.g. his *shockor* < 'cabbages' for Common Romani *šaxa* and so on). But on the basis of this non-existent /r/, Borrow assumes that the English Romani plural may be derived from the Romanian neuter plural {-*uri*}.[27] It is possible, however, that by Borrow's day, an intrusive /r/ could have found its way into a number of words, since in Angloromani as spoken in North America, it is clearly present in such words as *gorjer*, *vonger*, *kekker* and so on (where in British Angloromani these are pronounced *gawja*, *vonga*, *kekka* and so on). This behaviour of /r/ suggests that Borrow was dealing with south-eastern varieties of British Romani, since Welsh Romani is in the main rhotic (cf. *feder*, *určos*, *sår*). Rhotacism as a phonological feature of English began to disappear from the south-eastern dialects in the early modern period (1500–1700), but survives today in the south-western dialect area, in which the Kåle lived before moving into Wales. That phonological changes in English should affect the phonology of Romani spoken in that country suggests not only a high degree of bilingualism, but that the population probably became English-dominant early on. A similar sound shift in English which has affected Romani is that of [er] to [ar] (cf. sartain, varsity, sergeant, clerk), thus the original [er] in *erti-* 'forgive, excuse' (< Romanian) becomes *ātav-* in Welsh Romani, also demonstrating loss of postvocalic /r/, which is Borrow's *artav*, [er] in *verdo* 'waggon' (Common Romani *vurdon*) becomes Angloromani *va·da* or *vawda* and *terno* 'young' becomes Angloromani *tawno* with loss of /r/ and shift of

[a] to [aw], cf. Welsh Romani *tarno*, Common Romani *terno*. This latter, which is characteristically British Romani, also reflects a sound-shift which began in south-eastern (but not south-western) English in the early modern period, cf. [græs], [hæf], [læf] to [graːs], [haːf], [laːf]; also cf. southern Angloromani *gawja, yok, yog, yora* ('non-Romani', 'eye', 'fire', 'egg'), with northern (especially Scottish) *gadji, yak, yag, yaro*.[28]

Other misinterpretations which bear comment are Borrow's assumption that the genitive postposition, legitimately a nominaliser in Central and Northern Romani, in its various forms (*-engro, -eskro*) is a free morpheme meaning 'thing' or 'fellow', thus *boro drom engroes* 'highwaymen', (1851, 358), also listed with the same interpretation in his Hungarian Romani vocabulary (Winstedt, 1952: 110), and that the sociative postposition {*-sa*}, meaning 'with' or 'by', could be detached and made into a preposition: *come sar mande*, 'come with me'. It is entered as a separate word not only in his *Lavo-Lil* but also for Caló in the glossary in *The Zincali*, and turns up in Leland's *English Gypsy Songs*, and in Smart and Crofton. Sampson (1907a: 95) doubts that this ever existed as a separate preposition, suggesting that these various compilers, like Borrow himself, misinterpreted the postposition as they heard it.[29]

Sampson's inventiveness is betrayed by his poor knowledge of Romani grammar in his discussion of a verse he calls 'the oldest specimen of English Gypsy at present extant, and perhaps the purest … at least as old as the time of Elizabeth' (1923: 11). The lines in question, with his own translation, are,

Coin si deya,	'who's your mother,
Coin si dado	who's your father'
Pukker mande drey Romanes,	'do thou answer me in Romany
Ta mande pukkeravava tute.	and I will answer thee'

Coin is the form of Common Romani *kon* which he imported into the Romanichal dialect from his vocabulary of Spanish Romani, although it is not attested in any other dialect; *deya* and *dado* are both vocatives and cannot follow the verb *si*, the former taken from his Lovari wordlist, and not found in Britain (although he does have the British form *daiya* elsewhere in his book). In the second line, *Romanes* is an adverb, although he doesn't seem to have realised this; he has it glossed as a noun in his dictionary, and believing it to be a noun has it following the preposition *drey*. In the third line, he has the inflected forms *mande* and *tute* ('to me', 'to you') functioning as personal pronouns as they do only in Angloromani, while *pukkeravava* is a causative verb form, meaning 'I'm being made to tell'. The verses, in British Romani, ought to have read *kon si tiri daj, kon si tiro dad, phuker mange romanes tha (me) phukerava tuke.*

Borrow also treated the bound affix {*-i-sar*} (or {*-a-sar*}), a marker of loanverbs, as though it were a free morpheme, and entered it into his *Lavo-Lil* as the independent item *asarlas* 'at all'. However, his own example originates in the misanalysis of *we can't help asarlus*, which he glosses as 'we can't help at all', when the construction he heard was *we can't helpasar les*, 'we can't help it'. It is possible, however, that this development was in part a legitimate one in English Romani, since Smart and Crofton (1875: 52–4) list many examples of *asár* meaning 'also' which clearly demonstrate a reinterpretation of earlier {*-i-sar*}. But it is not paralleled in Welsh Romani, nor has the form and use seemed to have survived in modern Angloromani. This athematic morpheme is particularly characteristic of the Vlax group of dialects, and is used with loanverbs in Welsh Romani too, although with one exception only in imperative constructions (Sampson, 1926: 117–118). Another indication of Vlax influence is the non-final affix {*-n-*}, a marker of athematic adjective-derived adverbs, thus *drago, dragones, mundro, mundrones,* compared with thematic *baro, bares, tikno, tiknes,* without the {*-n-*}. Thus we have such Borromani forms as *weshenjugalogonæs, bolli-menggreskoenæs, dinnileskoenæs, dovodoiskoenæs* and so on. This last is compounded from *dovo* 'that', + *odoi* 'there', and is given to mean 'in that way', while that item and the two before it include *-(e)sko*, which consists of the singular masculine oblique nominal morpheme {*-es*} plus the Vlax genitive {*-ko*} (rather than the Northern Romani {*-k(e)ro*}), and followed by the adverbial {*-es*} linked with non-athematic {*-n-*}. In actual Angloromani, *dovodoi* is a legitimate determiner meaning 'that there', but not even in inflected British Romani could it combine with grammatical particles meant for nouns and adjectives. Yet such forms are presented as 'genuine Gypsy ... clear-sounding and melodious, and well-adapted to the purposes of poetry' (Borrow, 1874: 11; see also Hancock, 2003).

George Borrow probably never dreamt that his work would come under scrutiny a century and a half after it appeared; but at the time it was written, interest in Gypsies and the Romani language was marginal, and remained so until almost the end of the twentieth century. His writings were evaluated by his contemporaries not at all for the Romani they contained, but for his observations and descriptions and opinions in other areas. Those few individuals, such as Pott (1844), Ascoli (1865), Paspati (1870), Miklosich (1872) and Colocci (1889) who had an academic interest in Romani, on the other hand, used his material uncritically, and were scarcely interested in his writings otherwise.

Conclusion

Fifteen years ago, Angus Fraser summed up a talk he gave on George Borrow at the University of East Anglia[30] with the words, 'I wish I could feel sure that a new generation of Borrovians is growing up.' His wish has clearly been fulfilled; there is now a society and a journal dedicated wholly to Borrow's life and works, and an international conference on the man has become an annual event, although whether the impetus will be maintained since Fraser's death in 2001 remains to be seen. As specialists in Romani, we must be careful to separate our judgement of Borrow's linguistic expertise in that language from our judgement of him as a prose writer and raconteur. In the latter role, he holds a special place; and even as a linguist dealing with other languages, as Ridler (1996) has so magnificently documented, he demonstrated a remarkable genius.

It is all the more puzzling, therefore, that he dealt so inadequately with the one language for which he is remembered best of all.[31] As a student of Gypsies, he must only be regarded as the prime example of the term he himself created, a *Romany Rye* – for today, the word has been taken back by Gypsies, and is a term of disdain. It is no coincidence that Kalderaš Romanies in Europe and America use the word *rai* for a policeman or an authority figure, meanings also shared in England by the present-day descendants of George Borrow's Romani 'brothers and sisters'.

CHAPTER TWELVE

The concocters: creating fake Romani culture

To be fair, not all fake Romani culture has been faked deliberately. More often it is simply the result of misguided or misinformed hypotheses finding their way into the conventional account, and being repeated by subsequent writers unchecked. A prime example of deliberately faked tradition, however, is found in Manfri Fred Wood's much-publicised *In the Life of a Romany Gypsy* which appeared in 1973. Here (1973: 65–9) he summarised what was allegedly remembered of the original Romani religion. He begins, '[n]ow, as to Romany religion, there is not much anybody remembers of it today. There was a prophet called Soster, and a lot of the stories had to do with him.' Wood then goes on to relate the story of the creation of the Universe and the world out of a burst of fire, and of the two gods Moshto and Arivell, and Moshto's three sons, and the ginkgo or maidenhair tree, and of the two clay figures into whose mouths Moshto blew its seeds to give them life.

What is curious is that six years later, Leon Petulengro (Leon Lloyd) repeated the story in his own book *Romany Boy*, where the same account (1979: 136–7) – of a void within a void, and the explosion of a ball of fire, and of the two gods, Moshto and Arivell, and Moshto's three sons, and the two clay figures, and the ginkgo tree, is told. But this time the story is attributed to his paternal grandmother Anyeta who, he says (1979: 12), came from Romania. He had already introduced her a decade earlier as 'Anyeta, a Romanian Zingari, and a true Romany herbalist' in his *The Roots of Health* (1968: 15), although that book makes no

Originally published in Nicholas Saul and Susan Tebbutt (eds), *The role of the Romanies: images and counter-images of 'Gypsies'/Romanies in European cultures* (Liverpool University Press, Liverpool, 2004), pp. 85–97.

mention of Moshto or the old religion. In *Romany Boy* (1979: 24) her membership in a 'tribe' in Romania is referred to, as well as her being the head of that tribe, presumably also in Romania since he states that after coming to England, she 'did not live with us but with my father's cousin and his tribe, the Lovells'. Oddly, he has her speaking British Romani with native fluency on the same page. In 1936 his father, Gipsy (elsewhere Gypsy) Petulengro, 'King of the Gypsies' (1968: 15) wrote a book of his own entitled *A Romany Life*, but his mother Anyeta does not appear in it by name even though she is featured throughout quite prominently. He seems to have first introduced the actual name *Anyeta* in a chain letter he circulated in 1940.

On pages 2, 25 and 162 of *A Romany Life* she is referred to as a 'Berber', Petulengro Senior's own peculiar notion of Romani origins which he'd already spelt out in *The Listener* (1935: 649) a year earlier. In an essay there, he wrote that, 'The Romanies are not Egyptians, nor descendants of Egyptians, as many people seem to think. The Romanies are descendants of the Berbers, who trekked to practically every country in the world.'

There is much else to question in *A Romany Life* – thus the spurious jargon presented as Romani (pages 33, 49 and *passim*), and the use of uniquely British forms presented as Romanian Vlax (*boro-roy, tarno, rokkered*), contrasting with Continental Romani pronunciations presented as the dialect spoken in England (e.g. *yag-kash* for *yog-koshter,* 'firewood') in his *Listener* essays on British Romani life. In *The Roots of Health* the slogan *kooshti sante!* appears more than once as Romani for 'good health', although *sante* (*santé*) is a French word.

The question arises: who was the original owner of the Moshto story? Evidently Wood, since his version predates Petulengro's by six years. He linked it to general but fading community memory, while Petulengro on the other hand attributed it specifically to his grandmother from Romania, although in an account so similar to Woods' as scarcely to be coincidence.

The most detailed study of Romani spiritual belief among Romanian (Vlax) Romanies is Chatard and Bernard. Here (1959: 22–6) some of this story appears, although there is no reference to Moshto or Arivell by name. Instead, there are *O Pouro Del* and *O Bheng*, which is to say 'the old god' and 'the devil' in Vlax Romani. The two clay figures are mentioned, and called *Damo* and *Yehwah*, clearly Adam and Eve. They are brought to life not by the seeds of the maidenhair tree, but by *O*

Pouro Del's touching each of them with his wand. Wlislocki (1890) doesn't include the story, nor is it found in the imaginative works of Jean-Claude Frère (1973) or Françoise Cozannet (1973). The equally suspect Clébert (1961) relies on Chatard and Bernard, but does refer to a similarity with Zoroastrianism and Manichæanism, while Elysseeff (1890: 169), summarising Kounavine's concocted work, wrote that, 'The essence of the primitive beliefs of the Gypsies [is] borrowed from the different religions encountered by the Gypsies on their journey, and particularly those borrowed from the religion of Zoroaster.'

Kounavine was one of the boldest concocters of fake Romani culture, claiming that he found Brahma, Indra, Lakshmi, Ahriman and other deities being worshipped by name among Romanies in Russia, who (he said) had also retained a number of elaborate Hindu prayers. But we learn about his 'immense store of [Romani] materials' only at second hand in the same article by Elysseeff, none of which can be examined at first hand since Kounavine says he lost it all in the snows of Siberia. Sampson has already commented on Kounavine as 'not to be taken too seriously' (1907b: 7), pointing out that one of the alternative names he gives for Brahma is *Khakhava* (*XAXABA* in the original, that is, *xoxavav*, not to be confused with the *Kakkava* Herdeljezi festival amongst Turkish Roma) which in Romani means 'I deceive'; the word itself has passed into Russian slang with a similar meaning. Was this given him by a Romani interviewee who was having fun with the inquisitive *gadjo*, or was Kounavine himself having a private joke at the expense of his readers?

Correspondence within its inner circle during the early years of the Gypsy Lore Society contained a number of risqué exchanges, with 'Romani words providing a coded language' (Sampson, 1997: 111, where John Sampson's verses composed for Dora Yates provide just one example). These were not usually meant for its general membership but rather as in-group humour to be understood and appreciated only by the initiates. Did this sometimes deliberately find its way into material for a wider, although unsuspecting, audience, perhaps like Kounavine's *Khakhava* or Frank Elmény's heroine Gali Minsh (*kali mindž*) in his novel *Poor Janos*, thereby compounding the fun?

Some wordlists reflect legitimate misunderstandings recorded in earnest, such as Sinclair's (1915) *brokla* for 'cabbage' (actually the English word 'broccoli') or *kurrï, korrï* listed to mean 'cock, domestic fowl' (the actual meaning is 'penis'); Prince (1907), probably lifting from Smart (1863: 7) where the same mistake occurs, has *kovaskaruk* 'willow, laurel' when this is simply *kova's a ruk*, that is, 'that's a tree'. Even Manfri Fred Wood, in the wordlist at the end of his book (1973: 122), lists *becker* as 'fruit', evidently a misreading of the entry in a lexicon he had of English Romani collected by a site worker called Alice Bartlett, where she had it correctly glossed, although poorly handwritten, as 'frog'. Wood's mistake is now listed in Hayward's *Romany Dictionary* (2003: 38, 108). One may imagine Vasily Zuev pointing to a window in an attempt to collect the Romani word for 'glass', for which word he entered *xiv*, 'hole' instead in his wordlist (1789: 124). This latter is also used for 'window' (cf. Angloromani *dikin-hev*). Bryant (1785) lists *bauro beval acochenos* for 'storm' ('big wind a-catchin' us') and *porcherie* for 'brass' (actually *posh hori*, 'halfpenny'); Harriot (1830) has *charicklo* 'cage' when the word means 'bird' and *vailgoro* 'fair (skinned)' when it means 'fair, carnival'. Roberts (1836) has *chivya* 'tongs' when it means 'tongues'; Smart (1863) has *sorto-poov* for 'garden' when what he heard was *'sort o' phuv'*, 'sort of ground'. Leland (1882) has *gogemars* for 'swamps' (he heard the English word 'quagmires') and *kris* for 'mustard' (deduced from 'mustard and creese', 'cress' in the London dialect). Lexicography requires a certain degree of skill; some word-collectors found their lack of success more easily blamed upon their source than themselves. Ivanow wrote, '[i]t is very hard indeed to obtain from the average Gypsy any adequate linguistic material; their stupidity is sometimes beyond all description' (1914: 444).

Joseph Mitchell, at that time a Director of the Gypsy Lore Society, wrote two essays on Roma in the 1940s and 1950s for *The New Yorker* magazine, describing what he called the *bajour*, which Wikipedia defines as 'a gypsy word that refers to a con game in which lonely and unhappy women are swindled out of their life savings'. On this basis, a whole Broadway musical of the same name was performed in 1955, and the word was used in the 1956 Gypsy-themed film *Hot Blood*. A short story by Borden Deal, *The Big Bajoor*, appeared in 1962, and it was made into a film of the same name in 1996. However, there is no such word as *bajour/bajoor* in Romani. This was Mitchell's mishearing of *bužo*, which means a pouch or a small bundle of something. Deal's somewhat plagiarised story is about a Romani woman called Vanya (a man's name) and her husband Sandor, Hungarian/Vlax names for English Gypsies who speak *Calo* and talk about a *gajo* woman, 'dukkering' and 'cooring the drom'.

Detective Dennis Marlock (see further in Chapter 13 of this volume) published a 'law enforcement's guide to the secret language of the American Gypsy ... needed because Romany is only a spoken language. There are no Romany dictionaries or grammars in the city library, or in any library for that matter.' It is billed in the introduction by Concordia University Criminal Justice Operations Professor Joseph Andritzky as 'a concise, accurate and handy translation guide of the Romany language ... an outstanding example of original research that is contributing to our understanding of the Gypsy enterprise ... a must for every professional investigator of organised crime'. It is full of mistakes (e.g. *et-a-la* 'female', *et-a-low* 'male', when these mean 'here she is' and 'here he is', properly *eta la*, *eta lo* or *got-tay* 'hear', when it means 'here', properly *kathe*), although the words were 'carefully checked with numerous Gypsies, none of whom were aware that a study of their language was being conducted' (1993: 6). Perhaps being straightforward with them would have helped.

Sometimes these collectors were the innocent dupes of their informants and such errors were deliberately provided; Otto Duhmberg's 1870 wordlist of Siberian Romani for example has the entry *kari* glossed as 'grandson', *chamrimintsch* (*xa miri mindž*) as 'granddaughter' and *bremintsch* (*bari mindž*) for 'donkey'. Bryant (1785: 390) records *ming* for 'father'; Sampson (1891: 59) has written about the frequent offering of this particular word to lexicographers.

But to return to Moshto. Given that Clébert's very popular book became widely available in English in a Penguin paperback edition in 1967, the possibility must be considered that Manfri Wood, or else his ghost-writer John Brune, used this as a general source and subsequently sought out some literature on the Zoroastrian religion – and as a result, on the basis of the original *Zoroaster*, *Ahriman* and *Mazda*, created the names *Soster*, *Arivell* and *Moshto* (this last perhaps also influenced by the Romani word *mišto* 'well, good'). Six years later, Leon Petulengro (or perhaps his ghost-writer Betty Messenger) plagiarised it practically word for word.

Leon Petulengro's father was Walter Lloyd, a herbalist from Rochdale, who wrote under the name Gipsy (or Gypsy, and also sometimes Xavier) Petulengro. By his own account (1935: 80) his family name 'Lloyd' was a re-spelling of the Welsh word *llwyd* meaning 'grey' but which, he maintained, was in their case really an anglicisation of the Romani word for horse, *grai*.

For a while he also called himself Walter Smith. A smith is a *petulengro* in Borrovian Romani, more accurately *petalengro* (from *petalo*, 'horseshoe' – his own 'spelling pronunciation' of the word as *pet-yew-lengro* is evidence enough that he was not familiar with it as actually spoken), and he claimed to be a direct descendant of Borrow's Jasper Petulengro; the information that 'Gypsy Petulengro is the grandson of Tinker Petulengro immortalised by George Borrow' appears under his name in the *Listener* series, and in his book (on the second page) he recounts that, '[as a child in Romania] I could not speak English, although my father spoke English and Welsh being the son of Tinker Jasper Petulengro immortalised by George Borrow in his books'.

One wonders how he ever communicated with his father if he didn't speak English himself; his father, after all, revealed all of Anyeta's herbal mysteries to him 'when [he] was a boy' (1968: 15). Yet it could not have been in Angloromani, itself a register of English, and spoken very far away indeed from Romania. Furthermore, since Jasper Petulengro (George Smith in real life) was in fact from East Anglia, why would his son, Leon's father, necessarily have spoken Welsh?

Fred Wood's story has been picked up and woven into at least one published work of fiction, Charles De Lint's *Mulengro: A Romany Tale*, where Moshto is mentioned twice (1985: 87 and 277), as well as into several websites (Gypsy Phoenix Rising's 'Gypsy' site and another[32] providing two such examples); it has also found its way into academic treatises and been retold as though it were fact. Thus the late W.R. Rishi, in his book *Roma*, wrote (1976: 79), with his own additions, that,

> [T]he supreme god is Moshto (from the Romani word *mishto* meaning good) symbol of goodness, and Arivell (from Sanskrit *ari* 'enemy'), the symbol of evil. Moshto's three sons are the trinity of Hindu gods, Brahma (the creator), Vishnu (the sustainer) and Shiva (the killer of all that is evil).

At the same section in his book, Rishi also paraphrased and quoted Kounavine extensively as fact. Dennis Liggio dealt with it as real in an unpublished essay entitled *The Influences of Zoroastrianism and Manichæanism on the Romani Creation Myth* (1996), while John McLaughlin, a professor at the University of Illinois, recounts it in detail in his book *Gypsy Lifestyles* (1980: 4–7). Taking his cue, although maybe unwittingly, from Leon Petulengro, McLaughlin elaborated the story with embellishments of his own, stating (1980: 6–7) that, 'Moshto laid down strict rules of cleanliness to ward off disease, and many of these practices are still followed today by the gypsies … As will become clear later, the gypsies believe these stories, and they have a serious impact on gypsy life.'

At any rate Professor McLaughlin evidently believes that Romanies believe them, and his widely consulted book has certainly helped to entrench this concocted folklore yet more firmly in the ubiquitous and alternative Romani historical identity that continues to misdirect and misinform the interested scholar. I personally have not met nor heard of anyone, whether Romanichal or Vlax, who was acquainted with the Moshto story, and there is every indication that it originated with Wood, although likelier with the *gadžo* John Brune.

This is not the only spurious account of the original Romani religion. More recently, Patrick Jasper Lee has begun offering courses on 'Romany Gypsy Jal' through his now defunct Romani Life Foundation website, although curiously there is no mention of it in his earlier book (Lee, 2000). This is a philosophy which, he says, 'originated in India and was carried into Europe by the Romany Gypsies 500 years ago', and which he describes as 'the religion that became lost … the indigenous culture' of the Romani people. *Jal* is said to be cognate with the English word 'year' and the German *jahr*, and to mean 'to journey' or 'to go'; one meditational practice intended for self-empowerment is the *Nogo Jal Drom* or 'personal Jal road'. *Jal*, however, is a word specific to the Romanichal dialect, and while it does mean 'go', it originates in the Common Romani inflected form that means 'he goes' – Romani doesn't have infinitive verbs – and so this can hardly be an ancient term in the language. Still more specifically *English* Romani is the word *nogo;* it means 'own' in that dialect, but it isn't originally Romani at all, instead being a word adopted from German '*(mei)n eige(n)*' during the migration through northern Europe into the British Isles; several other German words have found their way into the Romanichal dialect as well, such as *waffodi* ('bad' < G. *böse*), *foshena* ('fake' < G. *falsch*) and *swegla* ('tobacco pipe' < G. *Schwegel*).

The late Henry Sherriff claimed to 'still speak the inflected puri chib, and thereby to be the last speaker in the country', and wrote extensive letters from prison in it to his lawyer friend Richard Wade, but upon investigation 'it quickly became apparent that huge chunks of [his] puri chib Anglo Romani were actually lifted, often verbatim, from other books, especially Smart and Crofton' (Dawson, 1988: *ix–x*).

The fact that some of these invented 'facts' originate with Romanies themselves – and we may add Ray Buckland, Lee Fuhler and Patronella Cooper to the list is distressing, since it gives the stamp of legitimacy to such misinformation and, when exposed, only reinforces the image of untrustworthiness we must live with. It also suggests that while these authors may indeed have one or more Romani forebears, that fact is only incidental to their real life, which clearly lacks any firsthand involvement with the day-to-day Romani world; they have accepted instead the 'magical' pop culture stereotype created by non-Romanies. If they are fully aware of what they are doing and are exploiting such misinformation solely for profit, then they do no credit to the people they claim to represent, and seriously hold back our effort to smash the stereotype.

Two more people who present themselves as Romanies and who provide details of Romani culture are Morrghan Savistr'i-Lovara, an 'American born Rom woman in her Mid 20s' and Allie Theiss, a 'descendant of Rom gypsies of Transylvania'. On her website, Ms Savistr'i-Lovara says she is a:

> ... practicing Chaos Mage as well as Shuvani (think Romani Shaman) [who is] currently working to devise some Roma rituals for cleansing and purification that are newer and less complex than the traditional ones ... most Rom do not do them because of the scarcity of materials as well as the amount of time they take to properly perform. [She is] owned by two cats names Fuzzface and Mr Pants. (http://twilightofmymind. chaosmagic.com).

Allie Theiss (2005a, 2005b) tells the reader,

> No matter their original origins, Gypsies, or Romas, are prized for their remarkable psychic abilities and the gift to attract good fortune or upset a life with a curse. All are born with such gifts, but what makes their powers so innate is their relationship with nature. Their bond with the spirits of the outdoors allow[s] their gifts to evolve naturally ... no longer do they wander the earth in a horse-drawn caravan, but are modernised and travel by car, bus and plane. The very definition of 'free spirits'...

Since that author refers to the *Porrajmos* (the Romani Holocaust) and the *Aresipe* (the arrival in Europe) she had evidently consulted Hancock (2002), the sole source in which both these words appear as chapter titles; yet she states that 'No one knows where the Roma originated', and that 'Roma are divided into three sub-groups, the *Domari* of the Middle East and Eastern Europe (the *Dom*), the *Lomavren* of Central Europe (the *Lom*) and the *Romani* of Western Europe (the *Rom*).' Like so many before her she mixes dialects, suggesting for example that all Romanies use *dukkerin* 'fortune telling' – from British Romani and *natsiya* 'nation' (she has 'nation*s*') – from Vlax Romani, although the two words do not coexist in any dialect. The same misunderstanding of the *Rom-Dom-Lom* distinctions appears in a more recently published novel by Barbara Nadel where, in wording remarkably like that found in Theiss, she explains that '[t]here are many spoken dialects [of Romani], three of which are to be found in Europe: *Dom*, spoken by the Domari in Central and Eastern Europe, *Lom* by the Lomavren of Central Europe and *Rom* spoken by the Romani of Western Europe' (2006: 335).

An example of the inaccurate, although probably not deliberate, presentation of Romani custom and belief is found in Barbara Walker's *Women's Encyclopaedia of Myths and Secrets,* which contains many Roma-related references throughout, all written in the past tense and all with a feminist (and often anti-male) bias. One example of this reads:

> [T]he matriarch was the centre of Gypsy tribal life; everything that went on around a tribal mother resembled the old pagan sex rites. Her husband was a drone, whose function was to impregnate her ... if he failed to beget perfect children, the tribe 'accidentally' killed him. (1983: 361)

Like other concocters, Walker based her statements not on firsthand acquaintance with Romanies, but on the writings of others, in this case Derlon (1977). An examination of that book reveals that Derlon's already lurid descriptions had been very freely elaborated upon further by Walker who, like Rishi and McLaughlin, could not resist the urge to editorialise, pad and reinterpret, a compulsion, whether conscious or not, to control Romani identity.

Elsewhere she states that 'together with "Smith", "Faa" is the most common gypsy surname, and means "fay" or "fairy"' (1983: 361). But this is in fact an old lowland Scottish surname and not Romani in origin at all, and was adopted only after Romanies arrived in Scotland in the late 1400s. Again, 'the popular gypsy surname Kaldera or Kalderas may have been derived from [the name of the Hindu goddess] Kali-Devi' (1983: 363). The reference given for this is Esty (1969: 67) which, on being consulted, actually says that 'the Kalderaš tribe, that huge group of Gypsies spread halfway around the world … governed in patriarchal fashion. There is no king or chief: all the men in the vitsa make all the decisions.' No mention of Barbara Walker's Kaldera, or of popularity, or of surnames, or of goddesses, although Esty does state incorrectly that Kalderaš Romanies have no leaders. The word itself is Romanian for 'coppersmith', and is cognate with the English word 'cauldron'. B.A. Robinson of the Ontario Consultants on Religious Tolerance seems to have accepted this as a reliable source in his 2008 posting on that organisation's website: '[T]he Roma were some of the last Goddess-worshipers in Europe. Their Goddess, Kali, was viewed as a trinity. Her symbol was a triangle. A male Horned God also played a prominent role. The similarities between ancient Roma belief and that of Wicca are obvious.'

Romani Studies has lent itself easily to scholarly fabrication, and the literature is replete with it; Decourdemanche's 'Romani script', reproduced uncritically by Clébert, is one well-known example, as are the off-colour sentences that appear inserted into one version of Andrew Boorde's 1542 text of early British Romani ('Mayde shew us yr tyttes' – Achae te sycke vesse meng itirrae berkes, 'Mayde prythee doff thyn knyckeres' – Achae te lelle patouty tirrae drawers, 'Allo darling give us one off ye wrysste then' – A pirani te des mai cabbe rancke), as sexist as they are mocking of Romani historiography. For those who want to learn our language, Marc Vandekeere (2006) offers *Subliminal Learn Romany*, a CD containing nothing but the sound of ocean waves breaking upon the shore. When contacted and asked to provide an explanation for this, Mr Vandekeere said that it was first necessary to find a Romani grammar somewhere to work with, while playing the CD in the background.

Other Romani 'facts' which, once claimed, may get repeated ad infinitum, have to do with the vocabulary of the language. These have without exception been made by people who don't speak Romani, but whose authority shows itself in their perceptions of what Romani should or should not be like. Elsewhere in this volume I document the repetition of the idea that Romani lacks words for 'possession' and 'duty' from ten different sources, each copying from its predecessor over a period of more than a century, and seemingly having originated with statements first found in Grellmann (1807). Eleanor Smith writes that 'in the gypsy language the words "divine" and "devilish" are the same' (1943: 59) – a novelist, incidentally, whom Angus Fraser called 'desperately fond of inventing fantasies about herself, [and who] liked to claim Gypsy blood' (1994: 29). These two words, both native to the language, could not be more different, viz. *devlikano* and *bengesko*. Similar statements from other writers maintain that Romani does not have words for 'truth', 'beautiful', 'read', 'write', 'time', 'danger', 'warmth' and 'quiet' (discussed in detail in Chapter 10).

Examples of the mystical Gypsy may be found at 'The Gypsy' (at http://larp.com/jahavra/ gypsy1.html) which informs the visitor that,

> Gypsies are normally dark skinned with bold flashing eyes; however it is not unusual to find golden or crimson haired Gypsies … most Gypsies live in travelling waggons called vardos … the campfire is the center of Gypsy family life; the three distinct nations of the Gypsy are the Lowara, the Ursari and the Kalderaša.

'Ultragypsy' in San Francisco (http://www.ultragypsy.com) explains in the poster for its 2008 'Hottest Dyke March' that,

> Gypsies, (pronounced *jip-sEs*) noun: [are] tight communities of artisans, musicians and dancers. Fiercely independent, they sometimes stay but never settle. Throughout history the word has come to include all who live outside societal norms and defy taboos to follow their passions.

Another example of what is probably a deliberate concoction is found in John Geipel's book *The Europeans* (1969). A serious historical and linguistic study, it includes Romani, stating in a footnote,

> A gipsy street seller of lucky charms recently told the author in the Portobello Road, 'Well, if you putches me, baw, cheeros is vassavo just now. We on'y bickins about desh cawlic matchkcrs in a sawler. Gi's a coupla tringerooshies for a cuppa mooter an' a packet o' tooves, wontcher?' ('Well, if you asks me, mate, times is hard just now. We only sells about ten black cats in a morning. Give us a couple of bob for a cup of tea and some cigarettes, won't you?') – a fantastic mixture of English, cant, Sanskrit, Turkish, Slavic and possibly German! (1969: 90)

While it's remotely conceivable that this could have happened, it is most unlikely that it in fact did. Why would a Romanichal use his ethnolect with a total stranger, and a non-Romani person at that, and expect him to understand it? The sentences appear to be a Borromani concoction, but they misinterpret *cheeros* as a plural noun, and Professor

Geipel has the man asking for a cup of urine. Like Winifred Lehmann, whose Romani sample in his linguistics textbook contains not a word of Romani (1983: 214), academic rigour can get less attention when it comes to Romanies and the Romani language.

In 1973, Dodgson drew attention to what he hoped might have been the very first documented sample of written Romani: a rhyme apparently published in 1517, a full quarter-century earlier than Boorde's sentences referred to above. He had come across the following bawdy incantation while thumbing through a (then) recently published book on witchcraft by Peter Haining (1972):

> *Dui rika hin mire mine*
> *Dui yara hin leskro kor*
> *Avnas dui yek jelo*
> *Keren akana yek jeles*

As his source for this, Haining listed a work of esoterica entitled the *Grimorium Verum*, for which he gave a publication date of 1517. Hodgson was unable to locate the *Grimorium* and so wrote to Peter Haining in care of his publisher. Haining replied that he had also been unable to find the book, but had been given the verses and that reference by an (unidentified) colleague. He also failed to provide a return address. Hodgson then passed the task along to the late Angus Fraser, who ascertained that the book is generally believed by scholars to be an eighteenth-, rather than a sixteenth-century work, but who was himself also unable to locate a copy.

The rhyme is in a remarkably standardised spelling for a sixteenth- (or even an eighteenth-) century Romani text, although it contains the misreading *mine* for *minč* in its first line. The dialect is a Central one, probably from the Hungarian-Slovak or the Transylvanian lands, and the orthographic conventions are English, not Continental, to judge from the evident values of the 'j' and the 'y'. Given its form, and that it is an incantation to ensure fertility in women, a few readily available sources from which it might have been lifted come at once to mind. The only one aimed at a popular market, however, is Leland (1891), and sure enough, the verse is to be found on page 100 of that book, with the following form:

Dui riká hin mire minč
Dui yārá hin leskro kor
Avnás dūi yek jelo
Keren akána yek jeles

Two sides has my *minč*
Two eggs has his *kar*
Two hearts came together
Now making one heart

Leland made no secret of the fact that many of the rhymes and incantations throughout his book, as well as their orthography, were taken from Wlislocki's various works. Consulting these, the original source for the rhyme in question is revealed in an article by him written in 1887 concerning birth, life and death beliefs among tent-dwelling Romanies in Transylvania.

While Leland is known for his creativity where Romani language and culture are concerned, the culprit this time would appear to be Peter Haining, whose lack of familiarity with Romani orthography, and whose failure to identify his source or to provide his own return address, make him another prime candidate for Concocter of Fake Gypsy History.

Leland himself was probably guiltier of sloppy investigative techniques and an active imagination than of intentionally creating academic hoaxes. He elicited some of his 'Romani' vocabulary from his informants by reading words from a Hindi dictionary to them and asking whether they sounded familiar. Being paid or treated to food and drink for their time, they clearly didn't want to disappoint their interrogator.

His contemporary George Borrow is also responsible for creating non-existent Romani words, which have been picked up from his books and reproduced elsewhere (for example by Pott, 1844 and by Miklosich, 1872) and he may well qualify for the category of deliberate concocter; well over half of the unsubstantiated words in Smart and Crofton's dictionary of English Romani (1875: 157–63) originate with Borrow (as detailed in Chapter 11 of this volume). Smart himself was not innocent of creating his own Romani material and 'commit[ting] it to the disintegrating waves of Gypsy tradition' unidentified as his own, as his notebooks reveal (Macfie, 1927: 143). An amusing although unintentional reinterpretation of a word is found in Sutton's 1982 reprint of Borrow's *Lavo-Lil*, where the original *hin* 'to void ordure' is glossed as 'to *a*void ordure'. This is modern Angloromani *hingger* or *hinder* 'defecate'.

Travellers don't have to be Romanies to be susceptible to a little fudging of the truth. 'T.J.' includes a version of the Lords Prayer in his account of American Traveller life 'which was recited to [him] by [his] Grand-Uncle Ned' (2007: 117), but which matches, word for word, (Hancock 1986: 207), itself a phonemicised respelling taken with acknowledgement from Macalister (1937: 139–40), e.g. for the English words 'but' <*bat*> and 'our' <*aur*>.

Two writers, Kogalnicean and Vaillant, who have shamelessly appropriated from each other's work, even to the extent of copying each other's mistakes, are represented in Romani lexicography; we find for example the English Romani word for 'hedgehog', *hochiwichi*, turning up in Romanian Romani wordlists such as that by Kogalnitchan who lists *hotschauitscha* (1837: 60), or Vaillant, who has *hoc'awiça* (1861: 108) – although the source of the word is in the regional English dialect *urchin* (cf. the prickly 'sea urchin'), and it exists only in Britain, having first been recorded by Roberts in 1836, Vaillant's and Kogalnicean's unacknowledged and respelt source. There is likewise scarcely a dictionary of Caló (Spanish Romani) that is original, each one copying freely from the one preceding it, mistakes and all, usually without a word of acknowledgement.

Roger Moreau has built an entire thesis around a misinterpretation. On the basis of the word 'Nawar', the place-name *Dasht i Nawar* is believed by him to mean 'Desert of the Nawar'. According to the standard Nelles 1:1,500,000 map of Afghanistan there is a Lake *Navar* about ninety miles west of Ghazni, and Moreau places his desert next to this. It is posited by him in his book to be the location to which three Indian peoples were taken from India as captives by Mohammed of Ghazni, three distinct ethnic groups who grew together over time to become the ancestors of the Romanies. 'Nawar' is an Arabic name for the Domari-speaking Gypsies in the Middle East. Their eventual date of departure for the West, he maintains, was at the end of the twelfth century:

> 'When do you think they left that terrible place on their journey West, Uncle?'

'The year following the Battle of Tarain – twenty-five miles north of Delhi – AD 1193 would be my guess. In fact I'd put Patsi's shirt on it' (1995: 111).

He continues (1995: 116), '[t]hey had entered Dasht i Nawar as three separate peoples. Three and a half centuries later they were leaving as a race, the appellations Lohar, Banjara and Kanjar forgotten. Their 'Romany roots' had taken hold.' But that entry into the region would have been in AD 843, over a century before Mohammed Ghaznavi was born.

Nawar is the plural of *Nuri*, elsewhere known as *Luri* and *Luli*, and probably adopted by Arabic from the Indian *luth*, meaning 'plunderer' (cf. *lur* 'robber' in Romani). One would assume, then, that the entire toponym were Arabic. However, 'Desert of the Nawar' would be *sahra'i nawar* in that language. The word *dašt* means 'rubbish' in Arabic. In Persian, long the lingua franca of Afghanistan, the word for 'desert' is either the adopted Arabic *sāhra* or the native *biaban*, while *Nawar* is an Iranian family name entirely unconnected with the Dom. The language indigenous to the area, however, is Pashto, and here, the word for 'desert' is *dašt*, and *nawār* in Pashto means 'a cultivated place, a habitation' – *Dašt-i-Nawar*, therefore, in the region's native language, means something like 'inhabited desert' rather than 'desert of the Nawar'. Alternatively, if the lake's name *Navar* is the source of the toponym, it is hardly likely that a lake in a non-Arabic-speaking country would be named with the Arabic word for 'Gypsies'. *If* the area is called *dašt* today (although *Dasht i Nawar* doesn't appear on the Nelles map) this is surely more recent, and must refer to the fact that the lakebed is now dry. The very name *Lake Navar* indicates that it held water in the past, and it is hard to imagine that 1200 years ago the area adjacent to it would have been a desert and named as such for the Lohar, Banjara and Kanjar that Moreau believes to have occupied it. (It was Roger Moreau too who, in his capacity as a self-proclaimed 'expert on Romany culture', provided *Cleo Magazine* with 'Your ancient Gypsy guide to wild sex'. It explains that '[t]he nomadic Romany people believe every man is ruled by one of 13 totem animals; to discover your ideal man, you must first identify his love totem' (Moreau, 2000: 83)).

Like the Moshto story which has been picked up and repeated as fact in works published subsequently, Moreau's account of Romani origins is likewise already finding adherents. Patrick Lee (2000: 27) says it provides:

[A] more feasible solution to the puzzle of the Gypsies' early days. Roger Moreau ... suggests that the Gypsies were taken from their homeland in vast numbers as slaves in the ninth century AD by the Afghan-Turks who used them to ferry booty out of India into Afghanistan. Three tribes, the Lohar, the Banjara and the Kanjar, who bore a great resemblance to the Gypsies in Europe and who were also at the lower end of the caste system in India, provided easy pickings for these ruthless marauders in their greed for India's vast wealth.

Besides questioning the actual meaning of *Dašt-i-Nawar*, and therefore the entire hypothesis that rests upon it, the date of the exodus proposed by Moreau (the ninth century) and the identity of the ancestors of the Romanies (from 'the lower end of the caste system in India') also bear scrutiny: regarding the date, the relocation of the Lohar, Banjara and the Kanjar into non-Indian-speaking territory in the first half of the ninth century does not coincide with the fact that the language or languages which subsequently developed into Romani were still a part of Middle Indo-Aryan at the time of its development into New Indo-Aryan at the beginning of the eleventh century (discussed in Chapter 5 in the present volume).

Regarding the caste identity of the pre-Roma, Bhalla (1992: 331–2), on the basis of bio-anthropological data comparing Romani and Indian blood groups, concludes that,

[T]he results of the distance analysis clearly refute the Dom theory. The gene pool of East European Gypsies is more in line with the stock of Indian people represented by Jat Sikhs, Panjabi Hindus and Rajputs, who share a common ethnic substratum. The dominant ethnic element in the Doms and Kolis, the two representatives of the low caste population, is Proto-Australoid, which is not reflected in any sizeable proportion in the genetic makeup of East European Gypsies.

This 'common ethnic substratum' is supported by recent and more rigorous serological investigation. A team of researchers at Cowan University's Centre for Human Genetics in Perth, after exhaustive blood samplings from fourteen Romani communities throughout Europe, concluded in a report dated June 2001 that,

Analysis of slow-evolving polymorphisms has identified a single paternal and a single maternal lineage of Indian shared by all [Romani] groups ... these lineages belong to a small subset of the known genetic diversity of the Indian subcontinent. Thus, Roma descend from a small ancestral ethnic minority in the Indian subcontinent that has subsequently fractured into multiple population isolates within Europe.

Elsewhere (Hancock, 2002) I discuss the need for higher academic standards in treatments of Romanies. The very latest authoritative volume, part of Gale Research's *Indigenous Peoples of the World* series (Sharp, 2003) still begins 'The Gypsies are a nomadic people ... living and travelling in caravans of colourfully painted waggons', and has all groups belonging to *vitsas*, a category and a word exclusive to the Vlax Romanies alone. That author also maintains that Romani is not a written language (2003: 49), despite abundant evidence to the contrary on the many websites she consulted in preparing the book. That certain authors demonstrate less attention to accuracy may well be a reflection, conscious or not, of the low regard in which they hold Romanies as a people, or the fierce urge to make us what they want us to be. As controversial as such findings as those of Bhalla and others may be, like the contemporary linguistic research being undertaken by Boretzky, Bakker, Matras, Friedman, Halwachs and others, they are the result of scientific investigation and analysis, and contrast as sharply with the non-academic literature as the image of 'gypsies' cultivated by the latter does with true Romani identity.

Indeed, a clear parallel is evident here between the two: those writing about Romanies generally maintain scholarly standards; those writing about 'small-g-gypsies' see no need to do so. The newcomer to the field has a difficult job discerning the two.

When the Cowan findings were made public (in Gresham *et al.*, 2001), the immediate response from a subscriber on one Romani/ Traveller listserver (posted 12: *xij*: 01) and himself an academic, was that they were just a 'newly souped-up version of racialist thought ... crap'. Such reaction and the debate it engenders is necessary; it moves the discipline forward and separates the useful lines of pursuit from those leading nowhere; but the arena is not mostly populated by specialists who are in a position to judge and critique the data. The overwhelming majority of those with even a passing interest in Romanies are the same people that might read Stephen King's *Thinner* or watch Walt Disney's *Hunchback of Notre Dame*.

Working with my own students over the years, I hear from them repeatedly that they cannot tell whether the sources they are consulting for their own research papers are reliable or not. Should a project on Romani religious belief rely on Wood? Should a study of gender roles use Walker as a source? Is Moreau a good book for early Romani history? All have been assumed to be trustworthy by my students. If there is to be a sincere concern for Romani Studies there must be a sincere concern for Romanies too, and the same criticism we do not hesitate to level at the work of our academic colleagues must extend to the popular treatments which, after all, reach a far larger audience and which help to shape the misconceptions and attitudes associated with our Romani people.

CHAPTER THIRTEEN

Gypsy Mafia, Romani saints:
the racial profiling of Romani Americans

The increase in racial profiling by the police directed at Romani Americans has led to some fumbling attempts on the part of their spokesmen to cover their bigotry by creating their own distinction between 'Gypsy' and 'Romani', on the model of the distinction between 'Mafia' and 'Italian'. But it is not working. Following is Ian's document in support of one such individual who has been the target of such categorisation.

[ed.]

Compared with the massive record of murder, theft, kidnapping and other crimes by non-Gypsies against Gypsies throughout history, Gypsy crime against non-Gypsies pales almost into insignificance, so that to prioritise the study of the latter over the former shows a twisted sense of values.
(Letter to Dennis Marlock dated 2 August 1990 from Dr Thomas Acton, Professor of Romani Studies, University of Greenwich, England)

It is evident that in the present case Mr Weems (a pseudonym) is being singled out on the basis of his ethnicity, and is therefore the target of racial animus. My review of selected discovery, which includes a bulletin issued by the Cherry Hill (New Jersey) Police written by Investigator John Thomson which refers to 'Gypsie' [*sic*] activity and a tape-recorded conversation with one of the investigating officers, as well as my knowledge of Romani history, confirms this conclusion. It is also clear that those law enforcement officers who focus on the people they refer to as 'Gypsies' and on 'Gypsy crime' are in violation of the constitutional protection afforded Romani Americans ('Gypsies'), who are shielded as a group from this kind of discrimination under the terms of Title VII of the 1964 Civil Rights Act. While an individual must be judged on the nature of his offense, he cannot pay a price for being what he *is*, although it is abundantly clear that in the US today, as in eighteenth-century England, simply *being* a Gypsy is enough to brand a person as a lawbreaker. I intend to establish in this report that this situation rests on a pattern of inherited treatment and attitudes that have become fixed over time, and on the vague understanding of what the perception of 'Gypsy' identity actually is on the part of the law enforcement body, which has resulted in the racial animus/targeting exhibited in this case.

The popular conception of the Gypsy is rooted historically in story and song, although it is mainly kept alive nowadays by the media. Despite the emerging awareness of Romanies as a real people, particularly as a result of the drastic changes that have taken place in the world since the fall of Communism, the fictional Gypsy still asserts himself. Thus an announcer on New York television station WABC eleven o'clock news on 6 October 2006 could still report on an incident involving 'real live Gypsies'. That she would never have referred to 'real live African Americans' or 'real live Jews' suggests a subconscious comparison with storybook Gypsies.

Discrimination against Romanies ('Gypsies') in America dates from colonial times; three were with Columbus on his second voyage in 1498 as unwilling transportees of the Spanish government. Romanies were shipped as slaves to Virginia, Jamaica and Barbados from England and Scotland (Dawson, 2001), and to Louisiana from France and Spain (Hancock, 1987 and 2002). Anti-Gypsy policies towards the end of the nineteenth century probably derived their impetus from the increase in discrimination evident at the beginnings of Reconstruction, following the abolition of slavery in America; there are several references to Romanies as a 'people of colour', as a visible minority, in the literature of that period; Lincoln's successor President Andrew Johnson vetoed the right to vote for Romanies, expressing his fear that the requirements of the Civil Rights Bill were designed 'to operate in favour of the coloured, and against the white, race [because they] comprehend ... the people called Gipsies as well as the entire race designated as blacks' (*Legislation for the Colored Man*, Philadelphia, February 1866).

Romanies are recognised as a distinct ethnic population of Asian origin by the federal government; five special Congressional sessions have been held in the past decade to address the increase of anti-Romani racial violence in Europe and the consequent increase in Romani asylum seekers coming to the US; acknowledgement of the substantial and growing Gypsy presence in our country is evidenced by the fact that the *Census 2000* forms were circulated for the first time in our Romani language.

There nevertheless remain laws on the books in various states and counties that continue to operate against Gypsies. Many of these laws, a list of which fills thirty-four pages (Gilbert, 1947: 567–601), were inherited from Europe and were intended to be used against the earlier Gypsy populations in the US; they have since found new application against the more recently arrived, and more visible, Eastern European Romanies escaping the post-Communist increase in racial violence in that region, many of whom are seeking political asylum here. Following is a selection of such laws (from Hancock, 1987), some of which remain in effect; the last such law in New Jersey was only repealed in 1998:

> [G]ypsies ... for each county ... shall be jointly and severally liable with his or her associates [to a fine of] two thousand dollars. (*State Code of Mississippi*, Section 27-17-191)

> The governing body may make, amend, repeal, and enforce ordinances to licence and regulate ... gypsies. (*New Jersey Statutes*, 40: 52–1)

> After the passage of this act, it shall be unlawful for any ... gypsies ... to ... settle within the limits of any county of this state [without having first obtained a yearly license to do so]. (*Pennsylvania Statutes*, Section 11810)

> Any person may demand of any ... gypsies that they shall produce or show their license issued within such county, and if they shall refuse to do so ... he shall seize all the property in the possession of such [Gypsies]. (*Pennsylvania Statutes*, Section 11803)

> Gypsies [in the State of Maryland] must pay jurisdictions a license fee of $1000 before settling or doing business. When any gypsy is arrested, all his property and all the property of members of any group with which he may be travelling, can be confiscated and sold to pay any fine a court may levy against the arrested gypsy. Sheriffs are paid a $10 bounty for any gypsy they arrest who pays the $1000 fee after he is arrested. (Logan, 1976)

> Whenever ... gypsies shall be located within any municipality ... the

county department of health or joint county department of health shall have power … to order such [Gypsies …] to leave said municipality within the time specified. (*Pennsylvania Title 53: Municipal and Quasi-Municipal Corporations*, Chapter xvii, Section 3701)

It is illegal in Pennsylvania to be a Gypsy without a license … Any Gypsy who insists on being what he was born – a Gypsy – without a license, is liable to up to $100 fine and 30 days in jail. A constable may confiscate and sell a convicted Gypsy's possessions to satisfy the sentence … any person may demand to see a Gypsy's license. If the Gypsy cannot produce a license, the person may turn the Gypsy in to any convenient justice of the peace. (Smart, 1969)

Upon each company of … Gypsies, engaged in trading or selling merchandise or livestock of any kind, or clairvoyant, or persons engaged in fortunetelling, phrenology, or palmistry, $250 [is] to be collected … [from those who] live in tents or travel in covered waggons and automobiles, and who may be a resident of some country or who reside without the State, and who are commonly called traveling horse traders and Gypsies. (*Georgia Acts and Resolutions*, 1927, Part I, Title II, Section 56, p. 3)

Texas law refers to 'Prostitutes, Gypsies and vagabonds' in the same breath, and charges the Romany people $500 to live there. (Bernardo, 1981: 108)

Be it enacted by the General Assembly of the State of Indiana, that it shall be unlawful for any band of Gypsies … to camp in tent, wagon or otherwise, on any public highway in this state, or lands adjacent thereto … Any person or persons violating the provisions of this Act shall be deemed guilty … and upon conviction shall be fined not exceeding twenty-five dollars or imprisoned in the county jail not exceeding thirty days, or both (*State of Indiana Statutory Regulations, Section I*). 'This statutory law has been used so often against the Gypsies in that state, that Indiana has not been visited by Gypsies for a long time.' (Marchbin, 1939: 152)

Smart (1969) pointed out the injustice inherent in such laws: 'Because a state does not require an Irishman to have a license to be Irish, or an Italian to have an Italian license, it is both un-American and discriminatory for the state to require a Gypsy to have a license to be a

Gypsy.' Steve Kaslov, who founded the first Romani benevolent society in the US, the *Red Dress Association* in New Jersey in 1927, and who met with Franklin D. Roosevelt to try to get some support for the plight in which he saw his people, believed that it was the police, enforcing such laws, who posed the greatest threat to American Gypsies:

> In county after county, state after state, troopers whisk unwanted Gypsies over the boundary ... Steve tells of one such journey: 'We were not allowed to stop for rations' ... Real tears ran down his cheeks at the bitter memory of that experience ... In New York, as in other places, the law is often applied to them with needless cruelty. Only a few weeks ago, a five weeks old nursing baby died of starvation in an unheated room when the mother, who was arrested on a charge of stealing a wallet, was held in the custody of the police for three days. (Weybright, 1938: 142, 145)

The most vocal crusader against 'Gypsy scams' is a Detective Dennis Marlock of the Milwaukee Police Department and creator of Professionals Against Confidence Crime, who maintains the *FraudTech* website and who lectures to police departments around the country on the topic. His attempts to define 'Gypsy scam' are, however, made entirely in the context of behaviour – what he sees as a culture of criminality. In his 1993 error-ridden book on our 'secret language' he defines *Gypsy* as 'a criminal lifestyle of thievery and deception dating back to 1000 AD', and *Romani* as 'of India; its people; a native or inhabitant of India, or a person of Indian descent' (1993: 6). Similarly guilty of mangling our language was J. Henry Strickland in a small book entitled *The Story of the Gypsy Life* written by his wife 'in the humble Gypsy way' (Adams and Strickland, 1941). He boasted in a newspaper interview that he was 'the first and only non-Gypsy ever to win their confidence ... I have learned everything you'd want to know about Gypsies'. But using that trust he goes on to say that he will 'benefit humanity by telling how Gypsies prey on people, and how they hornswoggle store owners' (*The Daily Oklahoman*, 1941). Not only Roma are capable of confidence trickery.

Kenneth Blachut (2005: 181) of the Kaplan online university defines 'Gypsy-type crime' as a 'crime of trickery or deception with a specific MO in the planning and commission of crime committed by the criminal element of self-proclaimed Gypsies'. Alexis Tarrazi, senior reporter on the New Jersey *Leader*, writes that 'originally, gypsy referred to a group of nomadic people who arrived in Europe from India. But, after many years, the term has become a pejorative, meaning any type of scam artist or swindler' (Tarrazi, 2008).

Marlock's influence has been far-reaching, and it is evident to me that statements made in the present case by Investigators Worst and Thompson have been very much influenced by his misguided rhetoric. Discovery of internal law enforcement records, including all training materials, would establish this link. The law enforcement's widespread identification of Gypsies as *any* people involved in 'crime on the run' became well rooted at a time when little was known about actual Romani history or identity. Now that an understanding of these areas is reaching the general public (including the police), the realisation has also hit home that statements about Gypsies have been made that one would never dare make about any other American ethnic minority. This has led to an attempt to cover the damage already done, resulting in the promotion of an entirely spurious distinction between 'Gypsies' and 'Romanies'. On the *Geraldo Rivera Show* on CBS Television, broadcast in April 1990, which dealt with Gypsy confidence crimes, one 'Gypsy expert' who appeared on that programme, Dr John Dowling, formerly of Marquette University in Wisconsin, asserted that,

> Eventually the Rom are going to be forced to do what the Sicilians did many years ago, terminologically distinguish between the broader population (Sicilians) and the smaller, criminal element (the Mafia). Using the ancient term 'Rom' for all those descendants of the exodus from India, and the much more recent term 'Gypsy' for the criminal element, makes sense and would permit the honest Rom to take pride in their ethnicity and their achievements by distancing themselves from the Gypsies.

Thus we can trace the origin of this new distinction directly to Dr Dowling and Detective Marlock who, on the same show, referred to 'those who once embraced the *Gypsy* life-style. In fact, the Gypsies who came to Milwaukee are now, quite by choice and on their own terms, abandoning their destructive life-style and becoming *Romani* citizens' (emphasis added). On that programme too, Professor Dowling asserted in all seriousness that 'Gypsies don't know the difference between right and wrong, like the rest of us do'.

Knowing that he should follow the Marlock and Dowling 'not-all-Italians-are-Mafia' line of reasoning, Mr Worst was aware that he should be contrasting 'Gypsies' (as the bad few) with something else (as the larger 'honest' group), but was unable to do so: nowhere in his exchange with Ms Copeland were the words *Romani* or *Rom* mentioned.

That recorded conversation shows unequivocal racial bias on the part of Cherry Hill's law enforcement team, and the targeting of Mr Weems. It takes very little effort to demonstrate that there is an institutionalised anti-gypsyism on the part of some law enforcement agencies in the US, and that there is profit to be made for some individuals by keeping this bigotry alive. Clearly it is in Mr Marlock's best interests to foster this relentless barrage of prejudice, since it enables him to travel around the country as a paid, invited speaker, educating his fellow police officers about 'Gypsy criminality'. We have in The Romani Archives and Documentation Center a flyer that was circulated nationally listing over twenty-five presentations on 'Gypsy crime' scheduled for just one year in different US cities, by different police department specialists. Based upon his extensive law enforcement seminar experience Detective Marlock has spoken to police departments in Pennsylvania and New Jersey, and is no doubt partly responsible for implanting anti-Gypsy attitudes among law enforcement personnel in those states; in any event his publications and his *FraudTech* website and others like it are available to everybody. But it is abundantly evident from the sources available that Mr Marlock, and the groups he addresses, remain nevertheless unsure of what a 'Gypsy' actually is, and *herein lies the root of the problem.*

In Austin, Texas in 2004 a national seminar was held by the APD entitled 'Gypsy Cops'. It dealt with police officers who moved from department to department. Like 'Gypsy scholars' and 'Gypsy chorus-line dancers', the word has nothing to do with ethnicity, only image. At least one interpretation of 'gypsy cop' was provided by Jane Pauley and Stone Phillips in their NBC special of the same name: 'Two officers were charged, accused of brutality, that's why they call them gypsy cops' (Pauley and Phillips, 1992).

Like Mr Marlock, Investigator Worst also believes 'Gypsy' to be a category of person defined by his behaviour rather than by his ethnicity. Caught off guard when reached on the telephone by Ms Gladys Copeland, and pressured by her to provide a definition of 'Gypsy', he evidently realised that he was required to make some sort of contrast between 'Gypsies' and something else, but was quite unprepared. What he said was what in fact he believes, that we were 'probably Hungarian

... a culture as such ... that's what a Gypsy is ... this is just a culture'. Ms Copeland reminded Investigator Worst that he had earlier told her that Gypsies were 'uneducated, and they traveled in a ring, that they were fraudulent', and asked him, 'is that their ethnicity?' His immediate answer was 'No'. And because *Gypsies* in Mr Worst's mind are criminals, and because Mr Weems is a Gypsy, he is therefore also a criminal. Mr Worst's negative analogies to 'Micks' and the Irish and to 'Guineas' and the Italians, demonstrate the racial animus he feels towards Gypsies.

Like Mr Marlock and Mr Worst too, sociologist Erdmann Beynon believes that anybody at all who pursues a certain means of livelihood can become a Gypsy, since 'one's membership in the pariah (i.e. Gypsy) group has tended to become identical with participation in their characteristic function' (1936: 358), a notion repeated by Terry Getsay, formerly head of the Illinois State Police Gypsy Activity Project, who was quoted as saying in the pages of *Spotlight: A Police Lifestyle Magazine* that '[t]he label of "Gypsy" refers to *any* family-oriented band of nomads who may be from *any* country in the world ... the only measure of respect a Gypsy woman can get is on her abilities as a thief' (1983: 59). Her success as a wife, a mother and a homemaker obviously count for nothing in Mr Getsay's eyes. Perhaps most egregiously, Joseph Sheley, Provost and Vice President for Academic Affairs at California State University and author of *Criminology: A Contemporary Handbook* includes the information that:

> ... emotionally dependent women are more easily persuaded by criminal men to 'do it all for love'. Among Gypsies, where traditional gender roles prevail and male dominance is absolute, Gypsy women do practically all the work and earn most of the money, and the culture dictates a large female-to-male involvement in thievery. (2000: 103)

The authority for this information is Peter Maas' fictional novel *King of the Gypsies* (1978); Professor Sheley's book is used in a class on criminology at my own university.

For these gentlemen, as Ralph Sandland wrote in the *Journal of Law and Society*, the word '*Gypsy* ... is merely a job description' (1996: 384). This was certainly the case in a story that ran in the Wisconsin *Capital Times*; it began 'Employees arriving at Bruegger's Bagels on Madison's west side were robbed by two black males and two black females described as "gypsies" early this morning' (Anonymous, 2007). In an April 2008 newsletter article entitled *More 'gypsy' scams* the Hammond, Indiana Chief of Police Brian Miller wrote of criminals 'described as Hispanic' but continues, after repeating the 'forging/stealing Christ's nails' story, by admitting that Gypsies 'look Hispanic and are often described as such'. The logic here, then, is that if the perpetrators look Hispanic, they must be Gypsies rather than actually Hispanic. Chief Miller adds 'What are Gypsies? I'm often asked that question. The original Gypsies come from Europe, more specifically, Romania.' In his support, it should be added that he does make a distinction between '*gypsies*' (his quotes and lower case 'g') and '*Gypsies*', but he must still be taken to task for perpetuating the label *gypsy* as representative of a behaviour and not an ethnic people.

In St Anthony, Minnesota, 'A Bulgarian delegation was ordered out of a grocer's store after the manager, who was worried about "gypsy-like" shoplifters, mistook the group for Gypsies; he said "put everything down and leave; we don't want your kind of people in this store"' (Anonymous, 1991a, 1991b). The proprietor said that he would apologise to the US Information Agency visitors 'if they *weren't* Gypsies … and if they were we'd certainly like to get them out faster'. His action was in response to a police department circular, a copy of which is in possession of the Romani Archives, which described individuals in 'gypsy-like' dress but who in fact were listed as 'Hispanic' and 'Spanish-speaking'.

In his telephone conversation with Mrs Copeland, Mr Worst defines *Gypsies* as 'those type of people who consider themselves to be … con artists', and tells her that we can be recognised by certain characteristics (which he attributes to Mr Weems by way of confirming that he is a Gypsy): thus we don't want to educate our children, we don't want to educate ourselves, and we're 'incapable' of reading and writing. When she told him that Mr Weems did not fit this description, and that he 'made goals and everything … he wanted his kids to go to school', Mr Worst replied, 'I'm told, and I haven't confirmed yet, he doesn't have any children … I'm telling, correct, I'm telling you what I'm told.' Mr Weems does in fact have children.

Apparently in an effort to head off any possible charges of racial prejudice, Messrs. Marlock and Dowling have created an entirely arbitrary distinction between 'Gypsies' and 'Rom'. They did so in their book *License to Steal* (1994) and again on Geraldo Rivera's television talk show referred to above. In Mr Marlock's words,

> [T]he term Gypsy is not meant to cast any aspersions on the majority of Romani, who are honest and active law-abiding members of American society. Gypsy is to Romani what Mafia is to Sicilians, a designation intended to separate the criminal from the noncriminal elements of Romani society.

While – in his terms – there may be individuals within the Romani population who are defined wholly by socially determined criteria, and whom he refers to as 'Gypsies', these are not typical of the Romani population, 'the majority of [whom]', he says on the cover of his book, 'have assimilated into American culture as honest and active members'.

I maintain that this is nothing more than a poorly conceived and insupportable example of the semantic manipulation of ethnic labelling, a scrambling to cover earlier uninformed statements, the purpose of which has been to allow Mr Marlock to indulge his apparent bigotry toward the Romani people while seeming not to be doing so. This is not a legitimate distinction. It is certainly not one recognised by members of the Romani community ourselves, for whom 'Gypsy' is by far the most common self-ascription when speaking English – nor is it one reflected in the principal dictionaries of the English language. Thus the *Oxford English Dictionary* defines *Romany* simply as 'a gipsy' without discussion (1956: 1750), and *Gipsy* in turn as 'a member of a wandering race (by themselves called *Romani*) of Hindu origin' (1956: 794); while the *Webster's New World Dictionary* entry for *Romany* lists simply 'a gipsy' 1966: 1750), this being further defined at that entry as 'a member of a wandering people with dark skin and black hair, found throughout the world and believed to have originated in India' (1966: 648). In neither of these leading standard dictionaries is there any indication that a semantic distinction exists between the words *Gypsy* and *Romani*; both works in fact list them as synonyms – variant names for the same thing. The two words are used interchangeably in the titles of a number of authoritative and scholarly works, some of whom are themselves Roma, and some of which are listed in the references (including Mazzone, Mirga, Rekosh and Weyrauch).

Indeed Mr Marlock himself seems to confuse his two labels at times. On page 16 of his book he refers to 'Gypsies, or Romani as they prefer to be called' (Marlock and Dowling, 1994: 16). He says he is sure (1994: 34–5) that having read thus far, the reader will realise that 'this book does not provide a complimentary view of the *Romani* society' (my emphasis). On page 281, he refers to '*Gypsies* in general, most of whom are honest, law-abiding citizens' (emphasis added); just three pages later, however, he speaks of 'the *Romani* who are beggars, cheats, con artists and thieves' (1994; emphasis added). On page 294 he refers to '*Romani* on both sides of the law'. He writes about 'dishonest Romani, the *true* Gypsies' (1994: 17), and cautions that 'no one is invulnerable to Gypsy crime' on the dust-jacket. Such crime, it says, 'has a feel, a smell and an aura that screams "Gypsy"' (1994: 5). His latest commentary on his *FraudTech* website is headed 'Scam in progress: *Romani* activists targeting US tax dollars'. In his own defence, however, Mr Marlock argues that 'the law enforcement organisation never *attributed negative attributes* to the *Romani* people [his emphasis] … only the organised criminal groups who call themselves Gypsies' (Marlock, 2002: 4). Clearly Mr Marlock is as confused about his terminology, and about which people he is really referring to, as I am.

Consider too that the word *Gypsy* should, as a proper noun, be written with a capital initial letter. If the word really referred to a person defined by behaviour, criminal or otherwise, it would be a common noun and written as such, with a lower case /g/. In Mr Marlock's book he writes *Gypsy* with an upper case initial throughout – suggesting that, despite his careful insistence that 'Gypsies' refers not to an ethnic population but to a behaviourally defined subgroup (criminals) within the larger number of Romani Americans, it's clear that he still regards, at least unconsciously, the word as applying to our people as a whole. Implicit too in his belief that Gypsies stand in relation to Roma in the same way that the Mafia stand to Italians, is the totally erroneous – let me say preposterous – idea that Gypsies constitute an actual structured, criminal organisation, a 'crime family' networking countrywide. In his most recent deposition, Detective Marlock could not provide a single instance in which he was able to 'prove' that a 'Gypsy' mafia actually exists.

Terry Getsay's input was responsible for an article in the *Chicago Tribune* with the headline 'Gypsies are new element in organised crime' – which also includes the information that 'the race['s] … origins have been traced to Egypt' (Elson, 1982: 2B). It is significant that while criminal activity associated with specific ethnic groups makes up many of the entries in *The Encyclopaedia of American Crime*, such as the '(Italian) Mafia' and the 'Jewish Mafia' (*Facts on File*: New York, 1982), there is no discussion of 'Gypsy crime', even at the entry on spiritualism. 'Gypsy crime' (as opposed to 'crime') is a created concept, and a concept created for a purpose, as I shall demonstrate; there are no crimes Romani Americans might commit which are unique to our people; there are more non-Romani fortune-tellers in the USA for example, than those who are ethnic Romanies.

An article on Gypsies published in the *FBI Law Enforcement Bulletin* in 1994, in wording reminiscent of the 1899 police conference in Germany which set the wheels in motion that ultimately led to their attempted genocide by the Nazis, stressed that 'interagency cooperation represents the greatest asset law enforcement can employ [against Gypsies]' (Mazzone, 1994: 5).

Sergeant Roy House of the Houston Police Department has spoken in the past about 'Gypsy crime' on Radio KPRC in that city, where he has been regularly introduced as 'the Gypsies' worst nightmare'. One need only replace the word 'Gypsies' with the name of any other ethnic or religious minority to realise how frighteningly oppressive such wording is, coming from a representative of the law, and how reminiscent it is of similar statements made in Hitler's Germany in the last century. Sergeant House has been known to wait outside Gypsy churches in Houston with his video camera, to capture local Romanies on film. The fact that some US law enforcement agencies are contributing to this state of affairs has escaped Detective Marlock, who otherwise seems to recognise on some level that something must be wrong somewhere: 'Just as numerous contemporary Jews fear almost irrationally the resurgence of anti-Semitism, Romani on both sides of the law [*sic*] have cause to dread a new wave of terrorism directed at them' (Marlock and Dowling, 1994: 284).

The targeting of Gypsies as a group, and the maintenance of unconstitutional legislation singling Gypsies out in state and county by-laws, and arguably the existence of ethnicity-specific police 'task forces', can be traced to one Dr Cesare Lombroso, a professor of psychiatry and criminal anthropology at the University of Turin, whose book, *Crime: Its Causes and Remedies* (1918) served as the basis for American legal attitudes and a model for law enforcement manuals in this country until 1940. In it, he devotes a chapter to Romanies who, he wrote (1918: 40) 'are a living example of a whole race of criminals'. The association of behaviour with race (a genetic association) is racism pure and simple, and yet such attitudes continue to be supported by representatives of our police to this day. No acknowledgement is made of the fact that the conviction rate for Romanies arrested for rape or murder is *far* lower than the national average; no acknowledgement is made of the fact that since the very founding of the country Romanies have been excluded *by law* from participating in the larger society, and have had to exist as a marginalised people in America.

Having established that by use of the word 'Gypsies', *the Romani American population as a whole* is included, the following examples take on a sinister aspect: Officers Alcantara and Boughourian, formerly both assigned to the so-called Gypsy Detail in the Los Angeles Police Department, say 'there is no such thing as an honest Gypsy fortune teller. Or an honest Gypsy for that matter' (Stumbo, 1985: 7B). In their article in the June 1975 issue of *The Police Chief* the same officers advised that '[s]trict laws and the enforcement of them will deter Gypsies from inhabiting your community'. This wording differs little from that found in an order issued to all police departments by the German Imperial Ministry of the Interior in 1888 that directly foreshadowed the Holocaust: 'The more that nomadic Gypsies are disconcerted and hampered in their freedom to move, the more they will avoid those regions which no longer provide them any room.'

The Spokane Police Department's *Gypsy File*, a document half an inch thick, has determined that crime constitutes our very culture: 'scams, theft and confrontations with law enforcement officials is a way of life with Gypsies' (dated 1986, on p. 9). The LAPD's *Gypsy Identification File* (1967) states that 'Gypsies are accomplished pickpockets'. This disdain is not restricted to the American police force. Announcement of Britain's 'Gipsy Roma Traveller History month' in June 2008 brought a swift response from representatives of the law, who called it 'political correctness off the scale', and asked, 'what planet [are we] living on?' (Wright, 2008: 1).

In a *Detroit News* article entitled 'it's Gypsy season, so don't get gypped!' (Willing, 1985), Detective Sergeant William Bradway of the Michigan State Police Gypsy Criminal Activity Task force is quoted as saying that 'Gypsies are domineering, very loud, outspoken, cunning and quick-witted; they are completely comfortable with a lifestyle centered around victimising others; they are not very nice'. I could go on. Only Craig Gunkel, Chief of the St Paul Police Department in Minnesota, had the wisdom to admit publicly that 'use of the term "Gypsy" in police reports refers to a type of crime, not the identity of the perpetrators. A crime committed by a Gypsy is not a "Gypsy crime"'.

József Vekerdi (1988: 14) noted that 'the mass media, in a veiled and often less-veiled form, goad opinion in an anti-Gypsy direction'. On several occasions during 2005, a journalist named Hector Becerra telephoned me for a series of interviews in connection with an article he was writing for the *Los Angeles Times* (2006). He even flew to Austin and spent an afternoon with me at the Documentation Center. I gave him contact information for Romani businessmen and community leaders, including a college professor and a psychologist, although he spoke to none of them, and while he was aware of Romani representation in the United Nations and on the US Holocaust Memorial Council, the Council of Europe and the US Department of State, he made no mention of any of that. I explained at length the nature and origin of Romani criminality, stressing that it was regarded as a serious issue within the Romani American population, although one greatly exaggerated by the media. Rather than deal with the situation in any responsible way, however, and providing a balanced picture, his article relied on sensationalism, and consisted of summaries of specific scams, and the liberal use of biased quotes from a certain Mr Sgro. I am still receiving anonymous attacks resulting from that article; an example is appended to this chapter.

The more recent publications issuing from these sources now attempt an air of scholarliness by including some 'serious' Gypsy history; but just as historians and sociologists should not pass themselves off as law enforcement officers, neither should the latter attempt the academic. Their sources are confused and they succeed only in repeating misinformation. For example, it is (of course) hard for them to resist including the story of the stolen nail which, so it goes, earned us the right to steal as a divine reward for sparing Christ some suffering. That our ancestors left India almost exactly a thousand years later than the time that Christ lived is neither here nor there. The story in any case is of non-Romani origin. It's not one of ours.

It is easy for conclusions of this kind to be reached by spokespersons such as those listed here, since by the very nature of their profession the *only* Romani Americans they routinely come in contact with are those who have been apprehended. Jack Morris, author of *Master Criminals Among the Gypsies* (1994) goes so far as to admit that he hasn't interacted personally with Romanies at all, that in fact in writing his book he 'has relied *entirely* on Rom Gypsy-related criminal records' (1994: 1, emphasis added). Yet on this basis alone, he felt qualified to discuss our society.

I have deliberately dwelt at some length on institutionalised anti-gypsyism within American law enforcement, and on Mr Marlock's complicity in it, in order to provide some perspective on his arguments, and to make the case that they are biased and therefore inadmissible. He is directly responsible for police attitudes throughout the country, including those of Investigators Richard Worst and John Thompson. Put simply, there is no such thing as a 'Gypsy fraud', any more than there is an 'Irish fraud' or a 'Swedish fraud' or an 'Anglo fraud'.

On his *FraudTech: Cons, Frauds and Other Lies* website, Detective Marlock reported on the international policy symposium organised by the late Senator Paul Simon on the contemporary plight of the Romani people in post-Communist Europe, and how our own government should be involved. Held at Senator Simon's Institute for Public Policy in Carbondale, Illinois, the keynote speaker was former Washington DC Attorney General Ramsey Clark. The principal targets of Mr Marlock's charges of fraud are myself and the chairman of the Canadian-based Roma Advocacy Centre Ronald Lee, who teaches at the University of Toronto. Despite my background having been intensively investigated over a period of several months by the FBI before my appointment to the US Holocaust Memorial Council by President Clinton, despite the credibility and integrity of a former US Senator and the former US Attorney General, we were nevertheless all 'players' (Marlock's word) complicit, he charges, in an elaborate scam to cheat the federal government. His almost neurotic obsession with 'Gypsy criminality' inserts itself into another report on the same website, this time of my visit in India at the personal invitation of His Holiness the Dalai Lama in March 2003. Summarising my own account of that visit, Marlock takes me to task because (he says) 'missing from Hancock's response is any mention of crime or other similar antisocial behaviour. Then, too, neither did he see fit to *attack* the Dalai Lama for suggesting that Romani people should integrate into the bigger national society' (emphasis added).

Relying on his colleague John Dowling for academic legitimacy, Mr

Marlock has more recently challenged objections to writing the word 'Gypsy' with a lower case 'g'. Dr Dowling is referred to as 'a tenured cultural anthropologist from Marquette University', and on the cover of their book as a 'professor'. However, he had never reached that academic rank, and had already retired as an Associate Professor when that book appeared over ten years ago. Detective Marlock too has only a two-year college background, and no academic credentials beyond that. Their arguments are weak at best, and carefully avoid drawing parallels with such expressions as 'jew down' or 'nigger-rigged'. Particularly, they fail completely to address the real issue being examined here. Mr Marlock also claims (without providing evidence) that I have 'a record for rewriting history to suit [my] own agenda, and for doing so in less than an honest fashion', and adds, 'Please be assured that it is not rumor or speculation that I base this seemingly harsh assessment about Professor Hancock's integrity, but on firsthand knowledge and experience'. He is no doubt referring to my manipulation of the federal government and of the Dalai Lama.

I am personally insulted and offended by Mr Marlock's statements regarding my integrity and the prejudice he directs at the ethnic group to which I belong. The Romaphobia generated by Messrs. Marlock, Worst, House, Morris, Bradway, Sgro, Getsay, Schroeder, Alcantara and others filters into the media and from there out into the general public; it has been difficult and painful for me to explain this state of affairs to my children while they were growing up. I doubt very much that Mr Marlock and his collaborator Mr Dowling would have dared produce a book on African American or Jewish American or Irish American crime, assuming such categories even exist, or that a publisher would have been willing to market such bigotry. I might add that I spent a month in Milwaukee, Mr Marlock's home town, in 1998, where I was recipient of the University of Wisconsin's Gamaliel Chair in Peace and Justice. He gives the impression in his books of maintaining a chatty and informal friendship with Roma in that town. In one 'philosophical discussion' with a local Rom he was told, 'you just keep up the hard work [of hounding us?], Dennis ... I've a car to buy' (2001: 20) – but in actual fact he is viewed with great suspicion by the Wisconsin and Illinois Romanies and everywhere given very short shrift.

I gave many talks both to organisations and on the radio in Milwaukee during that time, and invited Mr Marlock to meet with me in public debate on this issue. Not once did he attempt to make contact with me then (although I was told that he was present at some of my talks), nevertheless he claims that he has made 'repeated attempts' over time to do so. We shall extend a personal invitation for him to speak at our next organisational meeting, and I very much hope that he will accept.

Appendix 1

Message received anonymously on 23 September 2006 from 'Getaclue'.

Re: Gypsies and crime/L.A. Times article in Jan. 2006

You are utterly deluded if you believe that 'Roma' are not disproportionately involved in specific kinds of criminal activity and criminal activity in general, just as black men in the US tend to be. Any reasonably objective individual could tell you that Polish people do not approach me in shopping mall parking lots and ask if I want the dents in my car repaired and then throw insults at me if I refuse. Neither do people from Sri Lanka. And while we are on the subject, it is Muslims and not Presbyterians who generally hijack airplanes. So knock it off with your politically correct bullshit and deal with the unadorned truth. I certainly do not wish you or any group of people harm, but you would do well, as a leader of sorts for your community, to look honestly at what is wrong with your culture rather than to adopt a reflexively defensive posture every time someone points out something that is true but unflattering. That would entail MAINSTREAMING yourselves so that gainful employment is the norm rather than the exception in your community. You sir are not the norm in your community and you know it. You have an obligation as a scholar to look at things dispassionately and analytically. You have a second obligation as a leader to help your people and create positive change rather than denying what everyone knows is true.

CHAPTER FOURTEEN

The 'gypsy' stereotype and the sexualisation of Romani women

The Gypsy women and girls ... are capable of exciting passion of the most ardent description, most particularly in the bosoms of those who are not of their race, which passion of course becomes the more violent when the almost utter impossibility of gratifying it is known.

(Borrow, 1841: I: 88)

The fact that the representation of people of colour – and women of colour in particular – has been exoticised and sexualised in the Western perception is nothing new (cf. Burney, 1988; Grant, 2004; Jan Mohamed, 1985; Jiwani, 1992; Lalvani, 1995; Negra, 2001; Parmar, 1984; and Shohat and Stam, 1994). The Romani people, or 'Gypsies', have not escaped this portrayal and the literature that examines it is growing rapidly (cf. Awosusi, 2000; Briel, 1989; Champagne, 2002; Charnon-Deutsch, 2004; Esplugas, 1999; Gabor, 2003; Gordon, 2004; Hancock, 1996, 2002, 2004; Hund, 2000; Iordanova, 2003; Lemon, 1996; Malvinni, 2002; Mayall, 2004; McLaughlan, 2004; Needham, 1920; Nord, 1998, 2001, 2007; Pellegrino, 1998; Schrevel, 2003; and Bardi, 2007).

There are today some twelve million Romanies throughout the world, with between two and three million living in the Americas and elsewhere, and approximately eight million throughout Europe – thus constituting the largest and most widely dispersed of its many minority peoples. There are nearly twice as many Romanies as there are Danes or Swedes.

When Romanies first appeared in Europe, they were assumed to be a part of the Islamic spread into Christendom, and were identified with the

Ottoman Turks. 'Turks' as an exonym referring to Romanies is still found today in some places. Other misnomers that have stuck are 'Egyptians', resulting in such erroneous labels as *Gypsies* (earlier *'gypcians*), *(E)gitanos*, *Gitans* and so on, and the Byzantine Greek nickname *Ατσίγγανοι,* '(the) don't touch (people)', which has given rise to *Zigeuner, Cigan, Tsigane* and so on.

While there are mediæval and Renaissance references to an actual Indian origin this fact did not become generally known, and was eventually forgotten even by the Romanies themselves. As a consequence a great many incorrect, and sometimes bizarre, hypotheses were put forward. These included an origin inside the hollow earth, or on the Moon or in Atlantis, that Gypsies were the remnants of a prehistoric race, were Nubians, or Druids, or else were Jews coming out of hiding after the mediæval pogroms, or even that they were a conglomerate drawn from the fringes of European society that artificially dyed their skin and spoke a made-up jargon for the purposes of plotting criminal activity; it is the very existence of this nebulous identity that has contributed to the ease of its manipulation. The real origin was purportedly discovered fortuitously in the 1760s when a student at a Dutch university who had learnt some Romani from labourers on his family's estate in Hungary overheard some students from India discussing their own language (see Chapter 4 in this volume). Recognising similarities, he passed the information along and eventually it became public knowledge through the first book ever written on the subject (Grellmann, 1783).

The publication of Grellmann's book during the Enlightenment, and which appeared in an English edition in 1807, coincided with the emergence of a number of scientific disciplines, including botany and zoology. The need to categorise the plants and animals being encountered in the new European colonies overseas quickly extended to the classification of non-European human populations as well, and the nineteenth century saw a plethora of dissertations dealing with 'race' and the ranking of human groups – not only in terms of their perceived genetic, social, and technological advancement, but in terms of gender as well. Even Charles Darwin employed clearly biased language when he referred to 'the uniform appearance in various parts of the world of Gypsies and Jews ... contrast[ing] sharply with all the virtues represented by the territorially settled and "culturally advanced" Nordic

Aryan race'; he maintained further that 'man is more courageous, pugnacious and energetic than woman, and has a more inventive genius' (Darwin, 1871: 557).

The notion that 'race mixing' was dangerous both genetically and socially became to an ever-increasing degree the focus of such studies – not only because those born of unions between Europeans and colonised peoples of colour were thought to have aspirations of political equality that could eventually challenge European dominance overseas, but because it was already believed that the product of 'race mixing' resulted in the worst traits of both parents emerging in their offspring; thus describing their 'bastard brood', Smith (1744: 213) said 'whatever is bad among the Europeans and the Negroes is united in them, so that they are the sink of both'. Founder-gypsilorist R.A. Scott Macfie, writing about 'pure Gypsies' (1913: 73) said 'half-breeds – posh-rats as they are called – combine the vices of both nations, and by some malignant law of nature, shed the good qualities'. Bartels and Brun cautioned that 'nothing good has come from a crossing between a Gipsy and a white person' (1943: 5). In the American South the reaction to racial integration and the inevitability of intermarriage was most forcefully voiced by a judge who in a 1955 court case ruled that the state's purpose was 'to prevent the corruption of blood [and …] the creation of a mongrel breed of citizens' (*Naim vs. Naim*, in Sollors, 2002: 15; see also Zack, 1993, especially 77, 83–4).

That non-European blood would contaminate the gene-pool of Hitler's envisioned Aryan 'master race' was the underlying rationale for the intended extermination of Romanies and Jews during the Holocaust (Hancock, 2002: 34–52). The small African and Afro-European population in Nazi-controlled Europe was eradicated even before the Holocaust began.

Because of its forbidden nature, miscegenation acquired an attraction that journalists were quick to exploit; depictions of sexual encounters between colonised or enslaved women of colour and white males in their position of control found a ready place in Victorian literature. The erotic photography of the late nineteenth century consisted largely of naked African or Asian women (Stenger, 1931). That magazines such as *National Geographic* have traditionally never included photographs of unclothed *white* women merely helped carry that double standard into the twentieth century.

The oldest organisation devoted to the study of the Romani people is the Gypsy Lore Society, established in 1888 and still in existence. Some of its male members – all non-Romanies – referred to themselves as *ryes*, a self-designation interpreted to mean one who had gained privileged entrée into the Romani world, but which in Romani itself (as *rai*) means a person in a position of authority, including 'lord' and 'policeman'. For some ryes at least, it seems to have had a more specific in-group meaning: managing to bed a Romani woman. Thus in a letter dated 6 November 1908 Augustus John wrote to fellow gypsilorist Scott Macfie:

> I have recently taken it upon myself to confer the title of *Rai* upon a friend of mine – one Percy Wyndham Lewis, whose qualifications, the having coupled and lived in a state of copulation with a wandering Spanish *romi* in Brittany, seemed to me upon reflection to merit the honourable and distinctive title of our confraternity.

Westerners were (and still are) much more familiar with the enslavement of Africans in the Americas than they were with the enslavement of Romanies in Europe, and because of this, inaccurate portrayals of Gypsies relied upon the literary clichés of the period, describing in stereotypical terms the kind of slave a Victorian audience was more likely to have encountered in the literature. Ozanne wrote that the Romani slaves in Wallachia had 'crisp hair and thick lips, with a very dark complexion, [and ...] a strong resemblance to the negro physiognomy and character' (1878: 62, 65); St John wrote (1853: 140) that,

> [T]he men are generally of lofty stature, robust and sinewy. Their skin is black or copper-coloured; their hair, thick and woolly; their lips are of negro heaviness, and their teeth white as pearls; the nose is considerably flattened, and the whole countenance is illumined, as it were, by lively, rolling eyes.

An anonymous writer three years later wrote, 'on a heap of straw in the middle, in the full heat of the blazing sun, lay four gipsies asleep. They were all four tall, powerful men, with coal-black hair as coarse as rope, streaming over faces of African blackness' (1856: 273).

Sexual preoccupation also fixated on non-white *men*, believed to be consumed with lust for white women. That not all of the latter seemed quite so bothered by such a notion must simply have compounded this male insecurity; in contrast to Smith's dim view of the 'mulattoes' in

West Africa (above), one nineteenth-century visitor to the same region named Mrs Bowdich found them 'handsome, generally tall and gracefully formed, and very elegant' (Mahoney, 1965: 126). The early twentieth-century practice of castrating African Americans by racist mobs directly underscored a sexual fear, and male Romani slaves in the Balkans were likewise seen as a threat to white womanhood. Among them there was a category called the *skopitsi* (*scopiţi*), men who had been castrated as boys and whose job it was to drive the coaches of the women of the aristocracy without their being in fear of molestation. This was reflected in the Moldavian Civil code at that time, which stated that 'if a Gypsy slave should rape a white woman, he would be burnt alive' (Section 28), but if a Romanian should 'meet a girl in the road' and 'yield to love … he shall not be punished at all' (Section 39; Panaitescu, 1928: 14, see also Hancock, 1987).

Perhaps related to this emasculation of the non-white male is the literary tradition of having white men, in Gayatri Spivak's words, 'saving brown women from brown men' (1988: 294; see also Cooke, 2002). Shehrezade Ali (1996: 2) has strongly criticised the Disney film *The Hunchback of Notre Dame* for creating a subliminal racial bias in the developing social attitudes of children:

> To date, none of Disney's white female characters have been mated with Black or non-white suitors, yet the animated women-of-color are exclusively tied to white men, embracing them and ignoring their own races. Is this Disney's attempt to be inclusive? … Why does Disney put women-of-color in romantic situations with white men instead of men of color?, and what kind of subliminal message do you think it sends to little Black or Gypsy girls by repeatedly implying that the only hero or savior they have is a white male?, and what about little Black or Gypsy boys who have yet to see themselves in a strong hero role in a Disney film? What about their self-esteem? [it …] makes visual a continuing racist myth that every woman on the planet, whether Black or white, has only one everlasting hero – a white man.[34]

In her review of the 1919 silent film *A Day With the Gypsies*, Habiba Hadziavdic (2007) discusses the way the director manipulated this, depicting how the visitor to the community portrayed in that documentary posed a threat to the men, 'but who is *welcomed* by the Gypsy women, who cannot contain their pleasure and thrill at the prospect of spending a day with a white stranger'.

Image from a children's storybook

One recurrent feature in plots of this type is that the love interest turns out not to be a Romani after all, but a high-born white girl who was 'stolen by Gypsies' as a child and subsequently rescued, thus making the romantic attraction acceptable as well as admirable. The folk ballad *The Whistling Gypsy* tells of a young woman leaving her home to follow her roaming Romany; societal fears are allayed in the last verse: 'but he is no Gypsy my father dear, he's lord of these lands all over' (Quinn, 2001). This is in fact a literary cliché: the hidden identity revealed, thereby legitimising the union (Shakespeare's Fawnia in *The Winter's Tale* comes to mind, or Cervantes' Preciosa in *La Gitanilla*). A twist on this is entertainingly portrayed in Jennifer Lopez' musical video *Ain't It Funny*. Here, she strides uninvited into a Romani camp somewhere in the wilderness, although one with crystal ball and tarot cards prominently displayed, and 'becomes' Romani herself, changing her clothes, donning massive earrings, and takes control, proceeding to captivate all the young men employing strictly non-Romani behaviour.

Populations of colour were seen furthermore as unclean, both spiritually and physically. Hoyland repeated the Elizabethan belief that the Romanies' dark skin was simply due to dirt: 'Gypsies would long ago have been divested of their swarthy complexions, had they discontinued their filthy mode of living' (1816: 39–40). Celia Esplugas, in her grossly misinformed essay (which claims, for instance, that 'whether Gypsies originate in either Egypt or India is a matter that has not been settled') explains that 'the Gypsies' cleanliness and hygiene failed to meet English standards' (1999: 148).

Kenrick and Puxon believe that the present-day hatred of Romanies is a folk memory that dates from their earliest appearance in Europe, and stems from the mediæval conviction 'that blackness denotes inferiority and evil, [which] was well rooted in the western mind. The nearly black skins of many Gypsies marked them out to be victims of this prejudice' (1972: 19). European folklore contains a number of references to the Romanies' complexion: a Greek proverb says 'go to the Gypsy children and choose the whitest', and in Yiddish, 'the same sun that whitens the linen darkens the Gypsy', and 'no washing ever whitens the black Gypsy'. A widespread self-ascription in Romani is *Kalé*, which means 'Blacks', while Caucasian *gadjé* (non-Romanies) are referred to in the same language as *parné* or *parnorré*, 'whites', even by fair-skinned Romanies who might now be physically indistinguishable from them. The latter were remarked upon by the French traveller Félix Colson, who visited a slave-holding estate in Romania in the 1830s: 'Their skins are hardly brown; some of them are blonde and beautiful'; and while this resulted from the established practice of offering female Romani slaves as unwilling sexual entertainment to visitors, they were given such degrading house-names as *Bronze, Dusky, Dopey, Toad, Witch, Camel, Dishrag* or *Whore* by their owners (Colson, 1839: 49). In her novel, *Prince of One Summer*, set in the time of Romani slavery, Roberte Roleine (1979: 111) described this scenario:

> In the evening, the master makes his choice among the beautiful girls – maybe he will offer some of them to the guest – whence these light-skinned, blonde-haired Gypsies. The offspring from these unwelcome sexual unions automatically became slaves. It was this exploitation which was largely responsible for the fact that many Gypsies are now fair-skinned.

Illustration of a Carpathian Romani woman in flamenco attire (Labois, 1954: 18)

While she could be thus used, a Romani woman could not become the legal wife of a white man. Performing such a marriage was considered 'an evil and wicked deed', and a priest doing so was excommunicated, as stated in an anti-miscegenation proclamation issued in 1776 by Constantin, Prince of Moldavia:

[I]n some parts Gypsies have married Moldavian women, and also Moldavian men have taken in marriage Gypsy girls, which is entirely against the Christian faith, for not only have these people bound themselves to spend all their life with the Gypsies, but especially that their children remain forever in unchanged slavery ... such a deed being hateful to God, and contrary to human nature ... any priest who has had the audacity to perform such marriages, which is a great and everlasting wicked act ... will be removed from his post and severely punished. (Ghibănescu, 1921: 119–20)

Those who have written about the treatment of the slaves have believed, possibly as a salve to their own consciences, that Romanies were actually well-disposed to such barbarity: Lecca (1908: 181) maintained that 'once they were made slaves ... it seems that they preferred this state', and Paspati (1861: 149) wondered whether Romanies didn't in fact 'subject themselves *voluntarily*' to bondage because of the 'mild treatment' from their owners. Emerit (1930: 132) believed that 'despite clubbings which the slave-owners meted out at random, the Gypsies did not altogether hate this tyrannical regime, which once in a while took on a paternal quality'.

Together with imagined uninhibited pagan (that is, non-Christian) behaviour, the pathologised, Janus-faced image that emerged both fascinated and at the same time repulsed; George Borrow was said to have both 'despised yet intimately loved' Gypsies (Thomas, 1924: *vij*). The Augustinian phrase *inter urinam et fæces sedet amor* well reflects this paradox, which in the case of people of colour might also allude to skin pigmentation. Reference to the same two-way attraction but attributed this time to Gypsy men finds a place on the cover of Connie Mason's novel *Gypsy Lover* (2005): 'The arrogant gypsy had swept [the 'lovely Lady Esme Harcourt'] into his arms at a county fair, awakening both her desire and her disdain.'

Bayle St John (1853: 142), who based his anonymously written account wholly on Grellmann and who (like Carmen's creator Bizet) had never met an actual Romani in his life, wrote that Gypsies were 'a very handsome race, the women especially. These bold, brown, beautiful women only make one astonished to think how such eyes, teeth and figures can exist in the stifling atmosphere of their tents.' It was furthermore his painful duty to admit to his prudish Victorian readership that he was 'sorry to be obliged to add that both men and women are, as a rule, exceedingly debauched' – bongobongoistic editorialising expressly calculated to titillate and shock, as well as being a claim safe from academic challenge (Douglas, 1970: 15–16).

Esplugas writes that 'distrust of the Gypsies' moral standards extended to their sexual behavior', and that non-Gypsy men were 'attracted to the mystery of this roaming race, to the beauty of the Gypsy women, or to their free lifestyle ... [their] refusing to be tamed' (1999: 148–9, 152). Helbig (2004: 1) elaborates:

> The alleged lack of morals among the Gypsies was vehemently applied to the critique of their sexual practices and their disregard for decency and respect toward the body, especially by Gypsy women. In much of the art, music and literature of the 19th century, the female Gypsy in particular was characterised and stereotyped as free-spirited, strong, deviant, demanding, sexually arousing, alluring and dismissive. This romantic construct of the Gypsy woman may be viewed in direct opposition to the proper, controlled, chaste, submissive woman held as the Victorian European ideal. This 'oriental' fascination with the forbidden and taboo world of the Gypsy other in music is best characterised in the opera *Carmen*.

Judith Okely, who makes it abundantly clear how hygiene-conscious and conservative Romani culture actually is, points to George Borrow as being largely responsible for this pervasive stereotype, both in his books about English Romani life (1851, 1857), and particularly in his influential description of the Calé in Spain (1841). This latter, together with Carmen's enticing appearance in 1875 made that of the Spanish

Gitana the default image. Okely writes that 'in England, a stereotype of the Spanish Gypsy is often thought to be typical, and is often depicted in popular paintings: a black-haired girl in décolletage, with flounced skirts and swaggering walk, hand on hip … sexually available and promiscuous in her affections' (1983: 201). An illustrated novella about Romanies in Romania has the women in flamenco attire complete with castanets (Labois, 1954: 18; see also Charnon-Deutsch, 2004).

Male attitudes such as those of St John and others are still with us. In 1981 an article appeared in *Cosmopolitan* magazine written by martial arts specialist Dave Lowry entitled 'What it's like to be a Gypsy Girl'. A clue to the motivation for a grown white man to tackle the topic in the first place is in his references to 'male libido' and 'endless erotic fantasies' in his very first paragraph, and while he claims to have allowed a young Romani girl, 'Sabinka', to speak for herself, it's clear that Sabinka is Dave Lowry, who had gathered bits and pieces for his highly misleading story from the then easily-available sources – probably Gropper, Sutherland or Wood, all of which appeared during the previous decade. Another group of *gadže* has also recently discovered Romanies, and sought a sexual kinship with us. Kirstie Blair concludes her essay on 'Gypsies and lesbian desire' with the words, 'it appears the gypsy stands as an uneasy counterpart to the lesbian writer, an image for and of her desires, a strange yet familiar likeness' (2004: 160).

It will be a while yet before an accurate depiction of Romanies – and Romani women – is the one that comes first to mind; *The New Yorker* magazine recently referred in its pages to 'assertive women – "female scholars, priestesses, gypsies, mystics, nature lovers"' (Boyer, 2006: 36), as though all those categories were behaviours or occupations. The pervasiveness of this exotic image is nowhere more in evidence than on the *eBay* Internet auction site, where 'sexy gypsy-wicca blouses' and the like account for almost all of the over two thousand 'gypsy' offerings posted there daily. Another site, *The Gypsy*, informs the visitor that 'Gypsies are normally dark skinned with bold flashing eyes; however it is not unusual to find golden or crimson haired Gypsies … most Gypsies live in traveling wagons called vardos … the campfire is the center of Gypsy family life.' (Further examples of these sorts of sites are outlined in Chapter 12 above.)

Three titles recently acquired by the Romani Archives at The University of Texas are Sasha White's *Gypsy Heart* (2006) ('Can a man bent on settling down convince a free-spirited woman that doesn't believe in "happily ever after" to risk her Gypsy Heart? *Warning:* this book contains explicit sex explained in graphic detail with contemporary language'); Isabella Jordan's *Gypsies, Tramps and Heat: An Anthology of Erotic Romance* (2006) ('Lose yourself in the dark eyes and crystal ball of a gypsy lover'); and Alison Mackie's series *The Gypsy Chronicles* (2006) ('Upon each matrimonial bed that Tzigany de Torres makes, he bestows a potent charm, one which guarantees a lifetime of pleasurable love making ... with his matchmaker wife, Gitana'). The latter adds, 'What qualifies me to write about Gypsies? ... I had an Andalusian Gypsy nanny by the name of Ahalita' (2006: 182), a justification not unknown among white writers about the black experience (see, for example, Sue Monk Kidd's *The Secret Life of Bees* (2003)). Thus Romani identity still remains to a great extent controlled by the non-Romani world, by Hollywood and by novelists and journalists like those exemplified here.

That an ethnic label might be applied metaphorically is not necessarily offensive, but it often can be. Stereotypes need not be malicious as long as they are recognised as just that – stereotypes. We know that Hollywood gangland Mafiosi don't represent all Italians because we learn in school at the same time about the contributions of Botticelli, Leonardo and Michelangelo. Today, with increased media coverage and access to informative websites such as *Patrin* and *Radoc*, ignorance can no longer be used as an excuse if writers do their homework. The general public is coming to understand that the literary 'Gypsies' (or more usually 'gypsies') are something quite different from the actual Romanies, whose real story is both complex and moving – so reasons for the relentless perpetuation of the myth must be sought elsewhere, and the consequences of so doing examined. We don't want to say goodbye to Carmen and Esmeralda and their fictional sisters, but we should recognise them for who and what they really are.

Introduction to Section Five: Holocaust, racism and politics

In the chapter *Responses to the Porrajmos*, Ian discusses the deplorable tendency on the part of some scholars to deny the fact that the Romani people shared the fate of the Jews under the Nazis, or at any rate, to understate the Roma people's suffering. To express such ideas in the case of the Jews would invite immediate scholarly opprobrium, to say nothing of legal sentences; but in the case of the Roma, such negationist views are sometimes maintained even by mainstream scholars. It is interesting that in the immediate aftermath of the Second World War, a sense of solidarity prevailed between the victims, and the genocide against the Roma was usually explicitly acknowledged. Since the 1960s, however, a purely academic trend in historiography has emerged, which tends to minimise or deny the victimisation of the Roma, against the mounting evidence that has slowly but steadily bolstered the Romani case.

This disinformation campaign has succeeded, and the fact that the Holocaust affected the Roma as much as it did the Jews is not widely recognised, possibly because:

i.   Unlike the Jewish victims, the Romani victims were mostly of poorer backgrounds, and their suffering did not gain the same visibility.

ii. The Roma in diaspora outside Europe are divided into small self-contained communities, without much interest in politics, and not very influential in the countries in which they live. They were unable to lobby on behalf of their kin in Europe, partly due to a lack of means, and partly because they were not fully aware of the plight of their kin in Europe.

iii. No nation-state represents the Roma in international fora, or serves as a haven for fleeing Roma. Thus Romani victims and survivors are caught up in a continued struggle for survival, which leaves them with no leisure for promoting awareness or organising sustained campaigns for justice.

iv. The heritage of the Roma and their contributions to Western civilisation is relatively unknown to most Europeans. (This is partly because they were not – until recently – recognised as a people in most countries.) The contribution of Jews and Judaism, on the other hand, is well-known as being an important component of what is often termed Judaeo-Christian civilisation.

In excruciating detail, Ian compares the Jewish and Romani experience during the Holocaust. Whether we look at the sheer scale of the atrocities committed, the technology that was employed, the involvement of bureaucratic and state apparatuses, or the avowedly genocidal intent of the perpetrators,[34] it becomes obvious that the Roma underwent the same tragedies that befell the Jewish people. If the purpose behind the academic discipline of genocide studies is to ensure that such tragic events do not happen again, the genocide of the Roma – the *Porrajmos*, in Romani – must be fully acknowledged, and the memory of the Romani victims must be honoured in such institutions as the US Holocaust Memorial Museum.

The monograph *The consequences of anti-Gypsy racism in Europe* is based on a talk Ian gave in his capacity as the sole Romani member of the US delegation to the Organisation for Security and Cooperation in Europe (OSCE), in a seminar on the Roma (Warsaw, 1994). Ian takes stock of the bleak state of race relations in Eastern Europe, in the days after the fall of Communist governments, when racial animosities long suppressed under Communism suddenly found unfettered expression in the public domain. The events listed in the postscript, and the sharp increase in racially motivated murders in Europe at time of publication, grimly confirm Ian's predictions.

The last chapter in this book, *Our need for internal diplomatic skills*, appropriately focuses on the Romani interlocutors themselves. For the first time in their turbulent history, Roma are in a position to speak for themselves, in a limited way, and to attempt to be masters of their own fate. It is a novelty for Roma to be in this position with respect to the larger society. It is equally a novelty for the diverse Romani groups to speak with and on behalf of each other. To forge a unity of purpose and action between peoples of diverse backgrounds and expectations is very difficult, and there is much room for misunderstanding and alienation. Issues of identity and representation will have to be debated amongst the disparate Romani groups, and those wishing to be spokespersons for the Roma will have to tread very carefully, if they are not to shatter the fragile consensus that has been achieved with so much toil.

CHAPTER FIFTEEN

Responses to the *Porrajmos* (the Romani Holocaust)

... ignorance and arrogance are in full flower ... 'Holocaust' has been used to encompass more than the murder of the Jews. From the casualties in our Civil War to the wholesale murder of Gypsies in World War II.

(Alexander, 1990: 13)

... the [mistaken] notion that not only Jews ... but Gypsies were chosen by the Nazis for annihilation.

(Safire, 1983: 12)

... the whole Gypsy 'problem' was for Himmler and most other Nazis only a minor irritant.

(Bauer, 1994: 446)

Jews were not the only biologically selected target. Alongside Jews, the Nazis murdered European Gypsies.

(Friedlander, 1995a: *xij*)

Just four years after the fall of the Third Reich, Dora Yates, the Jewish secretary of the Gypsy Lore Society, noted in the pages of *Commentary* that,

It is more than time that civilized men and women were aware of the Nazi crime against the Gypsies as well as the Jews. Both bear witness to the

Originally published as 'Responses to the Porrajmos: the Romani Holocaust', in Alan S. Rosenbaum (ed.), *Is the Holocaust unique?: perspectives on comparative genocide* (Westview Press, Boulder, CO, 1996), pp. 75–102. First presented at the *Remembering for the Future International Conference on the Holocaust*, Berlin, 13–17 March 1994. I have been told that this essay is probably what caused me to be dropped, *sar tati kolompiri*, from the Project on Ethnic Relations' Romani Advisory Council and to be similarly distanced from a number of other Roma Rights organisations. My experiences with such bodies will be expanded upon in a forthcoming book. This is a somewhat updated version of the essay first published in 1996.

fantastic dynamic of the twentieth century racial fanaticism, for these two peoples shared the horror of martyrdom at the hands of the Nazis for no other reason than that they *were* – they *existed*. The Gypsies, like the Jews, stand alone. (Yates, 1949: 455)

And in the following year, the *Wiener Library Bulletin*, organ of what is now the Jewish Institute of Contemporary History in London, published the statement that 'Germany had in 1938 a gipsy population of 16,275. Of these, 85 per cent were thrown into concentration camps, and no more than 12 per cent survived' (Anonymous, 1950a: 18).

Despite these very early observations,[35] and despite the overwhelming amount of documentation relating to the fate of the Romanies in Nazi Germany which has been examined during the past fourteen years that the US Holocaust Memorial Council has been in existence, that body, more than any other, rigorously persists in underestimating and under-representing that truth, made plain forty-five years ago, a position reflected in the permanent exhibit in the Memorial Museum – whose staff, it should be said, have on the other hand generally been much more favourably disposed to the Romani case.

In their 1989 book *Holocaust: Religious and Philosophical Implications*, editors John Roth and Michael Berenbaum ask '[w]hy should the fate of the Jews be treated differently than the fate of the Gypsies or the Poles ... [t]he answer will be found in these essays' (1989: 6–7). But the answer to that question, at least for the Romani case, appears nowhere in any of the twenty-three essays the book contains. More recently still Martin Gilbert, in his foreword to Carrie Supple's *From Prejudice to Genocide: Learning About the Holocaust*, published in 1993 for use in British schools, refers to the Holocaust as 'the attempt by the Nazis to destroy all the Jews of Europe between 1941 and 1945', and then mentions the fate of the Romani victims as being among 'other attempts at genocide, such as the slaughter of the Armenians', placing Romanies with a group outside of the Holocaust altogether, echoing the statement in his *The Holocaust* (1985: 824), that '[i]t was the Jews alone who were marked out to be destroyed in their entirety'. And while Burleigh and Wippermann (1991) discuss in detail the 'Final Solution of the Gypsy Problem' in *The Racial State*, Antony Polonsky is still moved in his introduction to that book to maintain that '[a]s emerges clearly from the arguments of Burleigh and Wippermann, the mass murder of the Jews was unique in that every Jew, man, woman and child, assimilated or deeply orthodox, was singled out for destruction' (1991: xiv).

It is abundantly clear that some historians see only what they want to see, that a very blind eye is being turned in the direction of Romani history, and that where the Romani genocide in Nazi Germany is acknowledged, it is kept, with a few notable exceptions (e.g. Ehmann, 1981; Milton, 1990, 1991a, 1991b, 1992, 1994a, 1994b, 1995; Thurner, 1987; Young, 1994; Davis Lutz and Lutz, 1995; Friedlander, 1995a and 1995b; Fox, 1988 and 1995; and Stannard, 1996), carefully separated from the Jewish experience. Both Douglas (1985) and Lagrou (1997) have demonstrated that this ethnic exclusivity is an academic construction which dates only from the 1960s. It is evident, however, that from an outright rejection of the idea of Romanies sharing the fate of Jews, opinion is slowly moving in the direction of acceptance of the idea, voiced by Margot Strom (Henderson, 1986: 5C), that 'questions about who the Holocaust belongs to – whether it's only a Jewish concern – are superficial', although some writers continue to hover on the fence. Azriel Eisenberg, in his excellent edited volume *Witness to the Holocaust*, says in his introduction that:

> The focus of this book is on the Jews, but in point of fact precious human beings of other nationalities, faiths and ideologies were also annihilated by the millions – among them Gypsies, Czechs, Yugoslavs, Poles, Russians and French. However, it was Jews who were singled out for *total* destruction. (1981: 2)

Nevertheless, in the very next paragraph Eisenberg goes on to say,

> One people that shared the fate of the Jews were the Gypsies. They, too, had been persecuted through the ages and, like the Jews, the Gypsies were isolated and liquidated, country by country. Unlike the Jews, however, they left almost no records of the atrocities committed against them, which were no less horrible than those recorded in this book. When the bloodbath was over, only pitiful remnants were left alive. The world hardly knew of their sufferings, nor is it fully aware today of their disappearance. Except for the few survivors, a whole people, unique in its life-style, language, culture and art, was wiped off the face of the earth. There are no memorials to their dead or commemorations of their tragedy [in 1981]. The death of the Gypsy nation was more than physical; it was total oblivion. (1981: 2)

Others, such as Fackenheim and Meier, seem not yet to have made up their minds about whether to include Romanies or not:

> With the possible exception of the Gypsies, Jews were the only people killed for the 'crime' of existing. (Fackenheim, 1982: 12)

> Why ... does it seem important to insist on the uniqueness of the Nazi crimes? Because nowhere else but in Nazi-occupied Europe from 1941 to 1945 was there an apparatus so single-mindedly established to carry out mass murder as a process in its own right. And not just mass murder, but ethnic extermination – killing – without even a pretext of individual wrongdoing, an entire people (if gypsies [*sic*] are counted, two peoples). (Meier, 1988: 82)

Similarly, Breitman admits that Romanies might eventually also get higher billing once more details become available:

> The Nazis did try to wipe out virtually all Jews, whereas their murderous policies for other groups were more selective. In some cases, for example with the gypsies, further research is needed to show what distinctions were made, why some were killed and others spared. (1991: 19)

In the preface to one of the most recent treatments of the Nazi genocide, Friedlander (1995a: *xij–xiv*) states,

> Historians have categorised the Nazis' murder of the European Jews as totally different from the murder of other groups ... My research convinced me that this definition of Nazi genocide had to be slightly revised, because Jews were not the only biologically selected target. Alongside Jews, the Nazis murdered the European gypsies. Defined as a 'dark-skinned' racial group, Gypsy men, women and children could not escape their fate as victims of Nazi genocide ... I have provided a relatively detailed account of the murder of the gypsies because their annihilation has until now received little attention. [On the other hand] I have not covered the murder of the Jews, which has been the subject of much scrutiny and is relatively well known.

But despite the focus of that 421-page book, the Library of Congress' Cataloguing-in-Publication data, included following its title page, categorises it under the heading 'Holocaust: Jewish (1939–45)'.

Acknowledging what does and does not qualify for inclusion in the Holocaust is a profoundly emotionally charged issue, and one fraught with subjective interpretation and response. Assumptions are made, and repeated with confidence, by individuals who have no special expertise in Romani Holocaust history, and unqualified statements are reiterated which automatically assume a lesser status for Romanies in the ranking of human abuse. These take the form of entire articles, such as that by Katz (1988: 200–16), which systematically compares the fate of Jews in the Holocaust with (a) the mediaeval witch craze, (b) North American Indians, (c) Black slavery, (d) Romanies under the Nazis, (e) homosexuals during World War II and (f) Polish and Ukrainian losses during World War II, concluding (1988: 216) that 'all ... are to be fundamentally distinguished from the Holocaust, even when they reveal horrifyingly large casualty figures'. The same is found in the writings of Yehuda Bauer, who states with assurance in his entry on 'Gypsies' in *The Encyclopedia of the Holocaust* (Gutman, 1990; see also Gutman and Berenbaum, 1994) that '[t]he fate of the gypsies was in line with Nazi thought as a whole: gypsies were not Jews, and therefore there was no need to kill all of them'. Then, like Katz, he substantiates this claim by selectively citing sources, none of which is more recent than 1979, and makes no comparisons with Jewish populations which were also exempted from death, and for whom there was likewise 'no need to kill all'. More recently Michael Berenbaum told *The New York Times* that 'the Nazis targeted different groups, but singled out Jews for annihilation', and that 'Inclusion is not equivalence – not saying that their fate was equivalent. All the victims of Nazism are memorialised in the museum. The distinction between their fate and the fate of the Jews, is preserved' (Sengupta, 1996).

The three-and-a-half page entry for Romanies in the two volume, 2,000-page *Encyclopedia of the Holocaust*, incidentally, amounts to less than one quarter of one per cent of the whole book, despite the enormity of Romani losses by 1945, proportionately at least matching, and possibly exceeding, that of the Jewish victims. In his more recent book, Katz elaborates upon these comparisons, and expands upon the criterion of 'intentionality' which, he says, characterised the fate of Jews in the Holocaust but not that of any other victims of massive-scale murder. Indeed, he claims that 'the Nazi attack on the Jews was the only true genocide in history' (Katz, 1994; see also Nemeth, 1994).

Typically accompanying these statements and assumptions is the acknowledgement that yes, there were other victims of Nazism, but they belong under a separate heading of non-Jews, and their fate was different. Berenbaum places the Romani victims in a category we might easily call 'unnamed afterthought' in his own definition of the Holocaust: 'the systematic state-sponsored murder of six million Jews by the Nazis and their collaborators during World War II; as night descended, millions of others were killed in their wake' (1993: 1; see also Shermer, 1994: 33). Berenbaum presumed what the effect of the US Holocaust Memorial Museum upon the public consciousness would be fully five years before its opening, in *Newsday*, when he said '[p]eople had to grow. Jews had to learn to be sensitive to non-Jewish victims, and they, in turn, had to learn to be sensitive to the uniqueness of the Jewish experience' (quoted in Brenna, 1988: 3). The central issue rests squarely upon this notion of 'uniqueness', it was the basis of my presentation at the first *Remembering for the Future* conference in Oxford, which was published in an expanded version in *Without Prejudice* (Hancock, 1988a). Philip Lopate seems to be the only writer to have listed the criteria for 'uniqueness' in an unequivocal way:

> The position that the Jewish Holocaust was unique tends to rest on the following arguments: (1) scale – the largest number of deaths extracted from one single group; (2) technology – the mechanisation of death factories; (3) bureaucracy – the involvement of the state apparatus at previously unheard-of levels; (4) intent – the express purpose being to annihilate every last member of the Jewish people. (1989: 291–2)

I will enumerate these and other principal challenges to the Romani case that have emerged since the Oxford conference, which argue for categorisation separately from the Jewish case, and which thereby support the perceived 'uniqueness' of the latter, and comment upon each one in turn.

(1) *Jews were targeted to the last man, woman and child for complete extermination, a policy which held true for no other population.*

Jack Eisner is just one of many writers on the Holocaust who makes this distinction:

> Another misleading idea frequently advanced by those in the public eye is the conclusion that our concept of Holocaust should embrace several million non-Jewish civilians who perished at the hands of the Nazis along with six million Jews ... yet there is a crucial difference: As non-Jews they were not part of a race targeted for total extermination; that is the significance of the Holocaust. (Eisner, 1983: 153)

There were in fact numbers of categories of Jews who were exempt, and who escaped death. Hilberg discusses these in detail in the first chapters of his *The Destruction of the European Jews* (1961). As early as 1938, the German Reich asked various foreign governments to extend invitations to German Jews as a means of getting them out of the country, but this policy was not extended to include Romanies. Mention can also be made of the 1 September 1941 law confining Jews and Romanies to their place of residence which exempted Jews married to non-Jews, but which did not similarly spare Romanies. Smelser (1991: 55–6) discusses the Brand Mission of 1944, when Eichmann himself was prepared to spare the lives of one million Jews in return for 10,000 trucks, and the effort of the American Jewish Joint Distribution Committee, which successfully secured the release of 318 Jews from Bergen-Belsen in the same year. The US War Refugee Board was able to save over 200,000 Jews, bringing them to America from Europe beginning in 1944, but their programme did not even mention the Romani victims of Nazism. As the Holocaust intensified, most of these exemptions, for both groups, were progressively rescinded. When making statements of this kind, the year should be specified to incorporate policy changes. Ultimately, *only* Jews and Romanies were singled out for extermination (with the exception of certain exempted groups within each population) on the basis of race/ethnicity. No other targeted populations were thus identified, and for this reason Romanies must not be placed in the residual category of 'Others'. By the time that the Nuremberg Laws were fully in place, no other categories existed except 'Jews' and 'Aryans'. While the latter category was divided into numbers of specific populations, including Poles, the handicapped, homosexuals (some of whom also belonged to the former classification), Romanies were placed with 'Jews', and legislation directed at, and naming Jews henceforth automatically included Romanies.

In fact no written evidence has come to light indicating that Jews or any other targeted group were intended to be eradicated from the face of the earth, however passionate a Nazi vision that might have been. We find instead statements such as that in a letter from Thierack to Martin Bormann dated 13 October 1939, in which he refers to 'the intention of liberating *the German area* from Poles, Russians, Jews and Gypsies' [emphasis added]. Hitler's own statement, made publicly on 30 January earlier that same year, envisioned 'the annihilation of the Jewish race *in Europe*' [emphasis added].

(2) *Romanies 'come closest' to the Jewish situation but, as Messrs. Mais, Bauer, Wiesel, Berenbaum and others have said, close is still a miss.*

In this connection and most recently, Michael Berenbaum has said, in the introduction to *The World Must Know*, that,

> At the center of the tragedy of the Holocaust is the murder of European Jews – men, women and children – killed not for the identity they affirmed or the religion they practiced, but because of the blood of their grandparents. Near that center is the murder of the gypsies. Historians are still uncertain if there was a single decision for their complete annihilation, an enunciated policy of transcendent meaning to the perpetrators. (1993: 2)

He further says, 'Gypsies had been subject to official discrimination in Germany long before 1933, but even the Nazi regime never promulgated a comprehensive law against them' (1993: 51), a statement which seems to have been paraphrased from Luebke, who wrote that '[n]o comprehensive 'Gypsy Law' was ever promulgated' (1990: 3). To this might also be added Breitman's statement that 'Whatever its weaknesses, "Final Solution" at least applies to a single, specific group defined by descent. The Nazis are not known to have spoken of the Final Solution of the Polish problem or of the gypsy problem' (1991: 20). In fact the first document referring to 'the introduction of the total solution to the Gypsy problem on either a national or an international level' was issued under the direction of State Secretary Hans Pfundtner of the Reichs Ministry of the Interior in March 1936, while the wording *endgültige Lösung der Zigeunerfrage*, that is, the 'final (or "conclusive") solution of the Gypsy question' was made by Himmler in May 1938. What makes a decree calling for racial obliteration 'comprehensive' or not isn't discussed by Berenbaum, but his statement is neither correct nor serves in any way to relegate the fate of the Romanies to some less stringent category. But, as Kcablc (1995: 24) asserts in her refutation of those who claim that no so-called Gypsy Law ever existed, 'while denial threatens ... oblivion, facts require repetition if they are to remain facts'. There are numerous Nazi policy statements available to us calling for the total elimination of the Romani population, several of which I have included in my *Chronology*, together with references (Hancock, in Crowe and Kolsti, 1991: 11–30). Thus in the Auschwitz *Memorial Book* we find 'The final resolution, as formulated by Himmler, in his "Decree for Basic Regulations to Resolve the Gypsy Question as Required by the Nature of Race", of December 8th, 1938, meant that preparations were to begin for the *complete extermination* of the Sinti and Roma' (1993: *xiv*, emphasis added). In 1939 Johannes Behrendt of the Office of Racial Hygiene issued a brief stating that '[a]ll Gypsies should be treated as hereditarily sick; the only solution is elimination. The aim should therefore be the elimination without hesitation of this defective element in the population.' Müller-Hill writes:

> Heydrich, who had been entrusted with the 'final solution of the Jewish question' on 31st July 1941, shortly after the German invasion of the USSR, also included the Gypsies in his 'final solution' ... The senior SS officer and Chief of Police for the East, Dr Landgraf, in Riga, informed Rosenberg's Reich Commissioner for the East, Lohse, of the inclusion of the Gypsies in the 'final solution'. Thereupon, Lohse gave the order, on 24th December 1941, that the Gypsies 'should be given the same treatment as the Jews'. (Müller-Hill, 1988: 58–9)

Reinhard Heydrich, who was Head of the Reich Main Security Office and the leading organisational architect of the Nazi Final Solution, ordered the Einsatzkommandos 'to kill all Jews, Gypsies and mental patients' (Müller-Hill, 1988: 58–9). While there is no dispute about the Heydrich directive, which is also dealt with in Burleigh and Wippermann, both scholars draw attention to the fact that not all of the documentation regarding its complete details, relating to both Jews and Romanies, has been found:

> A conference on racial policy organised by Heydrich took place in Berlin on 21 September 1939, which may have decided upon a 'Final Solution' of the 'Gypsy Question'. According to the scant minutes which have survived, four issues were decided: the concentration of Jews in towns; their relocation to Poland; the removal of 30,000 gypsies to Poland, and the systematic deportation of Jews to German incorporated territories using goods trains. An express letter sent by the Reich Main Security Office on 17 October 1939 to its local agents mentioned that the 'Gypsy Question will shortly be regulated throughout the territory of the Reich.' ... At about this time, Adolf Eichmann made the recommendation that the

'Gypsy Question' be solved *simultaneously* with the 'Jewish Question,' ... Himmler signed the order despatching Germany's Sinti and Roma to Auschwitz on 16th December 1942. The 'Final Solution' of the 'Gypsy Question' had begun. (1991: 121–5)

The *Memorial Book* for the Romanies who died at Auschwitz-Birkenau interprets this somewhat differently:

The Himmler decree of December 16th, 1942 (*Auschwitz-Erlaß*), according to which the Gypsies should be deported to Auschwitz-Birkenau, had the same meaning for the Gypsies that the conference at Wannsee on January 20th, 1942, had for the Jews. This decree, and the bulletin that followed on January 29th, 1943, can thus be regarded as a logical consequence of the decision taken at Wannsee. After it had been decided that the fate of the Jews was to end in mass extermination, it was natural for the other group of racially-persecuted people, the Gypsies, to become victims of the same policy, which finally even included soldiers in the *Wehrmacht*. (State Museum, 1993: 3)

In a paper delivered at the March 1987 conference on the non-Jewish victims of the Holocaust, sponsored by the US Holocaust Memorial Council, Dr Erika Thurner of the Institut für Neuere Geschichte und Zeitgeschichte at the University of Linz stated that

Heinrich Himmler's infamous Auschwitz decree of 16 December 1942 can be seen as the final stage of the final solution of the Gypsy Question. The decree served as the basis for complete extermination. According to the implementation instructions of 1943, *all* Gypsies, irrespective of their racial mix, were to be assigned to concentration camps. The concentration camp for Gypsy families at Auschwitz-Birkenau was foreseen as their final destination ... opposed to the fact that the decision to seek a final solution for the Gypsy Question came at a later date than that of the Jewish Question, the first steps taken to exterminate the Gypsies were initiated *prior* to this policy decision; the first gassing operations against Gypsies did indeed take place in Chelmno as early as late 1941 or early 1942.

On 14 September 1942, following a meeting in Berlin with Minister of Propaganda Joseph Goebbels, Otto Thierack, Reichminister of Justice, wrote that 'with respect to the extermination of antisocial forms of life, Dr Goebbels is of the opinion that the Jews and the gypsies should simply be exterminated' (file no. 682–PS, US War Crimes Tribunal, 1946: 496).

Six years earlier, a memorandum was sent to Hans Pfundtner, State Secretary of the Interior, on 4 March 1936, which addressed the creation of a 'Gypsy Law' (the *Reichzigeunergesetz*), the purpose of which was to deal with the complete registration of the Romani population, their sterilisation, the restriction of their movement and means of livelihood, and the expulsion of all foreign-born, stateless Romanies.

(3) *Another argument, discussed in Fackenheim (1978) and most recently voiced by Israeli Rabbi Eliezer Schach, is that 'God used the Holocaust to punish Jews for their sins.'*

This would certainly exclude other groups, and is perhaps the most difficult defence of 'uniqueness' to address, from a non-Jewish perspective. But no doubt speaking for most of the Jewish religious community, Rabbi Yitzak Kagan of the Lubavitch Foundation of Michigan responded that Schach's statement 'borders on heresy' (DeSmet, 1990: B–3); we must wonder how the murder of innocent Jewish babies, thousands even unborn, can possibly be rationalised by this argument. It is of some significance that some Romanies today have succumbed to survivor's guilt, and have also wondered, rhetorically, whether the Holocaust was 'punishment' for imagined transgressions. There is also the argument, made, for example, by Vico (and discussed in Keable, forthcoming), that the Jewish experience cannot be compared to that of any other people because Jews alone 'dwell inside divine history' (or 'outside of history', as it has also been stated, for example, by Elie Wiesel). Such an argument is likewise a difficult one to reconcile with prosaic historical detail.

(4) *Certain Romani groups sedentary for two or more years were to be exempted from death* (Mais, 1988).

This two-year exemption was only a recommendation, and was never actually implemented, being overridden by Himmler's own directive, that all migratory Romanies should be killed, and sedentary Romanies worked to death in labour camps. In any case, this potential situation would only have applied to the USSR and the Baltic lands and nowhere else. A similar situation did, however, operate for Jews in these countries, thus Hilberg (1961: 142–4) writes of the *Gebietskommissar* for northern Lithuania in September 1941, complaining about the killings, explaining that 'the Jews were needed as skilled laborers'. Hilberg continues, '[i]n

October 1941, the *Reichskommissar* forbade the shooting of Jews ... [and] during the quiet months of the winter and spring of 1942, they began to adjust themselves to their hazardous existence'. By the end of 1943, 'some tens of thousands of Jews were being kept alive at Lida and Minsk in Byelorussia, and looked forward to evacuation or death'. Extermination of the Baltic Romanies was particularly effective, their having been destroyed almost in their entirety by 1945.

(5) *Some Romanies were even allowed to fight in the German army* (Mais, 1988).

Kenrick and Puxon (1972: 82) discuss Romanies who served in the armed forces, saying that 'Gypsies had officially been excluded from the army by law as early as November 1937 ... on the grounds of racial policy no more Gypsies should be called up ... [t]he release of servicemen took some time and Gypsies could still be found in the army as late as 1943'. The sentence following this, however, reads, '*Certain classes of Jews with mixed parentage were retained in the armed forces throughout the war*' (emphasis added).

(6) *Kenrick and Puxon discuss certain categories of exemptions which applied to Romanies* (Mais, 1988).

Kenrick and Puxon do deal with these in their book (Mais, 1988: 78), where they also include the statement that '[t]hese exemptions compare with similar arrangements for Jews'. If such an argument is to be used to characterise the treatment of Romanies, then it must likewise be used to characterise the treatment of Jews. And since it does apply to both populations, it cannot be used to support the 'unique' treatment of the latter.

Although Kenrick (1995 and elsewhere) has stated that anti-Jewish legislation generally preceded anti-Romani legislation, this was not typically the case. Being far fewer in numbers and more containable, Romanies often served as the test population for directives then later applied to Jews, e.g. attendance in schools, membership in trade unions, enlistment in the armed forces, sterilisation, Zyklon B experimentation, saltwater experimentation, genetic determination experimentation and so on.

(7) *It has been claimed, including by the German Government itself as a means of avoiding the payment of war crimes reparations, that Romanies were not targeted for racial, but for social, reasons.*

Yehuda Bauer has supported this argument also, stating that '[t]he gypsies were not murdered for racial reasons, but as so-called asocials … nor was their destruction complete' (Bauer, 1980: 45; 1994: 441). But this argument originates in the deliberate and despicable move on the part of the German Government to take advantage of the shattered condition of the surviving Romani population which was in no condition to contest it, and for which the Romani population is still suffering today. In fact in his most recent article (in Gutman and Berenbaum, 1994: 446), Bauer maintained that Romanies were murdered by the Nazis because 'they were a minor irritant' (a statement he repeated at the Scholars' Conference on the Holocaust and the Churches in 1996)!

The racial identity of the Romani people, and the genetically based rationale for their extermination, are abundantly documented and referenced (see e.g. Hancock, *Chronology*, in Crowe and Kolsti, 1991), and this was recognised in the press forty years ago: 'In his report on the matter, the Bonn Correspondent of the *Manchester Guardian*, 9: i: 56, points out that the Supreme Court's decision "is at direct variance with the known facts of Nazi policies for concentrating and later exterminating the gypsies"' (Anonymous, 1956). More recently, Professor Bauer has been quoted as saying that Romani claims to the extent of their victimisation in the Holocaust are 'all lies and fairy-tales' and that '[n]othing happened to them' (Katz, 1995); a statement which, if it were made publicly in Germany today about the Holocaust's Jewish victims, would result in a fine or a jail sentence. Indeed, as long ago as 1984, Yehuda Bauer dismissed Romanies from participating in the Holocaust, although without saying why, when he stated that '[t]he destruction of the Armenians and the Jews – but not of the Gypsies – which is a different problem again – belongs to the same category of Holocaust situations' (Bauer, 1994: 20).

At the 'task forces' meeting at the January 2000 Stockholm Holocaust conference, Bauer told an official from the Goethe Institute that 'Sybil Milton, Henry Friedlander [and others like them] had not been invited to Stockholm, because they belong to the last few examples of historians who still wrongly maintain that the Gypsies were victims of the Holocaust.' It is surely why I have not been invited back myself.

It is still the case that Romanies are widely believed to be a population defined by behaviour and social criteria rather than by genetic heritage or ethnicity. Professor Seymour Siegel, former chairman of the US Holocaust Memorial Council questioned, in the pages of *The Washington Post*, and in the context of their right to full inclusion, whether Romanies did in fact constitute a distinct ethnic people (Grove, 1984: C4), a particularly insensitive remark since Romanies have a far more demonstrable claim to a 'racial' identity than do Jews; this latter has been the subject of many studies (e.g. Coon, 1942; Petersen, 1988; Patai and Patai-Wing, 1989; Pollack, 2003; and see also Kohn, 1995). A report on the health of the Romani American population by a team of Harvard geneticists which appeared in the prestigious medical journal *The Lancet* concluded that, 'Analysis of blood groups, haptoglobin phenotypes and HLA types establish the Gypsies as a distinct racial group with origins in the Punjab region of India. Also supporting this is the worldwide Gypsy language Romani, which is quite similar to Hindi' (Thomas *et al.*, 1977: 379).

The fact remains, however, that whether Romanies and Jews are 'races' or not doesn't matter; Hitler believed both populations to constitute a racial threat, and race was his justification for their attempted extermination. It might be added here, that the oft-repeated argument that Romanies were the 'ultimate Aryans', having come from India, seems to be post-Holocaust folklore. The Nazis never claimed this, and in fact it was their own scholarship which attempted to demonstrate the Dravidian roots of the population. Pischel wrote about this as long ago as 1883, and Block repeated it in his 1936 treatise, which had a profound influence on Nazi anti-Romani policy. The notion seems to have arisen from the linguistic affiliation of the Romani language which (like Yiddish in fact), is an Indo-European (that is, 'Aryan') tongue. Bauer's further observation, that 'nor was their destruction complete', is a baseless and peculiar argument, since the same statement applies, mercifully, to Jews, over 300 times as many of whom survived the Holocaust than did Romanies (see (11) below).

(8) *Jews were a greater threat because they were responsible for Marxism and Capitalism, while Romanies posed no political or economic threat to the Third Reich* (Bauer, 1996).

This latter statement is certainly true, and it might be added parenthetically that Romanies have instigated no wars nor are recognised in the police records as perpetrators of major crimes such as murder or rape. The determination to eradicate the Romani population, therefore, was based *solely* on racial arguments, with no other mitigating factors.

(9) *Some families of 'pure' Romanies were to be preserved in special camps for future anthropologists to study* (Mais, 1988).

This has also been noted by Yehuda Bauer (1996), where he includes 'pure' Romanies with yet another category (apparently of his own devising: 'racially safe' Romanies – in direct contradiction of his reference in (7), above, to Romanies as a *non*-racially-targeted population) in his statement that 'Gypsies who were of pure blood, or who were not considered dangerous on a racial level, could continue to exist, under strict supervision.' In the US Holocaust Memorial Museum's published Holocaust history (Berenbaum, 1993: 51) we find the same argument made by Mais and Bauer repeated in slightly modified form, viz. that 'Pure gypsies were not targeted for extermination until 1942' (not true – but one might ask 'so what?'). The wording here gives the impression that there was an existing policy that was then revoked in 1942, rather than its having been (like (4), above) nothing more than a suggestion, by Himmler, which was mocked by his peers as 'one more of Himmler's hare-brained schemes' (Tyrnauer, 1985: 24) and rejected outright by Bormann. Thus on 16 December that same year, in compliance with this rejection of his idea, Himmler issued the order that 'all gypsies are to be deported to the Zigeunerlager at Auschwitz concentration camp, with no regard to their degree of racial impurity'. This order may even have been the result of a direct decision from Hitler himself (Milton, 1992: 10). SS Officer Percy ('Perry') Broad, who worked in the political division at Auschwitz, and who participated directly in the murders of several thousand prisoners there, wrote that 'it was the will of the all-powerful Reichsführer to have the Gypsies disappear from the face of the earth' (1966: 41). Richard Breitman reproduces the statement made by Security Police Commander Bruno Streckenbach following a policy meeting with Hitler and Heydrich held in Pretsch in June 1940, viz. that '[t]he Führer has ordered the liquidation of all Jews, Gypsies and communist political functionaries in the entire area of the Soviet Union' (1991: 164). Even if Himmler's Gypsy Zoo had been a reality, it would only have involved the lives of several dozen individuals, fewer by several hundred per cent than the 6,000 Karait Jews who were able to argue successfully for their own lives to be spared. The Karaits were 'a community who professed not only to be Jews but to be the authentic Jews since they accept no post-biblical Jewish texts as being authoritative, basing this ... on the words of a rabbinic decision' (Lang, 1997: 20).

(10) *Romanies received kinder treatment because parents and children were allowed to stay together in special family camps, unlike other prisoners.*

Lagnado and Dekel are among those who have referred to this: 'The Gypsies were allowed to stay together, perhaps because they were faithful Christians. Despite their inferior racial stock, it was their one privilege ... the Gypsies alone among the inmates had the comfort of being with their loved ones' (1991: 82). Their unqualified reference to Romanies as constituting 'inferior racial stock', their guess at their faithful Christianity, and their stunningly unfeeling description of the Romani camp in Auschwitz as resembling a 'vast playground, an ongoing carnival' can only reflect the authors' stereotypes about Romanies, and it is abundantly obvious that neither one of them ever spoke to a Romani survivor or was there at the camp at Birkenau. König (1989: 129–33) makes it very clear that the 'family camps' were not created out of any humanitarian motive, or desire to bestow any 'privilege', but because the Romanies became completely unmanageable when separated from family members. Zimmermann also discusses this:

> The Nazi institutions involved with the persecution of the Gypsies knew about the particularly close family ties in this ethnic group. If these family ties were not taken into account, as happened in part with the deportation of 2,500 Sinti to Poland in 1940, there were certainly difficulties for the police, which were recorded negatively. To this extent, the RSHA [the *Reichssicher-heitshauptamt*, or State Security Office] order of 29 January 1943 to deport the Sinti and Roma to Auschwitz 'in families' reflected efforts to keep the friction and resultant bureaucratic problems associated with the deportation and internment as small as possible. (1990: 107–8)

First Lieutenant Walther of Infantry Regiment 734 and head of the execution squad, wrote in his *Report on the Executions of the Jews and the Gypsies* that '[t]he execution of the Jews is simpler than that of the gypsies. One must admit that the Jews go to their deaths very composedly; they remain very calm. The gypsies, however, wail and scream and move about incessantly as soon as they get to the place of execution.' It was simply more expedient, and caused the guards less problems, to keep families together for processing. König writes of their sometimes having to smash the hands and feet of the Romanies, who even used loaves of stale bread as weapons, in order to render them docile as they were being herded to the ovens. Survivor Hermann Diamanski told jurists at a war crimes trial in Frankfurt in 1964 that,

> [T]housands of gypsies battled Gestapo guards [who were] driving them into the mass gas chambers of Auschwitz, but in the end they all died ... the gypsies fought with knives, razor blades and their fists against the Gestapo guards armed with submachine guns and other weapons ... the gypsies screamed all night; it was awful. Unlike the Jews, the gypsies fought. They sold their lives dearly. (Anonymous, 1964: B5)

König's book is a monument to Romani heroism and resistance in the camps, and should be required reading for any student of the *Porrajmos*. Romani families were not kept together in every camp, incidentally (cf. those shipped to Poland in 1940 referred to above by Zimmermann); this seems to have been a policy enacted at Auschwitz-Birkenau in particular. Jews transported to Auschwitz from Theresienstadt in September 1943, for example, were also allowed to remain together with their families.

(11) *'The denial of the right to live is what singles out the fate of the Jews from all other victims – Gypsies, Poles, Russian prisoners of war, Jehovah's Witnesses ... their fate was different from the fate of the Jews'* (Yitzhak Mais, in the brochure published by the Museums at Yad Vashem).

Michael Berenbaum, in a better position than most to know the details of the Romani Holocaust, repeats these arguments in his book (Roth and Berenbaum, 1989: 33), where he says

> Gypsies shared much, but not all of the horrors assigned to Jews. Gypsies were killed in some countries but not others ... Even though the Gypsies were subject to gassing and other forms of extermination, the number of Gypsies was not as vast ... In contrast, all Jews lived under an imminent death sentence of death [*sic*].

Jews were killed in some countries but not others too, and the number of Romanies was 'not as vast' because (according to the Nazis' own census conducted by Behrendt in 1939) there were nine times as many Jews as Romanies to start with at the outbreak of the Second World War, so obviously the numbers were greater. Steinmetz' argument that 'numbers decide' (1966: 44) would only be valid if the number of Jews and the number of Romanies had been equal to begin with. But when we discuss genocide we must do so in the context of the *destruction of entire peoples*, and in terms of overall *percentage*, the losses of the Romanies almost certainly exceeded those of any other group; their percentage was 'vaster'. If there had been 17.4 million Romanies in 1939 (the government's estimate of the number of Jews in that year), the Nazis would surely have murdered six million too; if there were only two Wisians on the planet and just one was murdered, that would be half of the Wisian population.

The question of the numbers of Romanies who were killed is a vexed one. Given the nature of their mode of life, no reliable estimate of the pre-war European Romani population exists. Similarly, the circumstances of their dispatch at the hands of the Nazis make this a question which can never be fully answered. I dealt with this in some detail in Hancock (1988a), but rely on König's statement that:

> The count of half a million Sinti and Roma murdered between 1939 and 1945 is too low to be tenable; for example in the Soviet Union many of the Romani dead were listed under non-specific labels such as *Liquidierungs-übrigen* [remainder to be liquidated], 'hangers-on' and 'partisans' … The final number of the dead Sinti and Roma may never be determined. We do not know precisely how many were brought into the concentration camps; not every concentration camp produced statistical material; moreover, Sinti and Roma are often listed under the heading of 'remainder to be liquidated', and do not appear in the statistics for Romanies. (König, 1989: 87–9)

In an article entitled 'Dutch World War II deaths higher than recorded' (*Dutch News nl* for Tuesday 9 October 2007), it was reported:

> The number of Dutch people who died in World War II is considerably higher than the accepted figure to date according to researchers at Utrecht University, reports ANP news service on Monday. The researchers say not 210,000 but 280,000 Dutch people died in the war. The discrepancy comes from the statistics of those who were deported. These are recorded as 'emigrants' while in reality they were Jews and Gypsies who were transported to the gas chambers in German concentration camps.

In the eastern territories, in Russia especially, Romani deaths were sometimes counted into the records under the heading of Jewish deaths. The *Memorial Book* for the Romanies who perished in Auschwitz-Birkenau also discusses the means of killing Romanies:

> Unlike the Jews, the overwhelming majority of whom were murdered in the gas chambers at Birkenau, Belzec, Treblinka and all the other mass extermination camps, the Gypsies outside the Reich were massacred at many places, sometimes only a few at a time, and sometimes by the hundreds. In the *Generalgouvernement* [the eastern territories] alone, 150 sites of Gypsy massacres are known. Research on the Jewish Holocaust can rely on comparison of pre- and post-war census data to help determine the numbers of victims in the countries concerned. However, this is not possible for the Gypsies, as it was only rarely that they were included in national census data. Therefore it is an impossible task to find the actual number of Gypsy victims in Poland, Yugoslavia, White Ruthenia and the Ukraine, *the lands that probably had the greatest numbers of victims.* (State Museum: 1993: 2 [emphasis added])

This means that statements such as 'somewhere between 20 and 50 per cent of the entire population of European Romanies was killed by the Nazis' (Berenbaum, 1993: 129), and the low figure of 250,000 Romani deaths displayed at the US Holocaust Memorial Museum must be considered underestimations. Several published estimates (referenced in Hancock, 1988b) put the figure in excess of one million, and even thirty years ago Pauwels and Bergier listed it at 750,000 (1960: 430). That perhaps an even higher number of Romanies were murdered in the fields and forests where they lived than were murdered in the camps has been recognised for some time. A reference to this appeared in the (London) *Financial Times* in an article by Tyler, who noted that 'between 500,000 and 750,000 were killed in the German death camps during the war, and another million may have been shot outside' (1994: 3). New information is reaching us all the time which is pushing the death toll upwards. Dr Paul Polansky of the Iowa-based Czech Historical Research Center recently published a report on his discovery of a hitherto unrecorded concentration camp at Lety in the Czech Republic, which was used for the disposal of Romanies. Now used as a pig farm, Lety and a chain of other camps processed mainly Roma, killing them on the spot or sending them on to Auschwitz. In Croatia between 80,000 and 100,000 Romanies are now estimated to have perished at the hands of the Ustaša, mostly at the

Jasenovac camp (Acković, 2006: 54). Numbers from here, like those from the Romani camps in northern Italy, have not yet been figured into the estimate (Strandberg, 1994: 1; Pape, 1997). We should nevertheless rejoice in the numbers of those who lived, and not glorify those of the dead in some horrible body-count; but if we are obliged to argue with numbers and quantity in this peculiarly American way, then let us look at the situation from the other side, and count the Romani *survivors* of the Holocaust, only 5,000 of whom are listed in the official register of the *Zentralrat Deutscher Sinti und Roma* in Heidelberg, and only four of whom have been located in the US, where over 80,000 Jewish survivors live today out of 350,000 still living worldwide. My respected colleague Donald Kenrick, co-author of *The Destiny of Europe's Gypsies*, the first full-length treatment of the *Porrajmos*, has claimed with some gladness that his own research points to the *lowest* figures for Romani deaths by 1945; in his revised edition, *Gypsies Under the Swastika* (Kenrick and Puxon, 2009), he estimates that they did not exceed 250,000, and in an article which appeared in *The Jewish Quarterly* he places it even lower, at 200,000 (Kenrick, 1995: 47). In his 1995 book *The Holocaust for Beginners*, Stuart Justman put it even lower: 'In addition to the Jews, the Nazis murdered prisoners of war, innumerable Russian civilians, political prisoners, common criminals, Jehovah's Witnesses, homosexuals, vagrants and some 100,000 gypsies, among others' (1995: 11).

If such estimates can be demonstrated as fact, then surely this is the dialogue we should be striving for, not a competition over whose losses were greater. Probably the most reliable statement regarding numbers was made at the first US Conference on Romanies in the Holocaust which took place at Drew University in November 1995, when Sybil Milton, senior historian at the US Holocaust Research Institute in Washington DC, stated that, 'We believe that something between half a million and a million and a half Romanies were murdered in Nazi Germany and occupied Europe between 1939 and 1945.'

(12) *Only Jews qualify as victims of genocidal action; other victimised groups were casualties of war.*

In Sidney Schiffer's play (see Hancock, 1988: 45) a Jewish objection was made to a Romani's referring to the Romani *Holocaust*, and a request followed that it be renamed the Romani *genocide*, since that word had already been taken. Now the word *genocide* itself seems to have become privileged property for some Holocaust historians; in their recent book *Auschwitz, 1270 to the Present*, authors Debórah Dwork and Robert Jan van Pelt refer to '[t]he genocide of the Jews and the mass murder of gypsies and Soviet prisoners of war' (1996: 374) in that camp. But not only does the treatment of Romanies under the Nazis qualify as genocide, the treatment *today* of Romani peoples in parts of Europe qualifies as genocide according to the United Nations' definition.

(13) *Although Romanies were likewise singled out for extermination, they weren't humiliated in the way that Jews were.*

This is one of the most recent arguments, and one which almost seems to be grasping to find a way to lessen the Romani experience. Avishai Margalit and Gabriel Motzkin, both of whom teach at the University of Jerusalem, maintained in an article published in 1996 that,

> The Nazis had plans for other peoples, and began to apply their programs to the Poles by liquidating the Polish elites. Gypsies and homosexuals also figured high on their list, and the whole process was given a trial run in the partial extermination of the mentally retarded … [h]owever, the mentally retarded, who were murdered through operation Euthanasia were not humiliated, nor were the gypsies, who were also the victims of planned extermination, humiliated in an elaborate structure of humiliation like the one the Nazis created for the Jews. (Margalit and Motzkin, 1996: 79)

The single source given for this information is Müller-Hill (1988). Nothing need be said except that the authors of this statement clearly know nothing of the history of the treatment of Romani peoples in Germany (see, for example, Hancock, 1989), and like so many of those who make such careless statements, they likely believed that no Romanies would read what they had written. Preaching to the converted yields no change.

(14) *The 'uniqueness' of the Jewish case should be defended at all costs because it justifies the existence of the Jewish homeland, Israel.*

On the main mall of the campus at my university stands a structure some nine feet high, erected by the Jewish Students' Association, which is a monument to Israel. It is covered with photographs and newspaper articles, and in the very middle of it is a yellow placard bearing the words 'Israel: The Six Million: Never Forget'. This is not a new argument, indeed it has been suggested to me by more than one well-disposed USHMC member, and Zygmunt Bauman explicitly refers to the way in which '[t]he Jewish state tries to employ the tragic memories as the certificate of its political legitimacy, a safe-conduct pass for its past and future policies, and above all, as the advance payment for the injustices it might itself commit' (1989: ix).[36] Lagrou has written more recently of the Holocaust's being 'gradually integrated as a cornerstone of Israeli national identity' (1997: 221). But it is a specious argument. Israel, a Jewish state, should exist under any circumstances; speaking as a member of a people without a country, I can feel very deeply the emotion associated with the possession of a homeland. To acknowledge that Romanies received the same treatment as Jews, as Miriam Novitch said, 'for the same reasons using the same methods', cannot take anything away from the enormity of the Jewish tragedy, or diminish the strength of the right to Israel. One is reminded of Dermot Mulroney's words in *Where the Day Takes You* (Rocco, 1992): 'What's mine is mine, and if I share it with you, it becomes less mine!' I cannot imagine that the rest of the world would interpret the Romani claim in this way, or see it as a threat to the right to the existence of a Jewish state.

(15) *No other group was viewed with such disgust and contempt, or so relentlessly and methodically persecuted, or was selected for total eradication from the face of the earth.*

Romanies don't match this, I have been told, because Romanies weren't mentioned in *Mein Kampf*, or at the Wannsee Conference, and because some Romanies were exempt from the death machine, and because a much higher number of Jews had died by 1945.

Romanies were not mentioned specifically in the documentation of the Wannsee Conference because by that time (20 January 1942), policies against Jews, subsequent to the directive of 24 December issued four weeks earlier, automatically included Romanies. The Wannsee Conference in any case was not a policy or decision-making meeting, although it has acquired that interpretation; its purpose was rather to coordinate existing policies. And no argument was necessary in *Mein Kampf* because it was totally unnecessary on Hitler's part to make any case for anti-gypsyism. There was simply no need to convince anybody of the subhuman status of Romanies, against whom laws were already firmly entrenched in Germany, despite the guarantees of the National

Constitution of the Weimar Republic. No public conscience ever provoked a defence of the Romani case, a fact Fraser comments upon in his book *The Gypsies*:

> From about 1937 onwards, [Nazi] pressures … on Gypsies built up swiftly and remorselessly, with no hostile public reaction, abroad or at home, of the kind which had made the Nazis a little more circumspect in their dealings with the Jews, at least in the early days, because of respect for world opinion. (Fraser, 1993: 261–2)

When the question of this indifference was raised following the war, one French physician commented, rhetorically, that 'everyone despises Gypsies, so why exercise restraint? Who will avenge them? Who will bear witness?' (Bernadec, 1979: 34). Nor can the excuse that the rest of the world was ignorant of what was happening be maintained in the Romani case:

> Whatever the real state of knowledge or ignorance among the German civilian population during the Second World War about the transport and the murder of millions of German and non-German Jews in Europe, the initial internment of the Roma was kept secret from no one. Concentration camps were built on the outskirts of the capital city, and the internment of the Sinti and Roma was not only covered by a number of Berlin newspapers, but was even joked about in their columns. Psychologists engaged in racial research paid official visits to Marzahn to study and take extensive film footage of the Romani children at play there. A major train line ran right past that camp, and its few survivors recall that train passengers who pitied their situation, and who knew or suspected that the interned Roma were surviving on only minimal rations, occasionally threw packages of food down into the camp enclosure as their train passed by. (Trumpener, 1992: 844)

While German anti-Semitism, like anti-gypsyism over the centuries, has bordered upon the pathological (see especially Wilson, 1982), there was no one to argue in support of the Romanies, unlike those who defended the Jewish position. As Burleigh and Wippermann make clear (1991: 36), anti-Semitism was *not* an undisputed part of the early [German] racial hygiene movement. Ploetz and a number of other racial hygienists, such as Wilhelm Schallmayer, fiercely denounced anti-Semitism; indeed, in his 1895 treatise, Ploetz classified Jews as a part of the superior 'white race' (Proctor, 1990: 144n.). On the contrary, in the early 1890s the Swabian Parliament organised a conference on the 'Gypsy scum' (*Das Zigeunergeschmeiß*), and in 1899 Alfred Dillmann established the Gypsy Information Agency (*Nachrichtendienst in Bezug auf die Zigeuner*) which began to collect data in the form of genealogical information, fingerprints, and photographs of Romanies throughout the territory. This led to the publication in 1905 of Dillmann's *Zigeuner-Buch*, which laid the groundwork for what was to come a quarter of a century later. It consisted of a lengthy argument for controlling Romanies, stressing their inherent criminality, and calling them 'a plague against which society must unflaggingly defend itself'. The bulk of the volume consisted of a register of over 5,000 individuals, which gave date and place of birth, genealogy, criminal record if any and so on. The third part of the book consisted of photographs of Romanies taken from police files throughout the German states. On 17 February 1906, the Prussian Minister of the Interior issued a directive to 'Combat the Gypsy Nuisance' (*Die Bekämpfung des Zigeunerunwesens*), and established bilateral, anti-Romani agreements with all neighbouring countries. Licences were required by all Romani people wanting to live and work in Prussia. In 1909 the Swiss Department of Justice began a national register of Romanies, while in Hungary it was recommended at a 'Gypsy Policy Conference' that all Romani people be branded on their bodies for easy identification. In 1912 France introduced the *Carnet Anthropométrique*, a document containing personal data (including photograph and fingerprints) which all Romanies were henceforth required to carry.

'The first anti-Jewish law was promulgated in 1933', (Burleigh and Wippermann, 1991: 4), at a time when scores of anti-Romani laws had already been in effect in Germany for centuries. In 1920, the Minister of Public Welfare in Düsseldorf forbade Romanies from entering any public washing or recreational facility, such as swimming pools, public baths, spas or parks; this restriction also came to be applied to Jews after 1933 (Burleigh and Wippermann, 1991: 77); more ominously in that same year, Binding and Hoche published their treatise on *Lives Undeserving of Life* (*Lebensunwertes Leben*), which argued for the killing of those who were seen to be 'dead weight' (*Ballastexistenz*) within humanity, including Romanies. This notion of 'unworthy life' was incorporated into Nazi law on 14 July 1933, less than six months after Hitler came to power, in his 'Law for the prevention of hereditarily diseased offspring'.

In 1934, Romanies were expelled from the trade unions. In June 1935, the main Nazi institution to deal with Romanies, the Racial Hygiene and Criminal Biology and Research Unit, was first established, the expressed purpose of which was to determine whether Romanies and Blacks were human or subhuman, groundwork on genetic evaluation which provided the model for the subsequent classification of Jews. Five months later, on 26 November, the Ministry of the Interior, which partially funded the Research Unit, circulated an order forbidding marriages between Germans and 'Gypsies, Negroes and their bastard offspring'. On 15 September 1935, the *Nürnberger Gesetze*, the 'Nuremberg Law for the Protection of Blood and Honour', was passed, making marriage between 'Aryan' and 'non-Aryan' people illegal. It stated that '[o]f the foreign blood common in Europe, there are only Jews and Gypsies'. In 1936, in preparation for the Olympic Games, and for fear of negative world opinion, 'anti-Semitic posters and placards were temporarily removed' from the streets of Berlin by the Nazis (Burleigh and Wippermann, 1991: 84), at the same time that Romanies were being cleared from those streets as an eyesore, because visitors had to be 'spared the sight of the "Gypsy disgrace"' (Zimmermann, 1990: 91), just as they were at the 1992 Olympic Games in Barcelona. Just before the Berlin games, six hundred Romanies were forcibly detained in a cemetery and next to a sewage dump at Marzahn, which was 'particularly offensive to a people hyper-sensitive about cleanliness' (Burleigh and Wippermann, 1991: 117); in Spain fifty-six years later, they were placed in the Campo de la Bota outside of the city, again because of the Olympic Games.

More significantly, we have now learned that Nazi propaganda encouraging public support for the incarceration of Romanies was widely distributed together with the programme for those games in 1936 (Sybil Milton, in personal communication). In 1938, more stringent criteria came to be applied to the definition of 'Gypsy'; if two of an individual's eight great-grandparents were even part Romani, that individual later was deemed to have too much 'Gypsy blood' to be allowed to live – a criterion twice as strict as that defining who was Jewish. Indeed, if criteria for the latter had applied equally to Romanies, some 18,000 (nine-tenths of the total Romani population of Germany at that time) would have escaped death (Kenrick and Puxon, 1972: 68; see also Ehmann, 1981: 10). One could argue, therefore, that Romanies in fact were seen as posing twice the genetic threat to the *Herrenvolk* that Jews did.

According to eyewitness accounts, in January or February 1940, 250 Romani children from Brno in the concentration camp at Buchenwald were used as guinea pigs for testing the Zyklon B cyanide gas crystals, a lethal insecticide which from 1941 onwards was used for the mass murders at Auschwitz-Birkenau. 'At Buchenwald then, for the first time, this gas was used for mass murder, and it was for the murder of innocent Gypsy children' (Proester, 1968).

(16) *There is no comparison between the wrath which characterised the Nazis' determination to destroy the Jews and the way they went about dealing with Romanies* (A point made by a member of the audience at the 'Encounters with the Holocaust' conference held at Texas A&M University in April 1997).

When questioned, the person making this assumption admitted that she in fact had no *actual* knowledge of the way in which the Nazis processed Romanies, but just 'felt' that it was surely the case that Jews were dispatched with more fury. If one thing typifies the way in which Hitler's genocidal policies were put into effect, it was the dispassionate, cold and clinical way in which the 'subhumans' were eradicated, both Jewish and Romani. It has been argued that if any anger was evident, it was an anger redirected, originating in the transference of feelings of guilt on the part of the Nazis.

The night of 9 November 1938 is remembered in the annals of the Jewish Holocaust as *Kristallnacht*, or 'The Night of Broken Glass', for it was on this night that, in response to the murder of a German embassy official in Paris by a Jewish teenager, over a thousand synagogues were desecrated and nearly a hundred Jews were killed, while thousands more were arrested. This blatant, public display of hatred marked the beginning of the open and official sanctioning of the persecution of an 'inferior race'. In effect, it sent a message to the general public that such violence had full state approval. From this date onwards, anti-Jewish hostility escalated steadily towards the Holocaust. Nor was this the first massive anti-Jewish outbreak in twentieth-century Germany; in November 1923, a violent attack took place in Berlin against numbers of Eastern European Jews who had come there to live (Peukert, 1987: 160). For the Romani victims, there were also mass round-ups and displays of military and police brutality, designed to show them, and the German public, exactly where they stood in the German hierarchy, and how they could be treated by ordinary citizens with the approval and encouragement of the government. As early as 1927, between 23 and 26 November, armed raids were carried out in Romani communities throughout Prussia, to enforce a decree issued on 3 November of that year which required that all Romanies be registered through documentation 'in the same manner as individuals being sought by means of wanted posters, witnesses, photographs and fingerprints' (von Hase-Mihalik and Kreuzkamp, 1990: 140). Even infants were fingerprinted, and those over six years of age required to carry identity cards bearing fingerprints and photographs. Eight thousand Romanies were processed as a result of that raid, more than a third of the entire Romani population in Germany. The second such action took place between 18 and 25 September in 1933, when the Reichsminister for the Interior and for Propaganda ordered the apprehension and arrest of Romanies throughout Germany, in accordance with 'The Law Against Habitual Criminals'. Many were sent to concentration camps as a result, where they were forced to do penal labour, and where some underwent sterilisation. The most significant military action, however, occurred during the summer of 1938, from 12 to 18 June, when *Zigeuneraufräumungswoche* or 'Gypsy Clean-Up Week' was ordered. Hundreds of Romanies throughout Germany and Austria were rounded up, beaten and imprisoned. In Mannswörth, Austria, three hundred were arrested in this way in a single night.

Following the collapse of the Third Reich, nothing was done to assist the Romani survivors, no effort made by the liberators to reorient them; instead, the terms of a 1926 pre-Nazi anti-Romani law which was still in effect ensured that those lacking a trade remained out of sight, hiding in the abandoned camps, for fear of arrest and incarceration. Since that time, all of the programmes used by the Nazis to deal with Romanies have been either suggested or implemented by various European nations – sterilisations in Slovakia, recommendations for incineration in a furnace from an Irish Government official, forced incarceration and deportation in Germany (Kinzer, 1992). Today, the Romani population faces its severest crisis since the Holocaust; neo-Nazi race crimes against Romanies have seen rapes, beatings and murders in Germany, Hungary and Slovakia; anti-Romani pogroms in Romania and Bulgaria, including lynchings and home burnings, are increasing. For my people, the

Holocaust is not yet over. The US Holocaust Memorial Museum has not yet done enough to educate the world about the Romani experience; there, the 'Gypsy' artifacts on display in the 'other victims' corner of the Museum's third floor, consist of a violin, a wagon and a woman's dress – more Hollywood than Holocaust – and very, very few of the Romani victims and inmates depicted in the photo exhibits (especially those involving Mengele's experiments with twins) are identified as such. Most galling of all was the total absence of the key words 'Gypsy', 'Rom', 'Sinti', 'Romani', 'Zigeuner' and so on in the computerised question-and-answer bank provided for the public to consult which led, in June 1993, to an organised protest at the Museum by a group represented by Ms. Mary Thomas of Adoptive Parents and Friends of Romani Children, demanding that more details of the fate of Romanies be included in the Museum. They argued that when their children grow older and begin to ask about their background and the history of their people, and about the Holocaust in particular, the US Holocaust Memorial Museum would not be the place to go for their answers; that the Romani story had been downplayed to the extent of differently representing historical fact, of revision by omission. That protest led to the circulation of a petition asking, among other things, that more Romani scholars (rather than non-Romani specialists) be directly involved; that more documentation on the Romani Holocaust be displayed and made available to visitors to the Museum; and has resulted in the inclusion of one or two Gypsy entries in the computerised data bank.

I have been both praised and criticised for bringing attention to these issues. The director of one Holocaust centre referred to me as a trouble-maker; another writer on the Holocaust called my discussion of the Romani case in the Jewish context 'loathsome'. A representative of the Memorial Council, whom I have never met, told a researcher who called to find out how to reach me that I was a 'wild man'; while its one-time director told the press that Romani spokespersons were 'cranks' and 'eccentrics' (Doolittle, 1984: 5), and his successor reported to the media that we were 'naïve' (Hirschberg, 1986: A16). People have stood up and walked out when it has been my turn to speak at conferences about the *Porrajmos,* and one former professor at my own university adamantly refused even to *mention* Romanies in his regular course on the Holocaust. Others have intimated that I should not be pursuing this because I am not a historian, and am therefore not qualified to engage in this kind of research. If you think these things don't hurt me, they do, deeply. There are those reading this essay who I'm sure are angered by what is being said in these pages, and who are ready to challenge me. Why should this be? I have tried to remain objective, and let the facts argue my case. If I can be proven wrong, I am happy to acknowledge that. I am well aware that for some people, insistence upon getting all the facts of the Romani experience properly acknowledged has been regarded as confrontational and even threatening; Yehuda Bauer (1990: 1) felt that 'anti-Gypsy sentiment' in Europe was, in his words, '*in competition*' with 'radical anti-Semitism' there, the 'sentiment' in question having led to the murders and pogroms against Romanies mentioned above, during the same period for which the 1990 *Country Report on Human Rights* reported 'no incidents of anti-Semitic violence' (for an extended discussion in this competitive vein, see Margalit, 1996). An August 1993 report issued by the Nemzetközi Cigány Szöveség on the other hand quoted a physician from the Romanian town of Teleorman, who said, 'our war against the Gypsies will start in the autumn. Until then, preparations will be made to obtain arms; first we are going to acquire chemical sprays. We will not spare minors, either' (Balogh, 1993). Events indicating that this persecution began to happen shortly thereafter were described in the 19 December 1993 issue of the *San Francisco Chronicle*, where the following appeared:

> An orgy of mob lynching and house-burning with police collaboration, has turned into something even more sinister for Romania's hated Gypsies: the beginnings of a nationwide campaign of terror launched by groups modeling themselves on the Ku Klux Klan ... 'We are many, and very determined. We will skin the Gypsies soon. We will take their eyeballs out, smash their teeth, and cut off their noses. The first will be hanged.' (Branson, 1993: A1, A15)

Anti-gypsyism is at an all-time high, and it can only begin to be combatted by sensitising the general public to the details of Romani history and suffering. My purpose in this paper, as a follow-up to that given at the last conference in Oxford, is to get these issues as they relate to the Holocaust out into the open, to air them publicly, and hope that a more accurate, and more compassionate, attitude will prevail.

Resistance to the Romani case must be due at least in part to the lateness of its arrival on the academic scene; scholarship on the *Porrajmos* is comparatively new, so much so that it has brought charges of 'bandwagoning' from some quarters. Our people are traditionally not disposed to keeping alive the terrible memories from our history – nostalgia is a luxury for others, and the *Porrajmos* was not the first, but the second historical attempt to destroy the Romanies as a people, following Charles VI's extermination order in 1721, and a meeting of European national representatives was held in 1908, to formulate 'an international plot legally to expel the gypsies from Europe' (Holroyd, 1975: 358). Romanies in the US, for example, have obliterated entirely from their collective memories all recollection of the five-and-a-half centuries of slavery in Romania which their great-great-grandparents came to America to escape during the last century (Hancock, 1988). Survivors of the Holocaust are today likewise reluctant to speak about their experiences, and so it is that the story is only now beginning to unfold. The task of those collecting testimonies is made the more difficult because for some groups, the Sinti in particular, there are cultural restrictions upon speaking about the dead.

It has to be said too that there is also an element of racism evident in the Jewish response; after all, Romanies are a 'Third World people of color', as Lopate coins the term in his discussion of the relative value of victimhood (1989: 292); Anton Fojn ('Bubili') wrote of the SS guards' whipping him and his father off the transport and through the gates of Dachau, and calling them 'Congo niggers' on account of their dark skin (Friedman, 1990: 18). I have been told – off the record – that some Council members do not want to be judged by the company they fear they might have to keep. The then-Director of the Holocaust Memorial Center in Dallas told me in 1987, apparently without intent to offend, that she believed that Jews did not want to be associated with Romanies in the Holocaust because it would 'detract from its solemnity'. In every single public opinion poll, including that conducted in the US (and reported in the 8 January 1992 issue of *The New York Times*), 'Gypsies' are listed as the most discriminated-against minority, the most despised ethnic population, and some of the stereotypes have evidently rubbed off on some Council members. At one presentation I gave at a Hillel Center, I was interrupted by a woman who leapt to her feet and angrily demanded why I was even comparing the Romani case to the Jewish, when Jews had given so much to the world and Romanies were merely parasites and thieves. On another occasion a gentleman in the audience stood up and declared that he would never buy a book on the Holocaust written by a Romani. I learned from James Michael Holmes of Phoenix Productions International that two Hollywood studios have already declined to consider an updated script of the 1947 film *Golden Earrings*, because it is a screenplay about the Holocaust which does not deal with its Jewish victims. When research revealed in a book published recently that 'Esther', the girl peering forlornly from a transport wagon leaving for Auschwitz, and who was assumed to be Jewish, was in fact a twelve-year-old Sinti girl named Settela, the Jewish community in The Netherlands became furious (Wagenaar, 1995). Jan Morris began her review of a newly published book on Romanies in the New Europe, with the words '[t]he Jews are tragically conspicuous by their absence, the [G]ypsies are all too often maddeningly present' (Morris, 1995: 4).

Working to alter attitudes of this kind is a mighty task indeed, and was one reason behind my co-founding the Romani-Jewish Alliance some years ago, which works to dispel anti-Jewish and anti-Romani stereotypes, and to educate both populations about the other's experience. I should say here, incidentally, in answer to an often-asked question, that there are many Romanies who are Jewish, and many more Romani–Jewish marriages. During the war such 'marriages' characterised one concentration camp in eastern Serbia in particular, where Romanies and Jews were held before transportation. Even popular attempts to document our story can do more harm than good; an example is the film version of Ramati's *And the Violins Stopped Playing* (1988), which is so full of misrepresentation and distortions of the truth that it would have been better left undone; among other things it suggests that Romanies were murdered in Auschwitz, for example, lest they survive as witnesses to the fate of the Jewish prisoners.

It might also be acknowledged that some resistance is grounded simply in disbelief, in the assumption that 'If this is true, why haven't we heard about it before?' I must admit that, for a very long time, as I'd search through the 'shelves tightly packed', through the innumerable books on the Holocaust looking for references to Romanies, I would skim right over those sections dealing with the non-Romani victims; I am ashamed to say that they just were not as important to me, so consumed was I with my search. It was only later that I began to take the time to learn about what happened to other groups, and to be appalled and aggrieved by what I read. When the existence of one's entire people is threatened so barbarously, anything else simply gets in the way. But others have come to do as I did, and are examining the cases of those besides their own without prejudgment, and I am encouraged by the responses forthcoming from those who have made the effort, with an open mind, to examine the details of what Romanies suffered at the hands of the Nazis. I have said many times that only Jews can really come close to understanding the impact the *Porrajmos* has had on the Romani population, and I venture to think that only Romanies can come close, on an emotional level, to understanding the Jewish tragedy. The Holocaust, sadly, just doesn't seem to mean as much for anyone else. But neither Jew nor Rom can *fully* understand the other's experience, then or now, nor should either begin to presume to interpret for the other. For this reason I would like to see the individual 'uniquenesses', if you like, emphasised by a greater use of the ethnic terminology: *Shoah* or *Khurbn* for the Jewish Holocaust, *Porrajmos* for the Romani. The word 'Holocaust', I feel, is used too casually to have the meaning intended for it.

I have been deliberately critical of the US Holocaust Memorial Council and the Museum in this essay, and make no apology for that, for our relationship over the past decade has been a stormy one, and one which has caused me considerable personal frustration. It is, after all, the national memorial to the victims of Nazism, and an international educational resource. The 1987 Conference on other victims, for example, included a panel on Romanies, but no Romanies were invited to speak or even participate in its planning. And on 23 April 1996, the US Holocaust Memorial Museum organised a public panel discussion entitled 'Sinti and Roma during the Holocaust and Today', again in which no Romanies were invited to participate. The promotional wording in the calendar announcing the discussion stated merely that 'Sinti and Roma suffered greatly as victims of Nazi persecution and genocide', making no mention at all of their being, like Jews, specific targets of the Final Solution. In 1995, the Education Committee of the Holocaust Council prepared a brochure on the Romani victims of the Holocaust, which it distributed in its education package at the 23rd Scholars' Conference on the Holocaust and the Churches in March 1996; this was the first time that William Duna, the former and only Romani representative on the Council *and member of the education committee,* learned of the existence of the new publication. It is this assumption that we can be 'discussed' in our absence, and having non-Romani scholars talk about us rather than to us, which is the most hurtful and demeaning. I could not imagine that the Jewish academic establishment would tolerate for one moment a 'panel discussion' on the fate of Jews in the Holocaust conducted with no Jewish presence or input. I cannot imagine a Holocaust Memorial center with no Jewish participation. But we must bear this indignity, as though we are incapable of representing ourselves, of being in charge of our own history. On 21 September 2000, the Center for Advanced Holocaust Studies at the US Holocaust Memorial Museum held a symposium entitled 'Roma and Sinti: Under-Studied Victims of Nazism'. Not of the *Holocaust*, notice. I was asked to find the invited speakers – which I did – but the organisers insisted, against my very strenuous protests, that Guenther Lewy also be included on the programme. Lewy is a revisionist who not only denies that Romanies were a part of the Holocaust, but that they were not even the victims of genocide (see Hancock, 2001 for my review of his book). He said as much in Washington DC, but the closing speaker at the same symposium was Raul Hilberg, generally considered to be the pre-eminent scholar of the Holocaust. In his talk he not only pointed out the weakness of Lewy's position, he also emphasised the special relationship which exists between Jews and Romanies and their shared experience in the Holocaust. I sat on the stage and wept at his words. But when the *Proceedings* were published (Shapiro and Ehrenreich, 2002), Lewy's paper was included but Hilberg's was left out.

Many factors, many personalities, have been involved in the misunderstandings and anger generated by the dialogue between Romanies and the Council (see e.g. Wiesenthal, 1989: 218–220 and Linnenthal, 1995: 228–47). Speaking at the Council's 1987 conference on non-Jewish victims in Washington DC mentioned above, Erika Thurner drew attention to the evident lack of concern for the Holocaust's Romani victims:

> Gypsies have generally been forgotten or been reserved for the footnotes of historical investigation … this very position, as a fringe social group with negligible social status, is responsible for the fact that, after 1945, the Gypsy Holocaust was not acknowledged for so many years, and continues to be neglected to a certain degree to this very day. Ignorance as to the fate of the Sinti and Roma in the Third Reich has made historical

reconstruction especially difficult. It has led to further discrimination against Gypsies, and to the *refusal* to recognise their right to restitution of both a material and ideal nature. (1987: 7)

In the years since Erika Thurner made those observations, there has been a steadily growing acknowledgement of the Romani tragedy, and an acceptance of the fact that the Jews and the Romanies were equally victim to the techniques and policies of the Nazi death machine. But along with this recognition at the academic and historical level, so efforts to singularise the Jewish experience have gained, at least for some of its champions, an almost desperate impetus (for example, Katz, 1994). Perhaps we should be examining not what the challenges are to the procedural and historical details with which scholars attempt to make their case, but *why* it is so vitally important to some of them to privatise the Holocaust – why they strive so passionately to do so.

This is beginning to attract the attention of the outside world. There is a growing reaction in print to the Jewish exclusivist position (Fox, 1995; Rosen, 1995), and in an essay in *Z Magazine* in which he makes the case that uniquist scholars such as Deborah Lipstadt and Stephen Katz are as guilty of re-working the historical record by failing to acknowledge Roma, as revisionists are in denying that the Holocaust even happened; Ward Churchill goes so far as to suggest that Jews are directly responsible for keeping the details of the Romani Holocaust away from the public:

> Nothing at all was done to save the Gypsies from their identical fate, and in this connection international Jewish organisations have no better record than do the governments of the US, Great Britain and Canada. To the contrary, it was arguably Jewish organisations that served as the vanguard in obscuring what was happening to the Gypsies even as it happened, a posture they've never abandoned. (1997a: 44)

These words were edited out of the same essay reprinted in *A Little Matter of Genocide* (Churchill, 1997b).

I said in the earlier published version of this paper that I was confident that open recognition of the Romani position will continue to grow in Washington DC. I said that we have gone from having no representation at all on the Council, to having one member; but I spoke too soon. That member's term has expired, and the President has declined to reappoint him – or any Rom. This decision came in the same week that Mr Clinton assured the nation of his commitment to bring non-white minorities into the American mainstream, and to deal with issues of racial inequality in society. The Council did formally protest against anti-gypsyism in Europe at the administrative level (Meyerhoff, 1992), but it will be a long time before my hope that we will eventually be moved out of the category of 'other victims', and be fully recognised as the only population, together with Jews, which was slated for its eventual eradication, will be realised. Now, without even representation, we are back to square one.

I want to be able to thumb through any of the many published treatments of the Holocaust at my local bookstore and find comprehensive information in them about what happened to my people – at present, we're usually not listed in their indexes at all. One of my most recent purchases was Louis Snyder's *Encyclopedia of the Third Reich*, but not only does it contain not one single reference to Romanies, neither do Robert Ritter or Eva Justin or Gerhard Stein or Sophie Erhardt find a place in its list of entries. This is true also for Wheal, Pope and Taylor's *Encyclopedia of the Second World War*, Wistrich's *Who's Who in Nazi Germany* and Keegan's *Who Was Who in World War II*, as well as for most other books on the Holocaust. On the same page that he writes of Himmler's 'conclusive solution to the Gypsy question' (the sole mention of Romanies in the book), Lang discusses the *Endlösung* only in terms of its being 'the term by which the Nazis chose to designate their genocidal war against the Jews' (Lang, 1990). It is an eerie and disheartening feeling to pick up such books, and find the attempted genocide of one's people written completely out of the historical record. Perhaps worse, in the English-language translation of at least one book, that by Lucjan Dobroszycki of *The Chronicle of the Lodz Ghetto*, the entire reference to the liquidation of the Romani camp there (entry No. 22 for 29 and 30 April 1942, in the original work), has been deleted deliberately. Such deliberate omission has been remarked upon by Sybil Milton, who says (1991a: 2),

> Analyses of the concentration camps by Martin Broszat and others ignore the pre-1939 *Zigeunerlager* (special internment camps for Gypsies) as well as the simultaneous presence of Gypsies in virtually the entire expanded concentration camp system after 1939. The most blatant example is Eberhard Kolb's deletion of any reference to Gypsies in his history of Bergen-Belsen. Parallel lacunae are evident in current literature about the

ghettos in Poland, the Baltic, and the occupied parts of the Soviet Union, although memoir literature does include contemporaneous accounts of the simultaneous incarceration of Gypsies. One example suffices to illustrate this point: although Adam Czerniakow's diary records the presence of both German and Polish Gypsies in the Warsaw ghetto in April and June 1942, Yisrael Gutman's study avoids even passing mention of them.

Similarly, the preoccupation with anti-Semitism as a central motivation in Nazi policy has resulted in Michael Marrus's failure to include Romanies in his recent analyses of the historiography of the Holocaust, although literature is available. This oversight is also found in such new studies as Robert Gellately's analysis of the patterns of racial denunciation, which unfortunately does not mention relevant Romani cases.

I have been told, but have not yet verified, that translations of other works on the Holocaust have also had entries on Romanies removed. Furthermore, I do not want to read references to the US Holocaust Memorial Museum in the national press and learn only that it is a monument to 'the plight of European Jews', as *The New York Times* told its readers in its 23 December 1993 issue. I want to be able to watch epics such as *Schindler's List* and learn that Romanies were a central part of the Holocaust too; or other films, such as *Escape From Sobibor*, a Polish camp where, according to its Kommandant Franz Stangl in his memoirs, thousands of Romanies were murdered, and not to hear the word 'Gypsy' except once, and then as the name of somebody's dog. This latter example is not merely offensive, it is cruel and callous. Camp survivor B. Stawska (in Fickowski, 1989: 43) is one who has described the transportation of Romanies to Sobibor:

In November 1942, the pogrom against the Jews and Gypsies began, and they were shot on a mass scale in street executions. The Gypsies were driven into the square at the fore of the crowd, and after them the Jews. It was cold, and the Gypsy women were weeping loudly. They had all their possessions on their backs, including eiderdowns; everything that they had, but all of that was taken away from them later. The Jews behaved very calmly, but the Gypsies cried a lot – you could hear one loud sobbing. They were taken to the station and loaded into goods wagons, which were sealed and taken to stations beyond Chelm, to Sobibór, where they were burnt in the ovens.

National Public Radio in Washington DC covered the 50th

anniversary of the liberation of Auschwitz-Birkenau on 26 January 1995 extensively, although Romanies were never once mentioned, despite being well-represented at the commemoration, at least outside the camp. In his closing report on the NPR *Weekend Edition* on 28 January, Michael Goldfarb described how 'candles were placed along the tracks that delivered Jews and Poles to their death'. But it is little wonder that Romanies weren't mentioned; they were not allowed to participate. An article on the Auschwitz commemoration in the British (but not the American) press dated 28 January included a photograph of a group of Romanies staring mournfully through a wire fence, with a caption reading 'Cold-shouldered: Gipsies, whose ancestors were among Auschwitz victims, are forced to watch the ceremony from outside the compound' (Stapinska, 1995: 5). In a speech given at that ceremony, Elie Wiesel said that the Jewish people 'were singled out for destruction during the Holocaust'. Nor was that the first time; in an article in *The New York Times* five years before that, entitled 'At a death camp, Gypsies confront indifference', writer Marlise Simons wrote of the Romani victims at Mauthausen being treated as a 'dismissive afterthought' in a commemorative ceremony that year (Simons, 1990), quoting one Holocaust historian who said that 'prejudice against Gypsies has permeated all levels of our society, the academic world, the bureaucracy'. British coverage of the present volume in the *Times Higher Education Supplement* focused entirely upon the Romani issue (Cornwell, 1996), while the three-page review in the US equivalent, the *Chronicle of Higher Education*, Romanies are referred to just once in a nine-line paragraph (Shea, 1996). In a CNN news feature on the Romani suit against the Swiss banks televised on 9 June 1997, based upon numerous information-seeking phone calls to the Romani Union office, the number of Romanies murdered in the Holocaust was announced as 'two hundred and fifty thousand', despite the US Holocaust Research Institute's current estimate of 'between a half and one and a half million' being provided to them. The BBC *World at War* segment entitled 'Genocide' mentions the 1935 law forbidding Aryans from marrying Jews, but fails to say that the very same law also referred to Romanies; it mentions the Polish victims repeatedly, but remains completely silent about Romanies, against whom – unlike Poles – the Final Solution *did* operate. The first group of concentration camp inmates pictured in that documentary is of Sinti prisoners at Buchenwald, but the viewer isn't told this. But as Reimer and Reimer point out, 'considering that the Gypsies are still discriminated against throughout Europe, including Germany, it is perhaps not surprising that they have been virtually excluded from films on the Holocaust' (1992: 165). And in Germany, where it all began, Romanies have even yet to be included in the national Holocaust memorial, an omission which attracted the international media (Anonymous, 1992), even though the Chairman of the Jewish community in Berlin, Heinz Galinski, speaking at a ceremony commemorating the Romani victims of the *Porrajmos* fifteen years ago, acknowledged publicly that 'Jews and Gypsies were both singled out as "lives unworthy of life"' (1980: 77). Surely genocide of the magnitude suffered by the Romani people deserves acknowledgement far beyond that which it now receives.

CHAPTER SIXTEEN

The consequences of anti-Gypsy racism in Europe

You talk about the race problem, the immigration problem, all sorts of problems. If you are liberal, you say that Black people have problems. If you are not, you say they are the problem. But the members of the new [Europe] have only one real problem; that problem is white people. Racism, of course, is not our problem; it is yours. We simply suffer the effects of your racism.

Salman Rushdie[37]

Honoured Ambassador, Mister Chairman, respected fellow delegates. I have chosen as the topic of my address before this meeting the issue of racism. Specifically, the nature and consequences of racism in Europe directed at the Romani population.

Racism must be recognised as a cancer which, if not checked, will lead us surely and inevitably into a catastrophic situation which has the potential to destroy Europe in a twenty-first century chaos. I don't wish to be charged with hyperbole, but I believe that the points I raise here cannot be made too forcefully.

The Eastern European nations have, since 1989, joined the West in establishing democratic systems of government. This ongoing change is not an easy one, for it must incorporate adjustments in many areas. Its slowness alone frustrates many people who, rather than make an effort over time to adjust, express their desire for a return to the older regime – the Communist system of government that places responsibility and

Text from the US Delegation to the OSCE Office for Democratic Institutions and Human Rights's Human Dimension Seminar on Roma in the OSCE Region, Warsaw, 20–23 September 1994. Originally published in *The Belgrade Circle*, 1–2 (1995).

decision-making with the State rather than with the people. We have already seen one success for the Communist Party this past year in Hungary.

Communism also placed the State above the individual, and regarded any expression of ethnic, rather than national, identity as anti-social. A consequence of this was that demonstrations of ethnic and racial resentment were suppressed. This did not mean that they didn't exist – merely that they were more or less contained. With the collapse of Communism, ethnic tensions and hatreds have been able to surface, with the disastrous consequences we are witnessing in parts of Europe today. A sad repercussion of this is that those groups who have little defensive power, and who are being particularly harshly victimised – and I refer here to the Romanies ('Gypsies'), are especially anxious to return to that earlier political system which offered them a measure of protection, and which also provided them with jobs.

The move to democracy, if it is to be successful, must incorporate *all* aspects of the democratic system. If the transition in that direction is only a partial one, then the system will be incomplete, and will never function properly. Frustration and resentment will remain.

One part of the democratic ideal which *must* be given priority is the granting of basic human rights. Since 1989, the human rights record in parts of Eastern Europe has been abysmal. Eastern European nations cannot simply pick and choose, selecting those aspects of democracy which appeal to them while ignoring those which don't; if the post-Communist nations are to embrace democracy fully and successfully, the recognition of the equal worth of all human beings must become fundamental. The alternative can only be disaster.

As the only Romani member of the US Department of State Delegation and American member of the Romani Advisory Council of the Project on Ethnic Relations, I want to draw a parallel between the Romanies in Eastern Europe and the situation of African Americans in the US. There is a lesson to be learnt here, and one that must be heeded at all costs.

No system is perfect in practice. The US is the leading democratic republic in the world, but it, too, has problems. Not because of discrimination in the law, but because of difficulties resulting from social attitudes that have become ingrained into the society. We are trying to cope with a racist legacy instituted long before America became a nation.

We recognise the origins of racism in our country's past, and we also recognise how fundamentally wrong and destructive racism is, and our system of government is constantly trying to demonstrate this to the public through our educational system and by means of workshops, public service announcements in the media and so on. Thus to understand the roots of the racial problems in the US, we must look to history. The African American population was held in slavery for nearly three centuries, and during that time was systematically dehumanised as a people. Following abolition, extra-legal forms of peonage, as well as segregation in education, transport, healthcare and so on have existed well into the twentieth century. A recent public opinion poll indicated that three-quarters of the White population in the US continue to harbour racist attitudes towards Black people. Any population that has been devalued to the point of losing its identity as human beings, over a period of centuries, will not automatically be seen as equals simply by passing a law. Generations of prejudices must be eradicated, and this is not easily achieved.

Racism is defined as 'the belief in the superiority of a particular race'. This tends to reinforce particular patterns of the behaviour of the majority over the minority, the dominant over the weak. Racism is prejudice plus power, and no one can deny the existence of racism in all areas of administration. It is legitimised in society by its very institutional nature. It ensures that, in a racist society, some citizens automatically have opportunities for success and security in life that are available to them in a routine way, while other citizens must struggle for those same opportunities or else not have access to them at all. A dominant, racist population sets up so many barriers in race relations that those excluded from full participation in the system come to feel like a surplus population, worthless and frustrated.

In the US, the long-term consequence of the racism directed at the Black American people has resulted in a deep-rooted bitterness within sections of that population, a sense of its having been cheated, a resentment and an anger which has robbed the present generation of any sense of hope or self-worth. This manifests itself in many ways, above all in anger, and in a desire to strike out at anybody and anything. Recent studies of this phenomenon routinely conclude that the majority of young Black Americans feel an overwhelming hopelessness about their prospects for the future. Unemployment among this section of the population is the highest in the country. The despair this generates translates into violence and an escape into drugs and alcohol. When questioned, such young people say that they don't expect to live long in the present system, and that there are no positive prospects for them, but they will go out protesting. This protest is tragically turned back onto the same African American population, a population devoid of a sense of dignity, angry at its own powerlessness. Fanon, describing European oppression in Africa, writes[38] of the police who 'beat the African, insult him and make him crawl' without fear of a hostile reaction, while at the same time the same African will 'reach for his knife at the slightest hostile or aggressive glance cast at him by another African, for his last resort is to defend his personality *vis-à-vis* his brother'. One consequence of this kind of racism is the evidence of widespread psychological problems: depression, self-hatred, rage, despair, and lack of the means to seek the kind of mental healthcare available to the middle classes. Another is evidence of crime and sabotage of the system. Over a hundred years ago, Friedrich Engels said that 'those members of the "surplus population" who, goaded by their misery, summon up enough courage to revolt openly against society, become thieves and murderers. They wage open warfare against those who have for so long waged secret warfare against them.'

There are other consequences too. If racist attitudes among some individuals prevent any feeling of concern for the population thus targeted, then consider five more widely relevant consequences of hate: (1) it destroys any sense of patriotism within the victimised group, and therefore presents a clear threat to national unity – indeed, it can result in the emergence of two separate nations within one land; (2), racism is very expensive. Not simply in a direct way (consider the hundreds of millions of dollars' worth of damage the Los Angeles race riots cost the country in 1992), but also the maintenance of separate physical facilities, legal costs in race-related law suits, the cost of welfare and unemployment payments; (3) racism, combined with a lack of skills, has resulted in an unemployment rate among Romanies which is as high as 90 per cent in some parts of post-Communist Europe. All of this costs money. The *wastefulness* of racism alone will undermine Europe, if we do not do something *now*; (4) a huge section of the national workforce is not being used in a maximally productive way; its potential is being denied; and (5), racism makes the whole country simply *look* bad; one may point to the universal condemnation of South Africa for so many years, and how it was excluded from participation in world events and world trade.

Racism as directed at Romanies in Europe has many origins. Colour prejudice is just one of them. But colour was not the reason for the initial enslavement of Romanies in the fourteenth century. Like the enslavement of Africans, Romani slavery grew out of the desire for a large and unpaid labour force. In order to keep that force from leaving the Balkans, which by the fifteenth century it was beginning to do, laws came into effect that turned those same workers into property. The dehumanising process began only after this event, as I have documented in my book, *The Pariah Syndrome* (1987). In contemporary Romania, anti-gypsyism is simply a continuation of discriminatory practices that Whites started in the 1300s. Elsewhere, it is a legacy of similar repressive policies in effect over centuries. A Romanian woman, asked about the recent murders in Hădăreni, claimed that killing Gypsies wasn't murder, because murder was when you killed human beings. And if you believe that this kind of thinking is restricted to Eastern Europe, I remind you of the member of the British Government who declared publicly a few years ago that Romanies were 'not human beings in the normal sense'. In America too, a university professor specialising in Roma, told the nation on public television that American Gypsies had not yet developed genetically 'like other people' to the point of being able to distinguish right from wrong. This month, his co-authored book on the same subject has just been published, on the cover of which is the warning that 'no one is safe' from my people. How do you imagine that I, as a university professor and a Romani, feel when I hear myself being described in this way? What do I tell my children?

Another book which has relevance here is Sheldon Ekland-Olson's treatment of capital punishment in the US legal system.[39] Dr Ekland-Olson, who happens to be Provost at The University of Texas, found that racism towards Black Americans, and the rate of arrests and convictions, was consistently higher today in those same states which were slave-holding states in the nineteenth century. His point, and the point I am emphasising here, is that the oppressive treatment of a population over an extended period of time will create discriminatory attitudes, the effects of which will continue to assert themselves in the actual population long after laws have been changed. It is no coincidence that we are hearing about the most overt examples of anti-gypsyism from Romania, Europe's one-time slave-holding nation.

I have been interested for some years now in the parallels between the experience of Africans and Romanies in the western world. Some of those similarities perceived by the larger population are documented in my book,[40] and turn up in factual accounts as well as in fictional literature. In this last connection, I should mention that the literary tradition has helped weave anti-gypsyism into the fabric of Western culture, where novels, folktales, proverbs, songs, jokes, cartoons, nursery rhymes and so on have helped create an unreal and damaging image of the Gypsy in the minds even of people who have never met one.

I am particularly interested in the parallels evident in the development of political awareness in both populations; I believed for a long time that we were running perhaps forty years behind the African Americans in our attempts at political self-determination, but in terms of outward expression of anger, I think we are maybe only half as many years behind – within twenty years, if we do not address the problem now, we will surely see race riots and destruction on a massive scale here in Europe as the pressure cooker can contain itself no longer. Already, one Romani political party in Slovakia is advising its members to arm itself in preparation for a conflict which it sees as inevitable. 'An increase in acts of retaliation and self defence' among Romanies has been reported from the towns of Pardubice, Brno, Jihlava, Budejovice and Ostrava in the Czech Republic, following a wave of murders and drownings by so-called 'death squads' organised mainly by skinheads. Romanies in Bulgaria and Romania are physically resisting organised white hate groups in both countries which call themselves the 'Anti-Romani Ku Klux Klan'. How long do we have?

Europe faces an uphill climb, and the sooner the issue of anti-Romani racism is addressed the better the chances will be of averting a catastrophe. For if the African American experience is a reliable indication, this is not something which will disappear simply by providing the economic and educational means for the Romani population to aspire to the middle class. The anger caused by racism is still evident in the African American middle class – indeed, this was the cover story of the 15 November 1993 issue of *Newsweek*, entitled 'The hidden rage of successful Blacks'. A best-selling book this year is Feagin and Sikes' *Living Racism: The Black Middle-Class Experience*, and Grier and

Cobbs' book *Black Rage* has sold consistently since 1968. It is not simply the system that has to change, and opportunities to be equalised, but we must also work to change peoples' attitudes. How can this be achieved?

Feagin and Sikes suggest that a place to start is by using the law. This makes perfect sense to me. After being fined a few times, with substantial, financially painful – I would suggest even crippling – penalties, racist administrators, companies and individuals will learn that racism is expensive. While this in itself will not have any immediate effect on changing people's attitudes (a recent *Times Mirror* poll indicated that white Americans' support for civil rights for African Americans has declined nearly ten per cent since 1992), it will give Romanies the chance they need at least to show what they can do in an equal opportunity environment. People in the West, as well as in Eastern Europe, want changes to come overnight, and that cannot happen; there is a danger that programmes will be abandoned before their effects begin to be felt (this has already begun to happen in some places). Thus Romanies will not be able to compete in the workplace unless they have had equal access to schooling, which means that the educational systems must be monitored too. It will take time before Romanies will be able to compete educationally with the rest of the population. In some of the countries whose representatives are here today, Romani children are placed in special schools for retarded children, where their failure to acquire any kind of useful education is guaranteed, even though a Swedish study in 1985 demonstrated that classroom problems for Romani children have their origins in the fact that those same children speak Romani and are not fluent in the national language. The same study demonstrated that in a balanced situation their intelligence quotient is no lower than the national average. If a population is regarded as worthless, then only the most minimal measures will be taken to deal with it; it is easier to separate Romani children into special classes than to develop linguistically and culturally sensitive educational curricula to accommodate their special needs. The media too must play its part. Journalists and newscasters routinely demonstrate their own biases when they editorialise instead of straightforwardly reporting the news; does it really help to repeat the words of a Hungarian skinhead, as a recent article in the *San Francisco Chronicle* did – 'there's too much of this scum; they screw their sisters and daughters and make children who are too stupid to do anything but steal' – without also saying something about the effort Romanies in that country are making to establish schools and work programmes for themselves?

As Asante has said, racist language makes the victim the criminal. The notion that a particular race is inferior to one's own carries with it an assumption of automatic incompetence on the part of members of that race, and they are then treated accordingly. Obviously Romanies are not incompetent; our very survival in an environment of unrelenting hostility says something about our spirit of determination. Given an equal opportunity, which has only been possible for those people light-complexioned enough to be able to hide their ethnicity, it is clear that we are as hard working and as diligent as anybody else. In the US, schoolbooks and social studies classes now contain material teaching all American children about the contributions of all Americans; few Europeans are really aware of the contributions our people have made to the world, in music particularly, but in other areas as well. Together with the Association for the Advancement of Democracy through Education, a team of us is preparing educational packages on the Romanies for use in European classrooms. Similar programmes are being initiated in France and the Czech Republic. The Project on Ethnic Relations is also preparing a handbook along similar lines. The way to combat racism is through education, and through the close monitoring of, and penalising of, those countries which fail to take active steps to eradicate it.

Democracy has brought with it capitalism, and as a consequence advertising, and the boycotting of companies sponsoring programmes which Romanies feel are offensive must also be implemented by vigilant media-watch organisations. But if we ignore the consequences of doing nothing about it, then it will be too late to do anything at all. And whatever negative repercussions will be borne by the Romani population because of anti-gypsyism, *all* European populations will be victims too.

I delivered the above address over a decade ago. Below are some reports issued since the year 2000. At the present time Roma in Italy are being killed and brutalised in ongoing racist attacks and are being arrested and fingerprinted by the Italian Government.

Roma remain to date the most persecuted people of Europe. Almost everywhere, their fundamental human rights are threatened. Racist violence targeting Roma is widespread in the last years. Discrimination against Roma in employment, education, healthcare, administrative and other services is observed in most societies, and hate speech deepens the anti-Romani stereotypes typical of European public opinion. (European Roma Rights Centre, 2001: 5).

Romanies in Europe were 'at the bottom of every socio-economic indicator: the poorest, the most unemployed, the least educated, the shortest-lived, the most welfare dependent, the most imprisoned and the most segregated. (*The Economist*, 2005)

Roma are the most prominent poverty risk group in many of the countries of Central and Eastern Europe. They are poorer than other groups, more likely to fall into poverty, and more likely to remain poor. In some cases poverty rates for Roma are more than ten times that of non-Roma. A recent survey found that nearly 80 per cent of Roma in Romania and Bulgaria were living on less than $4.30 per day ... Even in Hungary, one of the most prosperous accession countries, 40 per cent of Roma live below the poverty line. (*World Bank Report*, 2006)

In September 2001, the Council of Europe 'issued a blistering condemnation of Europe's treatment of the Roma Gypsy community, saying they are subject to racism, discrimination and violence ... the United Nations says they pose Europe's most serious human rights problem. (BBC, 2001)

On 1 February 2008, the Associated Press issued a statement released by the European Union beginning, 'The Roma, also known as Gypsies, remain frequent targets of racist attacks, abuse and police harassment.'

On 3 February 2008, ERIO, the European Roma Information Office, posted the following: 'During 2007, several events reflected the continued fragility of the fundamental rights of citizens of Roma origin: racist riots against Roma in Bulgaria, the collective expulsion of Romanian citizens in Italy, and the extreme patterns of social exclusion faced by the large numbers of Roma throughout Europe indicate the urgent need for fundamental changes in EU and national policies.'

A Czech fascist party which plans to be vying for power in future elections is releasing a 'Final Solution' for the Roma. The Czech National Party wants to succeed in the general elections in 2010 with radical anti-Romani rhetoric formulated in a 150-page study called 'The Final Solution to the Gypsy Issue in the Czech Lands' that it will present this month (August 2008). The nationalists claim they do not want to kill the Romanies, but that they want to buy land in India and to relocate Romanies there.

CHAPTER SEVENTEEN

Our need for internal diplomatic skills

Diplomacy is defined as 'the management of international relations by negotiation; the method by which these relations are adjusted and managed by ambassadors and envoys; skill … in the conduct of international intercourse and negotiations' (Onions, 1968: 514). While the assumption was that we met in Geneva to discuss diplomacy between Romani and non-Romani agencies, I want to take a step back and address issues of diplomacy solely within the Romani world.

A diaspora people, we as Romanies exist in a great many distinct groups and are both geographically and politically dispersed. We have become fragmented by complex social and historical factors, with far-reaching consequences – thus the above definition from the *Oxford English Dictionary* must apply equally well to us: we must be able to talk to each other before we are in a position to talk to anyone else.

At present, different Romani organisations representing different interest groups meet with various non-Romani agencies to address mutually agreed-upon issues. However, the Romani groups involved in each situation do not and cannot speak for all Romanies everywhere. They represent either their own shared agenda (such as the rights of the child) or their own group (for example, human rights training of Roma in Sweden). They do not speak for Romanies as one global people.

This, of course, is to be expected and is not what I am addressing here. What I want to focus on is why, even within such single-topic contexts, we find it difficult to find common ground amongst ourselves. I was in

Originally published in Valeriu Nicolae and Hanna Slavik (eds), *Roma diplomacy* (The International Debate Education Association, New York, 2007), pp. 49–56.

Stockholm not long ago, where at least five different Romani groups resident in Sweden had come together to discuss Roma-related issues; the lack of cooperation amongst them almost led in one case to a death threat. More recently still, I was in St Louis, Missouri, where nearly 3,000 Roma have settled, part of a much larger population of some 45,000 Bosnian refugees in that city. They must deal with hostility from the non-Romani Bosnians, with learning English, with finding jobs and establishing homes. Yet they exist in three distinct groups, who maintain their separateness and distinctiveness from each other despite sharing the fact of being a minority within a minority in a new land. At one of our international meetings, the Romani delegates from one particular country sat outside the conference hall angry and threatening to leave because they could not understand the Vlax dialect being used in the presentations.

It is this divisiveness that I want to concentrate on, because it causes us the most problems. I repeat, before we can talk to the rest of the world, we must be able to talk to each other. In order to talk to each other, we must know who we – and each other – are: what separates us and what we have in common.

Are Roma one people? The fact that we met in Brussels and are here today in Geneva – from many different parts of the world – is an indication that we are now treated as though we were, regardless of how we have been traditionally regarded.

Who's in charge of identity?

The definition of Romani identity rests in many hands, although hardly in our own. The media, and even some academics, regard it as based solely on social behaviour. Like Cher with her 1971 hit song *Gypsies, Tramps and Thieves*, in a recent issue the *New York Press* referred to 'hoboes and gypsies' as if they were the same thing, and *The New Yorker* magazine wrote about 'assertive women: female scholars, priestesses, gypsies, mystics, nature lovers' (Boyer, 2006: 36), evidently assuming that all of those labels refer to behaviours or occupations. One academic specialising in Roma, Professor Ralph Sandland of Nottingham University, says the word *Gypsy* 'is merely a job description' (1996: 384), while *The Centurion: A Police Lifestyle Magazine* defines 'Gypsies' as 'any family-oriented band of nomads' (Schroeder, 1983:

59). The Romani Archives and Documentation Center in Texas receives the *Google Search* links to 'Gypsy' in the press every day. For 23 January 2006, the Center received four items: one dealt with moths, one with Broadway chorus-line dancers, one with an Irish soccer team, and the last with recreational vehicles. Not one of them had anything to do with Roma.

The academics and folklorists who recognise an ethnic identity have, nevertheless, set their own limitations, traditionally wanting us to be illiterate and living under the hedges in order to be authentic. Even the great Paspati maintained that 'it is in the tent that the Gypsy must be studied, and not in the villages of the bastardized sedentary Gypsies' (1870: 14); his contemporary, Pischel, too believed that 'the Gypsy ceases to be a Gypsy as soon as he is domiciled and follows some trade' (1883: 358). This would disqualify most of us, and it is clear that educated, settled Roma pose a problem. The Czech sociologist, Jaroslav Sus, claimed that it was an 'utterly mistaken opinion that Gypsies form a nationality or a nation, that they have their own national culture, their own national language' (1961: 89). The former sub-editor of the *Journal of the Gypsy Lore Society* mocked the same notion as nothing but 'romantic twaddle' (Vesey-Fitzgerald, 1973: 2). Dora Yates, former Honorary Secretary of that organisation, asked, 'except in a fairy tale, could any hope [of a Romani nationalist movement] ever have been more fantastic?' (1953: 40). Yet another member, Werner Cohn, wrote in his book *The Gypsies* that we 'have no leaders, no executive committees, no nationalist movement ... I know of no authenticated case of genuine Gypsy allegiance to political or religious causes' (1973: 66) – and these are the experts. A firm denial of the nationalist movement also originates with the Gypsy Lore Society. One member, Jiří Lipa wrote:

> To be exact, there is no one Gypsy culture nor one Gypsy language ... If in the process of looking for native assistants and for training them [the gypsilorist finds that] literary talents should appear, so much the better ... [I]n reality, however, it is mere toying, a waste of energy and material means which are not abundant for Gypsy studies. While a missing attribute is being artificially contrived, which is supposed to make the Gypsies an ethnic minority in the conventional sense in the eyes of wishful thinkers and bureaucrats, irreplaceable values of Gypsy culture are being lost in our time. (1983: 4)

The question of who speaks for us is one constantly addressed.

Although sympathetic to our position, a non-Romani took it upon himself to 'forgive' a non-Romani Auschwitz survivor for anti-Roma statements made in his book (Weiss, 2007). At The University of Texas in April 2007, the promotional flyer for a conference on Romani women in Turkey entitled *Reconfiguring gender and Roma ('Gypsy') identity through political discourses in Western Turkey* noted that 'Rom and non-Rom men's voices speak for Roma women', although the 'reconfiguration of Roma identity' in this presentation was made on our behalf by a *non*-Romani woman, and not by a Romani herself. In a new book on world music, the passages on Romani music are illustrated by two non-Roma Balkan music specialists (Naylor, 2006: 89–90). A week-long 'Gypsy' conference at the University of Florida in March 2007 consisted mainly of singing and dancing and dressing up by various non-Roma, but included no Romani participation. When they were questioned in this regard, the response was that they 'couldn't find any Gypsies'. They have since received a complaint from members of the Miami Romani community.

So who are we?

While some of the earliest Roma told the Europeans that we had come from India, this fact was not generally known, and was eventually forgotten even by our own people. As a consequence, a great many incorrect, and sometimes bizarre, hypotheses gained currency. Some *gadže* have written that we originated from inside the hollow earth, or on the Moon, or in Atlantis, that we were the remnants of a race of prehistoric horsemen, were Nubians, or Druids, or even that we were a conglomerate drawn from the fringes of European society and that we artificially dyed our skin and spoke a made-up jargon for the purposes of plotting criminal activity.

The problem I am focusing on here is that we ourselves are as uncertain about our origins as is the general *gadžikano* population – and that uncertainty serves only to sustain the universal Hollywood image. Some of our own people have said that we are Berbers or Jews or Egyptians, or were a presence in the Roman Empire, thus giving the stamp of legitimacy to such claims.

In my book *We Are the Romani People* I complained that degrees have been awarded to graduate students whose theses and dissertations were supervised by committees the members of which had no expertise whatsoever in Romani studies. An article that appeared in a published collection of scholarly essays about Roma in 1999 maintained that 'whether Gypsies originate in either Egypt or India is a matter that has not been settled' (Esplugas, 1999: 43). Since 1997 at least three 'Gypsy' courses have been established at different American universities by faculty who have no qualifications in the area, who have never met any Romanies, and whose list of readings contain non-academic and misleading titles. Books and articles about Romanies number in the tens of thousands, but practically every single one of them has been written by an outsider – and most of those by people who have never actually met any Roma in their lives. It would be hard to imagine a book about modern-day Poles or Slovaks being taken seriously, had it been written by someone who had never visited Poland or Slovakia and who had never met anyone from those countries.

Recent scholarship is forcing a serious re-examination of our origins. My own sociohistorical and linguistic work supports genetic research conducted by Kalaydjieva and others, who found that 'confirming the centuries-old linguistic theory of the Indian origins [of Roma] is no great triumph for modern genetic research', but that 'the major, unexpected and most significant result of these studies is the strong evidence of the common descent of all Gypsies regardless of declared group identity, country of residence and rules of endogamy ... the Gypsy group was born in Europe' (2005: 1085–6).

This European perspective is fundamental to the discussion. Three hitherto unconsidered aspects of the contemporary Romani condition rest upon the facts of our history, and must be acknowledged if we are to understand our problems of identity and in-group communication or lack of it.

Accommodating our dual heritage

The extent to which our 'Asianness' should play a part in the discourse is a matter of some debate. We are unique among world populations in having the Indian ingredients in our early makeup come together in the West; we are both an Asian and a Western people, but with no Asian experience or (hardly any) presence. Mirga and Gheorghe have noted that some of us 'eagerly affirm [our] European roots and heritage and consider [our] Indian past as irrelevant to the current Romani causes and claims' (1997: 22); while Šaip Jusuf said his feelings of affinity with India were so intense that he refused to recognise that we belong to any European country (Sharma, 1976: 29–30). The late Matéo Maximoff (1994) stridently claimed that if you did not speak the Romani language you could not claim Romani identity.

In a very real sense, we are as European as anyone else. 'European' is not a nationality or an ethnicity; Europeans are composed of a multitude of these. 'European' does not mean being originally from a part of Europe; if that were true, the Saami and Hungarians and Finns and Estonians would not be Europeans. Having a country is not a qualification; if that were true, then the Basques, the Catalans and the Frisians would not qualify.

While the knowledge of our Indian origins is important, just as it is important for any nation to know its own history, it is not a body of knowledge kept in mind on a daily basis. In fact, most of us do not even know about it and some of us do not believe it when we first hear about it. When skinheads carry placards that say 'Gypsies Go Back to India', this is an informed but unrealistic bigotry; European Romanies regard Europe as home, not India. Our own spokespersons, who believe we should refrain from bringing too much attention to our Indian connection argue that if we stress our non-Europeanness, it will merely serve as justification for those who would like us to leave. In any case, in light of the details about our history that are now emerging, we may not even have begun to be an ethnic population until our ancestors reached the West, and the time spent in Europe and beyond accounts for practically the entirety of the Romani experience.

Despite the emphasis on Europe, it is important to remember also that we are a diaspora people found all over the world; we are a global population, with between a quarter and a third of our total number outside of Europe. The exclusive focus of Romani-related organisations on populations located only in Europe fails to acknowledge our existence internationally. With the constant (especially post-communist) migration of members of European Romani families to North and South America and to Australia, and with the tremendous increase in the use of the Internet, contacts linking us around the world will continue to grow.

At our follow-up meeting in Geneva, a document was circulated that I found entirely relevant to our own situation. It was the text of an interview by Eugen Tomiuc (2006) with the Chairman of the British Muslim Council for Religious and Racial Harmony, Dr Abduljalil Sajid, part of which is worth reproducing here:

> Muslims are a multifarious and multifaceted people throughout the world, and Europe is not separated from the world. Muslims are divided, as all human beings are ... and Europe is also divided. We didn't come here as a monolithic, collective group in Europe. We all are coming from different backgrounds and we all have to cement our differences and work out together what are our issues, common challenges, common problems, and how we can bring a common approach to deal with those challenges. That will be our strength. I think we can form a permanent body of European imams' councils. That would be a great strength. There we can debate our issues and bring common resolution to those issues to the whole world, and especially to the European people that we are going to be our partners in faith, in belief and in citizenship. And you have nothing to fear from the Muslims of Europe. [Regarding my identity as either] a Muslim in Europe or as a European Muslim, I'm both. I consider myself a European Muslim. My identity is in my geography, my area, but I myself also consider that my first and foremost duty is to the identity of my faith, believing in God. So I am a Muslim in Europe as well as a European Muslim. I do not see a contradiction in either of these two terms, and we should not be asked and forced to choose one against another. We can be both.

Everything that Sajid maintains for Muslims in Europe (a good many of whom are in fact Roma) also holds true for us. While not linked by a common religion, we share a common origin, but we are divided as the result of many factors, above all physical separation and lack of education. Both have kept us from taking charge of our place in the global community. This is now changing. Our leaders and representatives from all parts of the world are able to meet in person or communicate via the Internet. More scholarly works on our history and socio-political situation have been published in the past twenty years than ever before. Courses in Romani studies are being offered at the highest level, and educational grants for young Roma are now a reality. We have what we need to improve our situation, and to speak for ourselves in the international forum. But before we can be fully equipped to do that, we must speak to each other.

Endnotes

1. Although I am only speaking for myself in the present monograph.
2. The same statement is repeated in Elšík and Matras (2006: 425). Matras' article would seem to contain a number of misinterpretations and outright errors; for instance, translating the Indian word for 'sword' as *čhuri* ('knife') rather than *xanrro*. He also 'corrects' the very title of my book *Ame Sam e Rromane Džene* (*We Are the Romani People*) to *Ame Sam e Řom* (*We Are the Rom*), unmindful of the 1930s magazine published in Romania with the same Romani wording, and a distinction I clearly make in the book itself since not all Romanies use Rom endonymically (2002: *xix*). While he suggests my academic credibility will be damaged by pursuing the present hypothesis, I remain firmly committed to it. It has already been responded to by Acton (2005). Dr Matras is in good company: Dennis Marlock, editor of the *FraudTech* anti-Roma website, also accuses me of having 'a record for rewriting history to suit [my] own agenda, and for doing so in less than an honest fashion' (www.fraudtech.bizland.com).
3. 'Pan-Roma-ism' has led to the application of the word *Roma* to Romani populations that have never called themselves that, and even to populations which are not Romani at all. Thus a Reuters story released on 16 July 2003 carried the headline 'The Pogrom starts again: Roma-hunting in Iraq', although the population, called *Kawaliya* locally and which says it originally came from Syria, is presumably Kauli. In the same way, other reports of the same incident (such as El-Liethy, 2003) refer to the population as 'Gypsies', thus creating an association in the minds of Western readers with the stereotype of 'Gypsies' in their own countries. Gafarová (2003) does this when she writes about the Liuli Gypsies of southern Kyrgyzstan, describing them as 'freedom-loving people' who are characterised by 'brightly coloured clothes, hot passion, together with singing and dancing around the campfire', and referring three times to international human rights organisations paying attention to Roma and Sinti. The article, however, states that the Liuli came into Kyrgyzstan from Iran, where 'for many centuries they had moved from place to place'. There is now even an NGO affiliated with the International Organisation for Migration, called Premier Urgence, 'the first to deal with Roma people's

issues [in Iraq … and] to have a better view of the Roma situation, culture, etc. all over the world'.

The situation in Iraq as Gafarová describes it is terrible and in desperate need of attention. But the Liuli are not Romanies, and it is clear that the link with Romanies has been made solely on the basis of the common label 'Gypsy', which has been applied to a great number of unrelated peoples. That is now evidently starting to be the case for Roma.

4. In his typically biased way, Vekerdi (1981: 245, 250) writes: 'The complete lack of terms for agricultural activity indicates that the Gypsies' Indian ancestors were not concerned with any kind of agricultural productive work … the etymological analysis of the Gypsy vocabulary proves that the Gypsies' ancestors did not pursue either agriculture or hunting … their livelihood seems either to have been based on primitive gathering … or to have been entirely dependent on the producing society … Romani *čōr* 'thief' comes from Old Indian *cōra*, and the corresponding verb *čōrel* also goes back directly to an Indian verb.'

5. At this period the attacks on India were by the Huns; Islam had not yet begun its spread into India, which did not start for another two centuries when the Chālukyan armies drove back the Arab Muslim invasions at Navasari, in Maharashtra, in AD 732.

6. May 2008, http://www.religioustolerance.org/roma1.htm

7. The Armenian words in Romani for 'godparent', 'incense' and 'Easter' (*kirvo, xung, Patradji*) point to Armenia as the place where Christianity was first encountered.

8. Kochanowski actually argues for two separate migrations, the first following AD 855 when the Jatts joined forces with the Byzantine army against the Muslims, eventually giving rise to the Sinti and the Kalé Romani populations (both shown by Bakker (1995) to belong to the Northern group, Courtiade's (1994) Stratum 1), and the second, described here, which developed into the Rom (Kochanowski, 2003: 327). He derives the word *Sinti* from *Sindhi* and the word *Jatt* (*Zutt*) from *Goth*. If the modern Romani population is in fact a blending of two migrations separated by nearly 340 years, then it leaves unaddressed a number of fundamental linguistic questions. In the framework of the hypothesis presented in this paper, Kochanowski's first date is too early, and his second too late.

9. Sway (1988: 32) says, 'Linguistic evidence indicates that after one hundred years … the Dom separated into two major groups … the Ben Gypsies [i.e. Domari] wandered into Syria [and the …] ancestors of the European Gypsies, the Phen Gypsies, traveled from Persia to Armenia.' Marushiakova and Popov (2000: 5) write only of their 'wandering for several centuries throughout the lands of what are today Pakistan, Afghanistan and Iran, and to the south of the Caspian Sea'. As I've said in several places before, 'wandering' is a luxury afforded only those with the freedom and time to engage in it.

10. It would be useful to examine the sources of the metalworking vocabulary of this group (see Appendix 1); I have maintained that the metalworking terms in Romani are preponderantly of Greek origin because this skill was

acquired as a profession only after reaching Byzantia. One counter-argument has been that the lexicon would naturally be drawn from the local language since the Romanies' commercial interaction was with the host population. However, there is no need for customers to be acquainted with such specialist terms as 'bellows' or 'forge', and the words they would be most likely to have used in any commercial exchange, such as 'gold', 'silver' and (especially) 'iron', are the *only* Indic terms in the list, without non-Romani synonyms. It might also be argued that if this held true for metalworking terms, it would surely also hold true for other semantic areas as well.

11. I am indebted to Ronald Lee for pointing this out to me. It is also possible that *beš-* does not descend from OIA, *upaviśati*, 'sits down', as Turner has it (1966: 105) but from *vásati*, which has produced words for both 'reside' and 'sit' in the NIA languages (e.g. Marathi *bas-*, 'dwell', Tirahi *bāz-*, 'sit'). In the Dardic languages Kumari (*basno*) and Nepali (*basnu*) it means both 'sit' and 'reside'.

12. Elčík (in personal correspondence) maintains that the Istriani dialect could well have had the same Greek items as other dialects but lost them over time, and that it does not otherwise differ significantly from the non-Istriani Romani dialects spoken around it. It would be most unusual, however, if only Greek items disappeared and not items adopted from other languages, and that only this dialect should have lost such a substantial proportion of items from Greek in particular. That it is otherwise structurally like non-Istriani dialects neighbouring it is typical of the balkanisation which typically affects Romani dialects in contact.

13. Tcherenkov and Laederich (2004: 18) 'are of the opinion that Rroma departed from Persia before the arrival of the Arabic invaders in the mid-seventh century or right around that time'. They also (wrongly) maintain that all of the Persian words in Romani have their Old Persian (Pehlevi) form, indicative of their early acquisition.

14. Tikkanen (in personal correspondence) has challenged this source for the word *Lom*, however, which he states emphatically could not be derived from any form exhibiting an initial *r-*, and various alternative etymologies have been proposed for *Rrom* (such as Sinclair, 1909). A convoluted discussion of the various applications of the Indian word *ḍomba* is found in Gamonet, 2008. As an ethnonym, the word *Rrom* almost certainly dates only from the Byzantine period, during which time its inhabitants referred to themselves as Ρόμιοι (pronounced 'Romi'), *Romiti* or *Romaivi*, that is, inhabitants of Rûm (the Roman Empire). While the most oft-repeated argument for an Indic origin for this word is that Romani /rr/ is the reflex of OIA /ḍ/, it is also the case that /rr/ is traceable to /r/ in items derived from Persian (*burr*), Kurdish (*korr*), Greek (*rricini, rrutuni*), Slavic (*rribizla*), Romanian (*rrajo, rrobo*) and so on, and is therefore not automatically Indic. Of the over eighty entries for /rr/ (their <ŗ>) in Gjerdman and Ljungberg (1963: 331–6) only four are Indic; of the over 130 entries for this phoneme (their <ř>) in Boretzky and Igla (1994: 248–52) only four are likewise Indic; furthermore, one item is a reflex of OIA /d/, not /ḍ/ (*rran*, 'twig', < OIA daṇḍa-), and two items with /r/ rather than /rr/ are from OIA

sources with /ḍ/ (*rig*, 'side', < OIA ḍhig, *rod*-, 'seek', < OIA * ḍhunḍhati).

15. Most of the references here are concerned with Romani education in the US. For sources dealing with Romani education in Europe, see Tong, 1995: 95–124.

16. The newly democratic countries in Europe lag far behind in their acknowledgement of – and skills to address – multiculturalism, bilingual education and the culture of poverty. A recent report from Bulgaria concluded that education was a 'waste of time for Bulgarian Roma' (Ilieva, 2008: 1). This was based upon responses to a survey taken among 760 Roma 'from twelve ghettos in the country'. Such reported findings reinforce public attitudes to Romanies since they will be interpreted as evidence of their laziness and disinterest. But it is commonly understood amongst Bulgarian Roma that obtaining a degree does not guarantee either a job or respect: What do you call a Rom with a doctorate? A *tsigan*.

17. http://www.eliznik.org.uk/RomaniaHistory/minorities.htm

18. This might also be translated as 'who *laughs* at me from his rainbow', which would be an entirely different interpretation of the statement.

19. The original is in Hansard (see Wells, 1961).

20. Borrow's observations on the Iranian element in Romani (1841(*ii*): 111–112) are worth reproducing (as an adjunct, for example, to Hancock, 1995b):

     a. 'Still more abundant … than the mixture of Greek, still more abundant than the mixture of Sclavonian, is the alloy in the Gypsy language, wherever spoken, of modern Persian words, which circumstance will compel us to offer a few remarks on the share which the Persian has had in the formation of the dialects of India, as at present spoken.'

     b. 'The modern Persian, as has been already observed, is a daughter of the ancient Zend, and, as such, is entitled to claim affinity with the Sanscrit, and its dialects. With this language none in the world would be able to vie in simplicity and beauty, had not the Persians, in adopting the religion of Mahomet, unfortunately introduced into their speech an infinity of words of the rude coarse language used by the barbaric Arab tribes.'

21. The age and identity of Jasper is the topic of an article by Fraser (1996: 7–12).

22. Borrow was probably poisoned not by 'Mrs Hearne' (Martha Boss in real life) but by her daughter Joni (Borrow's 'Leonora'). See Fraser, 1996: 7–12.

23. It is interesting that Borrow should have given this impression, considering his disdain for others who have done the same thing. Describing himself in *The Romany Rye* as one who 'affects to be neither Frenchman, nor German', he scorns those who 'affect the airs of Spaniards [and who …] make Tom-fools of themselves by sticking cigars into their mouths, dressing themselves in *zamarras*, and saying *carajo*!' (1857, II: 273). Armstrong (1950: 79, 83) writes amusingly of him as a schoolboy who 'posed as a Gypsy himself and sometimes stained his face with walnut juice to the Gypsy swarthiness', and of his headmaster asking him, 'Borrow, are you suffering from jaundice, or is it only dirt?'. The nineteenth-century Romanologist Liebich, trying to get a Rom to admit that he was one in

court, told him 'you are a Gypsy and so am I, speak the truth!' (1863: 23). In his introduction to *Wild Wales* (1974: 6), Brian Rhys comments on this: 'This delusion of Borrow's [is] part of the man's very essence … we find that he is not displeased to pose as Father Toban to the Irish, as a Spaniard, as a Pennsylvanian, a man from the South [of Wales] in Anglesea … as a man from Anglesea in the South.'

His adversary Charles Godfrey Leland actually became angry at being referred to as a non-Romani (1882: 121–2): 'As we came up the street, I saw the man talking with a well-dressed, sporting-looking man, not quite a gentleman, who sat cheekily in his own jaunty little waggon. As I passed, the one of the waggon said to the other, speaking of me, and in pure Romany, evidently thinking I did not understand – dikk'adovo Gorgio, adoi! (Look at that Gorgio, there!). Being a Romany Rye, and not accustomed to being spoken of as a Gorgio, I looked up at him, angrily, when he, seeing that I understood him, smiled, and bowed politely in apology. I laughed and passed on.'

Like the use of *salo* ('brother-in-law') among Balkan Romanies as a disparaging term for a cuckolded husband – also found in India – the designation *rye*, for some ryes at least, seems to have had a more specific in-group meaning: managing to bed a Romani woman. Thus in a letter dated 6 November 1908 Augustus John wrote to fellow gypsilorist Scott Macfie: 'I have recently taken it upon myself to confer the title of *Rai* upon a friend of mine – one Percy Wyndham Lewis, whose qualifications, the having coupled and lived in a state of copulation with a wandering Spanish romi in Brittany, seemed to me upon reflection to merit the honourable and distinctive title of our confraternity.'

24. In Kalderaš Vlax these words are *trézneto* or *rróndjeto* for 'thunder' and *bábica* for 'hail', both from Romanian, and *strélica* for 'lightning', from Slavic; no Lovari Vlax wordlist contains Borrow's three items.

25. The same metaphorical compounding, especially typical of Northern Romani, is found in Sinti, thus 'thunder' is *devleskero čiro* ('God's noise') and 'lightning' is *devleskeri jakh* ('God's eye').

26. *Bor* (from Old English *bār*, and retained in the word 'neighbour') is listed by Wright (1898-I: 345) as meaning 'a term of familiar address', and localised to Cumberland, East Anglia and Essex. Borrow's created plural should have been **boror* rather than 'bau-or'.

27. The Rumanian-derived plural morpheme {-*uri*} does, however, seem to have made its way into British Romani otherwise; see Hancock, 1984: 103 and 1995a: 30.

28. Scottish Romani, on the other hand, appears to have entered Britain via Scandinavia rather than from the northern European coast; see Hancock, 1977.

29. Sampson (1907a) demonstrated convincingly that *sar* in British Romani was a literary creation, although Peter Bakker (in personal correspondence) points out that this may not be the case for Caló, referring to texts collected by de Luna (1951) in which *sar* is used prepositionally. Norbert Boretzky has also documented its prepositional use in some Balkan Romani dialects

30. 'George Borrow: The romance and the reality', 12 June 1981.

31. This would suggest strongly that he worked best from written materials, and perhaps had a photographic memory; Romani was the only language in his working repertoire for which he had no access to a comprehensive grammatical description.
32. www.geocities.com/Athens/Sparta/ 7313/gyps.html; http://riverendell.fortunecity.com/legions/379/fullstory4.html
33. For Disney, the message is there even where *non*-human females are involved. The mermaid Ariel rejects her 'merman Talassio who's so boring he'll put you to sleep' and grows legs in order to be with Prince Alex, 'tall, dark-haired and incredibly handsome … the most beautiful human she'd ever seen!' (McLain, 2003: 26, 31). It was Disney too who perpetuated the 'Gypsies steal children' myth with the character Stromboli in his *Pinocchio*, and the image of Gypsies as robbers and cheats in his version of *Robin Hood*. Gypsies as thieves and sorcerers have also been stock material in such children's cartoons and movies as *Scooby Doo*, *The Smurfs*, *The Simpsons*, *Pee Wee's Big Adventure*, *Daddy Daycare*, *Corsican Brothers* and many more.
34. These four criteria were proposed by the historian Philip Lopate to argue that the Jewish experience during the Holocaust was unique.
35. Earlier references to the situation of Romanies in Nazi Germany are Sultzberger (1939), Max (1946), Kochanowski (1946), Maximoff (1946) and Molitor (1947).
36. Timothy Luke has discussed this issue in connection with the construction of the US Holocaust Memorial Museum, the exhibits throughout which 'stress the plight of Jews under Nazi persecution as well as reemphasise the necessity for Israel's sovereign autonomy as a nation State after World War II' (1996: 125).
37. In M. Banton *et al.*, *Teaching about prejudice* (Minority Rights Group, London, 1983), 59: 4.
38. F. Fanon, *The wretched of the Earth* (New York, 1968), p. 52. For an extended discussion of this phenomenon, see P. Freire, *Pedagogy of the oppressed* (New York, 1970).
39. *The rope, the chair and the needle: capital punishment in Texas* (University of Texas Press, 1994).
40. *The pariah syndrome* (Ann Arbor, 1988).

Bibliography

Anonymous (1856), 'The Gipsies of the Danube', *Chambers' Journal of Popular Literature*, 122

Anonymous (1861), 'The Gipsies of Notting Dale', *Queen* magazine, 16 November

Anonymous (1879), 'Gypsy life round London', *The Illustrated London News*, 29 April

Anonymous (1950a), 'How the Gipsies were persecuted', *The Wiener Library Bulletin*, 4(3/4)

Anonymous (1950b), 'Caravans of mystery', *Coronet*, August

Anonymous (1956), 'Romanies in the Third Reich', *The Wiener Library Bulletin*, 10(1/2)

Anonymous (1964), 'At Auschwitz, Romanies fought Gestapo killers', *The Lubbock Avalanche Journal*, 20 March

Anonymous (1965), 'We don't want Gypsies in our schools', *Daily Mail*, 7 September

Anonymous (1973), 'Prejudice in the classroom', *Romano Drom – Gypsy News*, 8

Anonymous (1979), 'Gypsies', *MD*, 23(7)

Anonymous (1984), 'Spain's oppressed minority', *The New York Times*, 25 October

Anonymous (1991a), 'Bulgarian officials mistaken for Gypsies', *The Wenatchee Safety Valve*, 1 April

Anonymous (1991b), 'Mistaken identity', *The New York Times* editorial, 16 April

Anonymous (1992), 'Holocaust memorial omits Gypsies', *The Atlanta Constitution*, 15 July

Anonymous (2007), 'Armed robbery at Bruegger's Bagels', *The Capital Times*, 31 May ab Hortis, S.A. (1775), 'Von den heutigen Zustande, sonderbaren Sitten und Lebensart, wie auch von den übriben Eigenschaften und Umständen der Zigeuner in Ungarn', *Zeitschrift Kaiserlich Königliche Allergnädigste Privilegierte Anzeigen aus Sämtlichen Kaiserlich Königliche. Erbländer*

Abbas, S. (2002), 'Language of the armies: Urdu: a derivative of Persian and Aveston, *The Iranian*, 11 June

Achim, V. (2004), *The Roma in Romanian history* (Budapest)

Ackerley, F.G. (1942), 'Review of Potra, 1939', *Journal of the Gypsy Lore Society*, 21(1)

Acković, D. (2006), 'Suffering of the Roma in Jasenovac', in Lituchy (2006)

Acton, T. (1971) (ed.), *Current changes amongst British Gypsies and their place in international patterns of development*, Oxford, Proceedings of the Research and Policy Conference of the National Gypsy Education Council

Acton, T. (1980), 'Gypsylorism in the Far East: time for the end of an ideology?', privately circulated unpublished *ms*

Acton, T.A. (2000) (ed.), *Scholarship and the Gypsy struggle: commitment in Romani Studies* (Hatfield)

Acton, T., and Kenrick, D. (1984) (eds), *Romani rokkeripen to-divvus: the English Romani dialect and its contemporary social, educational and linguistic standing* (London)

Acton, T.A. (2005), 'Has Rishi gone out of style? Academic and policy paradigms in Romani Studies', *Roma*, summer issue: 56–7

Adams, L. and Strickland, J.H. (1941), *True story of the Gypsy life: facts on the life and ways of the American Gypsy* (revised 1952, West Texas State Teachers' College, Canyon)

Alexander, E. (1990), 'Review of Lopate', *Congress Monthly*, May/June

Ali, S. (1996), 'Author boycotts Disney's "Hunchback" cartoon because it disrespects women of color', The Afrikan Frontline Network (Los Angeles)

Allen, F. and Williams, N. (1991), *Pat Collins, king of showmen* (Wallsall)

Allingham, P. (1934), *Cheapjack* (New York)

Anderson, G. and Tighe, B. (1973), 'Gypsy culture and health care', *American Journal of Nursing*, 73(2)

Anisha, B. (Agnes Vranckx) (1997), *The declaration of a lost people* (Wolverhampton)

Anthony, P. (1988), *Being a green mother* (New York)

Armstrong, M. (1950), *George Borrow* (London)

Arnold, H. (1967), 'Some observations on Turkish and Persian Gypsies', *Journal of the Gypsy Lore Society*, 46(3/4)

Asante, M. (1988), *Afrocentricity* (Trenton)

Ascoli, G.J. (1865), *Zigeunerisches* (Halle)

Awosusi, A. (2000) (ed.), *Zigeunerbilder in der Kinder- und Jugendliteratur*

(Heidelberg)

Bailey, G. (1938), *Studies in north Indian languages* (London)

Bakker, P. and Courtiade, M. (1991) (eds), *In the margin of Romani: Gypsy languages in contact*, Institute for General Linguistics Publication No. 58, University of Amsterdam

Bakker, P. (1995), 'Notes on the genesis of Caló and other Iberian Para-Romani varieties', in Matras (1995)

Bakker, P. (2001), 'Typology of Romani numerals', *Sprachtypologie Univ. Forschung*, 54(2)

Balfe, C. (2008), 'A quip too far from Brundle?', *Pitpass*, 9 June

Balogh, S. (1993), 'Following in the footsteps of the Ku Klux Klan: Anti-Gypsy organization in Romania', *Nemzetközi Cigány Szövetség Bulletin*, No. 5 (New York)

Bamberger, E. (1994) (ed.), *Der Völkermord an den Sinti und Roma in der Gedenkstättenarbeit* (Heidelberg)

Bamberger, E. and Ehmann, A. (1995) (eds), *Kinder und Jugendlicher als Opfer des Holocaust* (Heidelberg)

Barany, Z. (2002), *The East European Gypsies* (Cambridge)

Bardi, A. (2007), 'The Gypsy as trope in Victorian and modern British literature', unpublished doctoral dissertation, The University of Maryland, College Park

Barkan, E. (2001), *Making it in America: a sourcebook on eminent ethnic Americans* (New York)

Bartels, E. and Brun, G. (1943), *The Gipsies in Denmark* (Copenhagen)

Bauer, Y. (1980), 'Whose Holocaust?', *Midstream*, November

Bauer, Y. (1990), 'Continuing ferment in Eastern Europe', *SICSA Report*, 4(1/2)

Bauer, Y. (1994), 'Was the Holocaust unique?', *Midstream*, 30(4)

Bauer, Y. (1996), 'The trauma of the Holocaust: some historical perspectives', keynote address, 26th Annual Scholars' Conference on the Holocaust and the Churches, University of St Thomas, 3 March

Bauman, Z. (1989), *Modernity and the Holocaust* (Cambridge)

Becerra, H. (2006), 'Gypsies, the usual suspects', *The Los Angeles Times*, 30 January

Behlmer, G. (1985), 'The Gypsy problem in Victorian England', *Victorian Studies*, 48(2)

Behrendt, J. (1939), 'Die wahrheit über die Zigeuner', *NS Partei Korrespondenz*, 10

Benninghaus, R. (1991), 'Les Tsiganes de la Turquie Orientale', *Etudes Tsiganes*, 3

Bercovici, K., (1928) *The story of the Gypsies* (London)

Bercovici, K. (1983), *Gypsies: their life, lore and legends* (New York, originally published 1929)

Berenbaum, M. (1993), *The world must know: the history of the Holocaust as told in the US Holocaust Memorial Museum* (Toronto and London)

Bernadec, C. (1979), *L'Holocaust oublié* (Paris)

Bernardo, S. (1981), *The ethnic almanac* (New York)

Bernasovský, I. and Bernasovská, J. (1999), *Anthropology of Romanies (Gypsies): auxological and anthropogenetical study* (University of Prešov Minority Research Centre)

Berzin, A. (2006), *The historical interaction between the Buddhist and Islamic cultures before the Mongol Empire* (Berlin, originally published 1996)

Beynon, E. (1936), 'The Gypsy in a non-Gypsy economy', *American Journal of Sociology*, 42(3)

Bhalla, V. (1992), 'Ethnicity and Indian origins of Gypsies of Eastern Europe and the USSR: a bio-anthropological perspective', in Singh (1992)

Bignell, A. (1977), *Hopping down in Kent* (London)

Binding, K. and Hoche, A. (1920), *Die Freigabe der Vernichtung Lebensunwerten Lebens* (Leipzig)

Bischoff, F. (1827), *Deutsch-Zigeunerisches Woerterbuch* (Ilmenau)

Blachut, K.B. (2005), 'Transient criminal subcultures and the crimes they commit against the elderly: implications for continuing criminal justice and community education', unpublished DE dissertation, University of Illinois

Blair, K. (2004), 'Gypsies and lesbian desire: Vita Sackville-West, Violet Trefusis and Virginia Woolf', *Twentieth Century Literature: A Scholarly and Critical Journal*, 50(2)

Bloch, J. (1953), *Les Tsiganes* (Paris, reprinted 1969)

Bloch, J. (1965), *Indo-Aryan, from the Vedas to modern times* (Paris)

Block, M. (1938), *Gypsies: Their life and their customs* (London)

Boretzky, N., and Igla, B. (1994), *Wörterbuch Romani Deutsch Englisch* (Wiesbaden)

Borrow, G. (1841), *The Zincali, or an account of the Gypsies of Spain* (London, republished 1924)

Borrow, G. (1851), *Lavengro: scholar, Gipsy, priest* (London, republished 1910)

Borrow, G. (1857), *The Romany Rye: a sequel to 'Lavengro'* (London, republished 1924)

Borrow, G. (1862), *Wild Wales* (London)

Borrow, G. (1874), *Romano Lavo-Lil, word book of the Romany or English Gypsy language* (London, republished 1910)

Borrow, G. (1974), *Wild Wales* (London and Glasgow, originally published 1862)

Bosworth, C.E. (1961), 'Ghaznevid military organization', *Der Islam*, 63

Bosworth, C.E. (2001) (ed.), *The history of the Seljuq Turks, from the Jani al-Tawarik: an Ilkhanid adaptation of the Saljuq-nama of Zahir al-Din Nishapuri* (Richmond)

Boughourian, G. and Alcantara, J. (1975), 'Gypsy fortune-tellers and your community', *Police Chief*, 42(6)

Bowdre, K.M. (2006), 'Racial mythologies: African American female images and representation from minstrelsy to the Studio Era', unpublished doctoral dissertation, University of Southern California, Los Angeles

Boyer, P.J. (2006), 'Hollywood heresy', *The New Yorker*, 22 May

Braham, R. (1983) (ed.), *Perspectives on the Holocaust* (Boston, MA)

Braithwaite, P. (1999), *A palace on wheels* (White Waltham)

Branson, L. (1993), 'Romanian Gypsies being terrorized', *The San Francisco Chronicle*, 19 December

Breitman, R. (1991), *The architect of genocide: Himmler and the Final Solution* (Hanover and London)

Brenna, S. (1988), 'Housing the memories of genocide', *Newsday*, 2 September

Briel, P.-G. (1989), *Lumpenkind und Traumprinzessin: zur Sozialgestalt der Zigeuner* (Giessen)

Briggs, G.W. (1953), *The Doms and their near relations* (Mysore)

Broad, P. (1966), 'KZ Auschwitz: Erinnerungen eines SS-Mannes', *Hefte von Auschwitz*, 9

Brockhaus, F.A. (1841), *Bilder-Conversations-Lexicon für das Deutsche Volk* (Leipzig)

Brode, D. (2005), *Multiculturalism and the mouse: race and sex in Disney entertainment* (Austin, TX)

Brown, F. (1988), *Fairfield folk: a history of the British fairground and its people* (Malvern, Upton upon Severn)

Brownlee, C. (2004), 'Genetic evidence of Gypsies' Indian origins', *Science News: The Weekly News Magazine of Science*, 20 September

Bryant, J. (1785), 'Collections on the Zingara or Gypsey language', *Archæologia*, 7

Buddruss, G. (1967), *Die Sprache von Sau in Ostafghanistan* (Munich)

Burke, J. (1996) (ed.), Proceedings of the conference entitled *Romanies in the Holocaust: the Nazi assault on Sinti and Roma* (Madison, NJ)

Burke, P. and Porter, R. (1995) (eds), *Languages and jargons: contributions to a social history of language* (Cambridge)

Burleigh, M. and Wippermann, W. (1991), *The racial state: Germany, 1933–1945* (Cambridge)

Burney, E. (1968), *Black in a white world*, The Economist Brief Booklets No. 5, London

Burney, S. (1988), *The exotic and the restless: representation of the 'Other' in colonialist discourse* (Vancouver)

Burton, R. (1849), *A grammar of the Játakí dialect* (Bombay)

Burton, R. (1851), *Sindh, and the races that inhabit the Valley of the Indus* (London)

Burton, R. (1898), *The Jew, the Gypsy and El Islam* (Hollywood, CA)

Büttner, C. (1771), *Vergleichungstafeln der Schriftarten verschiedener Völker in der vergangenen und gegenwärtigen Zeiten* (Göttingen)

Button, M. and Reed, T. (1999) (eds), *The foreign woman in British literature: exotics, aliens and outsiders* (Westport)

Caldwell, R. (1856), *A comparative grammar of the Dravidian or South Indian family of languages* (London)

Cech, P. (2006), *Dolenjska Romani. The dialect of the Dolenjski Roma in Novo Mesto and Bela Krajina, Slovenia* (Munich)

Chamberlain, H.S. (1899), *The foundations of the nineteenth century* (London)

Champagne, M. (2002), 'This wild Gypsy dream: the Gypsy in nineteenth century British imagination', doctoral dissertation, University of Michigan, Ann Arbor

Charmley, J. (1993), *Churchill: the end of glory* (New York)

Charnon-Deutsch, L. (2004), *The Spanish Gypsy: the history of a European obsession* (Philadelphia)

Chatard, J. and Bernard, M. (1959), *Zanko – chef tribal* (Paris)

Chesney, K. (1970), *The Victorian underworld* (Harmonsworth)

Churchill, W. (1997a), 'Assaults on truth and memory', *Z Magazine*, December 1996 and February 1997

Churchill, W. (1997b), *A little matter of genocide: Holocaust and denial in the Americas, 1492 to the present* (San Francisco)

Clarke, A. (1878), 'Origin and wanderings of the Gypsies', *The Edinburgh Review*, 148

Clarke, M.W. (1967), 'Vanishing vagabonds: the American Gypsies', *Texas Quarterly*, 10(2)

Clébert, J.-P. (1961), *Les Tziganes* (Paris)

Clébert, J.-P. (1963), *The Gypsies* (London)

Coggins, J. and Pratt, F. (1952), *Rockets, jets, guided missiles and space ships* (London)

Cohn, W. (1973), *The Gypsies* (Reading, MA)

Collie, M. (1982), *George Borrow, eccentric* (Cambridge)

Colocci, A. (1889), *Gli Zingari* (Turin)

Colocci, A. (1907), 'Review of De Goeje (1903)', *Journal of the Gypsy Lore Society*, 1

Colson, F. (1839), *De l'État présent et de l'avenir des principautés de Moldavie et de Valachie* (Paris)

Conan Doyle, A. (1913), 'Borrow-ed scenes', *The Pall Mall Magazine*, 52

Cooke, M. (2002), 'Saving brown women', *Signs* 28(1)

Coon, C.S. (1942), 'Have the Jews a racial identity?', in Graeber and Britt (1942)

Cornwell, T. (1996), 'Massacre denied a page in history', *The Times Higher Education Supplement*, 12 July

Courtiade, M. (1994), 'Phonologie des parlers Rom et diasystème graphique de la langue Romani', unpublished doctoral dissertation, University of the Sorbonne

Courthiade, M. (2004), 'KannauZ on the Ganges, cradle of the Rromani people', in Kenrick (2004)

Courthiade, M. (2007), 'Rroma history in the world and in Albania', *Coexistence House*, March

Courthiade, M. and Kányádi, A. (2007), *Un dictionnaire rromani oublié: le 'Gyök-Szótár' de F. Sztojka* (Paks)

Cozannet, F. (1973), *Mythes et coutumes religieuses des Tziganes* (Paris)

Cribb, B. (2001), *Tarmac Warrior* (Edinburgh and London)

Croley, L.S. (1996), 'Wanderers and settlers: vagrancy, begging, and the English middle class, 1780–1867', unpublished doctoral dissertation, University of Pennsylvania

Crone, P. (1980), *Slaves on horses: the evolution of the Islamic polity* (Cambridge)

Crone, P. (2003), 'The pay of client soldiers in the Umayyad period', *Der Islam*, 80(2)

Crowe, D. (2008), *The Holocaust: roots, history and aftermath* (Philadelphia)

Crowe, D. and Kolsti, J. (1991) (eds), *The Gypsies of Eastern Europe* (Armonk)

Daftary, F. (2003) (ed.), *Language politics* (Flensberg)

Darlington, C.D. (1969), *The evolution of man and society* (New York)

Darwin, C. (1871), *The descent of man, and selection in relation to sex* (London)

Davenport, C.B. (1915), *The feebly inhibited: nomadism, or the wandering impulse, with special reference to heredity* (Washington DC)

Davis Lutz, B. and Lutz, J.M. (1995), 'Gypsies as victims of the Holocaust', *Holocaust and Genocide Studies*, 14

Dawson, R. (1988) (ed.), *Henry Dry-Bread: the Richard Wade papers* (Alfreton)

Dawson, R. (2001), *British Gypsy slavery to America and the Caribbean* (Alfreton)

de Gila Kochanowski, V. (1968), 'Black Gypsies, white Gypsies', *Diogenes*, 63

de Gila Kochanowski, V. (1989), 'Problems of the common Romani: problems of an international language', *Żanglimasqo Simpozium i Romani Čhib thaj Kultura* (Sarajevo) de Gila Kochanowski, V. (1994), *Parlons Tsigane: histoire, culture et langue du peuple Tsigane* (Paris)

de Goeje, M.-J. (1876), 'Bijdrage tot de geschiedenis der Zigeuners', *Koninklijke Akademie van Wetenschappen: Verslagen en Mendeelingen*, 2(5)

de Kogalnicean, M. (1837), *Esquisse sur l'histoire, les mœurs et la langue des Cigains* (Berlin)

De Lint, C. (1985), *Mulengro: a Romany tale* (New York)

de Luna, J.C. (1951), *Gitanos de la Bética* (Madrid)

de Peyster, J.W. (1887), *Gypsies* (Edinburgh)

DeVita, P. R. (1992) (ed.), *The naked anthropologist* (Belmont)

Decourdemanche, J.-A. (1907), *Grammaire du Tchingiané ou langue des bohémiens errants* (Paris)

Dellal, J. (1999), 'American Gypsy: a stranger in everybody's land', videodocumentary, Little Dust Productions, San Francisco

Demeter, N.G., Bessonov, N.V. and Kutenkov, V.K. (2000), *Istorija Cigan: Novij Vzgljad* (Rossiskaja Akademija Nauk)

Derlon, P. (1977), *Secrets of the Gypsies* (New York)

DeSmet, K. (1990), 'Comments outrage area Jews', *The Detroit News*, 31 December

Dillmann, A. (1905), *Zigeuner-Buch* (Munich)

Diwana, M.S.U. (1943), 'The Asuric civilization in the Asuric West', *Dharwar*, July

Djonedi, F. (1996), 'Romano glossar: gesammelt von Schir-Ali Tehranizade', *Grazer Linguistische Studien*, 46

Djurić, R. (1996), *Romanies and Europe* (Strasbourg)

Djurić, R. (2003), 'The language of the Roma: the oldest language still spoken', PEN Centrum press release, Berlin, 25 January

Dodgson, R. (1973), 'Early Romani', *The Journal of the Gypsy Lore Society*, 52(3/4)

Doerfer, G. (1970), 'Irano-Altaistica: Turkish and Mongolian languages of Persia and Afghanistan', in Sebeok (1970)

Doolittle, L. (1984), 'Gypsies say Holocaust project snubbing them', *The Dallas Times Herald*, 28 June

Douglas, L. (1985), 'Film as witness: screening "Nazi concentration camps" before the Nuremberg Trials', *The Yale Law Journal*, 105(2)

Douglas, M. (1970), *Natural Symbols* (New York)

Duhmberg, O. (1870), *Zigeunerisches aus Sibirien: Wörter der Zigeunersprache* (Tomsk)

Duncan, D. (1969), 'The rocky Romany road', *Quinto Lingo*, December

Dwork, D. and Jan van Pelt, R. (1996), *Auschwitz, 1270 to the present* (New York and London)

Edmonds, J. (2001), *Gypsies, tramps and ... strangers*, 1 (Norwich)

Ehmann, A. (1981), 'A short history of the discrimination and persecution of the European Romanies and their fate under Nazi rule', lecture, Institute of Contemporary Jewry, The Hebrew University, 27 January

Eisenberg, A. (1981), *Witness to the Holocaust* (New York)

Eisner, J.P. (1983), 'The Genocide bomb: the Holocaust through the eyes of a survivor', in Braham (1983)

El-Liethy, I. (2003), 'Iraq's Gypsies struggle for life after Saddam's fall', *Islam on Line*, Baghdad, 6 May

Eliot, J. (2008), *Settela's last road* (Victoria and Oxford)

Elšík, V. and Matras, Y. (2006), *Markedness and language change: the Romani sample* (Mouton de Gruyter, Berlin and New York)

Elson, M. (1982), 'Gypsies are new element in organised crime', *The Chicago Tribune*, 25 February

Elysseeff, A. (1882), 'Kounavine's materials for the study of the Gypsies' [in Russian], *Reports of the Russian Geographical Society*, 17

Elysseeff, A.V. (1890), 'Materials for the study of the Gypsies, collected by M.J. Kounavine', *Journal of the Gypsy Lore Society*, 2

Emerit, M. (1930), 'Sur la condition des esclaves dans l'ancienne Roumanie', *Revue Historique du Sud-Est Européen*, 7(7–9)

Encarta World English Dictionary (1999) (New York)

Esplugas, C. (1999), 'Gypsy women in English life and literature', in Button and Reed (1999)

Esty, K. (1969), *The Gypsies: wanderers in time* (New York)

Evans, K. (2003), *On common ground: Travellers in Sutton and Merton* (London)

Fackenheim, E. (1976), *The Jewish return into history* (Syracuse)

Fackenheim, E. (1982), *To mend the world* (New York)

Fallon, D. (2001), 'Gypsy political effort in post-communist Europe', at http://www.yourwords.com/fallond/325.html

Faruqi, S. (2001), *Early Urdu literary culture and history* (Oxford)

Fickowski, J. (1989), *The Gypsies in Poland* (Warsaw)

Finck, F.N. (1907), *Die Sprache der armenischen Zigeuner* (St Petersburg)

Fishman, J., Ferguson, C. and Gupta, J.D. (1968) (eds) *Language problems of developing nations* (New York)

Fonseca, I. (1996), *Bury me standing: the Gypsies and their journey* (New York)

Fox, J.P. (1988), 'The Holocaust: a "non-unique" event for all humanity?', in *Remembering for the Future*, II:1863–1878 (Oxford)

Fox, J.P. (1995), *The Nazi extermination of the Romanies: genocide, Holocaust, or a 'minor irritant'?*, paper presented at the conference of the Association of Genocide Scholars, Williamsburg, Virginia, 14–16 June

Fraser, A. (1989), 'Looking into the seeds of time', paper presented at the annual meeting of the Gypsy Lore Society, Toronto, 7–9 April

Fraser, A. (1992), *The Gypsies* (Oxford)

Fraser, A. (1993), 'Authors' Gypsies', *Antiquarian Book Monthly*, 20(2)

Fraser, A. (1994), 'George Borrow as a character in fiction', *The George Borrow Bulletin*, 8

Fraser, A. (1995), 'Borrow, the Palgraves, and the Worships', *The George Borrow Bulletin*, 9

Fraser, A. (1996), 'The parallel universe of Borrow's Gypsies', *The George Borrow Bulletin*, 11

Freire, P. (1970), *Pedagogy of the oppressed* (New York)

Frère, J.-C. (1973), *L'Egnime des Gitans* (Paris)

Friedlander, H. (1995a), *The origins of Nazi genocide from euthanasia to the Final Solution* (Chapel Hill, NC)

Friedlander, H. (1995b), 'Die Vernichtung der Behinderten, der Juden und der Sinti und Roma', in Bamberger and Ehmann (1995)

Friedman, I. (1990), *The other victims: first-person stories of non-Jews persecuted by the Nazis* (Boston, MA)

Furlong, R. (2008), 'Roma's struggle for fair education', BBC News, http://news.bbc.co.uk/2/hi/programmes/crossing_continents/7581969.stm, 29 August

Gabor, E. (2003), 'The stereotype caravan: assessments of stereotypes and ideology levels used to portray Gypsies in two European feature films', MA Thesis, Virginia Polytechnic and State University

Gafarová, S. (2003), 'Central Asian Gypsies', *The Times of Central Asia*, 16 July

Galford, E. (2001), *The genealogy handbook* (London)

Galinski, H. (1980), 'Dieses Gedenken sei uns Mahnung zum Handeln', *Sinti und Roma in Ehemaligen KZ Bergen-Belsen am 27 Oktober 1979* (Göttingen)

Gardner, S. (1857), 'Notes on the condition of the Gypsy population of Moldavia', *Proceedings of the Royal Geographical Society*, 1

Geipel, J. (1969), *The Europeans: the people – today and yesterday; their origins and interrelations* (New York)

Geipel, J. (1995), 'The "secret" language of the Gypsies of Spain', in Burke and Porter (1995)

Getsay, T. (1983), 'GYP-sies and their criminal propensity', *Spotlight*, 1(1), 1(2), 2(1)

Gheorghe, N. (1983), 'Origins of Romas' slavery in the Rumanian principalities', *Roma*, 7(1)

Ghibănescu, G. (1921), 'The excommunication of mixed marriages with Gypsies', *Ion Neculcea*, 1

Gibb, H. and Bechingham, C.F. (1994), *The travels of Ibn Battuta 1325–1354* (London)

Gilbert, M. (1985), *The Holocaust: a history of the Jews of Europe during the Second World War* (New York)

Gilbert, W.H. (1947), *Marginal minorities of the World* (Silver Spring, reprinted 1962)

Gilliat-Smith, B. (1909), 'Russian Gypsies in Lithuania, July 1908', *Journal of the Gypsy Lore Society*, 3(2)

Gjerdman, O. and Ljungberg, E. (1963), *The language of the Swedish coppersmith Gipsy Johan Dimitri Taikon* (Uppsala)

Gladstone, F.M. (1969), *Notting Hill in bygone days* (London)

Gordon, M. (2004), 'Forging the Gypsy identity in Victorian England', MA thesis, the University of Calgary, Canada

Grabitz, H., Bästlein, K. and Tuchel, J. (1994) (eds), *Die Normalität des Verbrechens* (Berlin)

Graeber, I. and Britt, S.H. (1942) (eds), *Jews in a Gentile world* (New York)

Graffunder, A. (1835), *Ueber die Sprache der Zigeuner* (Erfurt)

Grant, A. (1995) (ed.), *Creole linguistics and society* (Bradford)

Grant, A. (2003), 'Where East meets West: observations on a list of Greek loans in European Romani', in *Papers in contact linguistics,* Bradford Studies in Language, Culture and Society, 6, Interface

Grant, K.N. (2004), 'Alison Hinds and Marion Hall: positioning female sexuality from East to West', *Sargasso*, 2003–4(1)

Greenfield, H. (1977), *Gypsies* (New York)

Grellmann, H. (1783), *Die Zigeuner. Ein historische Versuch über die Lebensart und verfassung* (Dessau and Leipzig)

Grellmann, H. (1807), *Dissertation on the Gipseys* (London)

Gresham, D., *et al.* (2001), 'Origins and divergence of the Roma', *American Journal of Human Genetics*, 96

Grierson, G.A. (1922), *Linguistic survey of India* (Delhi)

Griffin, C. (2008), *Nomads under the Westway: Irish Travellers, Gypsies and other traders in West London* (Hatfield)

Groome, F.H. (1900), *Introduction to Borrow* (originally published 1851)

Grosvenor, A. (1908), 'Whiter's "Lingua Cingariana"', *Journal of the Gypsy Lore Society*, 2(2)

Grove, L. (1984), 'Lament of the Gypsies: forty years after Auschwitz, petitioning for a place', *The Washington Post*, 21 July

Gutman, I. (1990) (ed.), *Encyclopaedia of the Holocaust* (New York)

Gutman, I. and Berenbaum, M. (1994) (eds), *Anatomy of the Auschwitz death camp* (Bloomington and Indianapolis)

Güzel, H.C., Oğuz, C. and Karatay, O. (2002) (eds), *The Turks: Middle Ages* (Ankara)

Hadley, G. and Fitrut, M.M. (1801), *A compendious grammar of the current corrupt dialect of the jargon of Hindostan, commonly called Moors: with a vocabulary* (London)

Hadziavdic, H. (2007), *A day with the Gypsies*, paper presented at the annual Midwest Modern Languages Association, Cleveland, November

Haider, S.Z. (1990), *Islamic arms and armour of Muslim India* (Lahore)

Haines, S.M. (1989), *The Travellers*, privately circulated report on 'Gypsy Crime', Swindle Section, Dallas Police Department

Haining, P. (1972), *The warlocks' book* (London)

Haliti, B. (2006), *India and Roma* (Kosovo)

Hall, J. (1915), *The Gypsy's parson* (London)

Halwachs, D. (1996), *Verschriftlichung des Roman*, Working Paper No.2 of the Kodifizierung und Didaktisierung des Roman Project, Oberwart, Verien Roma

Halwachs, D. (2000), 'Romani: attempting an introductory overview', *Romani in Austria* (Graz)

Halwachs, D. and Menz, F. (1999) (eds), *Die Sprache der Roma* (Klagenfurt)

Hancock, I.F. (1975), 'Problems in the creation of a standard dialect of Romanés', *Working Papers in Sociolinguistics*, 25, The Social Science Research Council Committee on Sociolinguistics, Southwest Educational Development Laboratory, Austin

Hancock, I.F. (1977), *Problems in the creation of a standard dialect of Romanés – II (grammar and lexicon)*, presentation to the American Council of Teachers of Uncommonly-taught Asian Languages, San Francisco

Hancock, I.F. (1980), 'Gypsies in Germany: the fate of Romany', *Michigan Germanic Studies*, VI (2)

Hancock, I.F. (1981), 'Slavic elements in Texan Romani', unpublished privately-circulated manuscript

Hancock, I.F. (1984), 'The social and linguistic development of Angloromani', in Acton and Kenrick (1984)

Hancock, I.F. (1986), 'The cryptolectal speech of the American roads: Traveller Cant and American Angloromani', *American Speech*, 1(3)

Hancock, I.F. (1987), *The pariah syndrome: an account of Gypsy slavery* (Ann Arbor)

Hancock, I.F. (1988a), 'The development of Romani linguistics', in A. Jazyery and W. Winter (1988)

Hancock, I.F. (1988b), 'Uniqueness, Gypsies and Jews', *Remembering for the future: Jews and Christians during and after the Holocaust* (Oxford)

Hancock, I.F. (1988c), 'Reunification and the role of the International Romani Union', *Roma*, 29

Hancock, I.F. (1991), 'Gypsy history in Germany and neighboring lands: a chronology leading to the Holocaust and beyond', in Crowe and Kolsti, (1991)

Hancock, I.F. (1993), 'Antigypsyism in the new Europe', *Roma*, 39

Hancock, I.F. (1994), 'The history of the American Hungarian Roma and their language', *Roma*, 41

Hancock, I.F. (1995a), *A handbook of Vlax Romani* (Columbus)

Hancock, I.F. (1995b), 'On the migration and affiliation of the Ḍōmba: Iranian words in Rom, Lom and Dom Gypsy', in Matras (1995)

Hancock, I.F. (1995c), 'Standardization and ethnic defence', in Grant (1995)

Hancock, I.F. (1996), 'Duty and beauty, possession and truth: the claim of lexical impoverishment as control', in Tong (1996), and Chapter 10 in this volume

Hancock, I.F. (2000), 'The emergence of Romani as a *koïné* outside of India', in Acton (2000)

Hancock, I.F. (2001), 'Downplaying the Porrajmos: the trend to minimize the Romani Holocaust', *Journal of Genocide Research*, 3(1)

Hancock, I.F. (2002), *We are the Romani People: Ame Sam e Rromane Džene* (Hatfield)

Hancock, I.F. (2003), 'Language corpus and language politics: the case of the standardization of Romani', in Daftary (2003)

Hancock, I.F. (2004), 'The concocters: creating fake Romani culture', in Saul and Tebbutt (2004), and Chapter 12 in this volume

Hanks, P., Hodges, F., Mills, A.D. and Room, A. (2002), *The Oxford names companion* (Oxford)

Harriot, J. (1830), 'Observations on the oriental origin of the Romanichal, or tribe miscalled Gypsey or Bohemian', *Transactions of the Royal Asiatic Society*, 2

Haugen, E. (1974), 'Language planning: commentary', *Language Planning Session of the Eighth World Congress of Sociology* (Toronto)

Hayward, J. (2003), *Gypsy Jib: a Romany dictionary* (Wenhaston)

Heard, W. and Cameron, A. (1978), *Brentford and Chiswick as it was* (Nelson)

Hearn, J. (2001), 'John's Story', in M. Horner (ed.) (2001)

Heine, M.A. (2001), *Roma victims of Nazi regime may be entitled to compensation*, International Organisation for Migration, Office of Information report, Geneva

Helbig, A. (2004), *Carmen*, New York City Opera Project

Helyčai, A. (1972), *The British Traveller: the Romani civilization, its mythical presentation in the English literature, and the social problems today,*

Diplôme d'Etudes Supérieures d'Anglais, Université d'Aix en Provence

Henderson, K. (1986), 'College students learn the meaning of the Holocaust', *The Baltimore Sun*, 27 July

Heredia, J. de D.R. (1988), *Krisipén Serserí – Constitución Española* (Barcelona)

Higgie, B. (1984), 'Proto-Romanes phonology', unpublished doctoral dissertation, The University of Texas, Austin

Hilberg, R. (1961), *The destruction of the European Jews* (Chicago)

Hirschberg, C. (1986), 'Romanies lobby for representation on Holocaust Memorial Council', *The Washington Post*, 9 March

Hofman, N.G. (2008), 'Accessing Romani women study participants: collaborating with their gatekeepers and other NGO entrepreneurs', *Practicing Anthropology*, 30(3)

Holroyd, M. (1975), *Augustus John: a biography* (London)

Horner, M. (2001) (ed.), *The Romany and Traveller Family History Society, oral history series No. 2*

Hoyland, J. (1816), *A historical survey of the customs, habits and present state of the Gypsies* (London)

Hübschmannová, M. (2000), 'On the beginnings of Roma history', in Žařabová and Davidová (2000)

Hübschmannová, M. (2004), 'Origin of Roma', *Rombase Network* (Graz)

Hund, W.D. (2000) (ed.), *Zigeunerbilder: schnittmuster rassistischer Ideologie* (Duisberg)

Ibbetson, D.C.J. (1881), *Census report for the Punjab* (Calcutta)

Ikram, S.M. (1989), *History of Muslim civilisation in India and Pakistan* (Lahore)

Ilieva, K. (2008), 'Education: a waste of time for Bulgarian Roma', *News.BG* (Sofia)

Iordanova, D. (2003), 'Cinematic images of Gypsies', *Framework: special issue of The Journal of Cinema and Media*, 44(2) (Detroit)

Ioviţă, R. and Schurr, T. (2004), 'Reconstructing the origins and migrations of diasporic populations: the case of the European Gypsies', *American Anthropologist*, 106(2)

Ivanow, W. (1914), 'On the language of the Gypsies of Qainat (in Eastern Persia)', *Journal of the Asiatic Society of Bengal*, n.s., 10(11)

Jackson, M. (1995), *A home in the world* (Durham)

Jan Mohamed, A.R. (1985), 'The economy of Manichean allegory: the function of racial difference in colonialist literature', *Critical Inquiry*, 12(1)

Jansen, W.H. (1959), 'The esoteric-exoteric factor in folklore', *Fabula*, 2

Jarman, A. and Jarman, E. (1991), *The Welsh Gypsies: children of Abraham Wood* (Cardiff)

Jazyery, A. and Winter, W. (1988) (eds), *Languages and cultures: studies in honor of Edgar C. Polomé* (Berlin and New York)

Ješina, P.J. (1886), *Romáňi Čib, oder die Zigeunersprache* (Leipzig)

Jiwani, Y. (1992), 'The exotic, the erotic and the dangerous: South Asian women in popular film', *Canadian Woman Studies*, 13(1)

John, V. (2006), *Indian origins of Romani numbers: a case for koïnéization*, Romani Studies term paper, The University of Texas

Jordan, I. (2006), *Gypsies, tramps and heat: an anthology of erotic romance* (Denver)

Justman, S. (1995), *The Holocaust for beginners* (New York)

Kalaydjieva, L., Morar, B., Chaix, R. and Tang, H. (2005), 'A newly discovered founder population: the Roma/Gypsies', *BioEssays*, 27(10)

Kaldi, L. (1983), 'Alternative education for the Rom', *Explorations in Ethnic Studies*, 6(1)

Kasaipwalova, J. (1973), 'Modernizing Melanesian society: why, and for whom', in May (1973)

Katz, K. (1995), Letter to N. Trehan, Jerusalem, 17 September

Katz, S. (1988), 'Quantity and interpretation: issues in the comparative analysis of the Holocaust', *Remembering for the Future: Jews and Christians during and after the Holocaust*, Vol. 3 (Oxford)

Katz, S. (1994), *The Holocaust in historical context: Vol. I: the Holocaust and mass death before the modern age* (Oxford)

Kaufman, T. (1984), *Explorations in proto-Gypsy phonology and classification*, paper presented at the Sixth South Asian Languages Analysis Round-Table, Austin

Kaup, M. and Rosenthal, D.J. (2002) (eds), *Mixing race, mixing culture: inter-American literary dialogues* (Austin, TX)

Keable, P. (1995), 'Creators, creatures and victim-survivors', unpublished doctoral dissertation, University of Sydney

Keable, P. (forthcoming), *Creators, creatures and victim-survivors*

Kearney, J. (1981), 'Education and the Kalderash' in Salo (1981)

Keegan, J. (1978) (ed.), *Who was who in World War II* (New York)

Kenrick, D. (1976), 'Romanies in the Middle East', *Roma*, (4), 2(1), 2(2)

Kenrick, D. (1977), *A contribution to the early history of the Romani people*, Romani Institute Occasional Paper No. 3, London

Kenrick, D. (1994), *Les Tsiganes, de l'Inde à la Méditerranée* (Paris)

Kenrick, D. (1995), 'The Nazis and the Gypsies: a fresh look', *The Jewish Quarterly*, 41(4)

Kenrick, D. (2000a), 'Inflections in flux', *Slavophilia: Slavic and East European Resources*, 5 April

Kenrick, D. (2000b), 'Learning Domari: unit 2', *Kuri-DR Journal*, 1(3)

Kenrick, D. (2004), *Gypsies: from the Ganges to the Thames* (Hatfield)

Kenrick, D. and Puxon, G. (1972), *The destiny of Europe's Gypsies* (London)

Kenrick, D. and Puxon, G. (2009), *Gypsies under the swastika* (Hatfield)

Kent, L. (1992), 'Fieldwork that failed', in DeVita (1992)

Kester, P. (1897), *Tales of the real Gypsy* (New York)

Khullar, K.K. (1995), 'Urdu, the language of national unity', *India Perspectives*, March

King, S. (1985), *Thinner* (New York)

Kinzer, S. (1992), 'Germany cracks down: Romanies come first', *The New York Times*, 27 September

Kjeilen, T. (2003), 'Seljuqs', *Encyclopaedia of the Orient* (Stockholm)

Knapp, W.I. (1899), *Life, writings and correspondence of George Borrow, derived from official and other authentic sources* (London)

Knudsen, M. (2003), *Die Geschichte der Roma* (Hamburg)

Kobak, A. (1995), 'The Gypsy in our souls: review of Fonseca (1995)', *The New York Times*, 22 October

Kochanowski, J. (1946), 'Some notes on the Gypsies of Latvia', *Journal of the Gypsy Lore Society*, 25(1/2), 25(3/4)

Kochanowski, J. (1971), 'The future of Romani', in Acton (1971)

Kochanowski, J. (2003), *Précis de la langue Romani littéraire* (Paris)

Kohn, M. (1995), *The race gallery* (London)

König, U. (1989), *Sinti und Roma unter dem Nationalsozialismus* (Bochum)

Korobeinikov, D. (2004), 'Diplomatic correspondence between Byzantium and the Mamlūk Sultanate in the fourteenth century', *Al-Masaq: Islam and the Mediaeval Mediterranean*, 16(1)

Kostić, S. (1998), 'O dvou indických pojmenováních jiných etnik', *Romano Džaniben*, 5(4)

Kroeber, A.L. (1917), 'The superorganic', *American Anthropologist*, 19(2)

Labois, R. (1954), *Sur la piste des Carpathes* (Paris)

Lagnado, L.M. and Cohn Dekel, S. (1991), *Children of the flames: the untold story of the twins of Auschwitz* (New York)

Lagrou, P. (1997), 'Victims of genocide and national memory: Belgium, France and The Netherlands, 1939–1945', *Past & Present*, 154

Lal, K. (1994), *Muslim slave system in Mediaeval India* (New Delhi)

Lalvani, S. (1995), 'Consuming the exotic other', *Critical Studies in Mass Communication*, 12

Lang, B. (1990), *Act and idea in the Nazi genocide* (Chicago)

Lang, B. (1997), 'Metaphysical racism, or biological warefare by other means', in Zack (1997)

Lecca, O.G. (1908), 'On the origin and the history of the Gypsies', *Viaţă Rumînă*, 8

Lee, P.J. (2000), *We borrow the Earth: an intimate portrait of the Gypsy shamanic tradition and culture* (Lomdon)

Lehmann, W. (1983), *Descriptive linguistics: an introduction* (New York)

Leitner, G.W. (1877), *The languages and races of Dardistan* (Lahore)

Leland, C.G. (1882), *The Gypsies* (Boston, MA)

Leland, C.G. (1891), *Gypsy sorcery and fortune telling* (London, republished 1900, 1962, 1995)

Lemon, A. (1996), 'Hot blood and black pearls: socialism, society and authenticity at the Moscow Teatr Romen', *Theatre Journal*, 48

Lesný, V. (1916), 'Über die langen vokale in den Zigeunerdialekten', *Zeitschrift der deutschen Morgenländischen Gesellschaft*, 70

Levi, S.C. (2002a), *The Indian diaspora in Central Asia and its trade, 1550–1900* (Leiden)

Levi, S.C. (2002b), 'Hindus beyond the Hindu Kush: Indians in the Central Asian slave trade', *Journal of the Royal Asiatic Society*, 12(3)

Levinson, D. and Ember, M. (1997) (eds), *American immigrant cultures* (New York)

Levy, V. (2000), 'Proti Romům stejně jako kdysi proti nám', *Romano Džaniben*, 7(1/2)

Lewy, G. (2000), *The Nazi persecution of the Gypsies* (Oxford)

Liddell, A.K. and Scott, R. (1980), *A lexicon, abridged from Liddell and Scott's Greek-English lexicon* (Oxford)

Liebich, R. (1863), *Die Zigeuner in IhremWesen und in Ihrer Sprache, nach eigenen Beobachtungen dargestellt* (Leipzig)

Liggio, D. (1996), *The influences of Zoroastrianism and Manichæanism on the Romani creation myth* (Austin, TX)

Linnenthal, E. (1995), *Preserving memory: the struggle to create America's Holocaust Museum* (New York)

Lipa, J. (1983), 'Guest editorial on priorities in Romanological studies', *Newsletter of the North American Chapter of the Gypsy Lore Society*, 6(1)

Lituchy, B. (2006) (ed.), *Jasenovac and the holocaust in Yugoslavia: analyses and survivors' testimonies* (New York)

Logan, H.J. (1976), 'Maryland Gypsy laws', *The Washington Post*, 29 January

Lomax, A. (1977), 'Appeal for cultural equity', *Journal of Communication*, Spring

Lombroso, C. (1918), *Crime: its causes and remedies* (Boston, MA)

Lopate, P. (1989), 'Resistance to the Holocaust', in Rosenberg, (1989)

Lopez, J. (2003), 'Ain't It Funny', YouTube broadcast, http://www.youtube.com/

Lowry, D. (1981), 'What it's like to be a Gypsy girl', *Cosmopolitan*, 191(6)

Luebke, D.M. (1990), *The Nazi persecution of Sinti and Ròma*, US Holocaust

Memorial Museum Research Brief, 18 April

Luke, T.W. (1996), 'Memorializing mass murder: entertainment at the US Holocaust Memorial Museum', *Arena*, 6

Maas, P. (1978), *King of the Gypsies* (New York)

Macalister, R.A.S. (1914), *The language of the Nawar or Zutt: the nomad smiths of Palestine* (Edinburgh)

Macalister, R.A.S. (1937), *The secret languages of Ireland* (Cambridge)

Macfie, R.A.S. (1913), 'The Gypsies: an outline sketch', *The Romanitshels', Didakais' and Folk-Lore Gazette*, 1(3)

Macfie, R.A.S. ('Andreas') (1927), 'Bread and water', *Journal of the Gypsy Lore Society*, 6(3)

Mackie, A. (2006), *The Gypsy chronicles* (Port Charlotte)

Mahoney, F. (1965), 'Notes on the mulattoes of the Gambia before the mid-nineteenth century', *Transactions of the Historical Society of Ghana*, 8

Mais, Y. (1988), private correspondence with I.F. Hancock, 11 May

Malvinni, D. (2002), 'The Gypsy caravan: from real Roma to imaginary Gypsies in western music', unpublished doctoral dissertation, The University of California at Santa Barbara

Marchbin, A. (1939), 'A critical history of the origin and migration of the Gypsies', doctoral dissertation, University of Pittsburgh

Margalit, G. (1996), 'Antigypsyism in the political culture of the Federal Republic of Germany: a parallel with antisemitism?', *Analysis of Current Trends in Antisemitism No. 9*, The Vidal Sassoon International Centre for the study of Antisemitism, The Hebrew University of Jerusale

Margalit, A. and Motzkin, G. (1996), 'The uniqueness of the Holocaust', *Philosophy and Public Affairs*, 25(1)

Marklein, M.B. (2005), 'European effort spotlights plight of the Roma', *USA Today*, 2 February

Marlock, D. (1993), *Gypsy talk: law enforcement's guide to the secret language of the American Gypsy* (Littleton)

Marlock, D. (2001), *How to become a professional con artist* (Boulder)

Marlock, D. (2002), 'Law enforcement under fire', *FraudTech* (Milwaukee)

Marlock, D. and Dowling, J. (1994), *License to steal: travelling con artists, their games, their rules, your money* (Boulder)

Marsden, W. (1785), 'Observations on the language of the people commonly called Gypsies', *Archæologia*, 7

Marsh, A. (2003), *Ottoman Gypsies or Gypsies in the Ottoman empire: a brief summary and some new perspectives on Romani history*, unpublished monograph, The University of Greenwich

Marsh, A. (2008), 'No promised land: history, historiography and the origins of the Gypsies', unpublished doctoral dissertation, The University of Greenwich

Marushiakova, E. and Popov, V. (2000), *Gypsies in the Ottoman empire* (Paris)

Masica, C. (1991), *The Indo-Aryan languages* (Cambridge)

Mason, C. (2005), *Gypsy lover* (Leisure Books, New York)

Matras, Y. (1995) (ed.), *Romani in contact: the history, structure and sociology of a language* (Amsterdam and New York)

Matras, Y. (1999a), 'The state of present-day Domari in Jerusalem', *Mediterranean Language Review*, 11

Matras, Y. (1999b), 'Johann Rüdiger and the study of Romani in eighteenth century Germany', *Journal of the Gypsy Lore Society*, 5(9)

Matras, Y. (2002), *Romani: a linguistic introduction* (Cambridge)

Matras, Y. (2004a), 'Typology, dialectology and the structure of complementation in Romani', *Trends in Linguistics, Studies and Monographs: Dialectology Meets Typology*, 153

Matras, Y. (2004b), 'The role of language in mystifying and demystifying Gypsy identity', in Saul and Tebbutt (2004)

Matras, Y. (2004c), 'A conflict of paradigms', *Romani Studies*, 14(2)

Matras, Y. (2004d), 'Romacilikanes, the Romani dialect of Parakalamos', *Romani Studies* 5(1)

Max, F. (1946), 'Le sort des Tsiganes dans les prisons et les camps de concentration de l'Allemagne Hitlérienne', *Journal of the Gypsy Lore Society*, 25(1/2)

Maximoff, M. (1946), 'Germany and the Gypsies', *Journal of the Gypsy Lore Society*, 25(3/4)

Maximoff, M. (1994), Interview, *Jekh Čhib*, 17

May, R.J. (1973) (ed.), *Priorities in Melanesian development* (Canberra)

Mayall, D. (1988), *Gypsy-Travellers in nineteenth century society* (Cambridge)

Mayall, D. (2004), *Gypsy identities 1500–2000: from Egyptians and Moon-Men to the ethnic Romany* (London)

Mazzone, G.L. (1994), 'Travelling criminals (the Rom Gypsies)', *FBI Law Enforcement Bulletin*, 63

McLain, C. (2003) (*trans.*), *Once upon a Princess* (New York)

McLaughlan, A. (2004), 'Gypsies and Jews: George Eliot's use of "race" in *The Spanish Gypsy* and *Daniel Deronda*', MA thesis, University of Northern British Columbia, Prince George

McLaughlin, J.B. (1980), *Gypsy lifestyles: swindlers and swindling* (Lexington)

Megret, J.-C. (2000), posting on the *Patrin* list-serve about the origin of the ethnonym *Sinti*, 10 March

Meier, C.S. (1988), *The unmasterable past* (Cambridge and London)

Meyerhoff, H. (1992), 'Council decries Germany's treatment of Gypsies', *US Holocaust Memorial Council Newsletter*, Washington DC, Winter

Meyers, R.R. (1966), *George Borrow* (New York)

Miklosich, F. (1872), *Ueber die Mundarten und die Wanderungen der Zigeuner Europa's* (Vienna)

Miklosich, F. (1874), *Beiträge zur Kenntniss der Zigeunermundarten* (Vienna)

Milton, S. (1990), 'The context of the Holocaust', *German Studies Review*, 13(2)

Milton, S. (1991a), 'Gypsies and the Holocaust', *The History Teacher*, 24(4)

Milton, S. (1991b), 'The racial context of the Holocaust', *Social Education*, February

Milton, S. (1992), 'Nazi policies towards Roma and Sinti, 1933–1945', *Journal of the Gypsy Lore Society*, 2(1)

Milton, S. (1994a), 'Antechamber to Birkenau: the *Zigeunerlager* after 1933', in Grabitz *et al.* (1994)

Milton, S. (1994b), 'Sinti und Roma als "vergessene Opfergruppe" in der Gedenkstättenarbeit', in Bamberger (1994)

Milton, S. (1995), 'Der weg zur "Endlösung der Zigeunerfrage": von der ausgrenzung zur ermordung der Sinti und Roma', in Bamberger and Ehmann (1995)

Mirga, A. and Gheorghe, N. (1997), *The Roma in the twenty-first century: a policy paper* (Princeton)

Mirga, A. and Grocholski, A.M. (2000), *Roma and the law: demythologizing the 'Gypsy criminal' stereotype* (Princeton)

Mitchell, J. (1942), 'King of the Gypsies', *The New Yorker*, August

Mitchell, J. (1955), 'The beautiful flower', *The New Yorker*, 31

Mokri, M. (1951), *Gurani. La Grande Assemblée des Fidèles* (Teheran)

Molitor, J. (1947), 'The fate of a German Gypsy', *Journal of the Gypsy Lore Society*, 26

Monk Kidd, S. (2003), *The secret life of bees* (Harmondsworth)

Mookerji, B. (1927), 'The Gipsies and the spread of Indian culture', *Journal of the Department of Letters*, 15, The University of Calcutta

Morar, B., Gresham, D. *et al.* (2004), 'Mutation history of the Roma/Gypsies', *The American Journal of Human Genetics*, 75

Moreau, R. (1995), *The Rom: walking in the paths of the Gypsies* (Toronto)

Moreau, R. (2000), 'Your ancient Gypsy guide to wild sex', *Cleo Magazine*, 15

Morris, J. (1994), *Master criminals among the Gypsies* (Loomis)

Morris, J. (1995), 'The lost tribes of Europe', *The Sunday Times*, 15 October

Morse-Kahn, D. (2007), 'The plight of the professional gypsy', *The Minneapolis-St Paul Star Tribune*, 3 June

Morwood, V.S. (1885), *Our Gipsies, in city, tent and van* (London)

Mróz, L. (1992), *Geneza Cyganów i ich kultury* (Warsaw)

Müller-Hill, B. (1988), *Murderous science: elimination by scientific selection of Jews, Gypsies and others, Germany 1933–1945* (Oxford)

Nadel, B. (2006), *After the Mourning* (London)

Nagy M., Henke, L., Henke, J., Chatthopadhyay, P., *et al.* (2007), 'Searching for the origin of Romanies: Slovakian Romani, Jats of Haryana and Jat Sikhs Y-STR data in comparison with different Romani populations', *Forensic Science International*, 169(1)

Naylor, M.L. (2006), *Our musical world: a creative program to greet humanity's coming of age* (Ann Arbor)

Needham, M. (1920), 'Gipsies in English literature', unpublished Bachelor's Thesis, University of Illinois, Champaign-Urbana

Negra, D. (2001), *Off-white Hollywood: American culture and ethnic female stardom* (London)

Nelson, C. and Grossberg, L. (1988) (eds), *Marxism and the interpretation of culture* (Basingstoke)

Nemeth, D. (1994), 'Contrasting realities and the Gypsy Holocaust', *Newsletter of the Gypsy Lore Society*, 17(3), August

Nemeth, D. (2002), *The Gypsy-American: an ethnographic study* (Lewiston)

Nicolle, D. (1996) *Medieval warfare source book: Christian Europe and its neighbours* (London)

Nicolle, D. (1997), *The armies of Islam, 7th–11th centuries* (London)

Nord, D. (1998), 'Marks of race: Gypsy figures and eccentric femininity in nineteenth-century women's writing', *Victorian Studies,* 41(2)

Nord, D. (2001), 'Seen in rare glimpses: the phantom Gypsy in nineteenth century culture', paper delivered before the Locating the Victorians Conference, Cambridge University, July

Nord, D. (2007), *Gypsies and the British imagination, 1807–1930* (New York)

Okely, J. (1983), *The Traveller-Gypsies* (Cambridge)

Okely, J. (1990), 'The invention and inventiveness of Gypsy culture', paper presented at the Leiden University Fund Congress conference entitled *The Social Construction of Minorities and their Cultural Rights in Western Europe*, Leiden

Onions, C.T. (1968) (ed.), *The shorter English Oxford Dictionary on historical principles*, 3rd edn. (Oxford)

Ozanne, J.W. (1878), *Three years in Rumania* (London)

Panaitescu, C.I. (1928), *Robii: Aspecte Ţiganeşti* (Bucharest)

Papazian, P. (1984), 'A "unique uniqueness"?', *Midstream*, 30(4)

Papazian, V. M. (1901), *Armenskije Boša (Ciganje): etnografičeskij očerk* (Moscow)

Pape, M. (1997), *A nikdovám nebude vidit: dokument o koncentratním tabore Lety u Pisku* (Prague)

Pardoe, M. (1840), *The city of the Magyar, or, Hungary and her institutions* (London)

Paredes, A. and Stekert, E.J. (1971) (eds), [Introduction to] *The urban experience and folk tradition* (Austin, TX)

Parmar, P. (1984), 'Hateful contraries: media images of Asian women', *Ten* 8

Paspati, A.G. (1861), 'Memoir on the language of the Gypsies as now used in the Turkish Empire', *Journal of the American Oriental Society,* 7

Paspati, A.G. (1870), *Etudes sur les Tchinghianés ou Bohémiens de l'Empire Ottoman* (Constantinople)

Patai, R. and Patai-Wing, J. (1989), *The myth of the Jewish race* (Detroit)

Patkanov, K.N. (1887), *Cigani njeskoljko slovo narječijax za Kavkazskix Cigan: Boša i Karači* (St Petersburg). A shorter English version, 'Some words on the dialects of the Transcaucasian Gypsies – Boša and Karači' appears in the *Journal of the Gypsy Lore Society,* 1(3) (1908)

Pauley, J. and Phillips, S. (1992), 'Gypsy cops', *Dateline* transcript, NBC News, New York

Pauwels, L. and Bergier, J. (1960), *Le matin des magiciens* (Paris)

Pellegrino, G. (1998), 'A critical look at Carmen as Other', unpublished Masters of Music thesis, University of Northern Colorado, May

Petersen, W. (1988), 'Jews as a race', *Midstream*, February–March

Petulengro, G. (Gipsy or Gypsy or Xavier) (1935), 'Romany', *The Listener,* 17 April

Petulengro, L. (Leon Lloyd) (1968), *The roots of health* (London)

Petulengro, L. (Leon Lloyd) (1979), *Romany boy* (London)

Peukert, D. (1987), *Inside Nazi Germany: conformity, opposition and racism in everyday life* (London)

Phelan, J. (1951), *Waggon wheels* (London)

Piasere, L. (1988), 'De origine cinganorum', in Stahl (1988)

Pipes, D. (1981), *Slave soldiers and Islam: the genesis of a military system* (New Haven)

Pipes, D. (2000), *Military slaves: a uniquely Muslim phenomenon*, paper presented at the Conference on the Arming of Slaves from the Ancient World to the American Civil War, Yale University, New Haven, 16–18 November

Pischel, R. (1883), 'Der Heimath der Zigeuner', *Deutsche Rundschau*, 36:3, 353–75

Pollack, R. (2003), 'The fallacy of biological Judaism', *The Jewish Daily Forward*, 7 March

Porter, M. (1975), 'Review of Cohn (1973)', *Journal of American Folklore*, 348

Pott, A.F. (1844), *Die Zigeuner in Europa und Asien* (Halle)

Pott, A.F. (1846), 'Ueber die Sprache der Zigeuner in Syrien', *Zeitschrift für die Wissenschaft der Sprache*, 1 (Halle)

Pray, G. (1776), 'Anzeigen aus sämmtlich-kaiserlich-königlichen Erbländeren', *Wiener Anzeigen*, 6

Price, G. (2000), *Languages in Britain and Ireland* (Oxford)

Prince, J.D. (1907), 'The English-Rommany jargon of the American roads', *Journal of the American Oriental Society*, 2

Proctor, R. (1990), 'From *Anthropologie* to *Rassenkunde* in the German anthropological tradition', in Stocking (1990)

Proester, E. (1968), *Nacistická okupace: Vrazdeni Cs. Cikán v Buchenwaldu*, Report for Miriam Novitch, Document No. ÚV CSPB K-135 on deposit in the Archives of the Museum of the Fighters Against Nazism, Prague

Quinn, C. (2001), 'The whistling Gypsy', *Carmel Quinn's Ireland*, Rego Irish [compact disk], Dublin

Radu, D. (2009), *On the road: centuries of Roma history*, BBC documentary series beginning 7 July, http://news.bbc.co.uk/go/pr/fr/-/2/hi/europe/8136812.stm.

Ramati, A. (1988), *And the violins stopped playing*, screenplay distributed by Odyssey Films and based upon his documentary novel of the same name (New York, originally published 1985)

Randhawa, B. (2007), 'Illicit proximities: the conundrum of Creole identity in eighteenth century British literature', unpublished doctoral dissertation, Vanderbilt University, Nashville

Ransom, J. (1919), *Schools of tomorrow in England,* regarding the Caldecott Community (London)

Reid, A. (1962), 'The Travellers', *The New Yorker*, 18 August

Reimer, R.C. and Reimer, C.J. (1992), *Nazi retro-film: how German narrative cinema remembers the past* (New York)

Rekosh, E. and Goldman, K. (1997) (eds), *Legal Defense of the Roma (Gypsies) in Central and Eastern Europe* (New York)

Reyniers, A. (1998), *Tsigane, heureux si tu es libre!*, Série Memoire des Peuples, avec CD-ROM, Editions UNESCO, Paris

Reynolds, J. (1858), *The Kitab-i-Yamini* (London)

Rhys, B. (1974), 'Introduction', in Borrow (1974)

Ridler, A.M. (1981), 'Sidelights on George Borrow's Gypsy Luke', *The Bible Translator*, 32(3)

Ridler, A.M. (1996), 'George Borrow as linguist: images and contexts' (Published by the author for private circulation; original source: doctoral thesis submitted to the Council for National Academic Awards, Oxford, 1983)

Rikhye, R. (2006), *Mahmud Ghaznavi's seventeen invasions of India*, http://orbat.com/site/kings_master/kings/Mahmud_ghaznavi/Mahmud%20Ghaznavi.html

Ripley, G. and Dana, C.A. (1873–76) (eds) 'Gypsies, Gipsies or Gipseys', *American Cyclopaedia Vol. 8* (New York)

Rishi, W.R. (1976), *Roma: the Panjabi emigrants in Europe, Central and Middle Asia, the USSR and the Americas* (Patiala)

Roberts, S. (1836), *The Gypsies* (London)

Rocco, M. (1992), *Where the day takes you* (New Line Cinema)

Roerich, G.N. (1983), *Tibetan-Russian-English dictionary, with Sanskrit parallels* (Moscow)

Roleine, R. (1978), *Le prince d'un été* (Paris)

Rosen, P. (1995), 'A broader Holocaust curriculum', *The Genocide Forum*, 1(8)

Rosenbaum, A.S. (1996) (ed.), *Is the Holocaust unique?* (Boulder and Oxford)

Rosenberg, D. (1989) (ed.), *Testimony: contemporary writers make the Holocaust personal* (New York)

Ross, J. (2002), 'The sexualization of difference: a comparison of mixed-race and same-gender marriage', *Harvard Civil Rights – Civil Liberties Law Review*, 37

Roth, J.K. and Berenbaum, M. (1989) (eds), *Holocaust: religious and philosophical implications* (New York)

Rubin, S. (1980), 'The assimilation and education of Portland Gypsies', unpublished BA thesis, Reed College

Rüdiger, J. (1782), *Neuester Zuwachs der Teuschen, Fremden und Allgemeinen Sprachkunde in Einigen Aufsatzen, Bücheranzeigen und Nachrichten, Vol. 1* (Leipzig)

Sachau, E. (1888), *Alberuni's India* (London)

Sachdev, P. (2008), 'The "gypsy" as muse and metaphor: modernity, mobility and a people's struggle for subjectivity', doctoral dissertation, The University of California at Davis

Safire, W. (1983), 'On language: long time no see', *The New York Times Magazine*, 20 September

Saker, N. (1982), 'Down memory lane', *The News and Post*, 2 April

Salo, M.T. (1977), 'Gypsy ethnicity: implications of native categories and interaction for ethnic classification', unpublished manuscript

Salo, M.T. (1981) (ed.), *The American Kalderaš: Gypsies in the New World*, Gypsy Lore Society Publication No. 1, Hackettstown

Salo, M.T. (1997), 'Gypsies', in Levinson and Ember (1997)

Salloway, J.C. (1973), 'Medical care utilization among urban Gypsies', *Urban Anthropology*, 2(1)

Sampson, A. (1997), *The scholar Gypsy* (London)

Sampson, J. (1891), 'Minche', *Journal of the Gypsy Lore Society*, 3(1)

Sampson, J. (1907a), 'sar, "with"', *Journal of the Gypsy Lore Society*, 1

Sampson, J. (1907b), 'Gypsy language and origin', *Journal of the Gypsy Lore Society*, 1(1)

Sampson, J. (1911), 'Jacob Bryant; being an analysis of his Anglo-Romani vocabulary, with a discussion of the place and date of collection and an attempt to show that Bryant, not Rüdiger, was the earliest discoverer of the Indian origin of the Gypsies', *Journal of the Gypsy Lore Society*, 4

Sampson, J. (1923), 'On the origin and early migration of the Gypsies', *Journal of the Gypsy Lore Society*, 2(4)

Sampson, J. (1926), *The dialect of the Gypsies of Wales* (Oxford)

Sand, S. (2008), *Matai ve'ech humtza ha'am haYehudi?* [When and how were the Jewish people invented?] (Tel Aviv)

Sandland, R. (1996), 'The real, the simulacrum, and the construction of "gypsy" in law', *Journal of Law and Society*, 23(3)

Sárosi Bálint (1983), *Gypsy Music* (Budapest)

Satory, S. (1986), 'Hungarian Gipsies still second-class citizens', *The Guardian Weekly*, 9 February

Saul, N. and Tebbutt, S. (2004) (eds), *The role of the Romanies: images and self-images of 'Gypsies'/Romanies in European cultures* (Liverpool)

Schiffer, S. (1986), 'The far side of enough', unpublished manuscript, privately printed and distributed by playwright, New York

Schrevel, M. (2003), *Gypsy life in Dutch children's books*, International Institute of Social History

Schroeder, J. (1983), 'Gypsy crime in America', *Centurion: A Police Lifestyle Magazine*, 1(6)

Schultz, S. (1974), *A reconstruction of proto-Romani*, privately circulated monograph

Schweitzer, P. and Hancock, D. (1991), *Our lovely hops* (London)

Scrivens, K. and Smith, S. (2006), *Hancocks of the West* (Tweedale)

Seabrook, D. (2006), *Jack of jumps* (London)

Sebeok, T. (1970) (ed.), *Current trends in linguistics, 6: linguistics in South West Asia and North Africa* (The Hague)

Seenan, G. (2005), 'Pub raided in wild bird trade inquiry', *The Guardian*, 7 February

Sellah, A. (2004), 'Study: Gypsies came out of India', *ABC Science Online*, September

Sen, S. (1960), *A comparative grammar of Middle Indo-Aryan* (Poona)

Sengupta, S. (1996), 'A rift opens over "other victims" at Holocaust memorial', *The New York Times*, 18 August

Shapiro, P. and Ehrenreich, R. (2002) (eds), *Roma and Sinti: under-studied victims of Nazism* (Washington DC)

Sharma, S.K. (1976), 'Roma have ethnic and linguistic connections with India', *Roma*, 2(2)

Sharp, A.W. (2003), *The Gypsies* (Farmington Hills)

Shea, C. (1996), 'Debating the uniqueness of the Holocaust', *The Chronicle of*

Higher Education, 31 May

Sheley, J. (2000), *Criminology: a contemporary handbook* (Belmont)

Shermer, M. (1994), 'Proving the Holocaust', *Skeptic*, 2(4)

Shields, A.C. (1993), 'Gypsy stereotypes in Victorian literature', unpublished doctoral dissertation, New York University,

Shields, M. (1981), 'Selected issues in treating Gypsy patients', *Hospital Physician*, 11

Shohat, E. and Stam, R. (1994), *Unthinking Eurocentrism: multiculturalism and the media* (London)

Shorter Oxford English Dictionary on Historical Principles, The, third edition (1956) (Oxford)

Simons, M. (1990), 'At a death camp, Gypsies confront indifference', *The New York Times*, 7 August

Sinclair, A.T. (1909), 'The word "Rom"', *Journal of the Gypsy Lore Society*, 3

Sinclair, A.T. (1915), 'An American-Romani vocabulary', *Bulletin of the New York Public Library,* 10

Singh, K.S. (1992) (ed.), *Ethnicity, caste and people. Proceedings of the Indo-Soviet seminars held in Calcutta and Leningrad, 1990* (Delhi and Moscow)

Sirmarco, E. (2000), *Endangered cultures: Gypsies,* (San Juan Capistrano)

Sloan, M.I. (1981), *Khowar-English dictionary* (New York)

Smart, B.C. (1863), 'The dialect of the English Gypsies', [appendix to] *Transactions of the Philological Society*

Smart, B.C. and Crofton, H. T. (1875), *The dialect of the English Gypsies* (London, republished 1968)

Smart, J. (1969), 'A Gypsy can't be a Gypsy without a Gypsy license', *The Philadelphia Bulletin*, 11 April

Smelser, R. (1991), 'The "Final Solution" and the War in 1944', unpublished manuscript, University of Utah, Salt Lake City

Smith, E. (1943), *Caravan* (Garden City)

Smith, G. (1880), *Gipsy life: being an account of our Gipsies and their children, with suggestions for their improvement* (London)

Smith, L.A. (1889), *Through Romani songland* (London)

Smith, R. (1901), *Gypsy Smith: his life and work* (London)

Smith, W. (1744), *A new voyage to Guinea* (London)

Snyder, L.L. (1989), *Encyclopaedia of the Third Reich* (New York)

Sollors, W. (2002), 'Can rabbits have interracial sex?', in Kaup and Rosenthal (2002)

Soravia, G. (1988), 'Di alcune etimologie zingariche', *Archivio Glottologico Italiano*, 73

Soulis, G. (1961), 'Gypsies in the Byzantine Empire and the Balkans in the late

Middle Ages', *Dumbarton Oaks Papers*, 15

Spivak, G. (1988), 'Can the subaltern speak?', in Nelson and Grossberg (1988)

St John, B. (1853), 'The Gypsy slaves of Wallachia', *Household Words*, 185

Stahl, P.H. (1988) (cd.), *Recueil: études et documents balkaniques et méditerranéens* (Paris)

Stannard, D.E. (1996), 'The dangers of calling the Holocaust unique', *The Chronicle of Higher Education*, 2 August

Stapinska, M. (1995), 'Faceless, stateless, endless victims', *The Yorkshire Post*, 28 January

State Museum of Auschwitz-Birkenau (1993), *Memorial book: the Gypsies at Auschwitz-Birkenau* (Munich)

Steinmetz, S. (1966), *Oesterreichs Zigeuner im NS-Staat* (Frankfurt)

Stenger, E. *et al.* (1931), *Die Erotik in der Fotographie: die Geschichtliche Entwicklung des Aktphotos and des erotischen Lichtbildes and seine Beziehung zur Psychopathia sexualis* (Vienna)

Stewart, M. (2004), 'Remembering without commemoration: the mnemonics and politics of Holocaust memories among European Roma', *Journal of the Royal Anthropological Institute*, 10

Stocking, G.W. (1990) (ed.), *Bones, bodies, behavior: essays in behavioral anthropology* (Madison, WI)

Strandberg, S. (1994), 'Researcher claims thousands of Gypsies exterminated by Czechs', *The Decorah Journal*, 5 May

Strong, T.B. and Stondemire, S.A. (1953) (eds), *South Atlantic studies for Sturgis E. Leavitt* (Washington)

Stumbo, B. (1985), 'Gypsies, their traditions set them apart', *The Daytona Beach Morning Journal*, 12 August

Sultzberger, C.L. (1939), 'Nobody wants these wandering Gypsies', *The Evening Standard*, 23 August

Supple, C. (1993), *From prejudice to genocide: learning about the Holocaust* (Stoke-on-Trent)

Sus, J. (1961), *Cikánská Otázka v ČSSR* (Prague)

Sutherland, A. (1975), *Gypsies, the hidden Americans* (New York and London)

Sway, M. (1988), *Familiar strangers: Gypsy life in America* (Urbana, IL)

Taranatha, J. (1970), *Taranatha's history of Buddhism in India [ca AD 1600]*, translated from the Tibetan by L. Chimpa and A. Chattopadhyaya, D. Chattopadhyaya (ed.) (Simla)

Tarrazi, A. (2008), 'Police warn of summer scams and gypsies', *The Leader*, 16 May

Taylor, M.R. (1983), *A brief survey of the history of Travelling People in North Kensington and Hammersmith, 1850–1965* (London)

Tcherenkov, L. and Laederich, S. (2004), *The Rroma, otherwise known as*

Gypsies, Gitanos, γιφτος, Tsiganes, Ţigani, Çingene, Zigeuner, Bohémiens, Travellers, Fahrende, etc. (Basel)

Theiss, A. (2005a), *Gypsy magic: for the prosperity's soul* (Wooster)

Theiss, A. (2005b), *Gypsy magic: for the lover's soul* (Wooster)

Thomas, E. (1924), *George Borrow: the man and his books* (New York)

Thomas, J.D. *et al.* (1977), 'Disease, lifestyle and consanguinity in 58 American Gypsies', *The Lancet*, 8555, 15 August

Thomas, J.D. (1985), 'Gypsies and American medical care', *Annals of Internal Medicine*, 102(6)

Thurner, E. (1987), 'Nazi policy against the Gypsies', a presentation to US Holocaust Memorial Council conference 'The Other Victims', Washington DC, 22–25 February

Tilford, J.E. (1953), 'A note on Borrow's bookish dialogue', in Strong and Stondemire (1953)

Tomiuc, E. (2006), 'The challenges of European integration and Muslim identity', Radio Free Europe/Radio Liberty, text of broadcast 7 April

Tong, D. (1995), *Gypsies: a multidisciplinary annotated bibliography* (New York and London)

Tong, D. (1996) (ed.), *Gypsies: an interdisciplinary reader* (New York and London)

Trumpener, K. (1992), 'The time of the Gypsies: a "people without history" in the narratives of the West', *Critical Enquiry*, 18(4)

Tsaggas, N. (2006), *Μάντζικερτ – Η Ἀρχη τοί Τέλούς τοί Μεσάιωνικοι Ἑλληνίσμοι* (Athens)

Turner, R.L. (1966), *A comparative dictionary of the Indo-Aryan languages* (Oxford)

Tyler, C. (1994), 'Gypsy president', *The Financial Times*, 26 March

Tyrnauer, G. (1985), *The fate of Gypsies during the Holocaust*, Special Report prepared for The US Holocaust Memorial Council, restricted access document (Washington DC)

Tyrnauer-Stastny, G. (1977), *The Gypsy in northwest America* (Tacoma)

Uhlik, R. (1973), 'Govori jugoslovenskih Cigana u okviru balkanskog jezi kog saveza', *Godišnjak*, 10

Vaillant, J.-A. (1861), *Grammaire, dialogues et vocabulaire de la langue Rommanes des Cigains* (Paris)

Vandekeere, M. (2006), *Subliminal learn Romany* (Royal Oak)

Vekerdi J. (1981), 'On the social prehistory of the Gypsies', *Acta Orientalia Academiae Scientiarum Hungaricae*, 35(2/3)

Vekerdi J. (1988), 'The Gypsies and the Gypsy problem in Hungary', *Hungarian Studies Review*, 15(2)

Vesey-Fitzgerald, B. (1944), *Gypsies of Britain: an introduction to their history*

(London)

Vesey-Fitzgerald, B. (1973), *The Birmingham Post*, 14 July

von Hase-Mihalik, E. and Kreuzkamp, D. (1990), *Du kriegst auch einen schönen Wohnwagen: Zwangslager für Sinti und Roma während des Nationalsozialismus in Frankfurt am Main* (Frankfurt)

von Stroheim, E. (1935), *Paprika, the Gypsy trollop* (New York)

Voskanian, V. (2002), 'The Iranian loanwords in Lomavren, the secret language of the Armenian Gypsies', *Iran and the Caucasus*, 6(1/2)

Voss, K. and Rocco, M. (1992), *Where the day takes you* (Hollywood, CA)

Wagenaar, A. (1995), *Settela: het meisje heeft haar naam terug* (Amsterdam)

Walker, B. (1983), *Women's encyclopaedia of myths and secrets* (San Francisco)

Webster's New World dictionary of the American language (1966) (Cleveland and New York)

Weiss, P. (2007), 'Forgiving Elie Wiesel, somewhat, on his opposition to Gypsies in Holocaust Museum', *The New York Observer*, 2 January

Wells, J. (1961), [Comments regarding Borrow], *Hansard* (Commons), Vol. 650, cols. 829–30, 1 December

Weybright, V. (1938), 'Who can tell the Gypsies' fortune?', *The Survey*, 27

Weyrauch, W. and Bell, M. (1993), 'Autonomous lawmaking: the case of the "Gypsies"', *The Yale Law Journal*, 103(2)

Weyrauch, W. (2001) (ed.), *Gypsy law: Romani legal traditions and culture* (Berkeley, CA)

Wheal, E.A., Pope, S. and Taylor, J. (1989), *Encyclopaedia of the Second World War* (Secaucus)

Whistler, J. (1983), 'Gypsy bake sale; or, should we educate our Gypsies?', *Good Mental Health*, 247

White, S. (2006), *Gypsy heart* (Dothan)

Whiter, W. (1800), *Etymologicon magnum* (Cambridge)

Wiesenthal, S. (1989), *Justice not vengeance* (New York)

Willems, W. (1997), *In search of the true Gypsy* (London)

Willing, R. (1985), 'It's Gypsy season, so don't get gypped!', *The Detroit News*, 30 April

Wilson, N. (1986), *Gypsies and gentlemen* (London)

Wilson, S. (1982), *Ideology and experience: anti-semitism in France at the time of the Dreyfuss Affair* (London and Toronto)

Windfuhr, G. (2002), 'Gypsy dialects', *Encyclopædia Iranica Vol. XI*

Wink, A. (1991), *Al-Hind: The making of the Indo-Islamic World* (Boston and Leiden)

Winstedt, E.O. (1952), 'Borrow's Hungarian-Romani vocabulary', *Journal of the Gypsy Lore Society*, 29(1/2), 30(1)

Wistrich, R. (1982), *Who's who in Nazi Germany* (New York)

Wlislocki, H. (1887), 'Gebräuche der transsilvanischen Zeltzigeuner bei Geburt, Taufe, und Leichenbestattung', *Globus*, 51

Wlislocki, H. (1890), *Vom Wandernden Zigeunervolke* (Hamburg)

Wogg, M. (2006) (ed.), *Roma history: from India to Europe*, Council of Europe Directorate General IV, Education of Roma Children in Europe, Strasbourg,

Wolf, S. (1959), *Grosses Wörterbuch der Zigeunersprache* (Hamburg)

Wood, M.F. (1973), *In the life of a Romany Gypsy* (London and Boston)

Woodcock, H. (1865), *The Gipsies* (London)

Woolf, V. (1956), *Orlando* (New York and London, originally published 1928)

Woolner, A.C. (1914), 'The Indian origin of the Gypsies of Europe', *Journal of the Panjab Historical Society*, 2

Woolner, A.C. (1916), 'Studies in Romani philology', *Journal of the Gypsy Lore Society*, 2(9)

Wright, J. (1898), *The English dialect dictionary* (London)

Wright, S. (2008), 'Police fury as bosses tell them to "celebrate" Gipsies', *The Daily Mail*, 15 July

Yates, D. (1949), 'Hitler and the Gypsies', *Commentary*, 8

Yates, D. (1953), *My Gypsy days* (London)

Yoors, J. (1967), *The Gypsies* (London)

Young, D. (1994), 'A Mulano place: paradox and ambivalence in the Romani Holocaust', BA (Hons.) thesis, Macquarie University, Sydney

Zack, N. (1997) (ed.), *Race/sex: their sameness, difference and interplay* (New York)

Zack, N. (1993), *Race and mixed race* (Philadelphia)

Zahradnik, Dr, *et al.* (1908), *Interpellation: Abgeordneten Karl Iro und Genossen an Seine Exzellenz den Herrn Minister des Innern, an Seine Exzellenz den Herrn Minister für Landesverteidigung und an Seine Exzellenz den Herrn Justizminister, betreffend Massnahmen zur Einschränkung, beziehungsweise Beseitigung der Zigeunerplage* (Vienna)

Žařabová, Z. and Davidová, E. (2000) (eds), *Life in black and white* (Prague)

Zemo, A. (1997), *Marko*, The Facing History and Ourselves Summer Workshop on Racism and Anti-Semitism, Berlin

Zimmermann, M. (1990), 'From discrimination to the "family camp" at Auschwitz: National Socialist persecution of the Gypsies', *Dachau Review*, 2

Zuev, V. (1789), *Beschreibung seiner Reise von St Petersburg nach Cherson in den Jahren 1781. *'Vokabular zu Belgorod in Russland' pp. 123–34, unpublished

against Romanies in Europe 264–72
solutions to problem of 270–1
and violent attacks of Romanies 271–2
see also African Americans, Antigypsyism
Radoc (website of The Romani Archives and
  Documentation Center) 222
Rajputs
  as ancestors of Romanies 56, 87, 71–2, 92,
    100, 101, 104, 192
  date of departure from India of 83
  invasion and defeat of, by Ghaznavids 73,
    76–7, 79, 88
  religious and domestic customs of 79, 107,
    109–10
  see also Romani origins, Seljuqs
'Rajputic' language 77, 81, 90
Ridler, Ann M. 160, 163, 169–70, 176
Rishi, Weer 60, 100–1, 103, 111, 182, 185
Rodney, Walter xii
Roma National Congress 57
Romania 268
Romani Archives and Documentation Center
  201, 221
Romanichals 128, 130, 131 *see also* Travellers
Romani-Jewish Alliance 256
Romani language
  Angloromani 169, 171, 172, 173, 174, 175
  dialect variations of 55, 57, 61, 80, 83, 97–9,
    102–4, 118, 120–1, 171–5 *see also* Diaspora
  dialects, most representative 121–2, 126
  character of people reflected in, perception of
    150–7
  as evidence of origins 58–60, 61, 62–71,
    76–82, 92 *see also* Romani origins
  gender system of 62–7
  and German 64, 102
  Greek influences on 57, 61, 70, 81, 90, 117,
    126, 283n12
  as Gypsy language 97–9
  inaccuracies in study of 179–180, 181,
    188–91
  Indian origin of 51, 55–56, 58, 62–83, 97
  lack of virtuous terms in, perception of 151–7,
    186–7
  metalworking terms in 92–4, 282–3n10
  and military *koïné* hypothesis of origin 55,
    70–82, 92
  military terms in 77–8, 92
  numerals in 80–1, 90
  Persian influences on 61, 63–5, 77–8, 81–2,
    92, 98, 116, 127, 284n20
  similarities to Urdu 71, 76, 77, 92
  standardisation of 117, 118–127
  Vlax dialect as basis for standard 121–6
  ways to create standard 123–4, 126–7
  see also Domari language, Lomavren
    language, Indo-Aryan languages, *and*
    languages of specific ethnic groups
Romani origins

debate over time period of 55–6, 59–63, 82–3,
  88, 92
bizarre theories of 213
discovery of Indian 47–53
formation of identity in Byzantium 57, 70, 83,
  87, 88, 90, 99, 101, 116
genetic evidence for 72, 83
in Kannauj 71, 79–80
and migration from India 54–83, 88, 99, 101,
  213
and migrations, suggested terms for 119
and migration theories, single vs. multiple
  54–68, 92, 99
and migration to Anatolia 54–5, 57, 75, 83–89
  see also Byzantine Empire, Byzantium
and migration to/as unified group in Europe
  90–1, 277–8
military *koïné* hypothesis of 55, 56, 70–82,
  87, 88–9, 98, 101
misconception of Egyptian 45, 147, 213
shared origin with Dom and Lom, theory of
  54–6, 58–62, 98–102, 185, 192, 282n9 *see*
  also Dom, Domari language, Lom,
  Lomavren language
see also Ghaznavids, Rajputs, *Rrom*, Seljuqs
Romani Parliament 119
Romani people, Roma, Rom
  assimilation, resistance to 130, 134
  close family ties of 241–2
  communication and cooperation among
    118–20, 274, 278–9
  complexion of, reaction to 218
  discrimination and violence toward 142–3,
    195–7, 252–3, 254 *see also* Antigypsyism,
    Law enforcement, racism
  dehumanization of 268
  domestic customs of 29, 79, 108–10, 190–10
  education of 41–2, 131–144, 270–1, 284n16
    see also Schools
  encampments of *10*, 19–20
  enslavement of 38, 129, 132, 215, 219, 268
  faked/fabricated culture of 177–188
  family names of 22–3
  genocide of 246 *see also* Holocaust,
    Porrajmos
  and illiteracy 135–6
  imprisonment of 14–15
  legislation discriminating against 150
  manipulation of 38–9, 43
  manipulation of image of 147, 150, 193, 213
    see also Borrow, George, Gadžo, gadže
  marriage of *see* Marriage
  means of livelihood of 15–16, 19, 28
  medical care of 110–11
  migrations and resettlement of
    (contemporary) 19–22
  misnomers of 212–3, 281–2n3
  names of 96
  nationalism of 39, 57, 275, 277–8

The Holocaust in History and Memory is a new peer-reviewed journal published by the University of Essex (United Kingdom). It is linked to the theme of the events organised each year at the University of Essex to mark Holocaust Memorial Day, but we invite contributions on all aspects of the history as well as the memory, memorialisation and commemoration of the Holocaust and other genocides. The journal takes a broad (i.e. inclusive) view of the term 'Holocaust' without losing the sense of its origin and the significance of the Holocaust for the European Jewry and the Sinti and Roma.

Vol. 1 (2008) – Representing the Unrepresentable: Putting the Holocaust into Public Museums
with contribution by Suzanne Bardgett (Imperial War Museum London), Rainer Schulze (University of Essex), Peter Vergo (University of Essex) and Wilfried Wiedemann (Stiftung niedersächsische Gedenkstätten / Gedenkstätte Bergen-Belsen)

Vol. 2 (2009) – Bearing Witness: Testimony and the Historical Memory of the Holocaust
with contributions by Sanja Bahun (University of Essex), Diana Gring and Karin Theilen (Stiftung niedersächsische Gedenkstätten / Gedenkstätte Bergen-Belsen), Olaf Jensen (University of Leicester), Michele Langfield (Deakin University Melbourne), Ulrike Smalley (Imperial War Museum London); testimonies by Edith Balas (Pittsburgh, Pennsylvania), Dora Love (Colchester), Ladislaus Löb (Brighton), Anna Kaletska (interviewed by David Boder 26 Sep 1946); reviews; announcements; calendar note (9 Dec 1948: The UN Convention on the Prevention and Punishment of the Crime of Genocide).

Vol. 3 (2010 – forthcoming) – *The Porrajmos:* The Gypsy Holocaust
we are still accepting proposals and actively pursuing submission of additional contributions – so far contributions have been accepted from Sharon Kangisser Cohen (Jerusalem) Donald Kenrick (London), Stephen Smith (USC Shoah Foundation Institute, Los Angeles), Yvonne Robel and Kathrin Herold (University Bremen); poems by Julius Balbin and Charles Adès Fishman; artwork by Marty Kolb; testimonies, reviews, announcements; calendar note (2 Aug 1944: The Liquidation of the Auschwitz *Zigeunerfamilienlager*).

General Editor of the journal is Rainer Schulze, University of Essex. Enquiries should go to: rainer@essex.ac.uk.

THE HOLOCAUST
IN HISTORY AND MEMORY